English Prose of the Seventeenth Century

Longman Literature in English Series

General Editors: David Carroll and Michael Wheeler
Lancaster University

For a complete list of titles see pages viii-ix

English Prose of the Seventeenth Century, 1590–1700

Roger Pooley

Longman
London and New York

Longman Group UK Limited,
Longman House, Burnt Mill,
Harlow, Essex CM20 2JE, England
and Associated Companies throughout the world.

Published in the United States of America
by Longman Publishing, New York

First published 1992

ISBN 0 582 01658 4 CSD
ISBN 0 582 01659 2 PPR

British Library Cataloguing-in-Publication Data

A catalogue record for this book is
available from the British Library

Library of Congress Cataloging-in-Publication Data

Pooley, Roger
    English prose of the seventeenth century, 1590–1700 / Roger
Pooley.
        p.   cm. — (Longman literature in English series)
    Includes bibliographical references and index.
    ISBN 0–582–01658–4 (csd). — ISBN 0–582–01659–2 (ppr)
    1. English prose literature—Early modern, 1500–1700—History
and criticism.   I. Title.   II. Series.
PR769.P66   1992
828'.04809—dc20   92–8343
                                                      CIP

Set by 8 in 9½ on 11pt Bembo
Produced by Longmans Singapore Publishers (Pte) Ltd
Printed in Singapore

Contents

Longman Literature in English Series

General Editors: David Carroll and Michael Wheeler
Lancaster University

Pre-Renaissance English Literature

★ English Literature before Chaucer *Michael Swanton*
  English Literature in the Age of Chaucer
★ English Medieval Romance *W.R.J. Barron*

English Poetry

★ English Poetry of the Sixteenth Century *Gary Waller*
★ English Poetry of the Seventeenth Century *George Parfitt* (Second Edition)
  English Poetry of the Eighteenth Century 1700–1789
★ English Poetry of the Romantic Period 1789–1830 *J.R. Watson* (Second Edition)
★ English Poetry of the Victorian Period 1830–1890 *Bernard Richards*
  English Poetry of the Early Modern Period 1890–1940
  English Poetry since 1940

English Drama

  English Drama before Shakespeare
★ English Drama: Shakespeare to the Restoration, 1590–1660
  Alexander Leggatt
★ English Drama: Restoration and Eighteenth Century, 1660–1789
  Richard W. Bevis
  English Drama: Romantic and Victorian, 1789–1890
  English Drama of the Early Modern Period, 1890–1940
  English Drama since 1940

English Fiction

★ English Fiction of the Eighteenth Century 1700–1789
  Clive T. Probyn
★ English Fiction of the Romantic Period 1789–1830 *Gary Kelly*
★ English Fiction of the Victorian Period 1830–1890 *Michael Wheeler*
★ English Fiction of the Early Modern Period 1890–1940
  Douglas Hewitt
  English Fiction since 1940

English Prose

★ English Prose of the Seventeenth Century 1590–1700 *Roger Pooley*
  English Prose of the Eighteenth Century
  English Prose of the Nineteenth Century

Criticism and Literary Theory

Criticism and Literary Theory from Sidney to Johnson
Criticism and Literary Theory from Wordsworth to Arnold
Criticism and Literary Theory from 1890 to the Present

The Intellectual and Cultural Context

The Sixteenth Century
★ The Seventeenth Century, 1603–1700 *Graham Parry*
★ The Eighteenth Century, 1700–1789 *James Sambrook*
The Romantic Period, 1789–1830
The Victorian Period, 1830–1890
The Twentieth Century: 1890 to the Present

American Literature

American Literature before 1880
★ American Poetry of the Twentieth Century *Richard Gray*
★ American Drama of the Twentieth Century *Gerald M. Berkowitz*
★ American Fiction 1865–1940 *Brian Lee*
★ American Fiction since 1940 *Tony Hilfer*
★ Twentieth-Century America *Douglas Tallack*

Other Literatures

Irish Literature since 1800
Scottish Literature since 1700

Australian Literature
★ Indian Literature in English *William Walsh*
African Literature in English: East and West
Southern African Literature in English
Caribbean Literature in English
★ Canadian Literature in English *W.J. Keith*

★ *Already published*

Editors' Preface

The multi-volume Longman Literature in English Series provides students of literature with a critical introduction to the major genres in their historical and cultural context. Each volume gives a coherent account of a clearly defined area, and the series, when complete, will offer a practical and comprehensive guide to literature written in English from Anglo-Saxon times to the present. The aim of the series as a whole is to show that the most valuable and stimulating approach to the study of literature is that based upon an awareness of the relations between literary forms and their historical contexts. Thus the areas covered by most of the separate volumes are defined by period and genre. Each volume offers new and informed ways of reading literary works, and provides guidance for further reading in an extensive reference section.

In recent years, the nature of English studies has been questioned in a number of increasingly radical ways. The very terms employed to define a series of this kind – period, genre, history, context, canon – have become the focus of extensive critical debate, which has necessarily influenced in varying degrees the successive volumes published since 1985. But however fierce the debate, it rages around the traditional terms and concepts.

As well as studies on all periods of English and American literature, the series includes books on criticism and literary theory, and on the intellectual and cultural context. A comprehensive series of this kind must of course include other literatures written in English, and therefore a group of volumes deals with Irish and Scottish literature, and the literatures of India, Africa, the Caribbean, Australia and Canada. The forty-seven volumes of the series cover the following areas: Pre-Renaissance English Literature, English Poetry, English Drama, English Fiction, English Prose, Criticism and Literary Theory, Intellectual and Cultural Context, American Literature, Other Literatures in English.

David Carroll
Michael Wheeler

Author's Preface

Although there have been a number of distinguished book-length essays on seventeenth-century prose, this is, curiously, the first attempt at a critical introduction. In keeping with the rest of the series, it is selective rather than comprehensive, say in the manner of the Oxford volumes on the period by Bush and Sutherland. Though there might be agreement on what would constitute a core of prose writers of the period – Nashe, Bacon, Burton, Browne, Milton and Bunyan – prose raises tricky questions of canonicity. It's also a question of what a student away from major libraries can find. In England at least, the demise of the general prose anthology has meant a shift away from questions of period style and delicious extracts; on the other hand, the admirable archaeological wing of feminist criticism has brought to light other texts. So we may not be able to find much Restoration pulpit rhetoric in print any more, but we can discuss women's spiritual autobiography from the same period. I've attempted to say something about both. As I've been writing, some major scholarly editions have appeared – of Bunyan, Burton and Walwyn, for example. I hope before long students will be able to consult good modern editions of Overton and Margaret Cavendish, as well as more of Bacon, Behn, Hobbes and Traherne. With a few exceptions, I have tried to write about authors who are reasonably available. I have steered round works of literary criticism, as these are dealt with in a separate volume in the series.

I say something more about method and organisation of the material in the Introduction; my various and occasionally conflicting commitments to Christianity, history, stylish writing, ideas and genre will doubtless become apparent. Certainly a reader of seventeenth-century prose will need to adapt a motto of Gertrude Stein's into 'I love everything a sentence can do.' There is great enjoyment and wonder to be found in these sometimes recalcitrant texts.

On balance, I have decided to modernise spelling and, more conservatively, punctuation; I hope the gains in accessibility will outweigh the occasional losses in sound, meaning and emphasis. In the

notes and bibliographies, place of publication is London unless
otherwise stated.

My debts are numerous: to Keele University for a Research
Fellowship which enabled a clear stretch of writing; to audiences in
London, Liverpool, Durham and Purdue where some of these ideas got
their first airing; to librarians at Keele, the Shakespeare Institute of the
University of Birmingham and the Bodleian; and to many colleagues
and friends with bent ears. My wife Helen gave invaluable encouragement and space-clearing; I would never have made it without her. To
Brian Vickers, who first initiated me into the debates about
seventeenth-century prose, my thanks and humility topoi. Finally,
three scholars to whom I owe a great deal died in the course of writing
this volume: Raymond Williams, Roger Sharrock and Ray Selden. The
book is dedicated to their memory.

Roger Pooley
Keele University

Introduction: Reading Seventeenth-Century Prose

This book is an introduction to the great richness and variety of prose texts in England over a hundred and ten year period. The history of prose has necessarily to be a more miscellaneous affair than a history of poetry, or drama, or the novel, simply because of that variety. It is more than a history of changes in style; it has to attend to changes over a wide band of genres and ideas, too. Even more than other kinds of literary history, it has to be aware of changes in politics, religion, philosophy and science, not least because many of these changes were initiated in the prose writings themselves.

From the perspective of our own time, the history of prose could be written as a history of deliberate hiddenness. As Godzich and Kittay argue: 'prose . . . does not offer itself to view, and plays what could be described as a game of self-concealment'.[1] That in itself might be an incentive to write a history of what would rather hide: The Hidden Textuality of the Unliterary. So, this text may look like a Herbal, or an account of an experiment with an air-pump, but in fact it is an intervention in the history of a wider discourse about science or nature (by 'discourse' is meant a way of writing on a subject which defines the limits of that subject, acceptable methods, questions, decorum and so on). A mirror image of this approach would be to start from the standard of 'fine writing' as literature – the prose which advertises itself as good prose – and organise seventeenth-century prose according to a division, between utilitarian texts and those in art prose, Bacon versus Browne perhaps.

There are problems with such a division, even allowing for those pieces that would recalcitrantly straggle the divide. One is that the concept of 'literature' is rather anachronistic, so that one cannot imagine a seventeenth-century writer or reader wondering whether, say, a particularly impressive sermon might be a work of literature. A notion of 'literature' in that sense is really only intelligible from the second half of the eighteenth century. What we do find is a sermon connoisseur like Pepys remarking that Mr Messums 'made a very good sermon; but only, too eloquent for a pulpit'.[2]

'Eloquence': that suggests that a more historically appropriate category than 'literature' might be rhetoric, the art of persuasion that was a key part of education in the period. Almost everyone who wrote knew something of it, so much so that in some circumstances it might have been as invisible, as 'natural' a way of organising a text as chapters and paragraphs; equally, witty play with rhetorical schemes or figures would be the way to appeal to an educated audience. It was valued, too, not just as an ornament to speech, but as a crucial preparation for public life. The humanist ideal of scholarship at the service of civic virtue is clearest in the teaching of rhetoric.

Rhetoric is, first of all, an art of persuasion. The three types of classical oration, the judicial, the deliberative (political) and epideictic (praise or panegyric) are all meant to persuade, and also to move. So did the letter, another Ciceronian genre, which was developed throughout our period, most notably into the essay. In Bacon's formulation, 'the duty and office of rhetoric is, to apply reason to imagination for the better moving of the will'.[3] There is an increasing emphasis on the rhetorical appeal to the passions in the period, and a parallel faith in the power of the word – even in those who are suspicious of some of its effects.[4] Rhetoricians distinguished the three levels of style, Grand, Middle and Plain, according to their power to move as well as their decorousness, their appropriateness to the subject matter. Stylistic variation within the *œuvre* of individual writers can often be ascribed to their sensitivity to decorum and the levels of style.[5] Rhetoric taught a tight organisational scheme; for example, modern editions of Sidney's *Defence of Poetry* show how closely it follows the sequence of exordium (introduction), narration, proposition, division of the subject, examination or *confirmatio*, refutation, digression, and peroration or summary.[6]

What is most striking about Renaissance education in rhetoric, though, is its insistence on learning the figures, or tropes; reading texts in order to note them down for further use, as well as learning them from textbooks. They include imagery, wordplay, repetition and contrast, classified and distinguished in extremely precise ways. Renaissance rhetorical instruction delivered a large and subtle armoury of devices to the writer; readers of Renaissance prose need to pick up a few, at least, to discover what their writers knew they were doing.[7] Take this sentence from Robert Burton's *The Anatomy of Melancholy* (first published in 1621): 'If through weakness, folly, passion, discontent, ignorance, I have said amiss, let it be forgotten and forgiven.'[8] The list ('weakness' onwards) exhibits asynedeton (from the Greek meaning 'unconnected'), due to its omission of conjunctions; the sound parallel in 'forgotten and forgiven' is best described as parechesis (from the Greek 'likeness of sound'), though we might add that part of the effect comes from the inversion of the usual idiomatic order, 'forgive and forget', which links it to the figure of disconnectedness in the first half of the sentence, as well as to a whole range of figures of inversion, of which the most common is antimetabole (Greek for 'turning about'), which involves inverting the order of repeated words. Popular rhetorical textbooks were able to draw on contemporary writing rich in the figures and tropes; Sidney's *Arcadia*, for example, is the source for many of the illustrations in John Hoskins's *Directions for Speech and Style* (c. 1599) and Abraham Fraunce's *Arcadian Rhetoric* (1588).

It is even a rhetorical device to say one is not being rhetorical (like Mark Antony over Caesar's body), or that one's opponents are being excessively rhetorical (Puritans of Anglicans, or vice versa). Everything is rhetoric, expecially that which proclaims it is not. Almost always. A parallel problem is that even utilitarian prose is very interesting as prose in this period. Constructing what purports to be a transparency (prose like a window-pane, as Orwell hoped his would be) is a tricky business. As we shall see in greater detail later, the attempts of early scientists to find a plain way of describing their experiments are fascinating, even at the crude level of catching them using metaphors when they had said they wouldn't. The main, accepted developmental model of seventeenth-century prose style, that it became plainer towards the end of the century under pressure from scientific, political and theological shifts, is difficult to deny, but needs caution. It is a mistake to take the programme for the practice. In particular, it has often reinforced a questionable picture of scientific 'progress' from 1660 to the present, with science (hard, precise, rational) emancipating itself from rhetoric (emotional, imprecise, biased).[9] There are changes going on from the 1650s and 1660s; the extent to which they produced a recognisably modern world-view, with a modern prose to go with it, is discussed in Part Four. A lot did not change. Edward, Lord Herbert's dictum of the 1640s applies to most of the century:

> And this part of Rhetoric I much commend to every body,
> there being no true use of speech but to make things clear,
> perspicuous and manifest which would otherwise be
> perplexed, doubtful, and obscure. The other part of Oratory
> is to speak common things ingeniously or wittily, there
> being no little vigour and force added to words when they
> are delivered in a neat and fine way and somewhat out of the
> ordinary road, common and dull language relishing more of
> the clown than of the gentleman . . . .[10]

In other words, a plain statement of the complex, and an inventive description of the commonplace, are both attributable to a traditional view of rhetoric.

The study of prose style, and rhetorical strategies in prose, reveals more than stylistic and rhetorical devices, as that example suggests – style can be the mark of a gentleman. The ideological battles and changes of the seventeenth century are inscribed in some of them. Everyone wanted to be known as a plain stylist during the Restoration; in practice, the standard by which that plainness was measured reflected the party, theological and philosophical loyalties of the writers.

There is a danger of circularity in this kind of investigation of style and allegiance, of deciding beforehand what those issues were and, lo, discovering them, reproduced in yet another form. Earlier in the period, during the Marprelate controversy of 1589–90, the opposite happened, and Marprelate's deflationary satirical style was adopted by the hired pens of the established Church.

It is difficult not to get caught up in these old controversies. It might also be better to admit now that I am happier in the company of nonconformists than bishops in this period, for example, though whether they would be happy with me, or the other critics and historians who celebrate them these days, is another matter. Very few share that mixture of fury and faith that makes many seventeenth-century Christians so magnetic and yet uncomfortable. It is an academic vice to celebrate revolutionaries (and, in some quarters, reactionaries) at a safe distance, or as a pretext for contemporary political debate; a firm hold on the differences as well as the similarities with our own situation is essential if the excitement of comparison is to be illuminating, not just a call to the barricades – or the complacency of 'it didn't work in the 1650s, and it won't now'.

The seventeenth century raises the question of the relation of history to literature in a special way. What do we need to know about the history of the period to make the history of its prose intelligible? The history of the British monarchy and its Court, indispensible for a grasp of poetry and drama, is less immediately relevant for the early part of the period, the last years of Elizabeth and the reign of James I (1603–25). However, the great institutional changes brought about by the Civil War which began in 1642, the execution of Charles I in 1649, the years of the republic until the Restoration of 1660, and the effective deposition of James II for William and Mary in 1688, generated some of the most compelling prose of the period. After 1642 there is a growing sense that politics needs to be rethought; the note of exploration and experiment is even more noticeable than the anger. This is partly due to the conflicts being within the ruling classes, rather than a popular uprising. More radical ideas were expressed, and repressed. The collapse of censorship in the 1640s and 1650s meant that works were published which had not even got as far as being banned in earlier years. (It didn't last.) All this is inextricably bound up with changes in religious belief and practice. Much recent historical argument about the causes of the Civil War has concentrated on the structural weakness of the Crown.[11] However, to the extent that the Civil War was fought over religious differences, it had a very long lead-in. Two of the masterworks of late Elizabethan prose, the Marprelate tracts and Hooker's *Ecclesiastical Polity*, argue in startlingly different styles about the proper constitution for the Church of England. Elizabeth, and the more theoretically minded James, both recognised the importance to their rule of a settled, powerful Church which would resist the pressures of Catholicism, the dominant form of Christianity in Europe, and thus of England's political enemies. It would also be a hedge against Puritanism, until the 1640s largely a party within the national Church campaigning for a more radical process of reformation. In that sense, the newly defined 'Anglicanism' could characterise itself as a middle way. Its importance depended on widespread religious belief as much as on considerable legal powers; it was also one of the few national institutions with a presence throughout the kingdom. For modern readers in England and North America, where religion is of political importance only when certain issues are debated, the present-day places to compare with seventeenth-century England for the power of religion might be Islamic states. It is not a precise fit, but many features – the internationalism of the radicals, religion's educational, self-realising power for the under-privileged, as well as its complex of repressions, for example – run parallel. We must not reduce seventeenth-century religion to its political implications, either. For example, there is evidence from the 1650s onwards of articulate personal spirituality much further down the social scale than before. The vast majority of prose writing by women in this period is religious, and the sects which grew exponentially in the 1650s, particularly the Quakers, are largely responsible.

What of economic and social changes? The effect of them is much harder to assess than political or religious change, partly because they were understood less well. Some areas are easier to link with literature than others. Britain became much more active in international trade during the period; the evidence in prose begins in the 1590s, with the great compilations of exploration narratives. The evidence by the end of the seventeenth century is much more utilitarian, in Pepys' diary entries about the navy, or the Royal Society's interest in the usefulness as well as the curiosity value of objects from abroad. Books themselves are part of a commodity market; the increased appetite for practical works of instruction, as well as fiction, news and popular devotion is evidence of increased economic activity, apart from what the works themselves say. The appropriation of romance, an aristocratic form, to middle-class readers, if not yet middle-class heroes and heroines, at the end of the period, is a piece of social history to set alongside the changing fortunes of the aristocracy and the gentry, as well as the still largely inarticulate mass of the rural poor.[12]

There are, then, a number of histories which run in parallel to the history of prose. The recent 'new historicist' approach to prose so far has often been opportunistic, analysing, say, texts about spectacular punishments or colonisation as a route to understanding Marlowe and Shakespeare. In suggesting that marginal, 'non-literary' texts interact at a discursive level with 'great literature', such an approach has taken literary-historical scholarship an important stage further, and incidentally reopened the study of Renaissance prose. What is distinctive about new historicism is its appropriation of anthropological models of cultural otherness to define our distance from the Renaissance, to analyse its strangeness as well as its relevance. If history is to be some kind of master concept in criticism, true historicists must historicise their own position as well as that of the period they study; Stephen Greenblatt has made it clear that he is writing about America in Vietnam as well as Caliban and the West Indies.[13] We must remember, too, that history articulates continuities as well as gaps; it is not naive or unhistorical to be shocked, or seduced, or inspired, or converted, by seventeenth-century texts as a twentieth-century reader. Patronising the past is as bad as sentimentalising it. Many of the ideas are still alive, and worth contesting.

What, then, of that older but still vital approach: the history of ideas? A literary historian coming to the study of major thinkers such as Hobbes, or Boyle, may feel like a tyro in another professional area; it is tempting to offer a few remarks about style and bow out. In fact the debate among historians of political or scientific ideas does not sound so alien to a literary critic these days. The return of grand theory in the wake of structuralism may have made the professional language of the humanities rather daunting to the 'general reader' (as well as the undergraduate), but it is much more of a shared vocabulary across the disciplines than thirty years ago. The analysis of 'discourse', for example, crosses all sorts of traditional subject divides. The earlier work of Michel Foucault in particular, in *The Order of Things* and *The Archaeology of Discourse*, provides a framework that needs a lot of translation to work in the English context, but is one that suggestively links language and ideas. More importantly for the present study, the work of J.G.A. Pocock on the history of political language and concepts is far more pervasive in its influence than the occasional footnote might suggest. His approach is also a corrective to the 'great thinkers' approach to seventeenth-century prose; meanings exist for historically specific audiences:

> The author of a political statement may intend to be
> ambiguous; he is employing a language by its nature
> inherently ambiguous; but because the language and the
> range of its ambiguities are given him by society and exist in
> a context of use and meaning whose multivalency he cannot
> expect to control, his statement may convey meanings to
> others (especially after the processes of linguistic change have
> had time to proceed in some way) outside any range of
> ambiguity he may have intended.[14]

To such a problem of interpretation he brings a notion of 'paradigms' (prevalent patterns of thought) that we can use in retrospect to judge what kind of framework a seventeenth-century reader might have brought to a political or religious statement. There is also the record of contemporaneous controversy to help us judge – normally a book-length refutation, not just the hostile review in a journal we are used to. In extreme circumstances, books might be burnt or authors executed for possession of seditious manuscripts. It is usually easy to find what the rulers of Britain did not like, even if a wider 'public sphere' of debate about political ideas seems to advance and recede in the course of the century.

So, a history of seventeenth-century prose is a history of paradigms, of images, as well as of styles, of rhetorics, of ideas and faiths often in conflict. It is also a history of genres – autobiography, history, sermons, essays as well as fiction. Some of these terms are back-formations, descriptions attached in retrospect. Autobiography, for example: writing a history of the self at this time was an embryonic, strange idea, driven by only some of the motives of modern autobiography. Others, like the essay, are virtually invented before our eyes in the period. This is the period of the origins of the novel, too, but only by hindsight; it does not feel the same as the essay, where the writers are self-consciously producing and naming a new form. Prose fiction is as old as storytelling; though towards the end of the century it starts to acquire that fascination with novelty, or 'the news', which is part of being a novel. All too often our sense of genre in a particular period is distorted by our knowledge of what it became. However, by naming prose genres in this period, and seeing how they might be mixed to produce a range of expectations and reactions, we can trace one important way in which prose texts produced their meaning. It is also, perhaps, a more available way of approaching seventeenth-century prose than as the history of style based on Latin models, the dominant debate for the first half of the twentieth century.

Every educated person in the period was taught Latin; once beyond basic literacy, the seventeenth-century pupil at school and at university learned to compose and argue in Latin. Education was based to an almost stifling degree on the study of classical texts, and those texts were virtually all in Latin. Writing in Latin was also the way to reach an international scholarly audience. It is true that English gradually became acknowledged as a more prestigious and eloquent language in our period, but even the exponents of 'new' learning, scientists like Newton for example, were still composing in Latin at the end of the century.[15] There is an increasing sense that there was a literate, popular audience beyond the university graduates (and the occasional but important autodidacts such as Jonson and Baxter), as much as 30 per cent of the male population by the end of the century, with the number of women harder to estimate because they were often taught to read but not to write.[16] This was targeted by popular fiction and devotional works as well as practical manuals, newsbooks and papers. The large number of rhetorics published in English in the second half of the century points both ways: to the survival of Latin-based models of how to speak and write, even as the ability to read Latin itself can no longer be assumed.

Many of the writers discussed here – Milton, Bacon, Burton and Hobbes, for example – have a considerable body of work in Latin as well as English prose, often a sign that they wanted more than an English audience for their work. Burton even complains that his stationer (his publisher) will not let him compose in Latin for financial reasons. Much of this writing is available in translation these days, so they are not lost to those of us with no Latin. But what should we remember about this intensely Latinate culture when we are reading texts in English?

The dominant descriptions of prose style of this period were based on Latin models – Seneca and Cicero. Undoubtedly they were both immensely popular writers. Writing Ciceronian Latin, as opposed to the 'barbarous' Latin of medieval scholasticism, was one of the prime aims of an influential group of humanist scholars. Gabriel Harvey's *Ciceronianus* (1577) describes at one point how he was imitated, and the passage shows how many of the features of Cicero's high style can be transferred to English:

> How can I say how great and how perfectly pure a
> Ciceronian I was, in the choice of each and every word, in
> the composition and structure of sentences, the
> discrimination of cases and tenses, in the harmoniousness of
> set formulas, in the fashioning of phrases and clauses, in
> measuring my periods, in the variety and charm of rhythm

and endings, in the elaborate and accurate accumulation of elegances of every kind?[17]

The sentence itself, as a close translation, shows how a Ciceronian period can be constructed in English, with the syntactic features, such as parallelism of the accumulated clauses, particularly noticeable. Even the greatest admirer of Cicero must notice that he does not stay at this level for long, and indeed recommends that the orator should master the plain 'Attic' style as well (brilliantly described as the style which sounds like common speech, but is in fact more controlled and composed).[18] So one can find Cicero himself writing (as well as commending) 'Attic' prose, one of the categories opposed to 'Ciceronian' in Morris Croll's influential taxonomy of prose in the period.[19] To be fair, Croll recognises the problem, but at several key points there is no specific analysis of texts to explain, let alone reinforce, the nature of his categories. When he changes from 'Attic' to 'Baroque' to describe the same movement, the desire for expressiveness rather than formal beauty in prose, the expansiveness is gained at the expense of descriptive precision. It is easy enough to pick up examples of the 'curt style' intermingled with the 'loose style' in writers like Felltham and Browne, and it is certainly true that Bacon's call to study matter rather than words was highly influential. Equally, though, such writers did not turn their backs on the resources of parallelism and climax which are the hallmarks of the Ciceronian style of the sixteenth century. As described by Croll's follower and adaptor, George Williamson, the Senecan style is such a mixture as scarcely to constitute a 'style' at all. When such markedly different writers as Browne, Bacon, Felltham and Burton can be joined together one begins to doubt the helpfulness of the model. As Williamson notes, 'Seneca could furnish authority for either pointed wit or plainness, for either sententious brevity or unlaboured fluency.'[20] There is no single Senecan style.

Rather than following a taxonomy linked to Latin styles, it might be more helpful to extract some of the terms of the debate – parallelism, the links between syntax and logic, particularly in the loosely paratactic sentence, even the length of phrases and sentences, and start again. Winifred Crombie has suggested that 'baroque' style (like Donne and Browne's) is characterised by 'associative relations' like similarity, contrast, and the more complex and logical modes like denial and correction; whereas 'metaphysical' style (like Andrewes') is 'logico-deductive', concentrating on reasons and results, conditions and consequences. Puritan plain style (her example is Perkins) tends to mix 'logico-deductive' with narrative.[21] Following that, we might be able to link up with the crucial issue of Latinate versus English vocabulary, and see how one of the central creations of the seventeenth century was an English prose which had consistently raided Latin vocabulary to expand its technical range, but which had gradually emancipated itself from a need to imitate Latin syntactic patterns. For a modern readership without the seventeenth century's Latin education, there remains the problem that we are not going to hear the Latin behind the English, the translated phrases tucked in without acknowledgement, the imitated patterns.

Finally, there is a route through a number of these texts which follows the changing nature of the first person singular, the individual self. The new genres of autobiography, and the variations on the familiar letter, such as the essay, contribute to a new sense of self in the period, most notably in religious discourse. Not so much the Romantic self, defined in relation to nature and against society, but a self defined as a conflict between God and the Devil, flesh and spirit, and, increasingly, public and private.[22]

So, the reader of seventeenth-century prose needs to acquire one or two fresh habits of reading to go with the usual equipment of psychological close reading, historical background and ideological and moral censoriousness (the extent to which 'theory' has displaced this trinity is, in my view, limited). As with Lord Herbert's orator, there are witty descants on the commonplace to deal with, which may be as good as contentless, but utterly and beguilingly (or repulsively) stylish; and other texts which maintain their grip by sheer force of argument or emotion.

The four parts of the book suggest an approach to reading seventeenth-century prose which combines the history of genres and style with the history of ideas. The first deals with different kinds of narrative—prose fiction, concentrating on the two great productive periods of the late Elizabethan years and the Restoration; history, contrasting Ralegh with Clarendon; biography, again with one fairly early exponent, Fulke Greville, and a later one, Izaak Walton; and autobiography, of which there is virtually nothing until the 1650s, but then a great outpouring in various contexts, from diaries to conversion narratives. There is, obviously, overlap between this and the second part, on religious prose. Here I start with the 1611 translation of the Bible, and then go on to the sermon. Even for those readers who often hear sermons on Sundays, let alone those who would run away at the thought of one, the seventeenth-century sermon will be strange. It is always an exposition of a text from the Bible; and so, in the hands of its best exponents, like Donne and Andrewes, an imaginative re-creation and expansion of that text, to persuade and inspire. If that sounds too like literary criticism (or at least good literary teaching), that is a measure of how far literature has taken over, or at least supplemented, the role of religion since then. A section on meditative practice and inward religion in Donne and Traherne should be thought of as a parallel to the autobiographical works of the first section. Then the longest section, on politicised religion, emphasises how much public debate was inspired by religious conviction in the period. The third part, on essays and cornucopian texts, gathers together the forms of the provisional and the would-be encyclopaedic which share many features – bookishness, digressiveness, the love of the epigrammatic – though sometimes at opposite ends when it comes to size. Bacon appears as an essayist here, but also as the master inaugurator in the final part, tendentiously called 'The Discourse of Modernity' (it might have had a question mark) which investigates some of the new idioms in philosophy, science and politics, mostly from the later seventeenth century. If this seems to reinforce questionable theories about a break in the century around 1660 – call it 'dissociation of sensibility', call it progress – so be it. While works as diverse as *Leviathan* and *The Rehearsal Transpros'd* are still recognisably Renaissance rhetorical performances, they are also testimonies to the fact that nothing, not even the composition of prose arguments, could be the same after the English people executed their Archbishop and their monarch, and did not immediately replace them.

I was once taken aback by the remark of a former student of mine who had gone into sales management, that my job was like that of a salesman for old literature. He had a point, though I hope this book is something more than an exercise in niche marketing. One good pitch for seventeenth-century prose is simply a recital of favourite opening phrases: 'God made the first marriage, and man made the first divorce'; 'An empty book is like an infant's soul, in which any thing can be written'; 'Thus saith the Lord, I inform you, that I overturn, overturn, overturn'; 'As I wandered through the wilderness of this world . . .'; 'I am so great a lover of my bed my self, that I can easily apprehend the trouble of rising at four o'clock, these cold mornings'; 'Gentle Reader, I presume thou wilt be very inquisitive to know what antic or personate actor this is, that so insolently intrudes upon this common theatre to the world's view', and that leaves out the long ones.[23] Now read on . . . .

Notes

1. Wlad Godzich and Jeffrey Kittay, *The Emergence of Prose* (Minneapolis, 1987), p. 209.

2. Samuel Pepys, *Diary*, ed. R. Latham and W. Matthews, 11 vols (1970–83), 19 February 1660.

3. Francis Bacon, *The Advancement of Learning*, ed. G.W. Kitchin (1915), II. xviii. 2, p. 146.

4. See Brian Vickers, *In Defence of Rhetoric* (Oxford, 1988), pp. 276–86.

5. Austin Warren's 'The Styles of Sir Thomas Browne', in *Seventeenth-Century Prose: Modern Essays in Criticism*, ed. Stanley E. Fish (New York, 1971), pp. 413–23, is a good example of this kind of analysis.

6. *A Defence of Poetry*, ed. J.A. van Dorsten (Oxford, 1966); *An Apology for Poetry* , ed. G. Shepherd (Manchester, 1965).

7. The most useful modern summaries are Richard Lanham, *Handlist of Rhetorical Terms* (Berkeley, 1968), and the Appendix to Brian Vickers' *In Defence of Rhetoric*.

8. Robert Burton, *The Anatomy of Melancholy*, ed. Thomas C. Faulkner et al. (Oxford, 1989–), I, p. 112.

9. The best recent discussion of this is in Richard Kroll, *The Material Word: Literate Culture in the Restoration and Early Eighteenth Century* (Baltimore, 1991).

10. *The Life of Edward, First Lord Herbert of Cherbury written by himself*, ed. J.M. Shuttleworth (1976), p. 28.

11. Notably, the work of Conrad Russell, most recently in *The Fall of the British Monarchies* (Oxford, 1991); Ann Hughes, *The Causes of the English Civil War* (1991) is a telling survey of the 'revisionist' approaches to the Civil War and a defence of the contribution of longstanding ideological divisions to the conflict.

12. While the work of Lawrence Stone in *The Crisis of the Aristocracy, 1558–1641* (Oxford, 1967) is still of great interest, students might start with more recent studies, such as Keith Wrightson's stimulating and accessible *English Society 1580–1680* (1982). For the growth of consumer society in the period, see Joan Thirsk, *Economic Policy and Projects* (Oxford, 1978).

13. See his *Learning to Curse* (1990), e.g. pp. 166–7. There is a burgeoning debate; see, for example, the interesting criticisms from a deconstructive angle in Howard Felperin, *The Uses of Canon* (Oxford, 1990).

14. J.G. Pocock, *Politics, Language, and Time* (1972), p. 23.

15. The standard text is still R.F. Jones, *The Triumph of the English Language: A Survey of Opinions Concerning the Vernacular from the Introduction of Printing to the Restoration* (Stanford, 1953); this now needs balancing with J.W. Binns's survey of *Intellectual Culture in Elizabethan and Jacobean England: The Latin Writings of The Age* (Leeds, 1990).

16. See Ch. 2 of Margaret Spufford, *Small Books and Pleasant Histories: Popular Fiction and its Readership in Seventeenth-Century England* (Cambridge, 1981).

17. Translated by J.W. Binns, *Intellectual Culture*, p. 279.

18. Cicero, *Orator*, xiii. 76; see trans. by H.M. Hubbell in *Cicero* V (Loeb, 1939), p. 363.

19. See the essays of Croll reprinted in *Style, Rhetoric and Rhythm*, ed. J. Max Patrick.

20. George Williamson, *The Senecan Amble: A Study in Prose Form from Bacon to Collier* (Chicago, 1951), p. 193.

21. Winifred Crombie, *Free Verse and Prose Style: An Operational Definition and Description* (1987); there is a summary in her 'Two Faces of Seneca: Metaphysical and Baroque Prose Styles in the Seventeenth Century', *Language and Style* 19 (1986), 26–48. She starts from the Croll–Williamson distinctions, but ends up with a quite different taxonomy.

22. The best study is still Joan Webber, *The Eloquent 'I': Style and Self in Seventeenth-Century Prose* (Madison, 1968); Stephen Greenblatt, *Renaissance Self-Fashioning: From More to Shakespeare* (Chicago, 1980), is a crucial discussion, though confined to the sixteenth century; Francis Barker, *The Tremulous Private Body: Essays on Subjection* (1984) is an important Foucauldian intervention.

23. Donne, Funeral Sermon for Sir William Cokayne, *Sermons on the Psalms and Gospels*, ed. Evelyn Simpson (Berkeley, 1963), p. 219; Thomas Traherne, 'Centuries of Meditation', in *Poems, Centuries and Three Thanksgivings*, ed. Anne Ridler (Oxford, 1966), p. 167; Abiezer Coppe, *A Fiery Flying Roll*, in *Selected Writings*, ed. Andrew Hopton (1987), p. 21; John Bunyan, *The Pilgrim's Progress*, ed. Wharey and Sharrock (Oxford, 1960), p. 8; Dorothy Osborne, *Letters to Sir William Temple*, ed. Kenneth Parker (1987), p. 50; Robert Burton, *The Anatomy of Melancholy* I, p. 1.

Part One
Narrative

Chapter 1
Elizabethan Fiction

Sidney, Lyly, Greene, Nashe and Deloney

Many of the changes in recent fiction, even those associated with the postmodern, such as pastiche, the preoccupation with stylishness, and discontinuity, find a curious, partial echo in this earlier fiction. Elizabethan fiction seems principally designed for stylistic display – true of at least some of Sidney, Lodge, Nashe and Greene. Increasingly common as we move into seventeenth-century fiction is an avowal of plainness, in a product designed for a newly literate middle-class audience, or for women, or for a moment's leisure. Occasionally, as in the religious fiction of Bunyan, we get the sense of fiction as the individual's search through a landscape which is as much of ideas as of other people.

'Novel' as a critical term is seductive but elusive. Michael McKeon has signalled a return to the study of seventeenth-century fiction as the 'origins' of the novel.[1] However, as he demonstrates, there is no one clear line of filiation between seventeenth- and eighteenth-century fiction. The term existed in the period, but as a translation of the French *nouvelle* or Italian *novella*, a short form of maybe a hundred pages distinguished from romance by its commitment to (relatively) realistic story-telling and psychological analysis.[2] But modern, or nineteenth-century, expectations of realism and character will be disappointed; better to think about the fluidity of generic boundaries with Bakhtin:

> In its earliest stages, the novel and its preparatory genres had
> relied upon various extra-literary forms of personal and
> social reality, and especially those of rhetoric . . . . And in
> later stages of its development the novel makes wide and
> substantial use of letters, diaries, confessions, the forms and
> methods of rhetoric associated with recently established

> courts and so forth. Since it is constructed in a zone of
> contact with the incomplete events of a particular present,
> the novel often crosses the boundary of what we strictly call
> fictional literature – making use first of a moral confession,
> then of a philosophical tract, then of manifestoes that are
> openly political, then degenerating into the raw spirituality
> of a confession, a 'cry from the soul' that has not yet found
> its formal contours.[3]

The inclusiveness, the multi-voiced nature of the genre is a good way of looking at developments in prose fiction. In this period we might draw up a different list of forms within the form – rhetoric, certainly, and letters, poems, trial narratives and gallows confessions, sermons, political speeches, travellers' tales, allegory – additions which define the form, rather than additions to some generically secure core. Least of all can we be confident about the relation between realism, history and truth: many of these texts can bear a variation on the old disclaimer, 'Any resemblance to any living person is entirely intentional.' One of many reasons is that journalism and contemporary history are similarly embryonic; only in the 1690s can we trace a significant parallel between novel, news and novelty, and even then it is confusing.[4]

A more obvious generic place to start might be Romance, though, like the novel, it is easier to define by its inclusiveness than its boundaries. The eighteenth-century apologists for the novel defined the 'new' novel form by its anti-romance truthfulness, and, as late as Henry James's seminal preface to *The American*, romance and realism are presented as polar opposites within fiction. Anti-romance as a truth-telling topos is common in our period, too. Nashe attacks those who attempt 'to repair the ruinous walls of Venus's court, to restore to the world that forgotten legendary licence of lying, to imitate afresh the fantastical dreams of those exiled abbey-lubbers, from whose idle pens proceeded those worn-out impressions of the feigned nowhere acts, of Arthur of the Round Table . . . with infinite others'.[5] *Don Quixote*, the greatest European prose fiction of the period, translated into English as early as 1612, is posited on the contrast between book-learnt romance chivalry and real life. The joke in *Don Quixote* is that the modern world is just as full of illusion and enchantment (at least, in the hero's mind) as that of the romance.

Romance is both inclusive and formulaic. On the one hand, almost any incident, however strange, can find its way into the romance narrative; on the other hand, its characteristic topoi, such as wandering in an alien land, disguise, the quartet of lovers, or the last-minute reprieve, can seem like a fiction construction kit. The incredible coincidence is so much a part of the mode that it can be expected, as it were cheered on, by the experienced reader rather than dismissed as a fault. We might even say, with A.C. Hamilton, that the resulting amazement and wonder is actually what the romance writer wants, drawing readers into the text 'in order totally to absorb and possess them'.[6] Such 'possession' could be seen as dangerous. So we find the repertoire of romance usefully but tartly listed in an attack by the Quaker William Penn in 1669:

> Some strange adventures, some passionate amours, unkind
> refusals, grand impediments, tedious addresses, miserable
> disappointments, wonderful surprises, unexpected
> rencounters, and meeting of supposed dead lovers, bloody
> duels, languishing voices, echoing from solitary groves, air-
> heard mournful complaints, deep-fetched sighs sent from
> wild deserts, intrigues managed with unheard-of subtlety;
> and whilst all things seem at the greatest distance, then are
> dead people alive, enemies friends, despair turned to
> enjoyment, and all their impossibilities reconciled; things
> that never were, are not, nor shall, or can be come to pass.[7]

The almost biblical tone of Penn's conclusion indicates that he sees the threat of romance as an alternative mystery – perhaps that the resurrections and reconciliations of romance detracted from, rather than pointed to, the real thing.

Marvels and marriages may be the heart of Elizabethan romance, but, like Cheryl Summerbee in David Lodge's novel, *Small World*, we need to distinguish between the 'debased versions of the sentimental novel of courtship and marriage' which constitute present-day mass-market romances, and books which an Elizabethan might recognise as romance: 'Real romance is a pre-novelistic kind of narrative. It's full of adventure and coincidence and surprises and marvels, and has lots of characters who are lost or enchanted or wandering about looking for each other, or for the Grail, or something like that. Of course, they're often in love too . . .'.[8] The hero has already, and condescendingly, found it odd that she should be reading *The Faerie Queene* rather than 'Bills and Moon' romance, but that also reflects a feature of prose romance from the earlier period – romance is a genre written for women. As Caroline Lucas has argued, many Elizabethan romances show the traces of a male author addressing women readers. More speculatively, she suggests women readers of the romance 'might . . . have found a refuge from a reality of female powerlessness' in it.[9] Fictions of female power in this period are not confined to the romance genre, as every student of Jacobean tragedy knows; and with a queen

on the throne, heroic romance writers such as Spenser and Sidney
make much of Amazons. To adapt Spenser's phrase, fierce wars as well
as faithful loves moralise the position of women in Elizabethan
romance. But romance can still be put down, as only fit for women. If
Arcadia was read by chambermaids, should anyone else take it
seriously?[10]

Romance is also subject to humanist attack, as an inferior, less
serious mode to classical epic. In practice, the Renaissance epic, notably
The Faerie Queene, is very hospitable to the inclusive, interwoven style
of romance. The influence of the Italian romantic epics of Ariosto and
Tasso is considerable here. Puttenham defends less ambitious romances
as 'sundry forms of poems', not subject to the constrictions of unity or
high decorum like epic or tragedy.[11] The same might be said of the
prose romance.

The compositional history of Sidney's prose romance, the *Arcadia*,
demonstrates how close romance and epic became during the period,
although its original shape was that of a five-act pastoral tragicomedy
with poetic interludes. There are in effect three *Arcadias*. The first,
generally known as *The Old Arcadia*, written about 1577–81, circulated
in manuscript, but was not printed in full until 1926. *The New Arcadia*,
containing Sidney's elaborate revision of the first two and a half books,
was published posthumously in 1590 as *The Countess of Pembroke's
Arcadia*, dedicated to Sidney's sister who had become Countess of
Pembroke. It breaks off in mid-sentence. In 1593 a folio version
supervised by the Countess of Pembroke amalgamated the revised
fragment with the rest of the book in its first version, with some
further revision; this composite, often reprinted, is what people
regarded as Sidney's *Arcadia* until Bertram Dobell came across
manuscripts of the earlier version at the beginning of this century.

Both Old and New/composite versions have their fans. The main
factors in defence of the *Old Arcadia* is that it is complete, composed
and circulated as a whole (not a draft), and that it is less verbose – a
relative rather than an absolute virtue, as we shall see. The *New Arcadia*
is, however, a record of Sidney's second thoughts on the text, even if
he seems to have abandoned the revision some time before his early
death. It emphasises and amplifies the heroic aspects of the text. It has
epic ambitions.

In a notable essay on *Arcadia*, Virginia Woolf suggests that 'all the
seeds of English fiction lie latent' in it, 'romance and realism, poetry
and psychology'.[12] Despite this variety in the text, its startling turns of
plot and its emotional range, what might strike another modern reader
coming to it with experience only of later fiction is the prominence of
rhetoric. The characters are forever making speeches to each other.
Their emotion is eloquent. The command of rhetoric can be an index

to a character's self-control, as when Philanax's rage undermines 'his precise method of oratory' when prosecuting the heroes Pyrocles and Musidorus.[13] Or it can disclose a character's true class, as when Pamela sees through Musidorus' disguise as 'Dorus' by 'the matter Dorus spake and the manner he used in uttering it'.[14] As with Hamlet's soliloquies, the skill of arguing is as revealing as the content. At every turn of the plot, the ability to persuade others is as important as swordsmanship. Lions and bears are no match for Pyrocles and Musidorus in their physical valour, but when they are threatened by men well-framed words work best.

Twentieth-century readers may have to suppress a desire to say 'less talk and more action'. For Renaissance readers, Sidney's verbal artifice was a great recommendation. Before the book itself was published, Abraham Fraunce's *The Arcadian Rhetoric* (1588) used it as his principal source of English examples, inaugurating a tradition of Sidney in vernacular rhetorics that lasted long into the seventeenth century. Gabriel Harvey's recommendations in 1593 give an unusually full critical response for any work in the period. The *New Letter of Notable Contents* simply praises the style – 'Is not the prose of Sir Philip Sidney in his sweet *Arcadia* the embroidery of finest Art and daintiest Wit?' In *Pierce's Supererogation* (mostly an attack on Nashe), Harvey praises Sidney's interlinking of discourse, which he values for its didactic quality as well as its eloquence, and the plot, which he sees as a series of incidents more than a unity:

> Read *The Countess of Pembroke's Arcadia*, a gallant legendary,
> full of pleasurable accidents and profitable discourses: for
> three things especially very notable – for amorous courting
> (he was young in years), for sage counselling (he was ripe in
> judgement), and for valorous fighting (his sovereign
> profession was arms); and delightful pastime by way of
> pastoral exercises may pass for the fourth. He that will love,
> let him learn to love of him that will teach him to live, and
> furnish him with many pithy and effectual instructions,
> delectably interlaced by way of proper descriptions of
> excellent personages and common narrations of other
> notable occurrences . . . .[15]

Harvey does not just give us the reaction of a learned and sometimes pretentious connoisseur of rhetoric; he gives us a contemporary critical vocabulary. The stress on 'interlacing' of episodes is a useful account of romance plotting, and shows how they might be extracted as moral exempla, or 'heroical monomachies' (i.e. duels). Sidney's original readers were just as likely to enjoy the details of sword-fighting and horsemanship as those of rhetoric and ethical dilemmas: a gentleman would know of both.

The rhetorical set-pieces in the narrative have a variety of functions. They express love – friendship, courtship, ungoverned passion. They are judicial – arguing a case, discovering the truth, and allotting the right rewards and punishments. So, they are not just operatic set pieces, prose arias. There is a development through the book. The immaturity of Musidorus and Pyrocles is shown in the excess of their rhetoric as well as their instant susceptibility to passion. Here Pyrocles's *copia* (the richness and fullness of expression much desired in the Renaissance), in his rebuke to the unsympathetic Musidorus, matches the extremity of his erotic self-indulgence – as the narrator dryly notes, 'they that think themselves afflicted are apt to conceive unkindness deeply':

> 'Alas', said he, 'Prince Musidorus, how cruelly you deal
> with me! If you seek the victory, take it; and if you list,
> triumph. Have you all the reason of the world, and with me
> remain all the imperfections; yet such as I can no more lay
> from me than the crow can be persuaded by the swan to cast
> off his blackness. But truly, you deal with me like a
> physician that, seeing his patient in a pestilent fever, should
> chide him instead of ministering help, and bid him be sick no
> more; or, rather, like such a friend that, visiting his friend
> condemned to perpetual prison and loaden with grievous
> fetters, should will him to shake off his fetters, or he would
> leave him. I am sick, and sick to the death. I am prisoner;
> neither is there any redress but by her to whom I am slave.
> Now, if you list, leave him that loves you in the highest
> degree; but remember ever to carry this with you: that you
> abandon your friend in his greatest need.'[16]

One has to admire the aesthetics of these sentences. The parallelism within and between them is never too pat – compare 'I am sick . . .' and 'I am prisoner . . . .' Syntactic control is subordinated to intellectual control, even if Pyrocles's intellect is coming second to his resentment. At the end of the book their convolutions of disguise and deceit come up sharply against the virtuous, deliberative oratory of their father Euarchus (who, true to romance convention, does not recognise them, even if he is Solomonic in every other respect). His 'unpassionate nature' is just what a judge needs, 'showing in his face no motions either at the one's or the other's speech, letting pass the flowers of rhetoric and only marking whither their reasons tended'.[17] His verdict is in marked contrast to the highly figurative language of his son and nephew. In his speech, the role of comparisons is taken over by general precepts which govern the particular judgement; so, for example:

> . . . he that terms himself Timopyrus [Pyrocles] denies not
> he offered violence to the lady Philoclea, an act punished by
> all the Grecian laws with being thrown down from a high
> tower to the earth – a death which doth in no way exceed the
> proportion of the trespass; for nothing can be imagined more
> unnatural than by force to take that which, being holily
> used, is the root of humanity, the beginning and maintaining
> of living creatures, whereof the confusion must needs be a
> general ruin.[18]

In Euarchus, the Ciceronian link between oratory and wisdom is remade.

Another sixteenth-century critic, John Hoskins, noted how Sidney's rhetorical figures are closely linked to wider effects of psychology and structure.[19] He notes two favourites in particular. One is antimetabole, the repetition of the same words in a different order to produce a different sense; his example from the *New Arcadia* is 'they misliked what themselves did, and yet did still what themselves misliked'. The other is synoeciosis, or oxymoron, the composition of contraries, like 'witty ignorance' or 'delightful sorrow'. Both of them are chiasmic, cross-over terms; as John Carey notes, precisely suited to the central themes of inner conflict and defeated intention.

Defeated intention is what the story is all about. *The Old Arcadia* is set in the golden, pastoral world of 'ancient' Greece, the world of Greek prose romance as well as pastoral poetry. It begins with a Delphic oracle, obscurely predicting the action of the book, though Duke Basilius attempts to escape its threatening prophecy by retiring with his wife, Gynecia, and two daughters, Pamela and Philoclea, for a year. Though Sidney calls the oracle 'the woman appointed to that impiety', many have seen in the determinism of the plot the dynamic of providence or even Calvinist predestination. It could be like Greek tragedy, too. The ironies that result from Basilius's failure to circumvent the prophecy are not tragic, in the end, but death comes close.

Pastoral was well established as a vehicle for political comment. Should we, then, detect a note of political criticism in the portrait of Basilius? 'Not so much stirred with the care for his country and children as with the vanity which possesseth many who, making a perpetual mansion of this poor baiting place of man's life, are desirous to know the certainty of things to come.'[20] His inability to control his passion for the Amazon Cleophila (actually Pyrocles in disguise) is in sharp contrast to the 'unpassionate' Euarchus, who is pressed to take over as 'protector' towards the end of the story. His death-like sleep, which results from taking a potion by mistake, after imagining he had committed adultery (actually it had been Gynecia all along), could be a metaphor for his irresponsibility as well as a result of plain stupidity.[21] But the ruler who effectively deposed himself is welcomed back as a solution to Euarchus's paternalist dilemma: justice versus family affection. Shakespeare drew on *Arcadia* for the sub-plot of *King Lear*, but Sidney's ending is closer to *Measure for Measure*, with the original ruler back in place along with many of the problems. Euarchus may have decided, admirably, that justice comes first, but the plot decides otherwise, and Pyrocles and Musidorus are rewarded rather than punished. Sidney confronts the problems of justified disobedience but leaves them unresolved.[22] Elizabeth may have been tempted to let passion rule her political judgement, and the ups and downs of her favourites (Sidney's patron Leicester among them) testify to her passionate nature; but it rarely resulted in political disaster, and in the crucial matter of marriage she stood alone, as indeed Sidney recommended.

Alan Sinfield has linked Sidney's critique of absolutist tendencies, here and in his controversial letter to Queen Elizabeth against the proposed Alençon marriage, to his own ambivalent class position, the son of a gentleman, but for a while the heir of Leicester through his mother.[23] If the insecurity shows anywhere it is in the treatment of the lower classes. The shepherds in the main text are either comic or contemptible, and only in the interspersed Eclogues is there any sign of the wise shepherds of pastoral convention. As one of them, Philisides, is taken as a fictional construct of Sidney himself, that can hardly count. The death of one of the Phagonian rebels at the hands of Musidorus is notable. I suppose it is a fitting end for an enemy of civilisation in such a rhetorical text, but the joke is disturbingly heartless:

> A third, finding his feet too slow as well as his hands too
> weak, suddenly turned back, beginning to open his lips for
> mercy, but before he had well entered a rudely compiled
> oration, Musidorus's blade was come betwixt his jaws into
> his throat; and so the poor man rested there for ever with a
> very ill mouthful of an answer.[24]

In the end, though, the regulation of passion is less a political issue than a personal one. It is true that a sixteenth-century prince or an heir can never pretend that the consequences of his or her passions are wholly private. The complex bed-tricks in the dark cave and bedrooms of Book Three show how mistaken such irresponsibility, or furtiveness, can be. The loss, though, is of one's own love, or life, or at most the loved one's reputation, not a kingdom. The strength of the *Arcadia* in such circumstances is its extended description of feelings, like the self-reproach of Gynecia after Basilius goes into his coma, or in this description of Pamela:

> But Pamela who all this while transported with desire, and
> troubled with fear, had never free scope of judgement to
> look with perfect consideration into her own enterprise, but
> even by the laws of love had bequeathed the care of herself
> upon him to whom she had given herself, now that the pang
> of desire with evident hope was quieted, and most part of
> the fear passed, reason began to renew his shining in her
> heart, and make her see herself in herself, and weigh with
> what wings she flew out of her native country, and upon
> what ground she built so strange a determination.[25]

It starts from Petrarchan love psychology, but is on its way to the specifics of circumstance. It reminds us that the enduring strength and popularity of romance is not just due to its catalogues of amazements, or to its fantasies of the power of women, but to its culture of feelings. As in this extract, virtue and reason need to be in control, but the power of feelings, and thus of the character's, and the reader's, subjectivity gives romances like *Arcadia* its principal dynamic.

The influence of Sidney needs to be set alongside the influence of John Lyly in the history of Elizabethan fiction. The sub-title of Lodge's *Rosalynde*, 'Euphues' Golden Legacy', might stand for much romance fiction of the 1590s. Lyly's *Euphues: The Anatomy of Wit* (1578) and its sequel, *Euphues and his England* (1580) set a style for romance fiction, and in particular its vein of argument and moralising, that lasted into the 1590s. Euphuism is well described as a hypertrophy of style. It is a way of writing a sentence in virtually complete subjection to antithesis – though the story itself is a warning against morally empty stylishness. This sentence is a fair sample of the style as well as the narrator's attitude towards the witty young Euphues:

> An old gentleman in Naples, seeing his pregnant wit, his
> eloquent tongue somewhat taunting yet with delight, his
> mirth without measure yet not without wit, his sayings
> vainglorious yet pithy, began to bewail his nurture, and to
> muse at his nature, being incensed against the one as most
> pernicious, and inflamed with the other as most precious.[26]

The symmetries and antitheses operate at every possible level – syntax, sound and sense – and Lyly manages to sustain this for virtually the whole text, not just for the set pieces. As a fashion it was instantly imitable, and answered to the new value placed on eloquence. A fashion in writing is in itself significant, pointing to an organised, or at least substantial and intercommunicating literary world. Euphuism is also indicative of a young, ambitious group of humanist intellectuals, who, as G.K. Hunter argues, are moving away from the early humanist love of learning and eloquence as the path to virtue towards a more instrumental view, of skill in language as a saleable commodity.[27] It is also highly susceptible to parody; and to the critical view once expressed to me as 'if you've read one sentence, you've read them all'. The style may have had the fizz of novelty, but it is an extension of classical Latinate symmetries, in the way that fashion often echoes and stylises the past. The euphuistic sentence can be regarded as a symptom, an attempt to fit experience into neat patterns of language and feeling at a moment of great upheaval. 'It was a substitute for technology, and gave the same feeling of control', in the view of John Carey.[28] However, even following such a hostile account, one would expect to see the cracks in the control showing, and there is certainly a suspicion of wit as amoral intellectual facility even as it is so relentlessly displayed.

Euphues is still the humanist drama of education, with its picture of youth seduced from virtuous study by sensuality. The difference is that, unlike the hero of *Youth*, Euphues is his own vice figure. His wit is the seductive shape-changer, at least as much as Lucilla, whose changeability in love eventually produces the repentance that Euphues's older mentor Eubulus cannot. Lyly thus confronts the major tension in the humanist educational programme: the study of rhetoric is both the path to virtue, in reading ancient wisdom and being able to restate it, and also a training in the techniques of deceit. To certain extent Lyly can get round this by restating one of the central humanist prejudices, that male friendship is more reliable than a woman's love: 'Is not poison taken out of the honeysuckle by the spider, venom out of the rose by the canker, dung out of the maple tree by the scorpion? Even so the greatest wickedness is drawn out of the greatest wit, if it be abused by will, or entangled with the world, or inveigled with women.'[29] It is the fault of the woman, not the chameleon quickness of Euphues's wit. The repentant Euphues retreats to Athens, symbolic of learning, while his friend Philautus remains in the court world of Naples. Even the plot takes on the shape of a euphuistic sentence.

Robert Greene, the most popular fiction writer of the 1580s, began in the euphuistic vein with *Mamillia* (1585, perhaps earlier), but, like Sidney, became increasingly persuaded of the virtues of pastoral. This interest coincided with the translation of the Greek romances of Heliodorus in 1587, and Angel Day's version of *Daphnis and Chloe* in the same year. Because Shakespeare later adapted it for *The Winter's Tale*, his *Pandosto: The Triumph of Time* of 1588 is probably his best-known pastoral romance.

Menaphon: Camilla's alarum to slumbering Euphues (1589) is, as the long title suggests, a kind of farewell to Euphuism; it is also set in an Arcadia akin to Sidney's. Nashe's famous preface 'To the Gentlemen Students of both Universities' praises Greene's true eloquence against those of the 'art-masters' who have to borrow every image and idea from some classical or Italian source. It is more an advertisement for the 'extemporal vein' of his own *Anatomy of Absurdity* than *Menaphon*, but it is also interesting as defence of middle-style prose against the 'bombast' of dramatic verse. When we get to Greene himself, we can see the remnants of euphuistic echoing in some of his sentences, but it has lost the relentlessness of Lyly.[30] It is a resource for high points of emotion, for the narrator or character needing a touch of eloquence. Some of them might break into poetry or song for the same reason, true to their pastoral convention. Modern readers might be reminded of the conventions of the musical – or of Elizabethan drama. Greene is confident enough of these conventions to be ironic with them, as when Menaphon, finding his love 'able to support her state without his purse, became sick for anger, and spent whole eclogues in anguish'.[31]

Like *Arcadia*, the book begins with an oracle, which Democles has to interpret, but the political inflection is already different. He is no Basilius: he is 'as careful for the weal of his country, as the continuance of his diadem' and so calls a Parliament.[32] Responsibility doesn't make him any less melancholy, though. The scene shifts abruptly to Menaphon, the king's shepherd, in a more generally pensive mood. He gives hospitality to three victims of shipwreck, and falls for the beautiful 'Samela', only to lose her to Melicertus, actually the courtier Maximius and the real husband of Samela, who is really Sephestia. But she has to survive the unwittingly incestuous attentions of her lost son Pleudisippus and her father Democles before it is all sorted out. The change of name is enough to convince all three that her resemblance to Sephestia is not because she is Sephestia until the oracle which began the story sorts it all out at the end, courtesy of an old prophetess. Democles abdicates in favour of Pleudisippus (permanently, so no Basilius or Lear-like problems), and everyone else pairs off appropriately in the space of a page. Sexual and social proprieties are restored.

Within the cheerful improbabilities of the romance plot and the sometimes dangerous extremities of emotion, Greene focuses on the ability of language to persuade, express and hide. Sometimes he sets up conversations within the formal *quaestio d'amore* convention (where questions about the ethics or sincerity of love are debated in not entirely objective terms), or singing competitions as in the classical pastoral. However, as the story progresses, the style if not the situation becomes less formal, more conversational, more aware of the ironies and implications of the games that are being played.

The flexibility of *Menaphon* continues into Greene's later works, virtually into fragmentation. This can be fragmentation of plot, with bits of story strung together, or fragmentation of language. He often writes about the deceptive power of language. The 'coney-catching' pamphlets of the 1590s, for example, mingle stories about the cheats, thieves and confidence-men of London with accounts or little dictionaries of their argot, on the assumption that power over their language may be proof against deceit.[33] The imported language of thievery – like 'foist' and 'nip' for pickpocket and cutpurse – gives a strange liveliness to Greene's language, which is an interesting trade-off for his abandonment of the obviously inappropriate language of pastoral love. Like some of Greene's longer works, *Repentance* and *Groatsworth of Wit*, the theme resembles that of the prodigal son parable in Luke's Gospel, but not easily or neatly.[34] There may be a prodigal father, or at least an imperfect one, and the repentance may take the form of marriage as well as reconciliation with parents. In other words, Greene's concern with levels and uses of language is closely linked with his concern with social disruption, particularly in the family.

If Greene repented of romance in his later years, Nashe, who was concerned to take up his mantle as a stylist and satirist, is consistently anti-romance in his extraordinary fiction, *The Unfortunate Traveller*. There may be love-poems interspersed in the narrative in the manner of the romances, but how many of them go on to say this?

> Sadly and verily, if my master said true, I should, if I were a
> wench, make many men quickly immortal. What is't, what
> is't for a maid fair and fresh to spend a little lipsalve on a
> hungry lover? My master beat the bush and kept a coil and a
> prattling, but I caught the bird: simplicity and plainness shall
> carry it away in another world. God wot he was Petro
> Desperato, when I, stepping to her with a Dunstable tale,
> made up my market. A holy requiem to their souls that
> think to woo a woman with riddles.[35]

A Dunstable tale is a plain tale, and, with the proverbial phrase about beating the bush versus catching the bird, Nashe's strategy might seem to be simply that of the plain man who cuts through the courtly guff. The 'dapper monsieur pages' he addresses as his real audience, are, like his narrator, Jack Wilton, likely to appreciate such a victory over their employers and superiors. But Jack is more than a plain speaker. He writes with a supercharged colloquialism which is closer to the eloquence of inebriation than sober plainness. The gestures of plainness – the simple phrase in contrast to convention-bound elaboration, the proverb, the first person openness, are all there; but that is part of the problem. They are there in excess, along with the inventive comic name and the insistent doubling of epithets. In fact, Nashe is so much of a stylist that many of his most astute commentators, from C.S. Lewis to Jonathan Crewe, have suggested that is all he is: the subject is unimportant (Lewis) or 'themelessness' which turns his writing into 'pure performance' (Crewe).[36] But it is not, as both recognise in different ways, just the performance of the comic who needs to keep his audience reading to stay in work – though that can be desperate enough. It is performance to keep out the dark, a darkness that keeps breaking in, from the grotesque physical distress of the victims of battle, disease and execution, to the spiritual distress of doubt and despair. He may be vehement, satiric, self-advertising, but he is also (Arthur Kinney's word) unsettled.[37]

To consider style before plot and character is right for Nashe. However, although the plot of The Unfortunate Traveller seems improvisational, episodic and arbitrary, there are several potential coherences. One is the shape of Jack's journeys, ostensibly through the Europe of Henry VIII's time, with dates neatly jumbled so that he can witness a number of significant events – the Field of the Cloth of Gold, the Anabaptist rising at Münster and Luther's disputations, for example. They follow the itinerary of the Grand Tour, the educational travels in Europe that were coming into vogue for young noblemen.[38] This is doubly ironic, first by being a rogue's journey, a picaresque, as well; and by discovering the high noon of humanism to be flawed or impotent against the forces of evil and chaos. His disillusion with Erasmus and More, and his almost unhinged fury at the populist religion of the Anabaptists suggest a deep crisis in Nashe's key values: civilisation's need for humanist learning and the social and historical coherences provided by religion.

On this latter point, we might also read The Unfortunate Traveller as a tale of repentance. Such narratives tend to have a double form: the narrative functions as a series of examples for the exegesis of a key sacred text, as well as leading to a climax of conversion. So they can be both episodic but with at least a retrospective shape. But Jack's repentance is as speedy as the end of any romance, and does not begin to match the indignation of his earlier satire. Because his original stance is that of the trickster who sees through pretence, seeing through himself at the end is too contradictory. It also sounds a bit Puritan for a largely anti-Protestant, if not quite pro-Catholic author, who learned his trade from the Marprelate controversy.[39] Perhaps Margaret Ferguson's argument is more persuasive, that the ending of the book is an escape from a descent into hell, via the counterfeit paradise of Rome, through the purgatory of Heraclide's plague-house, to the house of the Jew Esdras.[40]

Moral satire, literary virtuosity, but most of all bodies. *The Unfortunate Traveller* is full of grotesque physicality. We see the sweating sickness – 'I have seen an old woman at that season, having three chins, wipe them all away one after another, as they melted to water, and left herself nothing of a mouth but an upper chap.'[41] Or the victims of battle – 'So ordinary at every footstep was the imbrument of iron in blood, that one could hardly discern heads from bullets, or clottred hair from mangled flesh hung with gore.'[42] The climax of the book is an execution on the wheel, with each physical detail grimly humourous – like the executioner, who 'at the first chop with his wood-knife would he fish for a man's heart and fetch it out as easily as a plum from the bottom of a porridge pot'.[43] We must agree with Neil Rhodes, that such grotesquerie is derived from 'the unstable coalescence of contrary images of the flesh: indulged, abused, purged and damned'.[44] It is festive (the executioner is like a cook), but it is also the site of retribution, and at a level of excess which, in the end, is not peculiar to Nashe but to the whole spectacle of judicial violence: 'The very excess of the violence employed is one of the elements of its glory . . . . Justice pursues the body beyond all possible pain.'[45] So does Nashe.

Thomas Deloney

Jack may be a picaresque hero addressing himself to an audience in the pub or below stairs, but he is still the courtier's servant, concerned with courtly modes of behaviour and the humanist ideals of the rhetorician, however ironised or brought into question. When we move to Deloney's fiction we are immediately aware his are the heroes of the middle-class, of early capitalism. But it is not like reading Defoe. On the one hand it is extremely readable: one of those odd moments when twentieth-century reading habits can cope with Renaissance prose with little sense of strangeness. This is partly due to Deloney's skill in dialogue – Merritt Lawlis has calculated that something like four-fifths of Deloney's fiction is in dialogue form.[46] Nor are they limp litanies of agreement that so often pass for dialogues in non-fiction prose. They have a contested or conversational quality, reminiscent of citizen comedy, and they carry the plot on more effectively than the authorial commentary, which is more often used for settings.

Jack of Newbury (or *The Pleasant History of John Winchcombe*) is set in the reign of Henry VIII, and concerns the rise to fortune of a broadcloth weaver. He is chosen as a husband by his mistress, a widow older than he; it is not her lust (like the brothers' view of the Duchess of Malfi) that moves her, as much as his obedience, and his 'good government and discretion'. Nor is he a Puritan; it is just that he spends no more than he budgets for at the tavern on Sundays and holidays, when he is 'as merry as pie'.[47] No one seems worried that she does all the courting, and takes him to church to be married. Jack's motives are carefully shown to be honourable; later, he gets the opportunity to demonstrate that he prefers modesty to wealth in women. Similarly, his generosity in forgiving debts is shown to be magnanimous rather than prudential by two examples, one where he gains, another where he loses.

Perhaps the most interesting example of the display of Jack's values is when he is visited by the king in his progress through Berkshire. Jack clothes his thirty household servants in blue livery, much like the nobleman's retainers; and, like many nobles of the period, Jack has arranged an emblematic entertainment for his monarch. The twist is that Jack's men are guarding an anthill against the 'idle butterflies, their sworn enemies, lest they should disturb this quiet commonwealth who this summer season are making their winter's provision'.[48] The implication is that the industrious weaver is more useful to the commonwealth than courtly butterflies, or warmongers like Wolsey, who bad-temperedly accuses Jack of Lutheran tendencies. The king, of course, agrees with Jack, and is liberal with his gifts on his tour of the workshops, so the workers can have a feast.

Jack refuses a knighthood at the end of the visit, but this is not a rejection of all the values of the court – he produced 150 soldiers for the king's defence, and his banquet is as sumptuous as a nobleman's. In fact the whole story is punctuated by banquets, as if to emphasise the communal, rather than bourgeois-individualist loyalties of Jack the successful earlier industrialist. They also give opportunities for frank speech towards the limits of decorum, which is important in Deloney's exploration of his characters' true values, not the least of which is Jack's plain-speaking.[49] In a brilliant analysis, Laura Caroline Stevenson suggests that Deloney is potentially turning the values of the élite inside out: that he is on the edge of suggesting that hard work is better than privilege, and thus money a more socially useful route to power than birth and royal favour.[50] However, he still stays within the ideals of magnanimity and chivalry rather than the distinctive new ideology of the tradesman's calling propounded in the late seventeenth century by Richard Steele, and subsequently by Defoe. It is as if both the rhetoric and the ethics of praiseworthy behaviour, have yet to respond to changes in society. Perhaps social change needs a language in which it can perceive itself before it can get very far. But we must also count the sale of honours under the early Stuarts, the revolutionary aspects of the 1650s, and, most of all, the multiplication of centres of manufacture in the seventeenth century, as determining factors in the growth of a distictive social consciousness addressed by Defoe. Deloney may have retreated from it somewhat in *The Gentle Craft* (about shoemakers), and his last work *Thomas of Reading* (about clothier heroes in the reign of Henry I), but he remained a bestseller in the seventeenth century, and a small chapbook version of *Jack of Newbury* appears in a trade-list of 1689, along with the jestbooks and the tales of chivalry that it partly derived from a hundred years earlier.[51] Clearly his unusual, even paradoxical blend of the values of romance and realism, of the court and the progressive individual, retained its readability – and its saleability.

Notes

1. Michael McKeon, *The Origins of the English Novel, 1600–1740* (Baltimore, 1987).

2. See Paul Salzman, *English Prose Fiction, 1558–1700: A Critical History* (Oxford, 1985) for definitions: especially pp. 7, 308–11.

3. M.M. Bakhtin, 'Epic and Novel', *The Dialogic Imagination*, ed. Michael Holquist (Austin, 1981), p. 33. The whole essay is highly suggestive for our period; McKeon makes interesting use of it.

4. See J. Paul Hunter, ' "News, and New Things": Contemporaneity and the Early English Novel', *Critical Inquiry* 14 (1988), 493–515.

5. *The Works of Thomas Nashe*, ed. R.B. McKerrow, rev. F.P. Wilson (Oxford, 1958), I, 11.

6. A.C. Hamilton, 'Elizabethan Romance: The Example of Prose Fiction', *English Literary History*, 49 (1982), 287–99.

7. William Penn, *No Cross, No Crown* (1669), p. 41.

8. David Lodge, *Small World* (Harmondsworth, 1985 edn), p. 258.

9. Caroline Lucas, *Writing for Women: The Example of Woman as Reader in Elizabethan Romance* (Milton Keynes and Philadelphia, 1989), p. 7.

10. For a brief compendium of such attacks, see the Introduction to Sidney, *The*

Countess of Pembroke's Arcadia (The New Arcadia), ed. Victor Skretcowicz (Oxford, 1987).

11. George Puttenham, *The Art of English Poesie* (1589), in *Elizabethan Critical Essays*, ed. G. Gregory Smith (Oxford, 1904), II, p. 44.

12. Virginia Woolf, *The Common Reader*, second series (1935), pp. 49–50.

13. Sir Philip Sidney, *The Countess of Pembroke's Arcadia (The Old Arcadia)*, ed. Jean Robertson (Oxford, 1973), p. 399.

14. *Old Arcadia*, p. 100.

15. *Elizabethan Critical Essays*, ed. G. Gregory Smith (Oxford, 1904), II, pp. 282, 263.

16. *Old Arcadia*, p. 24.

17. *Old Arcadia*, p. 403.

18. *Old Arcadia*, p. 406.

19. John Hoskins, *Directions for Speech and Style*, ed. H.H. Hudson (Princeton, 1935), written c. 1599, and quoted in Jonson's *Timber*. See John Carey, 'Structure and Rhetoric in Sidney's Arcadia' in *Sir Philip Sidney: An Anthology of Modern Criticism*, ed. Dennis Kay (Oxford, 1987), pp. 245–64; and Brian Vickers, *In Defence of Rhetoric* (Oxford, 1988), pp. 329–30.

20. *Old Arcadia*, p. 5.

21. Annabel Patterson's point in 'Under . . . pretty tales: Intention in Sidney's *Arcadia*' in *Sir Philip Sidney: An Anthology of Modern Criticism*, pp. 265–85 (also available in her *Censorship and Interpretation*).

22. This is the argument of Richard C. McCoy, *Sir Philip Sidney: Rebellion in Arcadia* (Hassocks, Sussex, 1979), a much subtler book than my one sentence might imply.

23. Alan Sinfield, 'Power and Ideology: An Outline Theory and Sidney's *Arcadia*', *ELH*, 52 (1985), 259–77. For the circumstances and text of the letter, see *Miscellaneous Prose of Sir Philip Sidney*, ed. Katharine Duncan-Jones and Jan van Dorsten (Oxford, 1973), pp. 33–57. Their introduction challenges the common view that Sidney's advice was intemperate and caused his temporary banishment from court.

24. *Old Arcadia*, p. 308.

25. *Old Arcadia*, p. 196.

26. 'Euphues: The Anatomy of Wit', *An Anthology of Elizabethan Prose Fiction*, ed. Paul Salzman (Oxford, 1987), p. 91.

27. G.K. Hunter, *John Lyly: the Humanist as Courtier* (1962).

28. John Carey, 'Sixteenth- and Seventeenth-Century Prose', in *English Poetry and Prose, 1540–1674*, ed. Christopher Ricks (1970), p. 364.

29. 'Euphues: The Anatomy of Wit', p. 146.

30. For a discussion based on Greene's *Card of Fancy* (1584) see Robert B. Heilman, 'Greene's Euphuism', in *Unfolded Tales: Essays on Renaissance Romance*, ed. George M. Logan and Gordon Teskey (Ithaca, 1989), pp. 49–73.

31. Robert Greene, *Menaphon* ed. G.B. Harrison (Oxford, 1927), p. 74. For useful

critical discussions, see W.W. Barker, 'Rhetorical Romance', in *Unfolded Tales*, especially pp. 84–8; and Walter R. Davis, *Idea and Act in Elizabethan Fiction* (Princeton, 1969), which regards *Menaphon* as Greene's masterpiece.

32. *Menaphon* , p. 21.

33. A number of anthologies give good texts; see, e.g., *Coney-Catchers and Bawdy Baskets*, ed. Gamini Salgado (Harmondsworth, 1972). Many university libraries will have the facsimile 'Bodley Head Quartos'.

34. The best discussion is that of Richard Helgerson, *The Elizabethan Prodigals* (Berkeley, 1976), Ch. 5. The authorship of *Greene's Groatsworth of Wit* has been questioned.

35. Thomas Nashe, *The Unfortunate Traveller and Other Works*, ed. J.B. Steane, (Harmondsworth, 1972), p. 308.

36. C.S. Lewis, *English Literature of the Sixteenth Century Excluding Drama* (Oxford, 1954), pp. 41–6; Jonathan Crewe, *Unredeemed Rhetoric: Thomas Nashe and the Scandal of Authorship* (Baltimore, 1982), p. 2 and *passim*.

37. Arthur F. Kinney, *Humanist Poetics: Thought, Rhetoric and Fiction in Sixteenth-Century England* (Amherst, 1986), p. 309.

38. Kinney's point; Philip Sidney's spectacularly successful tour is traced by James Osborne, *Young Philip Sidney* (New Haven, 1972), and see also the revised version of John Stoye, *English Travellers Abroad 1604–1667* (New Haven, 1989) for the idea of travel in this period as an art to be learned.

39. For Marprelate, see Ch. 2 below; for Nashe's 'discreet Catholicism', see Charles Nicholl, *A Cup of News: The Life of Thomas Nashe* (1984), pp. 158–60.

40. Margaret Ferguson, 'Nashe's *The Unfortunate Traveller*: The "Newes of the Maker" Game', *ELR* 11 (1981), 165–82.

41. *The Unfortunate Traveller* , p. 274.

42. *The Unfortunate Traveller* , p. 286.

43. *The Unfortunate Traveller* , p. 369.

44. Neil Rhodes, *Elizabethan Grotesque* (1980), p. 4.

45. Michel Foucault, *Discipline and Punish*, trans. Alan Sheridan (paper edn 1979), p. 34.

46. See the introduction to *The Novels of Thomas Deloney*, ed. Merritt E. Lawlis (Bloomington, 1961); Lawlis's critical comments are expanded in *Apology for the Middle Class: The Novels of Thomas Deloney* (Bloomington, 1960).

47. 'Jack of Newbury', in *An Anthology of Elizabethan Prose Fiction*, ed. Salzman (Oxford, 1987), p. 315.

48. 'Jack of Newbury', p. 343.

49. Cf. the discussion of banquet imagery in Ch. 4 of Mikhail Bakhtin, *Rabelais and his World*, trans. Hélène Iswolsky (Bloomington, 1984 edn).

50. Laura Caroline Stevenson, *Praise and Paradox: Merchants and Craftsmen in Elizabethan Popular Literature* (Cambridge, 1984).

51. See Margaret Spufford, *Small Books and Pleasnt Histories: Popular Fiction and its Readership in Seventeenth-Century England* (Cambridge, 1981), pp. 241–4, 265. Chapbooks were small, cheap books, often sold by pedlars.

Chapter 2
Restoration Fiction

Bunyan, Behn and Congreve

Leaping from Deloney to Bunyan involves skipping a wide range of fiction. There is Sidneyan romance, most strikingly *The Countess of Montgomery's Urania* written by Lady Mary Wroth, Sidney's niece. This appeared in 1621, but had to be withdrawn because its references to one contemporary in particular caused offence, and a long continuation has remained in manuscript until now.[1] The Elizabethan tradition of neo-Hellenic romance also continued, most interestingly in the autobiographical *Loose Fantasies* of Sir Kenelm Digby (written c. 1628, but not published until 1827–28). This mixes abstract, Platonic discourse about the nature of love with a fairly close account of his own love (as Theagenes, a character from Heliodorus) for Lady Venetia Stanley (Stelliana). The narrative which breaks through the speculation is lively and engaging.[2] The romance tradition also continued at a less exalted level in translation, particularly from the French. There were important translations of the greatest works of European prose fiction, Cervantes' *Don Quixote* by Thomas Shelton in 1612 and 1620, and Rabelais' *Gargantua and Pantagruel* by Sir Thomas Urquhart in 1652, completed by Motteux in 1694. Urquhart's prose is an impressive response to Rabelais' own inventiveness.

There are the accounts of fantastic voyages, some of them not easily classifiable as fiction, like many a traveller's tale. Bacon's *New Atlantis* is discussed in the context of his scientific writing below. Francis Godwin's *The Man in the Moon* (1638) is the story of Domingo Gonzales, who travels from the Canary Islands to the moon attached to a trained flock of birds (a diagram is included). The scientific details, such as weightlessness, are quite sophisticated; the encounters with the 'Lunars' consciously parallel the style of factual accounts of visits to faraway foreign courts. As with a number of travel narratives of the period, Godwin shows how the writer of fiction will invariably appropriate the style of historicity. Strangeness can even reinforce a claim to truth.[3]

There is a curious parallel between the greatest fiction writers of the Restoration period, John Bunyan (1628–88) and Aphra Behn (1640–89). Bunyan was a Nonconformist, jailed for twelve years, uncompromisingly Christian in every page he wrote. Behn was a Tory, a government spy for a while, erotic and scandalous – nonconformist in her openness about sexual matters, in the way that Rochester, her friend, was, as well as in her loyalty to the Stuart cause in the 1680s. Neither was university-educated – Bunyan because of his poverty and lack of secondary education, Behn because she was a woman. As writers of fiction, they both show an ability to pick up on different aspects of the romance tradition, criticise them and mix them generically to produce powerful and innovative fictions.

Bunyan had already published some twenty-five books of religious controversy, doctrine and poetry, including his remarkable spiritual autobiography, *Grace Abounding to the Chief of Sinners*, when the first part of *The Pilgrim's Progress* was published in 1678. He had once, he confesses, been a fan of popular romances and sensation literature – 'give me a ballad, a newsbook, George on horseback, or Bevis of Southampton, give me some book that teaches curious arts, that tells of old fables; but for the holy Scriptures I cared not'.[4] His conversion to Christianity was, in all sorts of important ways, a conversion to the Bible, to the Word. It brought out his embryonic literacy, gave him an identity (someone spoken to and welcomed), and gave him a source of homiletic and literary power. The power is needed for the contest. Everything and everyone in Bunyan's life, and in particular for Christian in *The Pilgrim's Progress*, has to be evaluated. Is it helping him to heaven, or hell? The journey 'from this world to that which is to come' is full of traps, by-ways, destroyers and, equally dangerous, false pilgrims. It is the Word and what it points to that sets Christian off and guides him. But it needs interpreting. Here is the impressive, direct, troubled opening of Part One, literally crying out for interpretation:

> As I walked through the wilderness of this world, I lighted
> on a certain place, where was a den; and I laid me down in
> that place to sleep: and as I slept I dreamed a dream. I
> dreamed, and behold *I saw a man clothed with rags, standing in*
> *a certain place, with his face from his own house, a book in his*
> *hand, and a great burden upon his back.* I looked, and saw him
> open the book, and read therein; and as he read, he wept and
> trembled: and not being able longer to contain, he brake out
> with a lamentable cry; saying, *what shall I do?*[5]

The italicised portion in the middle is unlocked by five biblical references in the margin, which explain the precise theological significance of each phrase. Bunyan's allegory can be read from the Bible because so much of it is generated from the Bible. It is not just at this micro-level, of individual phrases, or events, or characters, but the central images of the fiction – pilgrimage as exodus, for example.[6]

As an allegory, it does not need much translation anyway – not in the sense that Spenser needs a reader's guide. A biblical concordance, one of Bunyan's own tools, helps. But the jury who condemn Faithful in Vanity Fair, Mr Blind-man, Mr No-good, Mr Malice and so on, down to Mr Implacable, stand self-explained and self-condemned. In many of the difficult instances, Bunyan supplies an interpreter, in the emblematic spectacles of the House of the Interpreter, or with Evangelist who first sets Christian on his way. Yet Christian can forget, or misread; and some of the false pilgrims, in the testing case of Mr Ignorance in particular, can mistake the word fatally.[7] In Doubting Castle, perhaps the most haunting episode of all, Christian and Hopeful are beaten up by Giant Despair until they discover the key of promise which was in Christian's bosom all the time.

Christian's heroism, then, involves a heroism of interpretation, and of making the right choice – right from the beginning, when he reverses Adam's mistake, leaving his wife in the City of Destruction rather than sharing her damnation. Like Milton, Bunyan is redefining the heroic. It is a commonplace of Milton criticism to suggest that he redefined heroism under the pressure of political defeat by a monarchy he despised, and the tension inherent in both Renaissance and Reformation views of humanity, its mixture of greatness and fallenness, and the nature of Christ's example. Part One of *The Pilgrim's Progress* effectively does for popular romance what *Paradise Lost* does for classical epic. Not so consciously, perhaps, and not completely – in particular, the eroticism of romance is left for *Mr Badman*. In *The Pilgrim's Progress*, Bunyan transforms the crusader tradition of the hero of faith, as he found it in the seventeenth-century prose versions of the Sir Bevis and St George legends.[8] Bevis is simply a heroic swordsman; George is more of a legendary figure, with a miraculous birth (in Coventry) and dragons to fight. Their Christianity consists of killing Saracens and resisting the charms of eligible and remarkably unsecluded Moslem women, interspersed in George's case with a spirituality of the miraculous, and even an inward struggle.

Another of the Seven Champions of Christendom, St Anthony, has an experience in the 'vale of walking spirits' similar to the Valley of the Shadow of Death that Christian has to pass through. Bunyan's treatment, however, is much more extensive: he firms up the biblical detail, for example with a ditch on one side for the blind leading the

blind, and the bottomless 'quag' on the other side which King David
(who named the valley) once fell into. He is specific in a different way
from Johnson, who lists the 'horrible hearings' St Anthony has to
endure; Bunyan has the wicked one suggesting blasphemies to
Christian, who does not have 'the discretion either to stop his ears, or
to know from whence those blasphemies came'.[9] Then the counter-
voice of Psalm 23, 'Though I walk through the valley of the shadow of
death, I will fear none ill, for thou art with me' brings on the morning.
Bunyan is more precise in his biblical and psychological detail; he also
makes a different point about the hero's courage. William Empson's
poem 'Courage Means Running' says that it is 'usual for a man of
Bunyan's courage to respect fear'. St Anthony may be at his wits' end,
but 'having an undaunted courage, exempting all fear', he prays for
deliverance.[10] Christian may wield his weapons and cry 'with a most
vehement voice', but no reader can doubt that he is very scared indeed,
and that is part of his heroism. The popular romance or saint's life does
not admit that model of the hero. It may be the difference between the
piety of devotion to the saint who is already a supernatural being, and
the Puritan notion of the 'saint' as every justified sinner.

At the end of the Valley, the Dreamer sees 'blood, bones, ashes, and
mangled bodies of men, even of pilgrims that had gone this way
formerly' – victims of Giants Pope and Pagan. Bunyan might have
expected martyrdom while he was in prison, from prison fever if not
the gallows. In prison he had read Foxe's *Acts and Monuments*, which
gave him his Church history and, along with his Bible, Acts
particularly, a perspective on persecution. The 1665 *Prison Meditations*
contrast the valour of those 'That will not stick to have a touch/With
any in the land' with those who 'conquer when they . . . fall'. This is
precisely the victory of Faithful, put to death in Vanity Fair on the
spurious evidence of Envy, Superstition and Pickthank (a sycophant or
tell-tale).

Christian himself becomes a glorious predecessor for his wife,
Christiana, the heroine of Part Two (1686), produced after a number of
spurious hack sequels. There is more of a community feel to this right
from the start, with her children and her neighbour Mercy accompany-
ing her, when Christian had to go through the early part of his journey
alone, or in the company of waverers. Although this has its attractions,
and it makes for a much more 'realistic' story in terms of everyday
detail, there are two key limitations. One is the reduced stature of the
opposition; for example, no one gets imprisoned in Doubting Castle,
though they release Despondency and his daugher Much-Afraid.
Instead, Giant Despair and his wife are killed in instant combat, and
they take seven days to demolish the castle. Does this mean that no one
will ever despair again? Or simply that the community of the faithful is

a better hedge against despair than the individual pilgrim with his fallible memory? The other limitation is Bunyan's retreat from the spiritual self-sufficiency of the female pilgrims. For the second half of Part Two they become annexes to the exploits of their pastoral protectors, Great-Heart and Valiant-for-Truth, who in their spiritual sword-wielding are themselves reversions to the chivalric types Bunyan had earlier reworked more radically.[11]

At the end, both are redeemed by the re-emergence of Christiana in her own right, called in the same words as the Virgin Mary was, and the pilgrims' encounter with the last enemy, death. Here, too, Bunyan's writing moves into a high elegiac mode, owing much to his principle biblical source, Ecclesiastes, mixed with the heroism of the weak: this is Mr Despondency:

> My will and my daughter's is, that our desponds, and slavish
> fears, be by no man ever received, from the day of our
> departure, for ever; for I know that after my death they will
> offer themselves to others. For, to be plain with you, they
> are ghosts, the which we entertained when we first began to
> be pilgrims, and could never shake them off after. . . .
> When the time came for them to depart, they went to the
> brink of the river. The last words of Mr Despondency were
> 'Farewell night, welcome day.' His daughter went through
> the river singing, but none could understand what she said.[12]

It is part of Bunyan's greatness that he is gentle with the weak, bitingly humorous with the hypocrites and bullies.

Historically, we can see many of the obstacles to the pilgrims' progress as the problems of Bunyan's own church, as much as the particular inward experience of Bunyan's own conversion. For example, Mr Worldly Wiseman, introduced into the third edition, exemplifies the new, moralist Anglican position, with a tone of condescension towards common men with serious spiritual concerns: 'it is happened unto thee as to other weak men, who meddling with things too high for them, do suddenly fall into thy distractions'.[13] Christian follows his advice, but on the road to the village of Morality to meet Legality, his fears increase rather than decrease, and he is rescued by Evangelist, who points him again to the cross, instead of the 'cheat' of legalism. This corresponds to Bunyan's own period, prior to conversion, when he tried to amend his life by obedience rather than faith; but it also links with his attack on Edward Fowler, the Latitudinarian minister in Bedfordshire in *A Defence of the Doctrine of Justification, By Faith* (1672).[14] Bunyan's quarrel is not just personal, but pastoral; he sees such errors as attacks on his own flock. The irony is that 'Legality' in another guise had put him in prison for twelve years for preaching the true faith.

The power of *The Pilgrim's Progress* stems from a number of sources. Bunyan's grounding in the Bible and Foxe, as well as his critical reworking of romance and folktale elements combine with a sometimes disturbing aural and visual imagination. The conflicts of Part One in particular show how spiritual seriousness and satiric humour can be mutually reinforcing.

The original 'Part Two' to *The Pilgrim's Progress* was *The Life and Death of Mr Badman*, a dialogue between Mr Wiseman and Mr Attentive published in 1680. The form was common in religious tracts; Arthur Dent's best-selling *Plain Man's Pathway to Heaven* was one of the books Bunyan's wife brought with her as a dowry, and is one clear influence. The dialogue between two like-minded characters can itself lack dramatisation; fortunately Mr Attentive is keen to push on and get to details (particularly Badman's death) enough to make the device occasionally interesting.

The narrative itself is the life story of Mr Badman, from birth to death; but, while he passes from stage to stage of development in wickedness, the narrative thrust is interrupted, partly by the systematic nature of Bunyan's analysis of wickedness, akin to the earlier parade of the Deadly Sins; partly by the interspersed narratives, sometimes a couple of pages long, where stories of other wicked characters reinforce the message about whichever transgression Badman is committing at the time. Thus the style is closer to anecdotal conversation than continuous narrative. Badman is typical rather than a strongly characterised individual. This may make him less sympathetic than Christian, but there are plenty of sympathetic villains in literature, and they have a skewing effect on the most explicit of moral frameworks.

Badman's progress begins with the effects of 'original corruption'; children 'learn to sin by example too, but example is not the root, but rather the temptation unto wickedness'.[15] He then proceeds through lies, pilfering, swearing and cursing to more adult (or at least adolescent) sins such as drunkenness and whoring. There is a nice example where a gentleman proves to his drunken groom that he is worse than a horse – 'he will drink but to satisfy nature, but thou wilt drink to the abuse of nature . . . he will drink, that he may be more servicable to his master, but thou, till thou art uncapable of serving either God or man'.[16]

Badman's attitude to religion is the key to his condemnation: he has the opportunity to follow true Christianity, but refuses it. He has a good master and family; he goes to godly sermons, but falls asleep, giggles, or fixes 'his adulterous eyes upon some beautiful object that was in the place, and so all sermon-while, therewith be feeding of his fleshly lusts'.[17] Most heinously, he deceives a rich wife into marrying him with a show of piety. This scheme, with his swift reversion to drink and prostitutes, and her humiliation, is at once the most novelistically conceived part of the book and at one with its didactic framing. In this case, says Wiseman, Badman's wife should have consulted a godly friend or minister before getting tangled. However, in a characteristic Bunyan mix of biblical and folk proverbs, 'the bird in the air, knows not the notes of the bird in the snare, until she comes hither herself . . . therefore I fear, that but little warning will be taken by young girls'.[18]

There are strong links between these examples and the problems Bunyan's own fellowship in Bedford was experiencing. Just as damaging as sexual misdemeanours and 'mixed' marriages were the economic sins that Badman goes on to commit, 'breaking', or going bankrupt in order to cheat his creditors, and using deceitful weights and scales. Wiseman and Attentive are worried by the conflicting demands of the market and the Christian ethic (particularly towards the poor) when it is clear that the old 'just price' approach is neither biblical nor workable.[19]

Badman's death is a rebuke to the 'art of dying' tradition, which suggests that a peaceful death is a Christian death. Badman dies like a lamb, but the quietness is a judgement on his spiritual imperviousness. Bunyan is not original – similar remarks can be found in the Puritan William Perkins at the beginning of the century – but he dramatises the perception, that a good man can die in fear and a wicked one in peace, to great effect.

There are literary reasons why *Mr Badman* is relatively unpopular – the lack of real conflict, and the uneasy relation between dialogue, story telling, and sermonising. There are theological reasons too. *Mr Badman* represents the doctrine of reprobation, the Calvinist doctrine of those that are not elected to eternal salvation. Bunyan's judgement on Restoration society, its debauchery and disregard for the poor, represents a familiar mode of polemic. The fate of the individual, however, exposes a paradox in Calvinism, as Stuart Sim puts it: 'Predestination demands that the elect can take no credit for their salvation, whereas the reprobate, although similarly predetermined as to ultimate fate, must carry the blame for their own damnation.'[20] Bunyan closes the case against Badman, as much by the mode of the telling – external, judgemental – as by the cumulative weight of the list of his sins. At the end of Part One of *The Pilgrim's Progress*, there is 'a way to hell, even from the gates of heaven, as well as from the City of Destruction'.[21] In Bunyan's preaching there is a way to heaven from the gates of hell. But not for Mr Badman. As Attentive remarks, 'this is a staggering dispensation. It is full of the wisdom and anger of God'.[22]

Bunyan's last allegory, *The Holy War*, returns to the individual believer, transformed into Mansoul, a battleground between the armies of Emmanuel and Diabolus. There is a double focus in theological time, as it is the history of world salvation, from creation and fall to the second coming of Christ, and also the history of the ups and downs in the salvation of the individual soul. There are epic ambitions here, and the armies marching and countermarching, the lists of captains, and the speeches, are all part of that flavour. The allegory operates most often as a distancing, generalising effect; on the way, there are lots of incidental pleasures. The problem is that they tend to stay at the local level. The naming, say, might be witty, but the gain is not sustained or developed. For example, the trial of the Diabolonians, an anti-type of the trial in Vanity Fair, makes good play with the hypocritical renaming of the Diabolonians, like Covetousness 'covered' with the name of Good Husbandry. Bunyan's humour is usually at its most telling with false fronts. At a more epic level, there is some impressive speech-making for Emmanuel, and a good deal of relish in the military detail of marching and siege warfare. We remember that Bunyan served in the Parliamentary Army.[23] Is *The Holy War* an allusion to that?

Twenty years earlier, the millennialist flavour of some of *The Holy War* could have signalled a Fifth Monarchist message, a call to uprising. In fact the principal political allusion is to the remodelling of Bedford corporation – though the principal events happened shortly after the book was published.[24] Bunyan's politics were of principled opposition rather than insurrection; though, as Forrest and Sharrock argue, 'In *The Holy War* . . . the struggle for man's soul is seen as emphatically a political transaction.'[25] That transaction, those politics, are what mattered to Bunyan. It does not make him apolitical: a purely devotional and evangelistic picture of Bunyan is almost as much of a mistake as regarding his Christianity as a form of 'false consciousness' masking his political nonconformity. At the risk of minor anachronism, he is best described as a Puritan writer. In the very energy of his exclusions he found a fresh way of writing Christian fiction.

Mr Badman avoided good books for 'beastly romances, and books full of ribaldry, even such as immediately tended to set all fleshly lusts on fire'.[26] Had he survived, he might have found a suitably lusty tale in Aphra Behn's *Love Letters Between a Nobleman and His Sister* (1684–87), though, if his drinking and whoring had not completely destroyed his brain-cells and his sexual politics, he might have noticed that the sensuality leads to some unusual, and critical turns in the romance genre. Behn was already an established professional playwright and poet when she turned to original fiction late in her career. Many of her plays, as well as the novels she had translated from the French, were explorations of different aspects of romance.

The first of the three parts is entirely epistolary; fiction in letters is not Behn's invention, but she takes it to new levels of sophistication. But the convention breaks down when the lovers elope in Part Two, and a narrative voice is needed to describe them together, as well as linking the letters which remain crucial to the plot but become less frequent. By Part Three the narrator is entirely in control, marshalling the occasional letter from abroad, but increasingly obtrusive, ironic, and distant from her creations. The experience of reading the three parts thus involves a growing recognition of the hypocrisies of the lovers, a distancing compensated for by increased intimacy with the authorial voice.[27] To begin with, the affair between Philander (well, yes, the name is a give-away) and his cousin (the 'sister' of the title) is sensational, and the thrill of taboo-breaking is coupled with openly sexy writing. The pattern of anticipation, the description of sexual experience, and the post-coital anxiety that is repeated in all the sections has one reaching for words like 'soft pornography', though 'soft' is the keyword – not just because of the level of detail, but because 'softness' rather than violence is the way Behn writes about sex most of the time, males as well as females. There are, it is true, some odd jokes with pistols going off (real ones that kill and wound) in Part Three. Male impotence spoils the first sexual encounter in the book, too; a subject Behn also addressed in her poem 'The Disappointment', but in the context an indication that Philander may be literally 'clapped out', not on his first affair.

The language of passion is intense, excessive, bearing little relation to truth, though truthfulness is an issue – 'true love is all unthinking artless speaking, incorrect disorder, and without method, as 'tis without bounds or rules', suggests the narrator in Part Two, but this is after Sylvia has torn up her first draft.[28] True love may break the literary or social rules, but Sylvia is increasingly revealed as an artful rule-breaker. She is frankly, physically attracted to a number of men, and though she takes Octavio (to whom she has been temporarily entrusted) at the end of Part Two from lust for vengeance on the lying Philander (who has been making love to Octavio's sister) more than lust for his body, her approach is of sexual initiative tempered with the need of male protection. With old Sebastian towards the end it is no more than lust for his jewels.

As with seventeenth-century drama, there is, in the monastery or nunnery, a stark alternative to sex once the plot has been relocated in Catholic Europe. Both Calista and Octavio take that option, though the scene where he serenely takes his vows is suffused with 'softness', not just because he is joining the chaste but not particularly austere Bernardines, but because of the female reaction at the ceremony. Sylvia is close to collapse (though 'not a nature to die for love'[29]), and other women sigh for him more than they would at his funeral, collecting locks of his hair as he is tonsured. In a way his final undressing and taking the habit is just as erotic as earlier descriptions of Sylvia's loose negligées.

All this eroticism and European adventure would make *Love Letters* interesting, not simply sensational, in its reworking of the romance tradition by its conscious deployment of a female author-figure. Behn's major fiction is also interesting because of its relation to fact. *Love Letters* is virtually a *roman à clef*. The story of Sylvia and Philander is based on the abduction of Lady Henrietta Berkeley by her brother-in-law Forde, Lord Grey of Werke in 1682. Grey was a supporter of Monmouth, who appears in the book as Cesario, with his mistress, Lady Henrietta Wentworth, as Hermione, Shaftesbury as Tomaso, and so on. The rakes are thus neither Tory nor crypto-Catholic, but part of a Protestant rebellion. The move from Sylvia the seduced innocent to Sylvia the vamp is matched by an increased attention to the Cesario/Monmouth plot in the Third Part. Protestantism is satirised as black magic and superstition, compared to the reverent softness of the Catholic scenes. The final tone of the book is ironic; the sexual and political deceiver Philander is eventually pardoned 'and came to court, in as much splendour as ever, being very well understood by all good men'.[30]

Behn was undoubtedly a Tory satirist with Catholic sympathies, and was disillusioned with James II's political incompetence, when he seemed to stand for all she did. However, late seventeenth-century party attitudes are complicated, and Behn's best-known piece, *Oroonoko*, shows how a recognisably Tory respect for nobility and loyalty can translate into something very close to an anti-slavery tract.

The story is based on Behn's own experience in Surinam, but herein lies a critical pitfall. One can, with most of the Behn criticism, take a biographical path, and see it as a fairly reliable, if fictionalised, piece of history or autobiography. The opposite approach, looking at questions of narration and its relation to romance, is more fruitful for critical purposes – after all, no one criticises Defoe or Swift for twisting the facts to fit the fiction – but that, too, runs the danger of missing the hybrid nature of the book. Travellers' tales introduce themselves as reliable eye-witness accounts; so do fictions; so does everything in between. 'I was myself an eye-witness' is an ambiguous generic marker.[31] It might mean that Behn did not 'invent' anything in the story, simply observed and reported it; more plausibly, to adopt

Bakhtin, it demonstrates 'the novel's special relationship with extra-literary genres, with the genres of everyday life and with ideological genres'.[32] The tales of travel, of course, combine the everyday and the ideological; the everyday life of a primitive tribe inevitably contains an ideological comment on Western civilisation. The descriptions of Indians with which the book begins use the common trope of primitivism as prelapsarian as well as unadorned 'Nature': 'these people represented to me an absolute idea of the first state of innocence, before man knew how to sin: and 'tis most evident and plain, that simple nature is the most harmless, inoffensive and virtuous mistress'.[33] Such truthfulness is vulnerable to the colonisers' deceit, and it is that contrast, innocence versus 'civilised' promise-breaking, that constructs the plot and the ideology of the book.

Oroonoko, the royal slave from Africa, has a similar truthful nobility. It is complicated by the fact that he had a French tutor who taught him morals as well as languages back in Coramantien, and he has a Roman rather than a flat Negro nose. His owner nicknames him Caesar, which signals ownership, as well as inability to pronounce the name; but also a recognition of his heroic qualities.[34] Behn laments that his heroism only has her 'female pen' to celebrate it; though their shared powerlessness links them, for all Oroonoko's physical strength and bravery.

Much of the plot has a romance quality; twice Oroonoko loses his love Imoinda, once at home and once as a result of slavery, itself the punishment for their illicit love. Their native language of sighs is reinforced by Western romance formulas.

As Michael McKeon has argued, all this is epistemologically unstable.[35] Behn is torn between her admiration for primitive simplicity and her progressive, sceptical concern about native superstition and credulity. In a way, this is matched by her ambivalence about colonialism, supporting it and admiring its more honest exponents, and yet investing strong sympathy with the slave rebellion. Describing any sort of rebellion in the 1680s runs the risk of being decoded in different ways, as we have seen with Bunyan's *Holy War*. There is a tension between the language of liberty that Oroonoko uses to stir up his slaves, the language of the Civil War, and the description of his death, comparable to the cult of King Charles the Martyr.

In *Love-Letters*, Behn had moved from frank exploitation of the romance to sober, ironic revaluation; in *Oroonoko* passionate involvement produces a less settled mixture. That Oroonoko might be more truly 'royal' than the representatives of her own king links it with a whole range of literature in the Restoration about European expansion. There was a tangible link, the costume used in Dryden's *The Indian Queen* which Behn brought back from Surinam. Like the oxymoron of

Behn's subtitle, 'The Royal Slave', it symbolises the tension between aristocratic and mercantile values in conquest.[36] It is both noble in origin, and a commodity – just like the prose romance at the end of the seventeenth century.

The Preface to William Congreve's *Incognita* (1692) contains a well-known contrast between the romance and the novel, which appears to separate the two at least partly along aristocratic/bourgeois lines, while maintaining the sense of romance as wonder which we noticed in Elizabethan examples:

> Romances are generally composed of the constant loves and
> invincible courages of heroes, heroines, kings and queens,
> mortals of the first rank, and so forth; where lofty language,
> miraculous contingencies and impossible performances
> elevate and surprise the reader into a giddy delight . . . .
>   Novels are of a more familiar nature; come near us, and
> represent to us intrigues in practice . . . . Romances give
> more of wonder, novels more delight.[37]

The romance as the genre of amazement is familiar to us from Elizabethan examples. Congreve goes on to say that his novel will take its cue from the dominant form of the drama, certainly in the plotting; and we don't have to know that he was on the brink of a successful dramatic career to see the links with Restoration comedy (if Restoration is still the right label in the 1690s). The rapidly escalating complexes of mistaken identity, disguise and instantaneous falling in love sidestep any problems of characterisation. The 'unity of contrivance' which he proposes as the fictional equivalent of 'unity of action' is what counts.

The young, naive 'cavaliers', Aurelian and Hippolito, disguise themselves as each other for love and honour in a Florence where masking seems to be not just carnival but a way of life. Their contrivances, and those of their lady-loves, tend to be self-defeating, but they are rescued by the power of coincidence. We might acknowledge this as characteristic of a romance tradition, but, as Aubrey Williams has proposed, it might equally be seen as an exemplary tale of the workings of providence, fit to stand alongside Restoration preaching on the subject.[38] Romance 'error' and Christian providence are at least as old as *The Faerie Queene*.

The arch, ironic, self-aware narrator that leads us through all this is hardly a Restoration moralist, though. He owes a lot to Scarron, whose novels were published in English in 1665, and whose self-conscious jocularity with his characters was still in vogue in the 1680s and 1690s. Aphra Behn's *The Court of The King of Bantam* is one example; most of the *novelle* published in Peter Motteux's monthly *Gentleman's Journal* (1692–94) are in the same vein, though one could go back to Walter Charleton's *The Ephesian Matron* (1659) or even Nashe for parallels.[39] For Congreve it involves a mixing of styles, an almost epic description of dusk, followed by 'Now, the reader I suppose to be upon thorns at this and the like impertinent digressions, but let him alone and he'll come to himself, at which time I think fit to acquaint him that when I digress, I am at that time writing to please myself; when I continue the thread of the story, I write to please him.'[40] The manner is hardly ingratiating. It does, however, give Congreve a distance between the well-meaning naiveties of his heroes and his (and some of his readers') sophistication which is ironic but not cynical: as Paul Salzman puts it, 'the appeal of a pattern with the knowledge of its artificiality'.[41] The values implicit in the subtitle, 'Love and Duty Reconciled', are nowhere called into question. The knives may be out in Italy, but it is no longer the sink of moral values (and perhaps the pretext for prurience) that it was earlier in the century.

There is an inventive humour in the language describing the lovers, though, what in poetry might be called Clevelandism, which suggests an audience that is still reading for the language as well as the plot: 'Aurelian, as if he had mustered up all his spirits purely to acquit himself of that passionate harangue, stood mute and insensible, like an alarm clock that had spent all its force in one violent emotion.'[42] The inventiveness is largely spent on this kind of bathos, and of course the plot. There may be a dark series of potential disasters – rape, murder, and dishonour – but Congreve's tone rarely rises to such tragic possibilities.

To conclude, then, this brief survey of seventeenth-century fiction does not suggest a teleology, of the rise of what we now call the novel shifted back a few decades; nor, exactly, a sophisticated middle-class readership waiting for the novel to happen. What we see is a generically rich range of prose fiction, indebted mostly to the romance tradition and in debate with it. It is self-aware in its devices, both of plot and language, but remains above all devoted to language, as a means of persuasion, of self-expression, even divine revelation.

Notes

1. As I write, the whole is being edited by Josephine Roberts. Book One is available in *An Anthology of Seventeenth-Century Fiction*, ed. Paul Salzman (Oxford, 1991).

2. Kenelm Digby, *Loose Fantasies*, ed. Vittorio Gabrieli (Rome, 1968).

3. For an important discussion see Michael McKeon, *The Origins of the English Novel 1600–1740* (Baltimore, 1987), especially Chs 1 and 2.

4. John Bunyan, 'A Few Sighs from Hell' (1658), in *Miscellaneous Works* I, ed. T.L. Underwood and Roger Sharrock (Oxford, 1980), p. 333.

5. John Bunyan, *The Pilgrim's Progress*, ed. James Blanton Wharey, 2nd edn Roger Sharrock (Oxford, 1960), p. 8.

6. For Bunyan and the Bible, see particularly John R. Knott, 'Bunyan's Gospel Day: A Reading of *The Pilgrim's Progress*', *ELR* 2 (1973), 443–61 and 'Bunyan and the Bible' in *John Bunyan: Conventicle and Parnassus, Tercentenary Essays*, ed. N.H. Keeble (Oxford, 1988), pp. 153–170; and Brainerd P. Stranahan, 'Bunyan and the Epistle to the Hebrews: His Source for the Idea of Pilgrimage in *The Pilgrim's Progress*', *Studies in Philology*, 79 (1982), 279–96, and 'Bunyan's Satire and its Biblical Sources' in *Bunyan in Our Time* ed. Robert G. Collmer (Kent, Ohio, 1989), pp. 35–60.

7. For stimulating recent discussion of interpretation, see Valentine Cunningham, 'Glossing and Glozing: Bunyan and Allegory' in *John Bunyan* ed. Keeble; Dayton Haskin, 'The Burden of Interpretation in *The Pilgrim's Progress*', *SP*, 79 (1982), 256–78.

8. I have used Richard Johnson, *The Seven Champions of Christendom* (1616; numerous editions in the period) for St George; and, slightly anachronistically, *The Famous and Renowned History of Sir Bevis of Southampton* (1689), though it is a reprint of an earlier version.

9. *Pilgrim's Progress*, p. 64.

10. *The Seven Champions of Christendom*, p. 64.

11. The two best studies of this aspect of Bunyan are N.H. Keeble, ' "Here is her Glory, even to be under Him": The Feminine in the Thought and Work of John Bunyan', in *John Bunyan and his England 1628–88*, ed. Anne Laurence, W.R. Owens and Stuart Sim (1990) and Ch. 3 of Margaret Olofson Thickstun, *Fictions of the Feminine: Puritan Doctrine and the Representation of Women* (Ithaca, 1988).

12. *Pilgrim's Progress*, p. 308.

13. *Pilgrim's Progress*, p. 18.

14. See *Miscellaneous Works*, IV, ed. T.L. Underwood (Oxford, 1989), where the link is made with the character of By-Ends.

15. John Bunyan, *The Life and Death of Mr Badman*, ed. James F. Forrest and Roger Sharrock (Oxford, 1988), p. 17.

16. *Mr Badman*, p. 45.

17. *Mr Badman*, p. 41.

18. *Mr Badman*, p. 74.

19. *Mr Badman*, pp. 111–17; and cf. Christopher Hill, *A Turbulent, Seditious and Factious People: John Bunyan and his Church* (Oxford, 1988), pp. 235–6.

20. Stuart Sim, *Negotiations with Paradox: Narrative Practice and Narrative Form in Bunyan and Defoe* (Savage, Maryland, 1990), p. 71.

21. *The Pilgrim's Progress*, p. 163.

22. *Mr Badman*, p. 168.

23. For a review of the evidence, see Anne Laurence, 'Bunyan and the Parliamentary Army', in *John Bunyan and his England 1628–88*, pp. 17–29.

24. See Hill, *A Turbulent, Seditious and Factious People* , pp. 254–9.

25. John Bunyan, *The Holy War*, ed. Roger Sharrock and James F. Forrest (Oxford, 1980), p. xx.

26. *Mr Badman*, p. 40.

27. For the best discussion of Behn's narrating, see Jacqueline Pearson, 'Gender and Narrative in the Fiction of Aphra Behn', *Review of English Studies*, 3:42 (1991), 40–56, 179–90.

28. Aphra Behn, *Love Letters between a Nobleman and his Sister* (1987), p. 184.

29. *Love Letters*, p. 400.

30. *Love Letters*, p. 461.

31. Aphra Behn, *Oroonoko and other stories* , ed. Maureen Duffy (1986), p. 27. For Behn's biography and its relation to her fiction, see Duffy, *The Passionate Shepherdess* (1977), Angeline Goreau, *Reconstructing Aphra* (New York, 1980), and, more reliably because less speculative, Sara Heller Mendelson, *The Mental World of Stuart Women* (Brighton, 1987) Ch. 3; Jane Jones, 'New Light on the Background and Early Life of Aphra Behn', *Notes and Queries*, 235:3 (1990), 288–93, makes some important additions and subtractions.

32. M.M. Bakhtin, *The Dialogic Imagination*, ed. Michael Holquist (Austin, Texas, 1981), p. 33.

33. *Oroonoko*, p. 29.

34. It was common for West Indian slave-owners to give their slaves classical names. Derek Walcott, the St Lucian poet, reworks this in *Omeros* (1990). I owe the above point to remarks he made at a public reading from the poem in 1991.

35. McKeon, *Origins of the English Novel* pp. 112–13, 249–50.

36. This is close to Laura Brown's judgement, that Behn's female characters and narrators have a 'mediatory role between heroic romance and mercantile imperialism' and thus 'make possible the superimposition of aristocratic and bourgeois systems – the ideological contradiction that dominates the novella'. 'The Romance of Empire: *Oroonoko* and the Trade in Slaves' in *The New Eighteenth Century*, ed. Felicity Nussbaum (New York, 1987).

37. Congreve, *Incognita*, in *An Anthology of Seventeenth-Century Fiction*, ed. Paul Salzman (Oxford, 1991), p. 474.

38. See Ch. 5 of Aubrey L. Williams, *An Approach to Congreve* (New Haven, 1979).

39. On Congreve and Scarron, see Helga Drougge, *The Significance of Congreve's Incognita* (Uppsala, 1976); for the French influence on fiction of the period see Charles C. Mish, 'English Short Fiction in the Seventeenth Century', *Studies in Short Fiction*, 6 (1969), 233–330, and Gary Kelly, ' "Intrigue" and "Gallantry": The Seventeenth-Century French Nouvelle and the "Novels" of Aphra Behn', *Revue du Littérature Comparée*, 218 (1981), 184–94.

40. *Incognita*, pp. 479–70.

41. Salzman, *English Prose Fiction 1558–1700* (Oxford, 1985), p. 337.

42. *Incognita*, p. 508.

Chapter 3
History

Ralegh and Clarendon

In his *Defence of Poetry*, Sir Philip Sidney describes the historian as 'laden with old mouse-eaten records, authorizing himself (for the most part) upon other histories, whose greatest authorities are built upon the notable foundation of hearsay'.[1] He is accurate about the practice of much Medieval and Renaissance history, which is based more on previous accounts than original research, though historians were beginning to recognise the importance of archives. Although the modern Society of Antiquaries was founded in 1707, its forerunnner, the College of Antiquaries, started up in 1586, including such key figures in the accumulation of historical material as Camden and Cotton, and emphasised the importance of research and documentation. Nevertheless, Hobbes's definition of history (which includes 'natural history' like geology as well as what he calls 'civil history') as 'the register of knowledge of fact' seems a bit optimistic, even by 1651.[2] Seventeenth-century history is more literature than science; and, as Hobbes recognised, politically and theologically potent as well. James closed down the College of Antiquaries in 1605 from political suspicion. After all, divine right ought to render history immaterial – and history might reveal divine right to be more of a human invention than a divine revelation.[3] After the imprisonment of John Hayward in 1601 for his *First Part of the Life and Reign of Henry IV*, the Privy Council decided that no books on English history should appear without their approval.[4]

Sidney's comparison of history with poetry and philosophy is less accurate as a description of contemporary practice: 'the historian, wanting the precept, is so tied, not to what should be but what is, to the particular truth of things and not to the general reason of things, that his example draweth no necessary consequence, and therefore a less fruitful doctrine'.[5] On the contrary, history from our period is full of general reasons and doctrines, despite an increasing interest in the contingent. What gives the seventeenth-century historian such confidence is the thought that history ought to be readable as the reflection of God's providential purpose; or, in Ralegh's rather gloomier formulation, 'we may gather out of history a policy no less wise than eternal; by the comparison and application of other men's fore-passed miseries, with our own like errors and ill deservings'.[6]

Sir Walter Ralegh

For much of the period, historical writing often shares with poetry, prose fiction and drama the sense of stories and, in particular, the fates of their heroes as sources of immediately applicable examples. This rhetoric of exemplarity, as Timothy Hampton calls it, is central to the historical thinking inherited from the early sixteenth-century humanists.[7] Shakespeare's appropriation of Holinshed and Plutarch for his English and Roman history plays goes along with that; the direct applicability of the past is more evident than its otherness. As early as 1627, Richard Hakewill was arguing the opposite, in his *Apology or Declaration of the Power and Providence of God*, that the symmetry between past and present is inexact, and so analogy is difficult.[8] The pastness of the past is implicit in the humanist programme, but takes a long time to work through to actual historical writing. It was given further impetus by growing encounters with non-European cultures. If the past is another country, there is a contrast between those who regard the inhabitants of foreign countries and past eras as essentially the same as them, and those who see them as profoundly, even culpably, different. That is one reason why Sir Walter Ralegh (1552?–1618) is such an interesting historian.

Before he began his *History of the World* (1614) he was a colonist in Ireland and the New World. By all accounts he was rather more humane in his dealings with American Indians than he was with the native Irish, though the principles of plantation in the colony of Virginia that he helped found owed a lot to Elizabethan thinking about Ireland. One explanation is his overriding hostility to Catholic Spain (one of the supporters of the native Irish in their rebellion against England), a theme which runs throughout his career and eventually resulted in his execution.[9]

Ralegh's earliest published prose was contemporary history, written in a lively narrative style for polemic purposes. *A Report of the truth of*

*the fight about the Isle of Azores, this last summer, betwixt the Revenge, one
of her Majesty's Ships, and an Armada of the King of Spain* (1591) is
pamphlet length, describing a suicidal attack by Sir Richard Grenville
in the best light possible. Grenville was Ralegh's substitute; while he
was in Elizabeth I's favour, she would not let him sail. The expedition
had already been six months at sea, with many of the sailors sick, when
they were surprised by a large Spanish fleet while they were
reballasting. The other ships slipped away, and, as Ralegh makes clear,
so could the *Revenge*, but Grenville decided to make a fight of it by
sailing through the Armada. The ship was eventually surrounded and
as good as sunk, but Grenville, fatally wounded, had to be outvoted
not to scupper it with all hands on board. 'Out of the greatness of his
mind', Grenville appears as a kind of tragic hero.

The vigorous account of the fight is sandwiched between two
attacks on the Spaniards in high rhetorical style, the first against the
Armada, the second against their greed, cruelty and deceit in Ireland
and Portugal as well as in the New World. The tone is always excited,
but shows flexibility and control, between invective and brisk
narrative, buttressed by eyewitness accounts:

> . . . two of the *Revenge's* own company, brought home in a
> ship of Lyme from the Islands, examined by some of the
> Lords, and others: affirmed that he was never so wounded as
> that he forsook the upper deck, till an hour before midnight;
> and then being shot into the body with a musket as he was a
> dressing, was again shot into the head, and withal his
> surgeon wounded to death. [10]

The combination of narrative excitement and propagandist intent is
equally evident in *The Discovery of the Large, Rich and Beautiful Empire
of Guiana* (1596); but here Ralegh himself is the eyewitness. While it
was a great popular success, it failed to persuade its intended audience,
Queen Elizabeth, of the virtues of empire. Ralegh was trying to rebuild
his favour at court after his marriage. The reasons for his failure are
numerous – the increasing capriciousness of the old queen, the
uncertainties about colonisation and policy towards Spain, and even
Ralegh's own incompetence. When, after a major feat of navigation
and diplomacy, he arrives at a likely site for goldmining, he has no
tools or experts to assess it properly. There is an anxious tone to his
constant assurances that the Spaniards are the common enemy to the
tribes of the Orinoko basin, that it is easily conquered but easily
defended, and that it promises wealth in excess of the Spanish Empire.
Perhaps the anxiety transmitted itself along with the confidence.

As an example of the literature of colonisation, the book is fascinating. Consider this description, of the hill country they reach at the farthest extent of their journey inland:

> I never saw a more beautiful country, nor more lively
> prospects, hills so raised here and there over the valleys, the
> river winding into divers branches, the plains adjoining
> without bush or stubble, all fair green grass, the ground of
> hard sand easy to march on, either for horse or foot, the deer
> crossing in every path, the birds towards the evening singing
> on every tree with a thousand several tunes, cranes and
> herons of white, crimson, and carnation perching on the
> river's side, the air fresh with a gentle easterly wind, and
> every stone that we stooped to take up, promised either gold
> or silver by his complexion.[11]

The list, and the listing, are interesting. The sentence does not appear to be building to a climax, but the final item, the almost Arcadian ease with which gold and silver ore can be picked up, is clearly meant to cap it all. The accumulation is thus revealed as a rhapsody of colonial possessiveness, not just the miscellaneous sights of exploration. Accuracy may well have been sacrificed to the enthusiast and the copywriter. In his reprint of 1599, Hakluyt tacitly revised a number of Ralegh's statistics downwards. Ralegh's curiosity is often looking for commercial exploitation, even when it is linked in his own mind with liberation from Spanish oppression. That produces another tension in the text. Ralegh respects the Indians, particularly the tribal chief Topiawari, and is indebted to their hospitality and guiding. But what will England do to the country?

> To conclude, Guiana is a country that hath yet her
> maidenhead, never sacked, turned, nor wrought, the face of
> the earth hath not been torn, nor the virtue and salt of the
> soil spent by manurance, the graves have not been opened
> for gold, the mines not broken with sledges, nor their
> images pulled down out of their temples.[12]

As Greenblatt notes, the words are too strong – 'sacked', 'broken', 'pulled down'.[13] Is there a note of anticipatory regret? An easier explanation would be the surface one, that Spain has not yet ruined it, but would the irascible Ralegh have been different? His inclination to hang a treacherous guide has to be set alongside his friendship with the chiefs and his anthropologist's respect for their customs.

Again, his ability to advance an exciting story is evident. He describes with verve how they found their way through the maze of the Orinoco delta, native feasts and remedies, and the hardships of underequipped travel: 'for no man had place to bestow any other apparel than that which he wore on his back, and was thoroughly washed on his body for the most part ten times in one day'.[14]

After the excitement of the early pamphlets, the solemnity of *The History of the World*; after the rhapsody of empire, the elegy of final judgement, of 'eloquent, just and mighty death'. The *History* is a characteristic late Renaissance project, encyclopaedic but individual, and unfinished – he made it to 146 BC, though there are numerous allusions to contemporary history, and the Preface uses Tudor history as its chief source of examples. It was written in the Tower, where Ralegh was imprisoned, under a stay of execution for treason, and yet, paradoxically, in a position to be friend and adviser to Prince Henry, James's heir until his death in 1612, and the great hope of militant Protestants.

The History of the World does not seem to have been enthusiastically read by the other Stuarts. Instead it became a source-book for the opposition – Cromwell, Milton and Locke were among its admirers. The fact that Ralegh had been victimised by James no doubt contributed to its popularity in opposition circles.[15]

The reader approaching Ralegh's *History* for the first time might be advised to go for a selection such as C.A. Patrides'; the Preface deserves to be read in full, but there is a danger of getting beached in the biblical history of the earlier books. These are important, because they show how a devout Protestant (I am discounting the accusations of Ralegh's atheism, certainly at this stage in his career) might have a critical approach to biblical authority; it is expressed as an interest in second causes, rather than the short circuit of seeing God as the first cause, full stop.[16] He acknowledges disagreements and mysteries in the interpretation of Scripture. None the less, there is a marked change of tone, a more secular scepticism and modified respect for authorities when he moves in Book Three to 'secular' history.[17]

The Preface begins with the hurt eloquence of the unjustly imprisoned; before moving to the central theme, of history as a record of God's judgement: 'we may gather out of history a policy no less wise than eternal, by the comparison and application of other men's fore-passed miseries, with our own like errors and ill deservings'.[18] He then gives a series of examples from the English kings, starting with Henry I. There are a number of 'tragic actors' about, which suggests a history gathered as much from the theatre as the chronicles. Certainly his viewpoint is close to Elizabethan and Jacobean tragedy. The pictures gather in historical and judicial detail until Henry VII and, most openly, Henry VIII: 'if all the pictures and patterns of a merciless Prince were lost in the world, they might all again be painted to the life, out of the story of this King'.[19] He turns such dangerous talk deftly into a complimentary contrast with the current king. Then he is off to find similar patterns in France and Spain. He declines to write contemporary history: 'whosoever in writing a modern history, shall follow truth too near the heels, it may happily strike out his teeth'.[20] There is an important methodological excursus on 'Nature', refusing to take the Aristotelian view of it as an active entity.[21] He acknowledges the influence of Bacon in his theoretical formulations and his critical attitude. Points like these remind us that Ralegh is in many ways a moderniser, even if the eloquent passing of judgement, which is so important to the literary impact of the *History*, has an archaic ring. Nor was he as sceptical as some of his contemporary historians: Stow, for example, in his 1598 *Survey of London*, is concerned with establishing facts, not just the hierarchy of authorities which is the extent of Ralegh's critical approach.[22]

Ralegh's own experience is often introduced. Eden is compared with the New World, the Amazons of antiquity are compared to the account he was given in the Guiana expedition. In his account of Alexander, he comments: 'The magnificence and riches of those Kings we could in no sort be persuaded to believe, till our own experience had taught us, that there were many stranger things in the world, than are to be seen between London and Staines.'[23] He draws lessons for the present – how much a king can trust ministers, the importance of sea power, the loyalty of mercenaries, and so on. There are fragments of a political theory, more anti-tyrannical than anti-monarchical, with a certain amount of sympathy for the suffering of ordinary people as well as betrayed servants like himself. As in the earlier pamphlets, the potent mixture of deft narrative and eloquent polemic is the source of Ralegh's appeal.

It is debatable whether the gathering gloom of Book Five is due to the death of Prince Henry, and Ralegh's hopes with him, or the fact that his account stopped short of the Incarnation and the birth of the Christian hope. Ralegh, who himself faced death so bravely and theatrically, relishes death as the final answer to the wickedness of rulers:

> It is therefore Death alone that can suddenly make man to
> know himself. He tells the proud and insolent that they are
> but abjects, and humbles them at the instant; makes them
> cry, complain, and repent, yea, even to hate their forepassed
> happiness. He takes the account of the rich, and proves him a
> beggar; a naked beggar, which hath interest in nothing, but

in the gravel that fills his mouth. He holds a glass before the
eyes of the most beautiful, and makes them see therein, their
deformity and rottennness; and they acknowledge it.

O eloquent, just and mighty Death! whom none could
advise, thou hast persuaded; what none hath dared, thou hast
done; and whom all the world hath flattered, thou alone hast
cast out of the world and despised: thou hast drawn together
all the far stretched greatness, all the pride, cruelty, and
ambition of man, and covered it all over with these two
narrow words, *Hic iacet*.[24]

Death has the irresistible eloquence and political power that Ralegh
himself did not have. The irony is that his death, and the eloquence
that death drew from him, developed its own power. King Charles's
executioners had read their Ralegh.

Which brings us to Edward Hyde, First Earl of Clarendon
(1609–74), who, like Bacon and Ralegh, wrote history in a period of
political disappointment. His *History of the Rebellion* was begun in 1646
after the defeat of the Royalists. He had taken the story up to 1644,
when he rejoined Charles in Paris in 1648. In 1668, in exile in France,
he began to write his own *Life* to 1660, and a *Continuation*, dated 1672,
addressed to his family, and a much lengthier work, containing an
account of his years in power, 1660–67, and his exile up to 1668. In
1671, he returned to the *History*, which, without benefit of documents,
he completed to 1660. This involved dovetailing elements of the earlier
Life into the original history. The *History* was not published until
1702–04 (he had died in 1674), the *Life* in 1759. Since Macray's edition
of 1888 it has been possible to disentangle the 1640s *History* from the
Life. They can then be seen as separate in purpose, as well as different
in accuracy. The *Life* is more a justification for his role in events, and
more outspokenly critical of Charles I; it is also less reliable in detail,
being composed almost entirely from memory.[25]

Clarendon's opening sentences on the aims of his history are less
orotund than the high Ralegh style, but curiously harder to disentangle
because of the involved syntactical subordination and the running
negatives; they need to be taken slowly:

That posterity may not be deceived, by the prosperous
wickedness of these times, into an opinion, that less than a
general combination, and universal apostasy in the whole
nation from their religion and allegiance, could, in so short a
time, have produced such a total and prodigious alteration
and confusion over the whole kingdom; and so the memory

of those few, who, out of duty and conscience, have
opposed and resisted that torrent, which hath overwhelmed
them, may lose the recompense due to their virtue; and,
having undergone the injuries and reproaches of this, may
not find a vindication in a better age; it will not be unuseful,
at least to the curiosity if not the conscience of men, to
present to the world a full and clear narration of the grounds,
circumstances, and artifices of this rebellion: not only from
the time since the flame hath been visible on a civil war, but,
looking farther back, from those former passages, accidents,
and actions, by which these seed-plots were made and
framed, from whence these mischiefs have successively
grown to the height they are now at.[26]

Clarendon, then, is much more concerned with 'second causes' even
than Ralegh, and the detail of his treatment is consequently minute.
But he is just as concerned to pass judgement from a particular
theological and political position; though the judgement is on
kingdoms, not just kings. He is much less of a populist than Ralegh.
He laments 'the inferior sort of the common people' becoming JPs after
the Civil War, for example. However, he is not starry-eyed about the
kings he served, either. He came to Charles's side as a reformer loyal to
the idea of Parliament rather than a supporter of the personal rule of
the 1630s. He had co-operated with Pym and Hampden against
unparliamentary taxation. When it comes to the final verdict on
Charles I, he is full of praise for his personal qualities: 'the worthiest
gentleman, the best master, the best friend, the best husband, and the
best Christian, that the age in which he lived produced'.[27] But not the
best king. He was badly advised, suggests a man who had been one of
his shrewdest advisers, if not always listened to. Bad advisers is often
code, in this period, for criticism which it would be dangerous or
indecorous to make directly; for Clarendon, writing for posterity, in
exile after being effectively jettisoned by Charles II, it points more to a
genuine affection and respect clouded with disappointment. Charles I is
more the victim of bullying opposition; Charles II of the looseness and
debauchery of his court, which Clarendon, almost reverting to his role
as tutor, tells him to his face.

Clarendon's verdicts, then, tend to be more even-handed and subtle
than Ralegh's; the *History* is full of these judicious characterisations.
Laud, for example, another recipient of Clarendon's direct advice about
his abrupt manner, is described here at the beginning of his rise to
ecclesiastical power:

. . . too secure in a good conscience, and most sincere
worthy intentions (with which no man was ever more

plentifully replenished) thought he could manage and
discharge the place and office of the greatest minister in the
court (for he was quickly made Archbishop of Canterbury)
without the least condescension to the arts and stratagems of
the court, and without any other friendship, or support, than
what the splendour of a pious life, and his unpolished
integrity, would reconcile to him; which was an unskilful
measure in a licentious age, and may deceive a good man in
the best that shall succeed . . . .[28]

It is that phrase 'unpolished integrity' that is so telling; suggesting
Laud's vulnerability to the court that should have defended him, as
well as to the Calvinists who directly opposed him. Such an uncourtly
manner became a greater handicap when he became involved in wholly
secular politics, as a member of the Treasury committee. However, in
the end it is judicial injustice – for which Clarendon reserves his most
open distaste – that completes Laud's fall. These characterisations are so
strong that there is a danger of seeing the *History* as a gallery of
personalities, and Clarendon's political explanations as dependent more
on the accidents and imperfections of individual character than
anything more general. To be really astute about character you have to
be astute about more than character. A historian who is praised by
both Christopher Hill and Hugh Trevor-Roper for the precision of his
class analysis has to be taken seriously as a more comprehensive
commentator.[29] He knows how institutions such as Parliament work;
how lapses of attention by a majority are exploited by activists, for
example. Words like 'insolence' and 'bitterness' applied to Levellers
and Presbyterians show where his sympathies lie; but, even if he is
unwilling to admit to sincerity in the rebels, especially Cromwell, he
recognises their abilities.

Clarendon is recognisably a Renaissance Christian historian; both
'Machiavellian' in his grasp of the realities of political power and his
debt to Livy and Tacitus, and providentialist in his desire to understand
events in terms of the will of God. Undoubtedly he was influenced by
the Great Tew circle, the group of progressive Anglican intellectuals
that met at Lord Falkland's house near Oxford from the early 1630s,
and made the study of civil history one of the main planks of their
humanism.[30] The Arminianism of Great Tew combines with that
classical version of history to suggest that the action of human will was
the key to understanding public life as well as Christian commitment.
So the character study, the analysis of personality and motive, is
central. There is usually a detachment, even a level of abstraction,
about them; there are no small revealing physical details. The details

that are almost incidental to his central point, and his syntactical symmetry, are to be cherished, though; like his observation that Buckingham, when organising the opposition to Clarendon himself in 1666, 'took more pains than was agreeable to his constitution', is even more tartly effective than the more measured effects of his general analysis, that Buckingham's libertinism might be agreeable to many in Parliament, but its real design is closer to 'the levelling party'. The combination of incidental darts and fully marshalled contempt for hypocrisy and gullibility is devastating:

> His quality and condescensions, the pleasantness of his
> humour and conversation, the extravagance and sharpness of
> his wit, unrestrained by any modesty or religion, drew
> persons of all affections and inclinations to like his company;
> and to believe that the levities and vanities would be wrought
> off by age, and there would be enough of good be left to
> become a great man, and make him useful to his country, for
> which he pretended to have a wonderful affection and
> reverence; and that all his displeasure against the court
> proceeded from their declared malignity against the liberty
> of the subject, and their desire that the king should govern
> by the example of France.[31]

Clarendon defending himself is even more formidable than Clarendon defending the king or the Church of England. Passages like this might make one question Trevor-Roper's verdict, that Clarendon is untouched by the bitterness of exile, were it not for his uncomfortable habit of speaking his mind when he was in power as well.

So, curiously, Ralegh and Clarendon have a lot in common in their practice of history; but the nature of their achievements is separated by a wide gulf. Only in the brief *Guiana* pamphlet is Ralegh really useful as a documentary source; whereas historians of the Civil War still have to reckon with Clarendon. Indeed, using his label of the 'Rebellion' has become a kind of party badge among modern historians. Clarendon is not as exciting in his account of action, but there is an impressive organising force to his narrative which extracts can only hint at. He is, in the end, more modern than Ralegh, not just because his material is more contemporary, and so less dependent on revered sources, but because his approach to authority is more circumspect. Ralegh, not surprisingly, had a kind of manic-depressive approach to monarchs, planting all his hopes on them, or celebrating their tragic fall. Clarendon's moderate, cagey conservatism is only too aware of the possibilities of betrayal, and that moderates even his own disappointment.

Notes

1. Philip Sidney, *A Defence of Poetry*, ed. J.A. van Dorsten (Oxford, 1966), p. 30.

2. Hobbes, *Leviathan*, ed. C.B. Macpherson (Harmondsworth, 1968) I. 9, p. 148.

3. See J.P. Sommerville, *Politics and Ideology in England 1603–40* (1986) pp. 49ff; J.G.A. Pocock, *The Ancient Constitution and the Feudal Law: A Study of English Historical Thought in the Seventeenth Century* (Cambridge, revised edn 1987).

4. Herschel Baker, *The Race of Time: Three essays on Renaissance Historiography* (Toronto, 1967), p. 29.

5. *A Defence of Poetry*, p. 32.

6. Sir Walter Ralegh, *The History of the World*, ed. C.A. Patrides (1971), Preface, p. 48.

7. Timothy Hampton, *Writing from History: The Rhetoric of Exemplarity in Renaissance Literature* (Ithaca, 1990).

8. See F. Smith Fussner, *The Historical Revolution: English Historical Writing and Thought 1580–1640* (1962), pp. 173–5.

9. There are more biographies of Ralegh than anyone would want to read. I have used Robert Lacey, *Sir Walter Ralegh* (1973), though D.B. Quinn, *Ralegh and the British Empire* (1947) is still important, and Stephen J. Greenblatt, *Sir Walter Ralegh: The Renaissance Man and his Roles* (New Haven, 1973), while hardly a biography, contains imaginative and innovative accounts of a number of events in Ralegh's life.

10. Sir Walter Ralegh, *Selected Writings*, ed. Gerald Hammond (Harmondsworth, 1986), pp. 68–9.

11. Ralegh, *Selected Writings*, p. 110.

12. Ralegh, *Selected Works*, p. 120.

13. Greenblatt, *Ralegh*, p. 112.

14. Ralegh, *Selected Writings*, p. 113.

15. The fullest account of Ralegh's influence is Ch. 4 of Christopher Hill, *Intellectual Origins of the English Revolution* (Oxford, 1965).

16. For the problem of Ralegh's 'atheism', see E.A. Strathmann, *Sir Walter Ralegh: A Study in Elizabethan Skepticism* (New York, 1951), which makes extensive use of *The History*.

17. John Racin, *Sir Walter Ralegh as Historian: An Analysis of the History of the World* (Salzburg, 1974), suggests an earlier point, in Book Two: 'Ralegh as historian replaced Providence as the judge of history' (p. 147). See Greenblatt, *Ralegh*, p. 149, for the debt to Machiavelli.

18. Sir Walter Ralegh, *The History of the World* ed. C.A. Patrides (1971), Preface, p. 48.

19. Ralegh, *History*, Preface, p. 58.

20. Ralegh, *History*, Preface, p. 80.

21. Ralegh, *History*, Preface, pp. 74ff; cf. I. i. 10, p. 103.

22. See Fussner, *The Historical Revolution*, pp. 203, 223.

23. Ralegh, *History*, IV. ii. 12, p. 312.

24. Ralegh, *History*, IV. vi. 12, p. 396. 'Hic iacet' means 'here lies . . .'.

25. See the Preface to Edward, Earl of Clarendon, *The History of the Rebellion and Civil Wars in England,* ed. W. Dunn Macray, 6 vols (Oxford, 1888); Chs. 8 and 19 of R.W. Harris, *Clarendon and the English Revolution* (1983); B.H.G. Wormald, *Clarendon: Politics, History and Religion 1640–1660* (Cambridge, 1951); and H.R. Trevor-Roper, 'Clarendon and the Practice of History', in (with French Fogle) *Milton and Clarendon* (Los Angeles, 1965). The only edition of Clarendon in print is the *Selections*, ed. G. Huehns (Oxford, 1955), which follows the 1843 edition; I have generally quoted from this text.

26. Clarendon, *Selections*, p. 1. It is often pointed out that the opening of the *History* is a deliberate echo of Hooker's *Ecclesiastical Polity*, the intellectual foundation document of Anglicanism.

27. Clarendon, *Selections*, pp. 318–19.

28. Clarendon, *History* (Oxford, 1843), p. 27.

29. H.R. Trevor-Roper in *Milton and Clarendon;* Christopher Hill in 'Lord Clarendon and the Puritan Revolution', in *Puritanism and Revolution* (1958).

30. See H.R. Trevor-Roper, 'The Great Tew Circle', in *Catholics, Anglicans and Puritans* (1987), Ch. 4, with a section on Clarendon; and Harris, *Clarendon and the English Revolution*, Ch. 1.

31. Clarendon, *Selections*, p. 471.

Chapter 4
Biography

Greville, Walton, Burnet and Aubrey

In the 1605 *Advancement of Learning*, Francis Bacon surveyed the deficiencies of learning, and noted a lack of modern biography apart from monarchs:

> For lives, I do find it strange that these times have so little esteemed the virtues of the times, as that the writing of lives should be no more frequent. For although there be not many sovereign princes . . . yet are there many worthy personages that deserve better than dispersed report or barren elegies.[1]

In 1694 John Phillips was able to preface his *Life of Milton* with a survey of ancient and modern biography that singled out Greville, Walton and Thomas Stanley (the last for his extensive revisions of classical biography) as the modern masters, fit to stand with Machiavelli and the classics. We might add that they did not significantly change the form of biography either, or alter the central aim of exemplarity which we have observed in seventeenth-century history; though there is a gradual increase of interest in the private life of the great (and not so great).

During the liberalisation of publishing that marked the Common-wealth period, *The Life of the Renowned Sir Philip Sidney* by Fulke Greville, Lord Brooke (1554–1628) was published, in 1652. The title may not have been Greville's – one manuscript describes it as *A Dedication to Sir Philip Sidney*, and the text itself suggests that it was intended as a preface to some of Greville's own works, the two tragedies *Mustapha* and *Alam* and what is now known as *A Treatise of Monarchy*. *A Dedication* was probably composed around 1610 (Sidney died in 1586) at a time when he was in enforced retirement from public life; so there is an implied comparison between the reigns of Elizabeth and James, to James's disadvantage, which may be one reason why it was never published in the author's lifetime, particularly once he was back in favour after 1614. Greville was always cautious.

Is *A Dedication* biography, exactly? About two-thirds of it, eighty pages in the modern edition, are devoted to Sidney's life and death, several further chapters to Elizabeth's reign, with particular reference to the Essex affair. The final chapter discusses Greville's purpose in the two tragedies. One explanation for this odd shape is that Greville added the material on Elizabeth in 1611–12 when Cecil refused to allow him access to State Papers for a full-scale life of Elizabeth.[2] The reason that this material is relatively at home in the *Dedication* is that the narrative of Sidney's life is already subordinated to a wider, political purpose, which is to criticise James and his court. So, for example, the way Elizabeth managed Essex is contrasted with the 'latitudes which some modern princes allow to their favourites'.[3] Even more explicitly, the new, peaceful policy towards Spain, and the parallel decline of the navy, is attacked; both the militant Protestant and the former Secretary for the Navy in Greville is outraged.

Greville, then, has a complex personal stake in the book – it is a preface to his own works, an expression of his political and religious beliefs, and most of all a working out of his own deep friendship with Sidney. 'Friend to Sir Philip Sidney' was part of his epitaph in 1628; they had been brought up together, gone to school together and started court life together. This does not result in an intimate, anecdotal picture, though. The tone is much more distant and generalised. To adapt a title from one of Sidney's works, it is an apology for Sidney, a belated, extended, funeral oration. There are narrative moments, like the account of the aborted expedition with Drake, but the only substantial, heroic moment of Sidney's life is his death at the Battle of Zutphen. So much of his life is a might-have-been, at least in political terms. The testimonials to Sidney's promise from the great and the learned, from Languet the Huguenot scholar to William of Orange, only serve to underline the waste of potential. His literary achievement is subordinated to his life. The *Arcadia* is valued for its political and philosophical wisdom, turning 'the barren philosophy precepts into pregnant images of life'.[4] The next step in Renaissance humanist thinking, though, is to act out this educational achievement on the public stage:

> But the truth is, his end was not writing even while he
> wrote, nor his knowledge moulded for tables or schools, but
> both his wit and understanding bent upon his heart to make
> himself and others, not in words or opinion, but in life and
> action, good and great; in which architectonical art he was

such a master, with so commanding and yet equal ways
among men, that wheresoever he went he was beloved and
obeyed: yea, into what action soever he came at last at the
first, he became first at the last, the whole managing of the
business not by usurpation or violence, but (as it were) by
right and acknowledgement falling into his hands, as into a
natural centre; by which only commendable monopoly of
alluring and improving men, look how the sun draws all
winds after it in fair weather – so did the influence of his
spirit draw men's affections and undertakings to depend on
him.[5]

The art, then, is preparatory to the life; not just an attractive life of
action, but a Christian one, with the allusion to 'the first shall be last,
and the last first' as well as the more Aristotelian idea of the great-
spirited man. The negatives are there to emphasise the ethical substance
of Sidney's choices. The sentence is also a good example of the more
complex Greville style. It abounds in pairs and parallels. The
organisation is less logical than cumulative as it moves from art to life,
from greatness to attractiveness. The climax of the sentence is,
however, too extended to form a rhythmic cadence. Though Greville
is quite capable of such effects, as John Gouws has demonstrated,[6] he
does give the impression of wanting precise statements rather than
impressive ones at climactic moments. So, the affecting description of
Sidney's death concludes with 'Here this noble gentleman ended the
too short line of his life, in which path whosoever is not confident that
he walked the next way to eternal rest will be found to judge
uncharitably.'[7] Greville is often celebrated as a great 'plain style' poet,
and there is, perhaps, a parallel. Plain style is less an absence of
complexity, or rhetoric, or metaphor, or even emotion, than a visible
restraint of all these. In all his judicious, deliberative long sentences
Greville wants to tell the truth in a deceitful age. So, the whiff of the
old-fashioned which is part of that truth-telling strategy has to be
innocent of style for style's sake. Plain style, but not low style.

Every so often he permits himself an epigram as a clincher to a
longer period – 'his heart and tongue went both one way', for
example, or the description of Leicester as 'a wise man (under colour of
taking physic) voluntarily become prisoner in his chamber'.[8] The best
example of neat phrasing is his description of his own meeting with
William of Orange (brought in as a witness to Sidney's promise) who
was dressed so humbly as to be indistinguishable from the multitude:

Notwithstanding, I no sooner came to his presence, but it
pleased him to take knowledge of me; and even upon that (as

> if it had been a signal to make a change) his respect of a
> stranger instantly begat respect to himself in all about him –
> an outward passage of inward greatness, which, in a popular
> state, I thought the worth observing, because there no
> pedigree but worth could possibly make a man prince and
> no-prince in a moment, at his own pleasure.[9]

The fascinated description of change – 'an outward passage of inward greatness', 'prince and no-prince' – links with Greville's own search for true nobility, which is, ultimately, noble action, rather than the counterfeits resulting from the Stuart inflation of honours. Sidney was able to use a couple of minor offices to accomplish noble, if not major things. The contrast with the court favourites of James is implicit in this general condemnation of the times: 'Here I am still enforced to bring pregnant evidence from the dead, among whom I have found more liberal contribution to the honour of true worth than among those which now live and in the markets of selfness traffic new interest by the discredit of old friends.'[10] 'Selfness' here means 'selfishness', though elsewhere Greville uses it in a more positive sense. Greville shared Donne's view of the steady decay of the world since the Fall, his pessimism likewise accentuated by the death of a friend. Sidney's life was a bright, brief flaring before the end, like a fever in the world's fatal illness. That was one way of reconciling his early death with the workings of providence, a Protestant hero mysteriously but deliberately struck down by God. As with Milton's 'Lycidas', that other great seventeenth-century elegy to a talented might-have-been, the occasion is taken to satirise the poverty-stricken present.

Izaak Walton (1593–1683) wrote *Lives* which are sometimes even closer to hagiography than Greville, but the approach, and the feeling are quite different. They were not conceived as a unit; the first, the 'Life of John Donne', was prefixed to the edition of Donne's *LXXX Sermons* which Walton had edited with Henry Wotton; Wotton's life appeared with the *Reliquiae Wottoniae* in 1651; *The Life of Mr Richard Hooker* was published separately in 1665, after a request from Archbishop Sheldon; in 1670 the *Lives* appeared together for the first time, including a life of George Herbert; finally, the life of Bishop Sanderson appeared in 1678. This account grossly oversimplifies the bibliographic record; the lives appeared several times, in various contexts, and Walton revised them at each stage, usually by adding to them rather than correcting them.[11] All five were clerics, though Wotton only towards the end of his life, when he became Provost of Eton. Walton is just as strategic as Greville in adapting their lives to wider purposes; that is a more accurate description than 'hagiography', even if they all stand as examples of devotion.

The clearest example of this is the life of Hooker, written to counteract the 'dangerous mistakes' of a life by Bishop Gauden, published in 1662. Hooker's reputation as the hammer of the schismatics was more valuable to the clergy of the Restoration settlement than it was in the 1590s. The problem with Gauden's life was that it was dull and often uncomplimentary; worse, that it was prefixed to an edition of the later books of the *Ecclesiastical Polity* that Hooker had not lived to complete which were ambiguous on crucial questions of obedience to the king and the Church hierarchy. Walton's *Life* was thus part of a strategy to reposition Hooker as a saintly champion of the High Church cause. ('High Church' in this period is more a matter of ecclesiastical authority and the use of the Prayer Book, though with only some of the emphasis on ceremony and sacrament that characterises the 'Anglo-Catholic' nature of modern, post-Tractarian High Churchmanship.) In earlier years Walton had wide sympathies; he was an admirer of the great Puritan preacher Richard Sibbes. The experiences of 1640–60 appear to have hardened a sense that the only way to ensure peace in religion was by a strong framework of ecclesiastical authority. There is an increasing opposition in the post-Restoration lives between the sweet reasonableness of the Anglicans, with their desire for quietness often symbolised by rural retreat, and the greed and spiritual wickedness of the Puritans. The tone is similarly suspended between peace-making and point-scoring. It is easy to see how critical opinion of Walton the biographer has veered between an often sentimental admiration for his Anglican pastoralism and scholarly exposé of his partisan fictionalising.

Walton was a layman who had connections with the Church hierarchy through friendship and marriage; he had already written lives of Donne and Wotton, both of whom he had met, as well as *The Complete Angler; or, the Contemplative Man's Recreation*, which first appeared in 1653. He really only settled to the life of Hooker after he had located some acquaintances, particularly George Cranmer, one of Hooker's pupils; he preferred eyewitness (or 'earwitness') accounts to research in records, even though the vague generalities of Gauden's account seem to have stimulated a greater amount of fact-finding than usual. Hooker's early life is bolstered by accounts of his ecclesiastical patrons. Then comes the account of his marriage, which has been contradicted by modern scholarship, not least what Novarr calls the 'false and magnificent detail' of this episode from Hooker's time as parson of Drayton Beauchamp:

> . . . his two pupils, Edwin Sandys and George Cranmer,
> took a journey to see their tutor, where they found him with
> a book in his hand (it was the *Odes* of Horace) he being then

> like humble and innocent Abel, tending his small allotment
> of sheep in a common field, which he told his pupils he was
> forced to do then, for that his servant was gone home to
> dine, and assist his wife to do some necessary household
> business.[12]

The picture is impressive, but not quite true. In the *Life* it functions emblematically, as Hooker put upon by an unworthy wife, and yet surviving as the picture of learned innocence. It then leads to his being offered the Mastership of the Temple, which plunges him into controversy, but makes his gifts more publicly useful. At this point in his life Walton pauses to give an account of the 'character of the times' and the rise of Whitgift as the defender of the Church against the vicious attacks of the sectarians. This sets the context for Hooker's ideas of Church government, except that Walton does not discuss Hooker's ideas. He does give an example of the way he dealt with Travers, his fellow-preacher at the Temple who had been ordained by Presbyterians at Antwerp, and so tended to take an opposite view. The point is Hooker's 'great and clear reason, and equal charity'.[13] Walton is less interested in the substance than the tone, or the temper of controversy. Puritanism invariably appears as intellectually insubstantial discontent. Walton, partly by education as well as instinct, takes the position of his subjects in controversy as read; in the later *Life of Sanderson* the Oxford don resigns his fellowship to devote himself to country parishioners, 'not troubling their thoughts by preaching high and useless notions, but such plain truths as were necessary to be known, believed, and practised'.[14]

Walton's latitude in matters of fact leaves him exposed to one kind of modern, documentary scholarship. His artistic shaping of the accounts available to him is of no surprise to recent historiographers who have focused on the interrelations of subjectivity, rhetoric and narrative in the writing of history.[15] No surprise, and therefore there is no need to blame Walton, simply recognise that this is what narrative history tends to do. This might find a way through the difficulty of Walton's overt commitment to truth and reason being compromised by some massaging of the evidence – even if one admits that he comes out better than many in the period. Consider the two great lives of the poets, Donne and Herbert, which are also conversion stories, organised round the mid-point turn of ordination.[16] Hooker's story had been one of childhood piety and learning gradually fulfilled; Donne and Herbert were both intellectually gifted and interested in religion, but aimed at Court preferment before being pressed into the service of the Church. The saint's life is the most obvious model for Walton here, and the Donne life is full of reference to various analogous saints: Augustine,

Ambrose, Stephen and Paul. In view of Walton's usual polemical purpose, we might also see it as a response to the Puritan pattern of election, calling, justification and glorification, which became increasingly prominent as a mode of describing a life after the explosion in publishing conversion narratives in the 1650s and 1660s. *Donne*, first written in 1640, includes a kind of conversion to Anglicanism from a Catholic family background as well as the ordination at James I's request; *Herbert* is more polemically patterned, framed between two acts of Puritan destruction, and Herbert's Cambridge career set against that of Andrew Melville (Melvin in Walton's account), the 'sharp and satirical' Scots Presbyterian. Herbert's devotion to music and building constitute two implicit charges against the Puritans, who virtually banned music in church.[17] The emphasis on Laud's persuasion that made him accept the Rectorship of Bemerton, the period of 'the great sanctity of the remainder of his holy life', brings into play another icon of the Anglicanism that the Puritans sought to destroy.

These are not lives of the poets, then, so much as of saintly clergy who happened to be poets. But Walton makes great use of their aesthetic as well as intellectual and spiritual qualities; as Clayton Lein puts it, their 'lives are constantly blessed with epiphanies of beauty'.[18] Whole poems are transcribed into the text; and with Herbert in particular, phrases are lifted from the poems and prose and woven into Walton's text. The portrait of Herbert at Bemerton owes much to *The Country Parson*, Herbert's handbook; Walton assumes it was a description of Herbert's practice as well as a prescription, though he never draws attention to this assumption, and does not document it beyond the assurance 'that I have used very great diligence to inform my self, that I might inform him of the truth of what follows'.[19] Walton's artistry, then, is structural, closely textual, and, as the following example shows, brilliantly anecdotal. This is the last in a series of stories of Herbert's twice-weekly journeys to Salisbury to play music:

> . . . he saw a poor man, with a poorer horse, that was fallen
> under his load; they were both in distress, and needed
> present help; which Mr Herbert perceiving, took off his
> canonical coat, and helped the poor man to unload, and after
> to load his horse: the poor man blessed him for it; and he
> blessed the poor man, and was so like the good Samaritan,
> that he gave him money to refresh both himself and his
> horse; and told him, that if he loved himself, he should be
> merciful to his beast. Thus he left the poor man, and at his
> coming to his musical friends at Salisbury, they began to
> wonder that Mr George Herbert, which used to be so trim

and clean, came into that company so soiled and
discomposed; but he told them the occasion: and when one
of the company told him, he had disparaged himself by so
dirty an employment; his answer was, that the thought of
what he had done, would prove music to him at midnight;
and the omission of it, would have upbraided and made
discord in his conscience whensoever he should pass by the
place; 'for if I be bound to pray for all that be in distress, I
am sure that I am bound so far as it is in my power to
practise what I pray for. And though I do not wish for the
like occasion every day let me tell you, I would not willingly
pass one day of my life, without comforting a sad soul, or
showing mercy; and I praise God for this occasion: and now
let's tune our instruments.'[20]

The final speech may have been memorable enough for the
'earwitnesses' to have reproduced entire; certainly 'let's tune our
instruments' is a fine, disarming climax to the various musical
metaphors ('discomposed', 'discord') and occasions that make up the
story. The canonical coat and the later soiling take on greater
significance from the story of the tailor being sent for to make him a
coat to exchange for his silk and sword when he accepted Bemerton;
even the characteristic trimness and neatness has been sacrificed now.
The anecdote makes its affinity with parable clear in the Good
Samaritan reference. Walton is keen on the private, revealing anecdote,
but the intimacy usually turns didactic, an aid to piety.

Such small-scale smoothness is not matched on the larger scale,
whatever one might say about Walton's reworking of the various
generic models for biography. The *Lives* are disrupted, not just by
conversions and pauses to indicate wider historical contexts, but also
by documents. Their sometimes excessive length, holding up a
narrative or argument for pages so we can read a will, is part of
Walton's uncertainty with written sources, as well as an occasionally
awkward manipulation of suspense before a scene of holy dying, say.
But, in conclusion, we ought to recognise Walton's skill with
conclusions. The *Life of Donne* closes with a list of characteristics –
stature, humour, 'melting eye', and so on – a feature which derives
from Plutarch's *Lives*, well-known at the time in North's translation.
Walton presses it further into the Christian mould, as one might expect
from one of Donne's parishioners. The last two paragraphs take it
further still:

He was earnest and unwearied in the search of knowledge;
with which his vigorous soul is now satisfied, and employed

in a continual praise of that God that first breathed it into his
active body; that body which once was a temple of the Holy
Ghost, and is now become a small quantity of Christian
dust:
But I shall see it reanimated.[21]

Anyone who can so creatively rework the combined forms of the
character, the list and the epitaph has to be taken seriously as a prose
artist.

Christian biographies are often organised as conversion stories:
many of them come best in the autobiographical section which
follows, but we should also note Gilbert Burnet, *Some Passages of the
Life and Death of Rochester* (1680). Burnet really only knew Rochester in
his last year, and was instrumental in the rake's conversion. He
prefaces his account of that year with a brief account of his early life
and character, but one of the strengths of the piece is its understatement of Rochester's legendary dissoluteness in favour of the 'sedate and
quiet temper' which Burnet knew.[22] Most of the text is dialogue, a
record of Burnet's arguments for God's grace, and Rochester's
growing response to them. Even before the extended conclusion,
Burnet points the argument towards his audience – for example, that
hypocritical Christians in the Court (not least the clergy) gave the
wicked an excuse to conclude that religion was a cheat. More usually
his intervention is to assure the reader that the death-bed conversion
was genuine; it is an interesting exercise in the credibility of restraint.

Many of the memoirs that we now recognise as seventeenth-century
biography remained unpublished at the time. Lucy Hutchinson's
Memoirs of the Life of Colonel Hutchinson, for example, was written for
her family and not published until 1806. It is one of the most skilled
and sustained pieces of biography as defence; Hutchinson died in prison
in 1664, under the threat of death for signing King Charles's death-
warrant. It is prefaced by two essays, 'His Description' and 'His
Virtues' before the narrative.[23]

The best, or at least the most entertaining example of the increasing
tendency to focus on the private life of the subject is the gossipy *Brief
Lives* of the antiquarian and pioneer geologist John Aubrey (1626–97).
It did not get published until the nineteenth century, and then it was
bowdlerised. Aubrey himself was alarmed when some of his notes
went missing, fearing revenge from the living. But he was more than a
gossip; he was principal researcher for Anthony Wood's *Athenae
Oxoniensis*, a biographical register of writers and bishops who had been
at Oxford, and a pioneering reference book. In one of his notes to
Wood, he quotes General Lambert, 'the best of men are but men at the
best', and says 'of this, you will meet with divers examples in this rude

and hasty collection'.[24] When you tire of the relentlessly admirable in seventeenth-century biography, dip into Aubrey:

> Mr Ingelbert was the first inventor or projector of bringing the water from Ware to London called Middleton's water. He was a poor man, but Sir Hugh Middleton, Alderman of London, moneyed the business; undertook it; and got the profit and also the credit of that most useful invention, for which there ought to have been erected a statue for the memory of this poor man from the city of London . . . . This Sir Hugh Middleton had his picture in Goldsmith's Hall with a waterpot by him, as if he had been the sole inventor. Mr Fabian Philips saw Ingelbert afterwards, in a poor rug-gown like an almsman, sitting by an apple-woman at the Parliament-stairs.[25]

Notes

1. Francis Bacon, *The Advancement of Learning*, ed. G.W. Kitchin (1915), II. ii. 9, p. 77.

2. Ronald A. Rebholz, *The Life of Fulke Greville, First Lord Brooke* (Oxford, 1971), p. 205.

3. *The Prose Works of Fulke Greville, Lord Brooke*, ed. John Gouws (Oxford, 1986), p. 105.

4. *Prose Works*, p. 10. Joan Rees links this to Greville's preference for the revised *Arcadia* in Ch. 4 of her lively *Fulke Greville, Lord Brooke, 1554–1628: A Critical Biography* (1971).

5. *Prose Works*, p. 12. 'Architectonical' means controlling.

6. *Prose Works*, pp. xxx–xxxiii.

7. *Prose Works*, p. 83.

8. *Prose Works*, pp. 22, 36.

9. *Prose Works*, p. 14.

10. *Prose Works*, p. 13.

11. The fullest account is in David Novarr, *The Making of Walton's Lives* (Ithaca, 1958); subsequent biographers of the various figures are also worth consulting, most notably R.C. Bald, 'Historical Doubts Respecting Walton's *Life of Donne*', in *Essays in English Literature from the Renaissance to the Victorian Age Presented to A.S.P. Woodhouse*, ed. Millar MacLure and F.W. Watt (Toronto, 1964), pp. 69–84.

12. Walton, *The Life of Mr Richard Hooker*, pp. 31–2. (All quotations are from the Scolar Press facsimile of the 1670 edition of the *Lives*, which are each paginated separately.) See Novarr, *Walton's Lives*, p. 275; much of the research exposing Walton's errors on Hooker's marriage was done by C.J. Sisson, *The Judicious Marriage of Mr Hooker* (1940).

13. *Life of Hooker*, p. 85.

14. *Lives of Donne, Wotton, Hooker, Herbert and Sanderson* (Oxford, 1927), p. 364.

15. The work of Hayden White, especially *Metahistory* (Baltimore, 1973) and *Tropics of Discourse* (Baltimore, 1978), has been seminal here, and he has moved on from the structuralist framework of these texts to an interest in narrative and ideology; see, for example, 'The Question of Narrative in Contemporary Theory', *History and Theory*, 23 (1984), 1–33. I am more persuaded by the reflections of Dominick LaCapra; 'Rhetoric and History'; Ch. 1 of *History and Criticism* (Ithaca, 1985), is a good place to start.

16. See Richard Wendorf, *The Elements of Life: Biography and Portrait-Painting in Stuart and Georgian England* (Oxford, 1990), Ch. 2; on the 'mid-point' in Walton and Tudor biography (Cavendish on Wolsey and Roper on More), he draws on Clayton D. Lein, 'Art and Structure in Walton's *Life of Mr George Herbert*', *University of Toronto Quarterly*, 46 (1976/7), 162–76, and refs.

17. But see Percy Scholes, *The Puritans and Music* (Oxford, 1930) for an important corrective to the anti-art caricature.

18. Lein, 'Art and Structure', p. 172.

19. *The Life of Mr George Herbert*, pp. 41–2.

20. *Life of Herbert*, pp. 62–3.

21. *The Life of John Donne*, p. 81.

22. *Rochester: The Critical Heritage*, ed. David Farley-Hills (1972), p. 47; the *Life* is here printed complete, pp. 47–92.

23. There is a modern edition by James Sutherland (Oxford, 1973) and an important essay on its relationship with her autobiography by N.H. Keeble in *Literature and the English Civil War*, ed. Thomas Healy and Jonathan Sawday (Cambridge, 1991).

24. *Aubrey's Brief Lives*, ed. Oliver Lawson Dick (1949; 1987 edn), p. 109.

25. *Brief Lives*, p. 270.

Chapter 5
Autobiography

Bunyan, Fox, Pepys, Evelyn and Cavendish

The first English autobiography is probably *The Book of Margery Kempe*, dictated in the 1430s. Its vivid accounts of her travels and religious experiences have affinities with the tradition of Christian narrative testimony that goes back to St Paul and St Augustine. It also forms part of a more particular tradition, of vernacular spiritual writing for women; within that, its locating spiritual significance in the everyday and the domestic, while it has a particular resonance in the story of a woman, is also part of what we now call the genre of autobiography. The word itself comes suspiciously late – it is coined by Southey in 1809 according to *OED*, though the term 'self-biography' had appeared in 1796. The first English autobiography to label itself as such was published in 1834.[1] So, we need to be cautious in applying a critical term that was not part of the consciousness of the writers. In particular, the evolutionary model, that sees seventeenth-century autobiography as half-aware gropings towards the fully achieved self-consciousness of, say, *The Prelude* is going to tell a misleading story. It is true that the Anglicised version of the term, the 'life by himself' or herself, is not unusual in the later seventeenth century. Clarendon, who, like Margery Kempe, writes of himself in the third person, is one example of a public figure writing out his own life. He is also characteristic in not publishing in his lifetime, but leaving it to his descendants. What we now call seventeenth-century autobiography was to a large extent discovered and published in the following two hundred years, not at the time. Why what was regarded as private should now be moved into the public space remains a question about our own culture as well as that of the late eighteenth century. It also marks some of the distance between what we regard as interesting and important and what a seventeenth century reader would have looked for.

There was one key exception to the rule about publishing, and there is a very specific historical reason for it. Testimonies of Christian experience were required for entrance into 'gathered' churches (those that were constituted by shared convictions rather than parochial location), and as these grew in number in the 1650s, so did the printed evidence for them. Their ministers were often not ordained, or university educated, and so their right to preach was vindicated by describing their conversion and calling; these accounts, of which Bunyan's *Grace Abounding* is the most famous, were more likely to be printed as a validation of the minister, and his congregation. The motive of seventeenth-century autobiography, then, is often either that of the bequest or the entrance qualification. That is in addition to the exemplary quality of lives in contemporary biography and history, not instead of it.

Take one of the earliest collections, *Spiritual Experiences of Sundry Believers*, first published in 1651, where the members of the gathered church in Westminster, under Henry Walker's ministry, spoke of their experiences to each other at the beginning of the church's life. Some of them are conversion stories; some of them are hardly narratives at all, simply statements of belief and a desire to join with the people of God. The variety is interesting. Some Puritan writers had codified the process of conversion in such detail that we might properly apply Foucault's description of medieval confession, 'a technology of the self', to it.[2] There would be early signs of God's providential care, then deliberate sinfulness, a calling, usually from a sermon, or perhaps a book or an ordinary believer; then a 'legal' conversion, a disastrous attempt to appease God by doing good, before the true experience of grace and mercy, and perhaps a further period of relapse before assurance of salvation was settled. The fact that the process was felt to be predestined by the grace of God, but no one could really know what was in the mind of God, added to the intensity, even to neurosis, with which the signs were sought. Walker's fellow-believers knew where they stood, but do not sound like clones of each other, especially when they get down to stories. E.C., for example, sounds like a victim of post-natal depression, with her suicidal tendencies after childbirth, most notably by a pond near Leeds. M.K. has a more educated tone – she is able to characterise her story as a 'comical tragedy, or a tragical comedy'. She records Satan tempting her to atheism before she looked out at the view from her top window and realised 'they could not make themselves'.[3] In a moment of despair F.P. hears the Devil in a whirlwind: 'I could have wished myself a beast, a dog, or anything; because their misery would have an end.'[4]

So, ordinary believers in an Independent congregation in the 1650s were encouraged to think intensely and inwardly about their experience, and to express it in narrative form. In John Bunyan's *Grace*

Abounding to the Chief of Sinners (1666), addressed to the Bedford congregation while he was in prison for unlicensed preaching, we have the most sustained, riveting, even disturbing, fruit of this practice. The typically explicit seventeenth-century title page describes what it is:

> A brief and faithful relation of the exceeding mercy of God
> in Christ to his poor servant John Bunyan. Wherein is
> particularly showed, the manner of his conversion, his fight
> and trouble for sin, his dreadful temptations, also how he
> despaired of God's mercy, and how the Lord at length
> through Christ did deliver him from all the guilt and terror
> that lay upon him. Whereunto is added, a brief relation of his
> call to the work of the ministry, of his temptations therein,
> as also what he hath met with in prison.

So, the fact that we learn which two books of piety his first wife brought as a dowry, but not what her name was; or that his period of temptation after conversion in about 1650 coincided with the birth of his blind daughter, is not surprising, or even particularly egotistical.[5] It is not a suppression of the influence of women, either; his encounter with three or four poor women of Bedford, 'sitting at a door in the sun, and talking about the things of God' is a great turning point in his attempt to establish his own righteousness without grace:

> And me thought they spake as if joy did make them speak:
> they spake with such pleasantness of Scripture language, and
> with such appearance of grace in all they said, that they were
> to me as if they had found a new world, as if they were
> people that dwelt alone, and were not to be reckoned among
> their neighbours. At this I felt my own heart begin to shake,
> as mistrusting my condition to be naught; for I saw in all my
> thoughts about religion and salvation, the new birth did
> never enter into my mind, neither knew I the comfort of the
> word and promise, nor the deceitfulness and treachery of my
> own wicked heart.[6]

This spiritual 'new world' introduces a different range of relevance. Bunyan's silences about his family may be revealing, but they are consonant with his stated focus. As in this example, the recurring pattern is of an episode of experience, followed by reflection on its meaning and impact. There are plenty of particulars which enliven the episodes, which make the intervention of the voice of God memorable. Memory is a key to keeping on the right spiritual road. 'Have you forgot the close, the milk-house, the stable, the barn, and the like, where God did visit your soul? Remember also the word, the word, I say, upon which the Lord has caused you to hope' he says in the Preface.[7]

The word has to be as important as the experience, and, in the end, it has to govern it. *Grace Abounding* is one long journey in interpretation, in learning to read the words of God in the Bible and in direct revelation; that is one of many parallels with the later *Pilgrim's Progress*. For a long time the words seem hostile, blows more often than comforts. In particular, a text that long troubled him, a verse in Hebrews 12 which described Esau selling his birthright (he is often tempted to 'sell' Christ), is eventually reinterpreted according to 'the mind of God in a New Testament style' and he finds that it does not apply to him.[8] The disembodied texts alternately 'strike him down, as dead' and fill him with 'admiration at the fitness, and also the unexpectedness of the sentence'.[9] Bunyan is a victim of the Scriptures long before he can master them and preach them; the impact as well as the mastery are equally signs of authenticating grace. *Grace Abounding*, we should remember, is not simply meant as an inspiring conversion story, but as a defence of Bunyan's right to follow his calling to preach. Proper handling of the Scriptures is central to that claim.

What of the narrative shape? One of the curious aspects of *Grace Abounding* as a conversion narrative is that it is not clear when the conversion happens. To be more precise, there are a number of crises and turning-points, but none of them, not even the moment of deliverance after discovering the truth of the Esau question, is a resting point. At the time it seems so: 'Now did my chains fall off my legs indeed, I was loosed from my affliction and irons, my temptations also fled away.'[10] However, about a year and a half later the wicked thought returns, and needs dealing with again. The movement is further complicated by the tacked-on accounts of his call to preaching and his subsequent imprisonment, where inward struggle is just as prevalent as outward opposition. There is no conclusion to the struggle between the old man and the new man, the blasphemer and the preacher in Bunyan.[11] That is not to say that nothing has changed, but there is always a precariousness about Bunyan's feelings of spiritual security – even if a modern reader might be more struck by the confidence with which he reports the voices of God and the Devil. There is certainly no doubt about the existence of the spiritual world and its struggles; there is a direct, physical actuality to it.

The sense that Bunyan is pursued by God and the Devil in his life is complicated by his being in prison: so a simile like 'These words were to my soul like fetters of brass to my legs, in the continual sound of which I went for several months together' implies an analogy between the spiritual prison of ignorance (the reference is to another Esau text) and the physical prison of persecution from where Bunyan is writing.[12] In his early years in Bedford jail he was depressed by the thought of the gallows, and that his 'scrabling shift to climb the ladder' in a state of fear would be a gift to the enemy; the answer to his prayer for comfort remains hidden until he is able to identify himself with Job, 'never to deny my profession, though I have nothing at all for my pains'.[13] This is the final resting place of the narrative of *Grace Abounding*; though there are some conclusions, and we should also note the rather chirpier reportage of *The Relation of My Imprisonment*.[14] Without being reductive, we might want to reach for the language of psychopathology to describe the intensity of Bunyan's struggles. This early incident, during his attempt at 'outward reformation', teeters on the edge of comedy; it is certainly neurotic in the way that his mind scrupulously thinks out the threats:

> Now you must know, that before this I had taken much delight in ringing, but my conscience beginning to be tender, I thought that such a practice was but vain, and therefore forced my self to leave it, yet my mind hankered, wherefore I should go to the steeple house, and look on: though I durst not ring. But I thought this did not become religion neither, yet I forced my self and would look on still; but quickly after, I began to think, how, if one of the bells should fall: then I chose to stand under a main beam that lay over athwart the steeple from side to side, thinking there I might stand sure: but then I should think again, should the bell fall with a swing, it might first hit the wall, and then rebounding on me, might kill me for all this beam; this made me stand in the steeple door, and now thought I, I am safe enough, for if a bell should then fall, I can slip out behind these thick walls, and so be preserved not withstanding.
>
> So after this, I would yet go to see them ring, but would not go further than the steeple door; but then it came into my head, how if the steeple it self should fall, and this thought (it may fall for ought I know) would when I stood and looked on, continually so shake my mind, that I durst not stand at the steeple door any longer, but was forced to fly, for fear it should fall upon my head.[15]

'Steeple house' was a common Quaker term of abuse for Anglican churches, though the visitor to Elstow church will notice that the bell tower is separate, so it has a kind of descriptive appropriateness too. But the central point is the anxiety. Bunyan's faith does not dismiss the anxiety in the calming, condescending manner of Worldly Wiseman.

Like most successful theodicies (the Book of Job is the obvious biblical example), it does not answer the problems of suffering by explaining or rationalising, it transcends, even abolishes them by an act of new creation. This produces a Bunyan who is redeemed, who understands himself, and who is part of the community of believers to whom the text is addressed. The Preface to the Bedford church, with all its coded biblical references, reminds us that this is meant to be a comforting text as much as an awakening text, to use the language of Puritan preaching. But no easy, palliative comfort; after all, God had first called him as he was in the middle of a game. For the Puritans particularly, playing games, word-games included, stood in the way of truth: 'God did not play in convincing of me; the Devil did not play in tempting of me; neither did I play when I sank as into a bottomless pit, when the pangs of hell caught hold upon me: wherefore I may not play in my relating of them, but be plain and simple, and lay down the thing as it was.'[16]

Another prison document, less well-known but impressive, is *A Short Relation of Some of the Cruel Sufferings, for the Truth's Sake, of Katharine Evans and Sarah Cheevers*, first printed in 1662. The authors were members of the Society of Friends, or Quakers. The nickname was because the early Friends used to 'quake' under the influence of the Holy Spirit in their meetings – in this respect, as well as their evangelism, they were as much like modern Pentecostals as modern Friends. They had set out on a Pauline missionary journey to Alexandria and Sicily when they were imprisoned by the Inquisition in Malta. The early Quakers were the most prominent deployers of women as 'prophets' among the sects that burgeoned in the 1650s. Their account of their sufferings, and their resistance to threatening attempts to convert them to Catholicism by the friars, is as confidently scriptural as Bunyan, but in quite a different mode. Their identification with Christ and the words of Scripture is sometimes so complete that there is no sense of them having to stand outside the text and appropriate it; here, for example, is Katharine: 'My life was smitten and I was in a very great agony, so that sweat was as drops of blood, and the righteous one was laid into a sepulchre, and a great stone was rolled to the door, but the prophecy was that he should arise again the third day, which was fulfilled.'[17] She is not just with Christ in Gethsemane and the tomb, she *is* Christ. Her spiritual understanding of her suffering takes precedence over the mundane details. Their account does give us an idea of their interrogator's threats, and attempts to get them released, but there is a much greater sense of 'realistic' detail being suppressed as irrelevant than there is in *Grace Abounding*.[18] This extreme spareness sometimes results in a telling irony: 'He [a friar] said he had brought me a physician, in charity. I said the Lord was my physician and my saving health. He said I should be whipped and quartered and burnt that night in Malta, and my mate, too.'[19] There is no need for comment on his 'charity' after that.

Sometimes there is a sense of a private or group language, only properly understood by 'a child of wisdom'. The letters to their family and Friends appended to the account give further substance to this understanding and supportive community. At times this becomes a visionary, almost incantatory, style, deriving its power from simple accumulation.[20] Sometimes the utter simplicity of the narration in short, bare sentences opens up into a moment of tenderness, as in their fast: 'We were weak, so that Sarah did dress her head as she would lie in her grave, poor lamb.'[21] It would be wrong, even sentimental, to call this artless, because comparison with other Quaker texts show how much of it is a learnt, shared language. There is not even the art of understatement, though; their spiritually sustained courage in the face of constant pressure to convert over two years is laid out in a mixture of ecstatic highs, physical and spiritual lows, and the simplest of narrative sentences.

Undoubtedly the most important Quaker autobiography is the *Journal* of George Fox (1624–91). The text of 1694, prepared by Thomas Ellwood after Fox's death in 1691, is an edited composite of a number of manuscripts, some dictated by Fox at the time, but mostly in retrospect. Some of the manuscripts have survived, so the journal has been re-edited in a modern, less regularising fashion than Ellwood's – though his version is all we have of Fox's early years.[22] So what we have of Fox is largely the record of his oral, rather than his written style; and, except for some diaries of his trip to America, a record of his considered rather than immediate recollection of events. It has the serial quality of a diary, but it is far more public in voice than those seventeenth-century diaries which were never intended for publication. After the opening pages, it is an account of his remarkable and invariably controversial itinerant ministry.

Fox's early experience does not answer to the more traditional Puritan pattern of conviction and conversion. His word is 'convincement', reflecting his sense that a light within the individual needed to be awakened, in contrast to the Calvinist idea of humanity's total inability to please God. Unlike Bunyan, he does not start out as a childhood sinner: 'When I came to eleven years of age, I knew pureness and righteousness.'[23] In 1643, at the age of twenty-one, he left his relations and set off, travelling round the country; he records a number of unsatisfactory meetings with would-be spiritual advisers. It is hardly surprising that he turns to a more direct, we might say mystical, experience of God, though this leads him into direct attack on the established Church rather than monastic retreat. This particular pair of

'openings' (his description of revelatory moments) may help to explain
why:

> About the beginning of the year 1646, as I was going to
> Coventry . . . the Lord opened to me that, if all were
> believers, then they were all born of God and passed from
> death to life, and that none were true believers but such; and
> though others said they were believers, yet they were not.
> At another time, as I was walking in a field on a First-day
> [i.e. Sunday] morning, the Lord opened to me that being
> bred at Oxford or Cambridge was not enough to fit and
> qualify men to be ministers of Christ; and I stranged at it
> because it was the common belief of people. But I saw
> clearly, as the Lord opened it to me, and was satisfied, and
> admired the goodness of the Lord who had opened this thing
> unto me that morning . . . .[24]

There is something appealingly direct about this, but Fox is
frustratingly inexplicit about the process of his spiritual discoveries;
perhaps a long life of itinerant preaching and defending himself in
courts is partly to blame for the extent to which his formulaic
vocabulary leaves the reader with little more than his imperturbable
assurance. Fox must have been a frustrating as well as a deeply
impressive man to deal with; in the precise sense of the word,
charismatic. However, as Christopher Hill notes, these doctrines in
themselves do not distinguish Fox from other radical preachers of the
1640s and 1650s; what made the Quakers a particular focus of anger
was their resolute opposition to priests and their privileges, such as
tithes, openly disputing with them in their 'steeple-houses', and their
refusal of 'hat-honour', taking hats off in the presence of a social
superior.[25] There is an aspect of Quaker doctrine, as opposed to social
practice, that comes out in the early pages of the *Journal* which was
distinctive:

> Now the Lord God hath opened to me by his invisible
> power how that every man was enlightened by the divine
> light of Christ; and I saw it shine through all, and that they
> that believed in it came out of condemnation and came to the
> light of life and became the children of it, but they that hated
> it, and did not believe in it, were condemned by it, though
> they made a profession of Christ.[26]

This is not just anti-Calvinist; it explains why the opponents of
Quakerism, in Fox's words, 'cried up sin'. The centre of Christianity

has been moved sideways, from forgiveness to enlightenment; though Fox himself was concerned to distance himself from the antinomian 'Ranters' who claimed to be able to do anything, because they were free from the moral law.[27] The implications of this doctrine may help us to understand the particular narrative qualities of the *Journal*. There are no stages of enlightenment, so there is no sense of spiritual progress, no real teleology – so dipping is a good approach to reading after the initial process of convincement. In addition, this doctrine enables Fox to understand his opponents as wilfully ignorant, refusing to acknowledge what is inside them. Alternatively, as in his meeting with Cromwell, they are secretly wishing to agree with him. So he is never in any doubt as to what an incident means.

The most stirring, and sometimes amusing moments in the *Journal* tend to be the public ones, then, like the trial of 1664, when Fox had to deal with interrogators of equal but opposite assurance. The trial hardly gets going at all, because Fox refuses to swear the oath; when he is handed a Bible to swear on he looks up the text where Christ commands his followers not to swear.[28] Judge Twysden complains that Fox is shouting him down: 'I must call for three or four criers to drown thy voice; thou hast good lungs.' He loses his cool, but Fox is not to be outfaced:

> *Judge* Sirrah, will you take the oath?
> *G.F.* I am none of thy sirrahs, I am no sirrah, I am a
> Christian. Art thou a judge and sits there and gives names to
> prisoners? It does not become either thy grey hairs or thy
> office. Thou ought not to give names to prisoners.[29]

There is a documentary immediacy about all this; and, as with the modern documentary TV programme, the simple laying out of the facts has an emotive, adversarial edge to it. In reporting his life, Fox is making a case against his opponents.

As I have already mentioned, Fox's account of his American journey was made much closer to the events, and has a consequently different feel. The circumstantial detail is much richer, not least because it was so much harder to get about. Nature – or rather, the lack of roads and bridges across it – provides more opposition than the authorities.

At the end of the journey, though, we might have to concur with Owen Watkins, that this is more a book by a great man than a great book.[30]

Diary-keeping in the seventeenth century was recommended as a spiritual discipline. John Beadle's chirpy *The Journey or Diary of a Thankful Christian* (1656) has as one of its epigraphs Zechariah 4:10, 'Who hath despised the day of small things?' He recommends keeping a spiritual account book: 'every true believer is a Merchant Adventurer, whose returns must be greater than his ventures, or he cannot live'. The materials he recommends, though, are not just the expected private ones of the moment of 'effectual calling', assistance with temptations, and answers to prayer, but the individual's perception of public events. Examples here are the ruler's religion, remarkable judgements on notorious offenders, and what 'the national epidemical sin' is at the moment (after considering contention, ambition and hypocrisy he settles on 'a most violent opposition against the kingly government of Jesus Christ in his church').[31]

It is instructive to move from Beadle to the cornucopia which is Pepys's Diary from 1660–69, because there is much that corresponds. It is both a literal and a spiritual account book; at the end of each month's entries, and in greater detail at the end of each year, he looks over his financial situation, how he is getting on at work (a series of offices mostly in the Navy Office), the state of his family and servants, and public affairs, principally the king and his Court. In the early years particularly he is also concerned with Church affairs, and records his opinion of the Sunday sermon as well as the appearance of the congregation; but the real spiritual content of the diary is in the thankfulness, and the series of resolutions about drinking and play-going kept or broken. The moral quality declines (or mellows, according to your viewpoint) under a series of pressures: the Great Ejection of 1662, which resulted in fewer, less experienced preachers in London, busyness and success, family worries and sexual dalliance.

Pepys's writing has considerable range and variety, and the haste, ellipses and informality which even modern critics regard as faults contribute to the sense of crammed exuberance. Crisp comments on preachers – 'a lazy sermon, like a presbyterian', 'slept the best part of the sermon, which was a most silly one', and to his surprise, 'Elborough, my old schoolfellow and a simple rogue; and yet I find preaching a very good sermon, and in as right a parson-like manner, and in good manner too, as I have heard anybody' – contrast with his detailed delight at his progress in music. At another level, he masters the technical language of boat-making, very pleased with his own conscientiousness for the king's sake (his own purse is not his first consideration in his accounting).

He is clearly writing for no one but himself, and a sense of overhearing is part of the delight of reading him. The diary was written in one of the forms of shorthand invented for taking notes on sermons.[32] But there are times when the privacy of the already locked away is compounded by a kind of Franglais or Spinglés (if that is a word) when it comes to extra-marital sex (enjoying his wife is done in English): 'and then alone avec elle je tentoy à faire ce que je voudrais,' or 'Peg . . . did suffer me a la besar mucho et tocar ses cosas upon her breast.'[33] There is the guilt, the fear of being found out; but in that case, why write it down at all? Is he confessing, resolving not to do it again, or compounding the enjoyment by writing it down? He prays to God, but it is his conscience he answers to. Francis Barker, in a virtuoso discussion of the 9 September 1668 entry, identifies the decisive quality of the 'Pepysian moment' as its 'enclosure': 'The text itself rehearses the situation it discloses as it inlays seclusion within seclusion.' The paradox is that such an observant, sociable character is also deeply alone in his subjectivity:

> The *Diary*, for all the fulness of its days, despite being so
> richly populated with others and with the furniture of gossip
> and events, is thus the record of a terrible isolation. At the
> moment when the soul reaches out to appropriate the outer
> world, the very gesture reinforces the division by which it is
> other than that which it seeks to apprehend.[34]

Barker starts from an unusual entry, Pepys's description of reading and then burning a pornographic book. We could make a similar point about Pepys in his public role, the servant of the Navy Board, maintaining his integrity and his ambition in a world of chicanery and unfair patronage. Sociability, intimacy, isolation: the continuum inhabited by the modern self.

Evelyn's *Diary* spans a longer period than Pepys's, virtually the whole of his life from 1620–1706; though most of it was written up in retrospect, from notes taken at the time. Only from 1684 onwards is it a contemporary diary. The *Kalendarium*, the title on the manuscript, was written up in 1660 and again in 1680–84. So it is closer to memoirs than diary for much of its length.

Evelyn had much in common with his younger contemporary Pepys; they met, corresponded over scientific and antiquarian matters (they were both early members of the Royal Society), were both public servants. Evelyn is sometimes a rather dour writer by comparison. His entry for 10 September 1665 reads: 'Dr Plume at Greenwich on 3 Coloss: 5.6 showing how our sins had drawn down God's judgements [the Great Plague]; I dined with the Commissioners of the Navy, retreated hither, and with whom I had business.'[35] Pepys is much fuller, describing the occasion as a celebration of Sandwich's taking of several Dutch ships. Evelyn himself comes across as a much jollier figure than ever he portrays himself: 'Among other humours, Mr Evelyn's repeating of some verses made up of nothing but the various acceptations of may and can, and doing it so aptly, upon occasion of something of that nature, and so fast, did make us all die almost with laughing . . . .' The issue here is less reliability than selfpresentation; Evelyn might have had his family as readers in mind as well as what he thought was important about the day in a process of self-examination.

At other times we can recognise a livelier Evelyn. In the earlier part of the diary, describing his time in Europe, he is the eager, intelligent, omnivorous tourist. His time in the Netherlands coincided with the time of the Civil War, so it was midway between exile and the usual educational European journey.[36] Here he shows a curiosity, not just for the tourist sites, but for instructional differences, in the treatment of the poor by the state, for example. The mixture, of eclectic curiosity and an eye for the social applicability of what he saw, prefigures the interests of the Royal Society quite as precisely as the scientific circles in London and Oxford. He gets as close as any of his contemporaries to precise physical description:

> My father, named Richard, was of a sanguine complexion,
> mixed with a dash of choler; his hair inclining to light,
> which (though exceeding thick) became hoary by that time
> he had attained to 30 years of age; it was somewhat curled
> towards the extremes; his beard (which he ware a little
> picked, as the mode was) of a brownish colour and so
> continued to the last, save that it was somewhat mingled
> with grey hairs about his cheeks; which with his countenance
> was clear, and fresh coloured, his eyes extraordinarily quick
> and piercing, an ample forehead, in sum, a very well
> composed visage and manly aspect . . . .[37]

Even here, the physical specifics veer into a generality, even idealising, that says very little, and least of all about the father-son relationship. Evelyn's inwardness remains guarded. It is not surprising that the diary has been read more often as a historical source than as an episode in self-examination. It still has more than occasional narrative and anecdotal appeal, like the set-piece on the Restoration, or the story of Sir William Petty, when challenged to a duel in Ireland, 'though exceedingly purblind, accepted the challenge, and it being his part to propound the weapon, defied his antagonist to meet him with an hatchet or axe in a dark cellar; which he refusing, was laughed at for challenging one whom everyone knew was so short sighted'.[38] The humour as well as the neat circumspection of Petty's stratagem both appeal to Evelyn, or at least, what Evelyn chooses to reveal of himself.

Any account of aristocratic autobiography in the period would have to mention Clarendon's *Life*, with its invaluable record of public events and people closely observed; the text is so intertwined with the revisions of the *History of the Rebellion* that it is best thought of as an

appendix to that work, discussed above. For an older aristocratic view
we might turn to Edward, Lord Herbert of Cherbury (1582–1648). He
was a considerable poet, if overshadowed by the achievement of his
younger brother George, and an interesting philosopher in the
Renaissance humanist tradition; his *De Veritate* ('Of Truth') was first
published in 1624.[39] It is possible to assemble quotations from *The Life*
which he wrote for his 'posterity' which would confirm this picture of
the aristocratic intellectual – his discussions of education, for example,
after the account of his own. As Margaret Bottrall points out, there are
affinities with the educational 'courtesy book' of the Renaissance in
parts of his account of his upbringing.[40] But that misses the central
flavour of the book, which is that of a man looking back on his
glittering early life, with his self-critical faculties pretty constantly on
hold.

Armed not just with book learning, but with the other aristocratic
accomplishments of swordsmanship and horseriding, the young
Edward Herbert says goodbye to his wife (he had married very young)
and sets off for the Continent. From then on the *Life* is really a series of
adventures. He fights, or at least challenges, a series of duels for the
honour of ladies (James I had made him a Knight of the Bath and he
took his knight errantry seriously); he makes friends with nobility in
France and the Low Countries, and in between avoids assassination in
the streets of London on the (wrongful) accusation of adultery.
Although one might suspect retrospective embellishment, there is great
verve and immediacy in the stories. It is difficult to think of more
exciting, or convincing, fictional fight scenes in the period.[41]
Eventually he comes to act as a diplomat for King James in the French
Court at the time of Prince Charles's Spanish match. The narrative
breaks off at the moment when his public life suffered its first reverse
and he decided to publish *De Veritate*; it is difficult to see how
Herbert's tone of imperturbable competence, along with his self-
confessed choler, might have adapted to disappointment.

Finally, Margaret Cavendish, Duchess of Newcastle, a remarkable
polymath who wrote poetry, plays, short stories, a utopian fiction
called *The Blazing World*, a biography of her husband and some
scientific essays.[42] She was eccentric ('singular' is her word) only in the
sense that she went in for men's pursuits like writing and philosophy
rather than needlework; and she dressed so unusually as to be the
object of attention – 'all the town talk is nowadays of her
extravagancies', noted Pepys on 26 April 1667.

In 1656 she published *Nature's Pictures Drawn by Fancy's Pencil to the
Life*, a series of verse and prose tales, which is followed by *A True
Relation of my Birth, Breeding and Life*. She was thirty-three at the time,
and her principal achievements were to come. Many critics have

remarked how the self-assertion and self-definition which close the account are nonetheless in terms of her relationships to men:

> But I verily believe some censuring readers will scornfully say, why hath this lady writ her own life? Since none cares to know whose daughter she was, or whose wife she was, or how she was bred, or what fortunes she had, or how she lived, or what humour or disposition she was of? I answer that it is true, that 'tis no purpose to the readers but it is to the authoress, because I write it for my own sake, not theirs. Neither did I intend this piece for to delight, but to divulge; not to please the fancy, but to tell the truth. Lest after ages should mistake, in not knowing I was daughter to one Master Lucas of St John's near Colchester in Essex, second wife to the Lord Marquis of Newcastle; for, my lord having had two wives, I might easily have been mistaken, especially if I should die and my lord marry again.[43]

Only at odd moments like this do we see the sparks of assertiveness amid the generally apologetic tone, the approach expected of a woman, and which merges with her self-confessed bashfulness. However, *A Brief Relation* has a sustained interest as self-analysis in terms of upbringing and personality, quite apart from the contemporary models of spiritual development, or gentlemanly education. There is an extended comment on her mother's policies, of not pressing her to sew or practice other 'virtues' (what a subsequent age called 'accomplishments') when she preferred to read and write; and dressing the family up to their income rather than saving, so that her children did not develop 'sharking' qualities in later life. She does her best to say what she is like as a person; it sounds so commonplace now, but it is really unusual in all the autobiographical material I have read in the period. This is not startlingly good writing, but it is very careful and self-attentive, for example: 'When I place a particular affection, I love extraordinarily and constantly, yet not fondly, but soberly and observingly.'[44]

More often the self in this period is suspected rather than indulged as an object of attention; as a result, the genres of self-examination are either rigorously bounded, as in religious confessions, or scattered and provisional, in journals, family records, prefaces and appendices. In Christian thinking, for example, the goal of self-examination was more often self-denial than self-development. Yet because the self was the arena of conflict, the theatre of the spiritual, it became an object of interest. The increasing emphasis on conscience in the later part of the century reinforces this. At the same time, we need to be aware of historical and class circumstances. An aristocrat like Clarendon or even Herbert, forced into retirement would take to contemplation, not just out of necessity but out of classical training. A bourgeois public servant like Pepys or Evelyn would have a different view of private responsibilities. A seventeenth-century woman would be less likely still to regard the public world as a likely sphere for action. In these texts we are witnessing part of that long, long history of change from the sense of the private world as the scene of privation to that of plenitude.

Notes

1. Felicity A. Nussbaum, *The Autobiographical Subject: Gender and Ideology in Eighteenth-Century England* (Baltimore, 1989), p. 6.

2. Michel Foucault, *The History of Sexuality Vol. I: An Introduction* (1980); for the Puritan patterning of conversion, Ch. 3 of William Haller, *The Rise of Puritanism* (New York, 1938) is still a good introduction; see also Owen C. Watkins, *The Puritan Experience* (1972). The sources were intended to be popular and are almost as readable: for example, William Perkins, *A Golden Chain* (1600), Richard Sibbes, *The Bruised Read and Smoking Flax* (1630) and Arthur Dent, *The Plain Man's Pathway to Heaven* (1601).

3. *Spiritual Experiences of Sundry Believers*, intro. Vavasor Powell (2nd impression, 1652), p. 176. Henry Walker recorded, and one presumes edited, these oral testimonies.

4. *Spiritual Experiences*, p. 238.

5. For the second omission, see Nussbaum, *Autobiographical Subject*, pp. 236–7.

6. Bunyan, *Grace Abounding*, ed. Roger Sharrock (Oxford, 1962), §38–9, p. 15.

7. *Grace Abounding*, p. 3.

8. *Grace Abounding*, §225–7, p. 71; see Nussbaum, *Autobiographical Subject*, pp. 75–6 and John R. Knott, Jr, 'Bunyan and the Bible', *John Bunyan, Conventicle and Parnassus: Tercentenary Essays* ed. N.H. Keeble (Oxford, 1988), pp. 153–70; Christopher Hill, *A Turbulent, Seditious and Factious People: John Bunyan and His Church* (Oxford, 1988), pp. 68–71 draws attention to the link with poverty as well as 'selling out' in Bunyan's obsession with the text; Graham Ward, 'To Be a Reader: Bunyan's Struggle with the Language of Scripture in *Grace Abounding to the Chief of Sinners*', *Literature and Theology* 4 (1990), 29–49, demonstrates how the hermeneutic crisis is not totally resolved even then.

9. *Grace Abounding*, §185, 188, pp. 58–9.

10. *Grace Abounding*, §230, p. 72

11. See Vincent Newey, 'Bunyan, Experience, and Interpretation', in *John Bunyan, Conventicle and Parnassus*, especially pp. 198–208.

12. *Grace Abounding* §143, p. 44. I develop this in a slightly different context in 'Grace Abounding and the New Sense of Self', Ch. 8 of *John Bunyan and His England, 1628–88*, ed. Ann Laurence, W.R. Owens and Stuart Sim (1990).

13. *Grace Abounding*, §334, p. 100, §338, p. 101.

14. This was not published until 1765, but is now usually reprinted as an appendix to *Grace Abounding*.

15. *Grace Abounding*, §33–4, pp. 13–14.

16. *Grace Abounding*, pp. 3–4.

17. Katharine Evans and Sarah Cheevers, 'A Short Relation of Cruel Sufferings', in *Her Own Life: Autobiographical Writings by Seventeenth-Century Englishwomen*, ed. Elspeth Graham, Hilary Hinds, Elaine Hobby and Helen Wilcox (1989), p. 120.

18. For the general comparison of Nonconformist autobiographies along this line, see Dean Ebner, *Autobiography in Seventeenth-Century England: Theology and the Self* (The Hague, 1971).

19. *Her Own Life*, pp. 121–2.

20. For the best general account of Quaker style, see Richard Bauman, *Let Your Words Be Few: Symbolism of Speaking and Silence Among Seventeenth-Century Quakers* (Cambridge, 1983).

21. *Her Own Life*, p. 128.

22. *The Journal of George Fox*, ed. J.L. Nickalls (Cambridge, 1952, repr. 1986); see the Preface. Two of Nickalls's sources are available separately: the Spence MS, dictated 1674–75, as *The Journal of George Fox*, ed. Norman Penney (Cambridge, 1911), 2 vols, and *The Short Journal*, ed. Norman Penney (Cambridge, 1925), written or dictated in Lancaster Prison in 1664.

23. *The Journal of George Fox*, ed. J.L. Nickalls, p. 1.

24. *The Journal of George Fox*, p. 7.

25. Christopher Hill, *The World Turned Upside Down* (1972: 1984 edn), pp. 232–5.

26. *The Journal of George Fox*, p. 33.

27. There are numerous disputes with Ranters described in the *Journal*. See also Hill, *The World Turned Upside Down*, Ch. 10, 'Ranters and Quakers', and the confessions of Laurence Clarkson, *A Lost Sheep Found* (1660), who seems to have gone to bed with a 'pretty maid' who liked his preaching, *A Collection of Ranter Writings* ed. Nigel Smith (1983), p. 178.

28. *The Journal of George Fox*, p. 463; Matthew 5:34–7.

29. *The Journal of George Fox*, p. 468.

30. Owen C. Watkins, *The Puritan Experience* (1972), p. 198.

31. John Beadle, *The Journal or Diary of a Thankful Christian* (1656), pp. 25, 39.

32. Thomas Shelton, *A Tutor to Tachygraphy, or Short-Writing* (1642), available in facsimile with an introduction by William Matthews (Los Angeles, 1970).

33. *The Diary of Samuel Pepys*, ed. Robert Latham and William Matthews, 11 vols (1970–83), 20 December 1664, 28 November 1666.

34. Francis Barker, *The Tremulous Private Body: Essays in Subjection* (1984), p. 10.

35. John Evelyn, *Diary*, ed. John Bowle (Oxford, 1985), p. 205; this is the only edition currently in print, based on E.S. de Beer's standard edition (Oxford, 1955) 6 vols.

36. See John Stoye, *English Travellers Abroad 1604–1667* (rev. edn, New Haven, 1989), pp. 176–9.

37. Evelyn, *Diary*, p. 1. For Evelyn's observant side, see 'John Evelyn', *Essays of Virginia Woolf*, ed. Andrew McNeillie, Vol. III (1988), pp. 259–68.

38. Evelyn, *Diary*, pp. 253–4.

39. See R.D. Bedford, *The Defence of Truth: Herbert of Cherbury and the Seventeenth Century* (Manchester, 1979); there are also useful discussions of his thought in Basil Willey, *The Seventeenth-Century Background* (1934) and R.H. Popkin, *The History of Scepticism from Erasmus to Spinoza* (Berkeley, 1979).

40. Margaret Bottrall, *Every Man a Phoenix: Studies in Seventeenth Century Autobiography* (1958), Ch. 4.

41. See, e.g., *The Life of Edward, First Lord Herbert of Cherbury, written by himself*, ed. J.M. Shuttleworth (1976), pp. 62–4.

42. See Kathleen Jones, *A Glorious Fame: The Life of Margaret Cavendish, Duchess of Newcastle, 1623–73* (1988); Sarah Heller Mendelson, *The Mental World of Stuart Women* (Brighton, 1987), Ch. 1. Little of her work is in print, apart from poems in anthologies, e.g. *Kissing the Rod*, ed. Germaine Greer et al. (1988), pp. 163–74; *The Blazing World* is in *An Anthology of Seventeenth-Century Fiction* (ed. Salzman), extracts from her autobiography in *Her Own Life*.

43. Margaret, Duchess of Newcastle, *The Life of William Cavendish . . . to which is added The True Relation of my birth, breeding and life*, ed. C.H. Firth (1907), p. 178.

44. *A True Relation*, p. 175. Paul Delany, in *British Autobiography in the Seventeenth Century* (1969) suggests that her preoccupation with her own singularity is similar to Rousseau's.

Religious Prose

Part Two
Rehgoryis Prose

Chapter 6
The English Bible

> You can read it [the Bible] as literature only by a *tour de
> force*. You are cutting the wood against the grain, using a
> tool for a purpose it was not intended to serve.[1]

C.S. Lewis is not the only Christian writer to suggest that whoever
reads the Bible as literature is not really reading the Bible. The claims
the Bible makes to authoritative revelation of divine truth would
appear to make aesthetic considerations, of style or genre or wordplay, not only trivial but beside the point. That is, for believers, where
the choice might be simply to obey, or disobey and take the eternal
consequences. Unbelieving readers might be more like modern tourists
in a Christian cathedral or Buddhist temple, admiring the aesthetics,
but merely curious about the beliefs which inspired the art object. Thus
(in a gesture close to many modern critical theories) it might be argued
that an unbelieving reading of the Bible is likely to make it into
literature; a believer's reading might make it into a directory of faith
and conduct, the maker's handbook to the world.

Would seventeenth-century readers have recognised this opposition?
To begin with, they did not have the same category, 'literature'. They
had both a narrower, generic one – poetry, which could also include
drama – and a wider one – rhetoric, the art of persuasion. Not until
Robert Lowth's *Lectures on the Sacred poetry of the Hebrews* (published in
Latin 1753, in English 1787), it is generally argued, does the modern
idea of the Bible as literature get formulated.[2] But consider Martin
Luther's view, Luther who elevated the Bible above the Church as the
single source of Christian doctrine, and whose translation into German
was one lasting result:

> I am persuaded that without knowledge of literature, pure
> theology cannot at all endure, just as heretofore, when letters
> have declined and lain prostrate, theology too has
> wretchedly declined and lain prostrate; nay, I see that there

has never been a great revelation of the Word of God unless
he first prepared the way by the rise and prosperity of
languages and letters, as though they were John the Baptists
. . . .[3]

This is cognate with the confluence of Renaissance and Restoration we
call Christian Humanism, which suggested, notably in the work of
Erasmus, its greatest exponent, that the rediscovery of learning and the
revival of Christianity should be interdependent. The movement called
for a return to the original texts, of the classical as well as the Christian
era, as essential to revive thought and learning, as well as religion. One
early result was the Greek New Testament of Erasmus, first printed in
1516 with a Latin translation that corrects the Vulgate from
accumulated corrupt readings. The Vulgate was the fifth-century Latin
translation by St Jerome which had formed the basis of Catholic
doctrine and philosophy since then, particularly during the Middle
Ages, when knowledge of Greek and Hebrew in the West was virtually
extinct. However, it was only in 1546, rather against the tide of
European vernacular translations as well as the rise of Greek and
Hebrew scholarship, that the Roman Catholic Council of Trent,
heralding the Counter-Reformation, declared the Vulgate to be the
authentic text of Scripture.[4] Luther, already in rebellion against the
Catholic church in doctrine arising from his own re-reading of St Paul,
seized on Erasmus' scholarship to aid his own translating work in the
1520s. But I do not think the letter above simply refers to the revival of
philology as being essential to the study of the Bible, even if linguistic
study was much more the basis of literary study than it is now. At least
it implies that there is no conflict between regarding the Bible as
authoritative and regarding it as literature.

In what sense is the Bible literary? One could construct a list of
literary genres represented in the Bible – epic, elegy and epithalamion,
for example, or point to its variety of distinctively religious genres –
prophecy and apocalypse, for example, and yet again the popular
forms such as riddle and parable. The Bible is a collection of books of
widely differing styles and scope; while they can be synthesised into a
coherent historical and doctrinal whole, a favourite seventeenth-
century habit, they also demand a variety of reading skills which might
be classed as literary. One reason the Bible took so long to appear in
the English vernacular, and then for a long time as a forbidden text,
was the concern of ecclesiastical authorities that the appropriate reading
competence was beyond the unlearned (learning by definition included
the knowledge of Latin). From one side this is painted as a wise
pastoral decision – after all, look what happened to Christendom when
the Scriptures were available to be read beyond ecclesiastical supervi-

sion. From the other side it is seen either as a cover for the clergy's ignorance, or in the wonderful words of Tyndale, as hiding the truth:

> The causes that moved me to translate, I thought better that others should imagine, than that I should rehearse them. Moreover I supposed it superfluous, for who is so blind to ask why light should be shewed to them that walk in darkness, where they cannot but stumble, and where to stumble is the danger of eternal damnation?[5]

The fact that Tyndale had to move to Germany to do his translation, that the secretly imported copies were hunted out and burned, and that he was burnt for heresy suggests that the 'blind' were in positions of power. But not for long – at least in the sense that the Reformation of the 1530s meant the English Bible became increasingly available to the English people.

The 1611 translation of the Bible, known variously as the King James Version or the Authorised Version, is the culmination of the Reformation tradition of vernacular versions of the Bible. Although some fifty translations of the Bible or parts of it into English had appeared before 1611, it is appropriate to talk of the tradition in the singular, not least because of the influence of William Tyndale's achievement. Tyndale's translation of the New Testament (1525) and the first five books of the Old Testament, the Pentateuch (1530) is still recognisably a principal basis of the 1611 translation.

The 1611 Bible was commissioned at the Hampton Court conference of 1604. The conference had been convened by the recently crowned James I to deal with the increasing unrest of the Puritan wing of the Church of England. During a discussion of the catechism Dr John Reynolds, President of Corpus Christi College, Oxford, and a Puritan, suggested a new translation of the Bible. This immediately appealed to the king, who professed that 'he could never, yet, see a Bible well translated into English; but the worst of all, his Majesty thought the *Geneva* to be'.[6] That last is significant; the Geneva translation had been made by some of the exiles from Mary Tudor's persecution, and these formed the beginnings of the Puritan party on their return. It was important as a reasonably sized and affordable Bible – it was the one that Shakespeare used – but also as a source of radical Protestant interpretations of the Bible through its marginal notes. The translators were instructed to base their work on the Bishops' Bible (as might be guessed from the title, a previous attempt at an 'authorised' translation, mostly by a number of bishops, published in 1568, and ironically much indebted to the Geneva version). The fifty or so translators (lists vary) were divided into six companies to translate different parts of the Bible, and met in Oxford, Cambridge and Westminster; their versions were then revised by a group of twelve, and the finishing touches put in by Thomas Bilson and Miles Smith before printing. The list contains a number of Church and university scholars, some of whom were bishops either then or later on. All were eminent scholars, and they included some, such as Reynolds himself and Laurence Chaderton, who were Puritans. The translators were chosen for their linguistic skill, but most of them were also preachers, including the celebrated Lancelot Andrewes.

What did the translators think they were doing? They did not start from scratch, though they had the collective ability, unlike some of their predecessors, to do so. 'The Translators to the Reader', a preface which is much more interesting, but rarely reprinted compared to the praise of James in the 'Epistle Dedicatorie', suggests that they wanted 'to make a good one better'. Which one? Officially, the Bishops' Bible, but in practice Tyndale, Coverdale, Geneva, and (despite their anti-Catholic strictures) Rheims have a voice in the finished product, at least as strong as any of the committee. It is ironic, in view of James's stated preference against it, that the Geneva Bible should be so influential. Or perhaps he just disliked the radical Protestant marginal notes, which disappeared until an edition of the Authorised Version was printed with Geneva notes in 1642.

The vocabulary of the new translation was more conservative, even Catholic, in some respects. The old ecclesiastical words like 'Baptism' and 'Church' are preferred to the Tyndale/Geneva use of 'washing' and 'congregation'; both denoting areas of controversy in Church government during the century. Sir Thomas More had criticised Tyndale for translating *'presbyteros'* as 'elder' instead of 'priest' (the word adopted in 1611). He regarded it as a threat to the 'Church'. He was right. Tyndale was a threat to the Latin 'Vulgate', in a way more 'Authorised' than the so-called 'Authorised Version' ever was. The Catholic English translation (known as Rheims–Douai from the places of publication) described itself as 'Faithfully Translated into English out of the Authentical Latin' and sticks to Latinity in the vocabulary to a disabling extent. Philippians 2:7, for example, in 1611 translated as 'made himself of no reputation' is in the 1582 Rheims New Testament 'he exinanited himself'.

The 1611 preface steers a recognisably Anglican middle way between what it characterises as Puritan 'scrupulosity' and Catholic obscurity. The statement that they did not use the same English word for the same Hebrew and Greek word each time suggests not only a freedom in translation but also a desire to avoid setting up an exclusively 'religious' vocabulary. However, as Gerald Hammond has demonstrated, their reproduction of variation and repetition in Old

Testament vocabulary is often very close; within an individual passage the same Hebrew word will correspond with the same English word.[7] This is particularly important in poetic passages, where reproducing the Hebrew device of parallelism means that something of the variation in vocabulary, and perhaps the syntax of the original, needs to be reproduced if the effect is to be retained. The effect is no longer quite English, though. Some modern readers prefer it this way, arguing that the failure of modern Bible translations is in part due to the inertness of contemporary English, at least in its official versions.[8]

Is it more religious, then? The language of religion need not necessarily be more sublime than ordinary speech; as Auerbach argued, comparing the Old Testament with Homeric narrative, 'The sublime influence of God here reaches so deeply into the everyday that the two realms of the sublime and the everyday are not actually unseparated but basically inseparable.'[9] This siting of profound seriousness in everyday contexts is most evident in the Gospels: 'Now as he walked by the Sea of Galilee, he saw Simon, and Andrew his brother, casting a net into the Sea (for they were fishers.) And Jesus said unto them, Come ye after me; and I will make you to become fishers of men' (Authorised Version, Mark 1:16–17). Tyndale doesn't even have 'to become', which is a gain in directness; but the point is that there is no need for a special 'religious' language, even with the metaphorical 'fishers of men'. Yet the call and response is of eternal consequence, implicit at this early stage of the narrative. We should not confuse 'religious' with 'decorous'. John Carey has attacked the Authorised Version for preferring the 'rotund sentiment' to the jagged homeliness of Tyndale when it does make a change.[10] Instances such as this comparison from the Epistle of St James demonstrate that, four hundred years on, Tyndale can sometimes appear more modern than his revisers. The image is of a mirror:

> But whoso looketh into the perfect Law of liberty, and
> continueth therein, he being not a forgetful hearer, but a
> doer of the work, this man shall be blessed in his deed.
> (Authorised Version, James 1:25)

> But whoso looketh in the perfect law of liberty, and
> continueth therein (if he be not a forgetful hearer, but a doer
> of the work) he shall be happy in his deed.
> (Tyndale, 1525)

There are two differences; one is that Tyndale uses the bracket and a 'perfective' (I use Halliday's term) rather than imperfect participle to clarify a complex subordination. Second is 'happy' versus 'blessed'. To us now 'blessed' is the religious word. Even the *Good News Bible* (1976), which of all modern translations most explicitly tries for 'a standard, everyday, natural English', has 'blessed by God'. In I Corinthians 13 the Authorised Version has 'charity' where Tyndale has 'love'. It is arguable there (as it was in the sixteenth century) that the range of meaning of the original Greek word is better rendered by 'charity'. Not now, of course, because the primary meaning of 'charity' has shifted, to make an apparent contradiction of the Authorised verse 3: 'And though I bestow all my goods to feed the poor . . . and have not charity, it profiteth me nothing.'

Other changes show that the King James revisers were aware of the ambiguities in their originals, and in some cases attempted to preserve them in similarly ambiguous English, using the margin to indicate alternatives. The phrase, 'in that he feared', referring to Jesus in Hebrews 5:7, has a marginal alternative, 'for his piety'. The construction 'in that' can mean both 'because' and 'in the state of'; 'piety' reflects another possibility in the word translated 'fear', itself already suspended between 'awe' and 'anxiety'.[11] In such cases, the Authorised Version leaves open the question of interpretation by giving the English reader as many of the possibilities in the original as English will allow.

The translators were criticised by John Selden, the seventeenth-century antiquary, for translating words rather than sentences, producing something more like a crib than a translation; in following this Tyndale principle it appears that the King James translators were going against contemporary translating practice for other texts:

> There is no book so translated as the Bible. For the purpose
> if I translate a French Book into English I turn it into English
> phrase and not into French English (Il fait froid) I say it is
> cold; not it makes cold but the Bible is translated into
> English words; rather than into English phrase: the
> Hebraisms are kept and the phrase of that language is kept,
> as for one example (he uncovered her shame) which is well
> enough so long as scholars have to do with it but when it
> comes among the common people Lord what gear do they
> make of it.[12]

Selden may be right about the words; his fear of the common people's 'gear' (i.e., nonsense) shows that English translation of the Bible had let it out of the study, the pulpit, indeed most of the institutional controls on interpretation.

Another way of dealing with Selden's criticism would be to ask what happens to the larger-scale effects, such as narrative, as a result of the word-for-word tendency in the Tyndale/King James tradition. Tyndale's claim, that Hebrew 'agreeth a thousand times more with the English than with the Latin', is particularly true of syntax and word order. So he is able to reproduce much of the narrative flow. Hebrew has few connectives, most commonly 'waw', which Tyndale and his successors usually render as 'and'; the effect of this on narrative is to make it extremely deadpan, cutting the usual logical and interpretive pointers like 'however'. Another Hebrew idiom is to express the relation between concepts as 'noun plus noun' rather than 'noun's noun' or (sometimes) 'adjective noun'. Again, this transfers easily enough into English idiom, but its exclusive use does produce a distinctive effect, a 'biblical' English – 'the day of trouble', 'the valley of the shadow of death', 'the paths of the Lord', 'the oppression of the enemy' (all examples from the Psalms).[13]

A similar complaint to Selden's is heard in Robert Boyle's *Some Considerations Touching the Style of the Holy Scriptures*, though his main criticism is that the poetry and the figures of rhetoric tend to vanish 'in such literal Translations as are ours of the Bible'.[14] Boyle was one of the most distinguished members of the Royal Society. From the evidence of his scientific work we gather that he shared their ideal of a plain style; in religious writing, however, he sometimes had different priorities. He argues that the variety of Scripture styles is to catch different prey. The following extract is interesting for its attack on the proof-texting approach to Scripture which, armed with a concordance, reads each verse as confirmation or denial of a particular doctrine, which is countered by the argument that the aesthetic properties of the Bible have a religious impact:

> I use the Scriptures, not as an arsenal, to be resorted to only
> for arms and weapons to defend this party, or defeat its
> enemies; but as a matchless temple, where I delight to be, to
> contemplate the beauty, the symmetry, and the magnificence
> of the structure, and to encrease my awe, and excite my
> devotion to the Deity there preached and ador'd.[15]

Boyle's main target in *Some Considerations* seems to be educated objectors to the Bible, those who cavil at its supposed incoherence or triviality, but in particular those who dislike its style – defined by Boyle in the broadest way, 'almost the whole manner of an author's expressing himself'.[16] He argues that there are fashions in language, as in dress, which may hinder appreciation of an old work whose context has largely vanished. It is sometimes a translation problem – 'in many places strangely harsh and barbarous', he complains.[17] In the end, though, it comes down to plainness. He quotes Machiavelli in its defence – presumably no longer the bugaboo of earlier in the century – and suggests that, in the end, it comes down to persuasiveness: 'The Scripture, not only is movinger than the glitteringest human styles, but hath sometimes a potenter influence on men in those passages that seem quite destitute of ornaments, than in those where rhetoric is conspicuous.'[18] The English Bible, then, introduced a whole range of idioms from Hebrew and Greek into English simply because of the unusual translation practice introduced by Tyndale.

We need to bear this kind of response in mind when asking what difference the Authorised Version made. Not only is it difficult to disentangle the effect of that particular version from its predecessors; educated men continued to use the originals, or Latin (not necessarily the Vulgate; Milton, like many European Protestants, used Tremellius's 1579 Latin version). Over forty years on we find Bunyan beginning his writing career using the Geneva Bible for his quotations; three years earlier than that, in 1653, a Bill presented to the Long Parliament (though never acted upon) called for a revision to get rid of the inaccuracies and 'prelatical language' of the Authorised Version.[19] Yet it is in the remarkable upsurge of popular religious expression in the 1650s that we see the clearest evidence of English biblical style. I agree with Lewis, that Bunyan's style of writing is not biblical, even if his work is unimaginable without the Bible. Some of his more radical contemporaries did write in a biblical style, however, and the prophecies they made sound very like biblical prophecies. Here is Hester Biddle in 1662:

> Oh you high and lofty ones! who spendeth God's creation
> upon your lusts, and doth not feed the hungry, nor clothe
> the naked, but they are ready to perish in the streets; both
> old and young, lame and blind lyeth in your streets, and at
> your masshouse doors, crying for bread, which even melteth
> my heart, and maketh the soul of the righteous to mourn.[20]

At this early stage the language is not freighted with half-acknowledged biblical phrases which anyone might call on in such impassioned speech. Rather this is a challenge to authority. The language of the Bible, acknowledged by the authorities to be authoritative, is turned against them. There are other code words as well – 'masshouse' is a Nonconformist taunt at High Anglicanism – but this is the style, and the thought, behind such prophecies:

> Is not this the fast I have chosen? to loose the bands of
> wickedness, to undo the heavy burdens, and to let the
> oppressed go free, and that ye break every yoke?

> Is it not to deal thy bread to the hungry, and that thou
> bring the poor that are cast out to thy house? when thou
> seest the naked, that thou cover him; and that thou hide not
> thyself from thine own flesh?
>
> (Authorised Version, Isaiah 58:6–7)

The contrast between notional and visible religious observance, like fasting, and action to relieve the poor, which is what Isaiah's God demands as a sign of righteousness, is a constant theme of radical religion, to which we shall return. What I am suggesting here is that the impact of the English Bible in the seventeenth century is less on the well-educated, particularly the clergy and many that we might find prominent in the history of literature, and more on the laity, those who had not been to university, and those who challenged the powerful. However, this is not to limit the impact of the printed Bible from the sixteenth century on; simply to underline that the Bible for such as Andrewes the preacher (and translator), or Milton, was a Hebrew and Greek, and perhaps Latin text before it was the English version. Only from the relatively uneducated do we hear the idioms as well as the message of the English Bible unmistakably breaking through.

Notes

1. C.S. Lewis, *The Literary Impact of the Authorized Version* (London, 1950), p. 25.

2. See, e.g., Walter L. Reed, 'A Poetics of the Bible: Problems and Possibilities', *Literature and Theology* 1 (1987), 154–66.

3. *Luther's Correspondence*, ed. P. Smith and C.M. Jacobs (Philadelphia 1918), II, p. 176; cited by David Greenwood, 'Reading the Bible Literarily' in *Reading Literature: Some Christian Approaches*, ed. D. Barratt and R. Pooley (Leicester, 1984), pp. 13–30.

4. Walter Schwarz, *Principles and Problems of Biblical Translation: Some Reformation Controversies and their Background* (Cambridge, 1955), pp. 44–5.

5. Prologue to *The New Testament* (1525).

6. William Barlow, *The Summe and Substance of the Conference . . . at Hampton Court* (1604), quoted by Ward Allen, *Translating for King James* (London, 1970), p. 4.

7. Gerald Hammond, *The Making of the English Bible* (Manchester, 1982), p. 177.

8. I take this to be Ian Robinson's position in *The Survival of English* (Cambridge, 1973) and his essay 'The Word of God Now' *PN Review* 6:5 (1979), 223–7.

9. Erich Auerbach, *Mimesis*, trans. Willard R. Trask (Princeton, 1953), pp. 222–3.

10. John Carey, 'Sixteenth- and Seventeenth-Century Prose' in *English Poetry and Prose, 1540–1674*, ed. C. Ricks (London, 1970), p. 352. Similar criticism can be found in David Daniell's contribution to *The Cambridge Guide to the Arts in Britain*, ed. Boris Ford (Cambridge, 1989), vol. 4.

11. Ward Allen, 'The Translation of *apo tes eulabeias* at Hebrews 5:7', *Bulletin of the Institute for Reformation Biblical Studies* I: 1 (1989), 9–10.

12. *Table Talk of John Selden*, ed. Frederick Pollard (London, 1927), p. 11. Selden died in 1654; the *Table Talk* was first published in 1689.

13. I have no Hebrew; my knowledge is entirely derived from secondary sources, especially Hammond, *Making of the English Bible*; and Robert Alter, *The Art of Biblical Narrative* (1981), which indicates the limitations as well as the strengths of the King James version for a literary reading.

14. Robert Boyle, *Some Considerations Touching the Style of the Holy Scriptures* (2nd edn, 1663), p. 9.

15. Boyle, p. 78.

16. Boyle, p. 2.

17. Boyle, pp. 153–4.

18. Boyle, pp. 246–7.

19. Gordon Campbell, 'Bunyan and the Theologians', *John Bunyan: Conventicle and Parnassus: Tercentenary Essays*, ed. N.H. Keeble (Oxford, 1988), pp. 138–9.

20. Hester Biddle, *The Trumpet of the Lord Sounded forth* (1662), p. 12. I owe the reference to Elaine Hobby, *Virtue of Necessity: English Women's Writing, 1649–88* (London, 1988).

Chapter 7
The Sermon

Many seventeenth-century preachers had a captive audience. With fines for non-attendance, it could not be otherwise, and in a Puritan family you were likely to be catechised on the preacher's main points. Sermons would last for an hour, sometimes longer. Yet preaching generated excitement. People would travel miles to hear great preachers. Systems of shorthand were first devised in England to take notes from sermons. A congregation would hum loudly to express their approval or appreciation of a particular point.

One of the common complaints of the Puritan party was that there were not enough preaching ministers; but interest in preaching was by no means a Puritan monopoly. This was not just a taste for Christian doctrine memorably and movingly expressed, though sermons often took the place that today's newspapers, or rather current affairs programmes, might. There were sermons on special royal anniversaries – the Gunpowder Plot, for example, or the Gowrie Plot, which James had escaped before he came to the English throne. During the Restoration, the death of Charles I was commemorated by sermons. During the Civil War and part of the Interregnum, Parliament would often call special fast days: the sermons preached and printed from these days are, at one level, a guide to the political issues faced at the time which, in the period as a whole, were often seen and expressed in religious terms.

Take one example of the political sermon: William Barlow's sermon preached at St Paul's Cross (by the old cathedral) on the first Sunday in Lent, 1601. It was the first Sunday after the Earl of Essex's execution for treason. Barlow had been commissioned to give the official Court line – Paul's Cross was, indirectly, a government pulpit. In some sense every pulpit was; before and into our period, the Elizabethan *Book of Homilies* had provided a centrally sanctioned set of sermons to be read in church, which included the famous homily against rebellion as well as more familiar religious topics. The printed preface to this sermon suggests that Barlow had spent three days at court gathering information, and as one of Essex's private chaplains at the execution was able to reveal something of the dead man's confession. Although the sermon does expound a relevant text, Matthew 22:21, 'Render therefore unto Caesar, the things which are Caesar's', for a while, the substance of the sermon is a kind of moralised obituary of the dead rebel, linking him to biblical rebels such as Abimelech and Absalom, as well as English ones such as Ket and Tyler. There is even a comparison with Plutarch's life of Coriolanus, eight years before Shakespeare's play. The sermon provides a mixture of moral and political judgement and a privileged insight into the last words of the dead rebel, satisfying curiosity but also keeping it from developing into further unrest. Barlow's performance after the Gunpowder Plot was discovered four years later is interestingly much more of an exposition, and much less personal. Fawkes gets in only incidentally to the condemnation of Popery. The personality and status of Essex were obviously more germane to the importance of his act of rebellion than that of Fawkes and his co-conspirators. Barlow's sermons are responding as much to the political as to the religious implications of these rebellions.

Sermons were also great rhetorical performances, we might say literary events, and were admired as such. In London, where there was choice, preachers like Andrewes attracted the literary wits like Nashe and Lyly. Unfortunately, of the great poet-preachers of the century, Donne, Herbert and Crashaw, only Donne's texts survive, but they demonstrate a literary power and integrity which makes them much more than curious addenda to his poetry. Herbert's reflections on preaching, in *The Country Parson* and some poems in *The Temple*, are interesting. 'The Windows', for example, argues that the preacher's life is crucial to the impact of his sermon:

> Doctrine and life, colours and light, in one
> When they combine and mingle, bring
> A strong regard and awe: but speech alone
> Doth vanish like a flaring thing,
> And in the ear, not conscience ring.[1]

Herbert's remark 'A verse may find him, who a sermon flies', which was quoted in defence of practically every book of religious poetry that followed him, might also suggest that poetry and sermons run in parallel to the same purpose, and that poetry's appeal, its wit, its attempts at truth-telling, and its range from personal lyric to universal epic, might be looked for in the sermon.

However, the literary form which makes almost as much sense as a parallel is the drama, despite the hostility of many religious people then to the idea of drama, let alone its practice. The preacher-playwrights are few – John Marston is the only major figure; he abandoned the stage for the pulpit, and there are no records of his preaching. What sermons and plays share is a mixture of narration and persuasive oratory, bringing the audience to a central crisis of recognition. Thomas Nashe, an admirer of good preaching as well as a playwright, defends plays in similar terms to Sidney's defence of poetry. The final sentence of this quotation could equally apply to all sermons, but the earlier political message is a feature of many in the period, too:

> In plays, all cozenages, all cunning drifts over-gilded with
> outward holiness, all stratagems of war, all the cankerworms
> that breed on the rust of peace, are most lively anatomized.
> They shew the ill success of treason, the fall of hasty
> climbers, the wretched end of usurpers, the misery of civil
> dissension, and how just God is evermore in punishing of
> murder . . . . They are sour pills of reprehension, wrapped
> up in sweet words.[2]

In the following survey I will concentrate on a few major figures, but also attempt to map the arguments about sermon style as the century progressed. These form part of larger movements in prose style and, like them, cannot be isolated from other loyalties, religious and political.

Lancelot Andrewes

Beginning with Andrewes might seem tendentious, in view of T.S. Eliot's celebration of him.[3] It is still difficult to discuss Andrewes from a literary point of view except in dialogue with Eliot. What follows is not an endorsement of his view of Andrewes' preaching as being intrinsically superior or more spiritual than Donne's. However, he began preaching earlier; he rose higher in the Church hierarchy than Donne; and was more influential than any other single preacher on the style of preaching in the early seventeenth century. As catechist at Pembroke College, Cambridge in 1578 he was already creating wide interest by his lectures on the Ten Commandments. 'Lectures' in this context are not solely academic; many Puritan parishes had a 'lecturer' to expound the new doctrines. Though some of Andrewes' views, on Sabbath-keeping, for example, were close to the Puritans, he had an almost Catholic view of confession. William Alabaster, best remembered now as a devotional poet, described them as 'a certain mixture of all sides of religions, which by their very novelty now in England do begin to please again such men as have some affection to Catholic faith'.[4]

Andrewes' sermons were edited after his death by Buckeridge and Laud. While Andrewes lacked Laud's energetic intransigence, they shared many commitments, for example to royalty, and to order and beauty in the church, and Laud took Andrewes' devotions, the *Preces Privatae*, to the scaffold with him. It is reasonably clear that they only published those sermons which were available complete rather than in note form. This means that the Andrewes corpus may be misleadingly weighted towards special occasions, particularly court sermons. James I was a learned man, and something of a theologian, which points to a greater allusiveness as well as formality for these occasions. It is also difficult to recover the precise relationship between text and delivery. But it is clear that what we are reading is a script for an oral performance:

> What did they? Praised God. For *Angels* to *praise God*, is no
> new thing. From the beginning, it was their occupation, so
> to do. But, to praise him for a *child* in a *cratch*, that (lo) is
> new; A new thing; A new song; and (if you will) a new *sign*,
> too. For, never the like seen before. Before (in Job), their
> praise was for the creating; they had that only, then, to
> praise Him for: now, for the *restoring* of all things.
>   (Sermon 1 Of the Nativitie: Christmas 1618)[5]

The absence of the main verb in 'For, never the like . . .' might have worried a lesser linguist, but in oral delivery, who would notice? Even the italics seem deliberately placed for emphasis, an unusual habit for printing then. The same could be said of the punctuation, heavier in those days generally, but here particularly pointing to each pause and inflection. Notation for the spoken voice is the first thing we notice about Andrewes' style. This is what drives his version of the Senecan, or 'cut' style, as it was described at the time – producing a text for effective spoken delivery.

Andrewes' way with the text he is expounding is similarly to cut it into tiny pieces, usually a word at a time. This method has been variously praised by T.S. Eliot as extracting the last juice of meaning from a word, and criticised by George Herbert (who may have heard Andrewes preach at Cambridge or at Court) as 'crumbling a text into small parts'.[6] Partly it's a consequence of his relentless drawing out of the implications in a word; for example, in the sermon quoted above, he pauses on the word 'multitude' which describes the angels who 'sang' to the shepherds at the birth of Jesus. He argues that it emphasises their authority as witnesses, it made them a better choir, and the fact that it was an organised rather than a confused multitude is part of the evidence that it was the grand saviour of all rather than an ordinary one who would only need one angel to announce him. This kind of exposition has much in common with the virtuoso practical criticism of literature, though with a more committed sense that the density of meaning has implications beyond the complexity itself. In contemporary criticism, the ability of a text to sustain multiple interpretation is a sign of its literariness, or its classic status; the seventeenth-century preacher tends to drive beyond those multiple meanings into multiple applications, exhorting his listeners to change their lives.

Andrewes is not much of an image-maker – one reason that his sermons have been less popular than Donne's with literary readers. There are bursts of imagery: 'No reed, no cobweb-hope then; but helmet, anchor-hope'.[7] But they are incidental. Eliot remarked that Andrewes gives little joy to the anthologist, though this is mainly a point about the structure of the sermons: the text may be examined one word at a time, but the argument is tight, referring back, pushing forward, rarely making a point in isolation. It is, after all, God's word, so each word has some significance, and the whole will be coherent. Andrewes will take a 'yet' or a 'with' as crucial to the meaning of a text, or he will warn his hearers against cutting out bits of a text when it is inconvenient to them, for example in a sermon on fasting. This word-by-word approach can be a defence of the coherence of the text, even though one Scottish Lord, according to Aubrey, criticised Andrewes' sermons as a series of 'here's a pretty thing, and here's a pretty thing'.[8]

I shall now turn to three particular sermons; an early sermon, to show the method in embryo, a political sermon, and finally a sermon for a major Christian festival, which shows Andrewes at his best, tackling central Christian doctrines. Andrewes' first published sermon was preached at St Mary's Hospital in London in the Wednesday of Easter Week, 1588. The 'Spital' sermons, as they were known, like those at St Paul's Cross, were major public performances. The Mayor of London issued the invitations and sat with his aldermen and any bishops who might attend in a kind of grandstand. The contrast between them and the charity pupils of the bluecoat school who were obliged to turn up, as well as the rest of a London audience, shows in the choice of text ('lay up for yourselves treasure in heaven') and his charge to the rich to be generous. The drive to apply the text to his audience is more constant here than in later sermons, in fact; there is a dig at corrupt lawyers (and a nod towards the better ones), and an unusual suggestion that the 'moths' in the same passage are evil creditors – both aimed at a rich city audience. In view of Andrewes' later reputation, we must also note his praise of intellectual and rhetorical honesty. The constant Elizabethan fear of treason had been exacerbated the previous year by the Pope's declaration of a crusade against England; this seems more like a trailer for Marlowe's heroes, though: 'For when the minds of men will overreach their abilities, what must be the end, but as we have seen of late to prove traitors?'[9] This passage sets words against actions in religion, but could be taken as a stylistic manifesto: 'It were better reversed, if we were, as St Paul saith, "perfect in all good works", than perfect in certain curious and quaint terms and set phrases, wherein a great part of many men's religion do now-a-days consist; plain speech and sound dealing, plain speech and good works, best.'[10] In that last elision we can see signs of Andrewes' later, clipped manner. Most of this early sermon displays a more expansive, flowing sentence structure.

Andrewes is understandably more circumspect in his applications in the court sermons, which are our principal source for his later preaching. He was a conspicuous loyalist, if not an especially astute or interested Church or state politician, and he was a regular Court preacher from 1605 on. There are two main series of sermons with a potentially political edge, both commemorating the king's escape from an attempt on his life – the Gowrie conspiracy of 1600 and the Gunpowder Plot of 1605. They were very Jacobean occasions, answering to James's sense of himself as a theologian as well as the originator of the full Divine Right of Kings theory.

Andrewes' Gowrie sermon of 1622 discusses the incident in I Samuel 24: 5–8 where David cuts off part of the robe of Saul, the first King of Israel. His main point is that David refused to touch the Lord's anointed, even though he had threatened his life and was now in his power. Saul in his cave becomes a 'type' of James in the Gowries' castle at St Johnstone. Typology is most often used in the period to find New Testament ideas prefigured in the Old, but there is a political use as well. Stuart theory was taken with the theological privileges of Old Testament kingship; republicans preferred the prelude to the anointing of the first Israelite king, where God (through his prophet Samuel) is angry that his people want a king, just to be like everyone else in the pagan Middle East. This had the additional advantage of suggesting that people, as much as God, choose kings.[11] I suspect, though, that the original Court audience would have thought 'Catholic assassins' when hearing this: 'you see, it is no new thing, this, to kill Kings by divinity. This gear is but newly raked up from hell again.'[12]

Andrewes' way with the narrative part of the sermon is instructive, particularly for a preacher who is not renowned for it. He can characterise it in a word – 'It is all but a delivery . . . a delivery into their hands; a delivery out of them'[13] – which is an intellectual's way of reducing narrative into a concept, a lesson. But he can also expand it, dramatically:

> So up he rose and toward Saul he made, as softly and
> secretly as he could. And when he came at him, close behind
> him, out went his knife, as if he meant to use it. His men, I
> dare say, hoped to some other end. Stay here. And he that
> had seen David thus, in this wise, coming close behind the
> King's back with his knife drawn in his hand, would he not
> have taken him for Ravaillac? What difference? I promise
> you, this was not *bonum in oculis*, no very good sight. And
> then knowing Saul was his mortal enemy, and even now at
> this very instant time come forth to seek his life, and seeing
> them thus in a blind cave, and David hard at his back with a
> naked knife, would he not have given Saul for dead, past for
> ever *Abiit vitam suam*?[14]

The conclusion is that David does no more than cut off a piece of Saul's cloak. Notice how Andrewes varies the pace of his storytelling. 'Stay here' – a short sentence, at once David's command and the preacher's seizing his audience's attention. 'And then knowing . . .', a cumulative sentence, full of suspense. Much of the sermon, then, becomes an evocation of the passions of rebellion before they are, inwardly, resisted or restrained. We can see the occasion and the text forcing Andrewes into considering the mind of the potential assassin. Imaginative sympathy, and the ability to dramatise it, will need to be added to the picture of the intellectual, eirenic contemplative; and thus help to explain why he was a popular as well as a respected preacher.

Andrewes seems particularly at home in the Christmas sermons; perhaps it is the element of paradox in the Word made flesh, the mixture of joy and intellectuality that the festival permitted. In discussing Sermon 11 of the Nativity (1616) we might avoid the cliché of looking at the 1622 sermon which Eliot quotes in 'The Journey of the Magi', and which is consequently most anthologised, though of course that is a fine example of Andrewes' imaginative skills with a narrative. The 1611 sermon demonstrates his ability to structure a discourse round four abstract concepts – mercy and truth, righteousness and peace – in an exposition of Psalm 85 v. 10–11. The parallel is with the masque tradition, also a feature of the Court at Christmas, where apparently antagonistic abstract forces are reconciled in their personified forms.

> This *meeting* is of *four*. Four, which of themselves (*proprie
> loquendo*) are nothing but *attributes*, or *properties*, of the *divine*

> *nature*. But, are (here) by the Psalmist brought in, and
> represented to us, as so many *personages*. *Personages* (I say)
> inasmuch as they have here *personal acts* ascribed to them.
> For, to *meet*, to *kiss*, to *look down*, are all of them *acts
> personal*.[15]

But this is only a prelude to a drama of a fairly intellectual sort. The
very next paragraph shows one of the habits that distance Andrewes
from the popular Puritan preachers, and even his Restoration
successors, the use of Latin:

> At a *birth*, at *orta est*, these four meet here: at *orta est veritas*,
> the *birth of truth*; *de terra*, *from the earth*. For, two *ortus* there
> were: and this, not his *antesaecularis ortus de coelo*, his *birth
> before all worlds* from *heaven*; but, his *ortus de terra*, his *temporal
> birth, from the earth*.[16]

To quote in Latin to a learned audience was not particularly
obscurantist at the time; and Andrewes translates as he goes. The most
that could be said against it in the context would be that it flatters those
who do not need the translation – though it would be a different matter
in an ordinary parish church. So what is the effect? It slows the
movement of sense down, a movement which is already slow,
incremental, one word at a time. It offers a convenient mode of
repetition, always important in spoken discourse. In doing so, it
intensifies the play on the word birth/*ortus* – though 'wordplay' is
misleading; it is really concept-play.

John Donne

For a modern reader, it might seem curious that Donne was better
known in his own time as a preacher than a poet. He did not enter the
ministry until quite late in his life (1615), and then mostly on the
prompting of James I, who made him a royal chaplain, but had
indicated that other royal patronage would not be available. In 1621 he
became Dean of St Paul's. He preached to a variety of London
congregations, the Inns of Court, his parish church, noble families, and
the Virginia Company, as well as the royal courts and St Paul's

cathedral. Fifteen of his sermons were published in his lifetime, eighty in a posthumous volume of 1640.

The reader of the poetry might usefully enter the prose through the *Devotions*, which have a private intensity comparable to the *Songs and Sonets*, not to mention the divine poems. But some of the devices of immediacy of the lyrics appear in the sermons, too. The sermon preached at the funeral of Sir William Cockayne, Alderman and former Lord Mayor of London, in 1626 begins 'God made the first Marriage, and Man made the first Divorce'; particularly in the context of the funeral of a civic dignitary, as startling as 'I wonder what thou and I did, till we loved?'. What's missing in this example is the first person, but Donne is as free with that, singular and plural, as Andrewes is sparing.

Donne the preacher is a Christian psychologist, an investigator and mover of the emotions, an Augustinian who regarded love and fear as essential motives to the discovery and obedience of Christian truth. As Deborah Shuger so neatly puts it, in the Renaissance, you are what you love.[17] Donne's ambition as a preacher was to refocus that love onto God. The rationale for this comes from St Augustine, who argued that knowledge and love of God were reciprocal.

Donne's debt to Augustine, like him a rake turned preacher, is wide-ranging. He found him a kindred spirit as well as point of reference in such matters as his fascination with the details of death and resurrection, with the impotence of the will, his delight in the Psalms; a passionate, intellectual spirituality which matched his own feelings and the challenges he faced as a preacher. Not that Donne is uncritical of Augustine; and we may hesitate to endorse Walton completely over the conversion parallel. I am more persuaded by R.C. Bald's argument, that the seriousness and change of heart that marks a conversion experience is more in evidence after his wife's death in 1617 than in the years leading up to his ordination.[18]

This Augustinian process, of reaching for the knowledge and love of God, involved first self-scrutiny, then contemplation of God, which leads to a perception of the gap between God and the divine likeness in us marred by sin. This gap could only be crossed by God's mercy and grace. Take the Fourth Prebend Sermon, preached at St Pauls in 1626:[19] 'The looking upon God, by the first light of Nature, is, to catechize, and examine thy self, whether thou do govern, and employ thy natural faculties to his glory . . . .' The first step, self-examination, leads to a sense of sin. In this particular sermon, the process leads to a proper fear of judgement. Donne does not think that God's mercy removes fear – 'There is a holy fear, that does not only consist with an assurance of mercy, but induces, constitutes that assurance.'[20]

Many of Donne's sermons deal with that uncertainty of whether one is saved or not. The anxiety often has a Calvinist twist in the period – how can you know if you are one of the elect? On most theological questions Donne is Calvinist. However, in the Fourth Prebend sermon it arises in the context of the Sacrament of Communion, in itself a sign of the grace of God, but are we taking it as a John, a beloved disciple, or a Judas? We won't know until death. In Sir William Cockayne's funeral sermon one of its most famous passages describes the uncertainty of spiritual things in this world:

> When we consider with a religious seriousness the manifold
> weaknesses of the strongest devotions in time of prayer, it is
> a sad consideration. I throw my self down in my chamber,
> and I call in, and invite God, and his Angels thither, and
> when they are there, I neglect God and his Angels, for the
> noise of a fly, for the rattling of a coach, for the whining of a
> door; I talk on, in the same posture of praying; eyes lifted
> up; knees bowed down; as though I prayed to God; and, if
> God, or his Angels should ask me, when I thought last of
> God in that prayer, I cannot tell: sometimes I find that I had
> forgot what I was about, but when I began to forget it, I
> cannot tell. A memory of yesterday's pleasures, a fear of
> tomorrow's dangers, a straw under my knee, a noise in mine
> ear, an any thing, a nothing, a fancy, a Chimera in my brain,
> troubles me in my prayer. So certainly is there nothing,
> nothing in spiritual things, perfect in this world.[21]

It's a compelling account of distraction, with all the specifics of petty, and not so petty concerns crowding out 'God, or his Angels'. It is also a good example of how Donne's preaching can do similar things to his poetry, but differently, perhaps even better, because of the different scale and the slightly more relaxed disciplines of prose. The lists, for example, like the 'eyes, lips and hands' that a more spiritually loving couple miss less in 'A Valediction Forbidding Mourning'. In the poem they are significant, but crammed into a half-line. In the sermon, the list beginning 'A memory . . .' may seem at first sight organised, with its antitheses, but the last pair is not an antithesis, and it seems on the point of breaking down into the lack of control all these distractions are producing. But then the repeated 'nothing' reasserts control, and Donne is able to restate his point before moving on to the next.

This extract may also stand for another tension in Donne's preaching style. The labels critics use for this are numerous and slippery; but there is the restlessness, the inventiveness and the gap-bridging that we might call baroque, and there is also the organisation, the delight in antithesis and rounding off that is associated with the

Ciceronian style.[22] Both these styles are copious rather than restrained, and Donne's use of the briefer periods associated with Senecan style are more for occasional effect rather than a habitual resource. Or it may be, simply, that in his earlier sermons he was using sentences like Andrewes' until he had developed more of a style of his own. Certainly a sense of antithetical structure can produce memorable simplicities as well as extended rhapsodies: this, from the conclusion of the 1621 Christmas Sermon: 'To end all, we have no warmth in our selves; it is true, but Christ came even in the winter. We have no light in our selves; it is true, but he came even in the night.'[23] We must remember, though, that inserting a relatively simple statement in the middle of longer ones is different from being a 'plain style' preacher. Plain style can often get its best effects from appearing aginst a real or implied richness. In a sermon preached in 1623 Donne argues that a richer style is in line with the practice of the Bible: 'the Holy Ghost in penning the Scriptures delights himself, not only with a propriety, but with a delicacy, and harmony, and melody of language; with height of Metaphors, and other figures, which may work greater impressions upon the Readers, and not with barbarous, or trivial, or market, or homely language'.[24] Earlier in the sermon he suggests that the mistake of thinking biblical style to be homely rather than eloquent derives from the pioneering but unsophisticated scholarship of the early Reformation. It would be an exaggeration to say that Donne excludes homely or trivial language from his sermons – what of the distractions in the Cockayne sermon? Actually that may be the point. The homely is precisely that which distracts from the spiritual.

The richness is not just syntactic. Sometimes the imaginative flight seems to take off beyond decorum. As with some of Crashaw's poetry, too literal a reading would be stomach-turning, grotesque and messy: 'There we leave you in that blessed dependency, to hang upon him that hangs upon the Crosse, there bath in his tears, there suck at his wounds, and lie down in peace in his grave.'[25] Of course, read it as devotional code, and it works; but part of its power comes from skirting the boundaries of excess.

This stylistic tension in Donne is matched by a similar approach to structuring the sermons themselves. Most of them announce their organisation, that is, how the biblical text is to be divided up, early on. You ought always to know where you are in a Donne sermon. Yet, Stanley Fish argues, in *Death's Duell*, Donne's final sermon, the discrete categories become merged, and there is a progressive loss of confidence in the capacity of these structures, and thus our capacity to understand.[26] The structure stays in place, but the content seems to escape it, at times by paradox, as when he sees first life in the womb, then birth, as deaths: 'We have a winding sheet in our mother's womb, which grows with us from our conception, and we come into the world, wound up in that winding sheet, for we come to seek a grave.'[27] Fish, characteristically, exaggerates; in fact the sermon keeps to its structure while being aware of its limitations, just as Donne himself recognised the limitations of language in describing God. It is not so much a sceptical, self-consuming artifact as a self-dramatising artifact. But the self-dramatising is always linked to a persuasive purpose.

In the end, Donne's greatness as a preacher lies in his ability to capture the perceptions and feelings of a specific congregation for specific theological ends. He is adaptive, learned with the Inns of Court, deferential within limits to the king, expansive and direct in St Paul's. The paradox is that all these appeals to the will, all these cajolings, come from someone whose sense of the paralysis of the fallen will is still thoroughly Calvinist (and Lutheran, for that matter):

> But can we love God when we will? . . . every man may
> love him, that will; but can every man have this will, this
> desire? Certainly we cannot begin this love; except God love
> us first, we cannot love him; but God doth love us all so
> well, from the beginning, as that every man may see the
> fault was in the perverseness of his own will, that he did not
> love God better.[28]

Is it reasonable to see Andrewes and Donne as part of a 'metaphysical' school of preaching? In an area low on critical labels ('plain' is about the only other one), this is particularly tricky, because it can either mean everything we associate with the Metaphysical poets – the combination of directness with ostentatious wit, for example – or everything we don't associate with Puritan plainness (see below). Horton Davies's eleven-point checklist of the features of Metaphysical preaching may be over-schematic, and not all eleven have to be present for the sermon to count as 'Metaphysical', but it has the advantage of being rooted in a much wider sample than just Andrewes and Donne. Here is the list in summary: wit; patristic citations (to assert the continuity of Anglicanism with the undivided Early Church); use of classical literature and history; illustrations from 'unnatural' natural history; quotations in Greek and Latin, and use of etymology; a middle road between medieval four-level exegesis of Scripture and the Puritan insistence on a single level; use of division in sermon structure (though I am not convinced that this is significantly different to that of other kinds of preachers); Senecan sentence structure; the use of paradoxes, riddles and emblems; speculative doctrines and arcane knowledge; and finally, relating doctrine and devotion to the liturgy and the calendar of the Christian year.[29] This analysis emphasises two major tendencies: the use of wit and the display of (sometimes deliberately obscure) learning, and the commitment to the developing Anglican synthesis of the teaching and practice of the Early Church (approximately the first five centuries AD) with Reformation biblical theology. As so often in this period, style is a badge which indicates other loyalties, particularly in theology.

Puritan preaching

'Puritan' began as a term of abuse; and even now, is principally linked with the Parliamentary side in the Civil War. Until the 1640s, though, it is best to describe Puritanism as a party within the Church of England campaigning for Reformation principles, with a clearer break with Roman Catholic practice in ceremonies and vestments, and a demoting of the Prayer Book in favour of preaching and extempore prayer. There was a separatist movement, often forced to operate in exile, in the Netherlands or New England, and that generated much of the odium; Ben Jonson's stereotypical Puritan hypocrites in *The Alchemist* are off to Holland.

Preaching was at the top of the Puritan agenda for the English Church. The complaint of Puritans against many of the bishops was that they supplied too few godly and learned preaching ministers. Preaching, they argued, was the usual way that Christ arrives in the Church, in the individual believer: 'Preaching is the chariot that carries Christ up and down the world', wrote Richard Sibbes, 'Christ doth not profit but as he is preached.'[30] Bacon's complaint, that preaching was to the Puritans as the mass was to the Catholics, is theologically precise.[31] They are both God's principal media. Whereas Andrewes, for example, regarded preaching as a preparation, for prayer or the sacraments, it is hard to find a subordination of preaching among Puritans.

The Puritans were as definite about the appropriate style of preaching as they were about its purpose. It comes down to one word – plain. Plainness as openness, as concealed or even banished art, as frankness. William Perkins's *The Art of Prophesying* is representative of the advice they took. Perkins was an influential preacher in Cambridge in the 1590s, when it was the intellectual heart of Puritanism, and exemplifies the early Puritan characteristic of learning consciously adapted to the needs of the ordinary person.[32] Prophecy, in his definition, includes public prayer as well as preaching. The preacher's plainness should take its cue from Scripture, which 'is full of majesty in the simpleness of the words'.[33] There is a lot about rhetorical figures and how to keep a commonplace book – preaching is still a branch of rhetoric – but the drive is away from audible art and learning, whether the citation of philosophers or 'Greek and Latin phrases and quirks'. Stick to 'the natural sense' of Scripture, and apply it 'to the life and manners of men, in a simple and plain speech'.[34] So, you could tell Puritan preachers by the way they preached, plain and simple according to their manuals, endlessly and with a nasal voice according to their detractors. It was even a mark of conversion: John Cotton, the great New England divine, began to preach with 'as much quotation and citing of authors as might possibly be', but changed to a style 'after the plain and profitable way, by raising of doctrines, with propounding the reasons and uses of the same'.[35]

It isn't an invariable guide, though. Thomas Adams was Puritan in doctrine and morals; he began preaching in London in 1618 and occasionally appeared at St Paul's Cross and Whitehall. Some of his sermons, like *The Gallant's Burden*, went through several editions. His style, sometimes his whole approach, has as much in common with the drama of popular pamphleteers like Nashe and Dekker as it has with Perkins. Certainly his attitude to the theatre is ambivalent: for example, at the end of *The Two Sons* (on the parable of the Prodigal Son) he comments: 'What an excellent son had this been, if his heart and tongue had been cut out of one piece! He comes on bravely, but like an ill actor, he goes halting off.'[36] It is not just a conventional 'theatre of the world' topos, he does have a genuinely dramatising way of presenting his biblical and moral types. Yet, in the middle of one, the theatre appears in its more familiar Puritan moral clothing, as a place on the epicure's road to damnation, between the tavern and the stews. Adams shows just how misleading the popular stereotype of the Puritan preacher can be. The academic stereotypes, too; he is not afraid to put in a tag from Seneca or a couple of lines from Ovid. He will translate them, and the effect is not as intricately macaronic as Andrewes, it is part of a conscious attempt to address the educated as well as the ordinary members of the congregation, to reclaim the faithless as well as encourage the faithful. It is also characteristic of the English Renaissance habit of Christianising the classics, as when he translates *'vir'* as 'Christian'.[37]

A comparison with Nashe, himself not a complete stranger to the high moral tone, might help. Compared to Dame Niggardise in *Pierce Penniless*, Adams's usurer is less exuberantly and grotesquely portrayed, but he makes up some of the ground by attending to the victims: 'Usury, robbing, grinding, sucking blood, cutting throats, while he sits at the chimney corner, and hears of his zanies, whelps, underling thieves ending their days at the gallows.'[38] The most impressive of Adams's 'character' sermons, as we might call them, is *Mystical Bedlam*, which actually appears as two sermons in 1615, but is condensed into one for the collected edition. We might expect from the traditional physiological psychology that he really will take on the spiritual dimensions of madness – 'by the brains we feel, by the liver we love, but by the heart we be wise'.[39] In fact, that gets only passing treatment, and madness is seen as the state of every man, a frantic 'doing and undoing' out of ignorance and unfaithfulness. It is a spiritual bedlam he takes us round (Bedlam was the old London madhouse), with no fewer than twenty inmates ranging from drunkards and liars to Papists and separatists ('Protestants out of their wits'). Adams manages to be both playful and practical, to encapsulate a recognisable human type in a neat and dramatic prose without compromising the tone of warning.

Restoration preaching

Not everything was restored at the Restoration. Few tears were shed when the corrupt Court of Wards did not reappear, for example. There was no guarantee that the Church of England would have reappeared unchanged, either. Charles was restored by a Presbyterian Scots army, and had sheltered in Catholic France during the Interregnum. The Long Parliament had done away with bishops long before the monarchy, and with more support. The fact that the restored Church of England came back with the political and intellectual heirs of Laud in control shows as much as anything the size of the swing against revolution.[40] Its character as an alliance of Church and state was not the same after Clarendon's fall in 1667; the reign of James II added further complications by oscillating between Charles's early 'Laudian' policy and his later attempts to rely on a dubious alliance of Catholic and Dissenting interest. Restoration Anglicanism as a political establishment was no unchanging monolith.

It is Dissent, though, which more than anything defines the character of Restoration Anglicanism; because, even more than Catholicism, it provided a convenient and occasionally dangerous picture of what it was not. In 1662, with the re-imposition of the Prayer Book, Puritanism effectively became Nonconformity; no longer a party within the Church of England with a fringe of separatism, it became a separate set of churches (or 'conventicles') with a sharply circumscribed legal position, which amounted to persecution or toleration depending on the current aims of the monarch. Almost by definition, then, Dissenting churches were seen as the heirs of the political revolution of the 1640s and 1650s; of their spiritual leaders, John Owen and Richard Baxter had been Cromwell's chaplains. Many of them were also the doctrinal heirs of the Reformation; the doctrine of justification by faith, for example, the key to Luther's break with Catholic teaching, is at the heart of most Nonconformist teaching and experience in the period. Coupled with that is the strong emphasis on the individual, inward nature of religious experience, to be sought by every believer; and here the Quakers, who had moved a fair way from Luther and Calvin, were equally emphatic.

Turn to the sermons of the prominent Restoration Anglicans, and a different version of Christianity finds its expression. The difference in language is a key; justification by faith is pretty much a metaphoric expression, and the Nonconformists used a colourful language to celebrate it. Here is Bunyan, in dispute with Edward Fowler, a Bedfordshire Anglican minister who became Bishop of Gloucester: 'The Holy Ghost is not obtained by your description, that consisting only in principles of Nature, and putting forth it self in acts of Civility and Morality . . . .'[41] For Bunyan, nature is ineluctably the old nature of man, which has to be fought against; the new thinking sees it as a perfectly acceptable guide to conduct. This new thinking can be represented quite adequately by a series of abstract nouns (the capital letters are probably no more than seventeenth-century typography). Contrast this with Bunyan expounding St Paul to the Romans a few pages later, packing in the metaphors, not just as illustrations, but as statements: 'Ye are become dead to the Law: dead to the Law! Why? That you should be married to another: Married to another! Why? *That you should bring forth fruit unto God.*'[42] The metaphors aren't Bunyan's invention, of course, they are straight from St Paul; didn't the Restoration Anglicans like Fowler have the same Bible? Yes; but they didn't read it through the eyes of St Paul as much as the Reformers did. Look through the fifty-four published sermons of Archbishop Tillotson, and only seven are on texts from St Paul, and none from Romans or Galatians, the great epistles on justification by faith. Robert South, the eloquent defender of the Book of Common Prayer against the Nonconformists and, less promisingly for his spiritual reputation, a popular preacher at the court of Charles II, returns to the Wisdom literature of the Old Testament (Ecclesiastes and Proverbs particularly) much as Bunyan returns to Romans. South does preach on Romans, but on Chapter 13, about obedience to the powers that be. South as much as any Restoration preacher shows how arguments about the appropriate religious language are indices of far wider concerns. Language is certainly not neutral in his attack on Nonconformist extempore prayer, though his own preaching style has two distinct tones. One is an almost Baconian clarity, responding to the terseness of Scripture (the text is from Ecclesiastes, 'let thy words be few'):

> God said, Let there be light, and there was light . . . .
> Heaven, and earth, and all the host of both (as it were)
> dropped from his mouth; and nature itself was but the
> product of a word; a word not designed to express, but to
> constitute and give a being; and not so much the
> representation, as the cause of what it signified.[43]

The second half of the sentence shows how South links the sublime simplicity of Scripture (he cites Longinus on the sublimity of Moses in the passage) with the Restoration emphasis on the relation of language to things. He sounds even more Baconian in his praise of the aphorism in human speech:

> The truth is, there could be no such thing as art or science,
> could not the mind of man gather the general nature of
> things out of the numberless heap of particulars, and then
> bind them up into such short aphorisms or propositions; that
> so they may be made portable to the memory, and thereby
> become ready and at hand for the judgement to apply.[44]

Unfortunately, he does not share Bacon's belief in moderate language in religious controversy; when he comes to characterising Puritan prayer he becomes vociferous and heavy-handedly comic. His vociferousness may have been tactical, as he had showed some Presbyterian leanings at Oxford, though that would have been pretty conservative in the 1650s.

Stylistic changes in Restoration preaching are not simply a matter of metaphor, or concise sentences. There is also a shift in method. Isaac Barrow, Master of Trinity College, Cambridge as well as a Royal Chaplain, led the way here. His sermons are still expositions of texts, but his method is less to divide the texts in the old rhetorical fashion than to extract some proposition from them, and discourse on that. He translates 'Scripture-dialect' (a term which, oddly, he shares with Bunyan) into a maxim, which he then 'confirms' and 'illustrates'. His definitions have a certain rigour, very different to those contemporary preachers or speakers who begin with a quotation from the dictionary. Here he is on wisdom: 'a habitual skill or faculty of judging aright about matters of practice, and choosing according to that right judgement, and conforming the actions to such good choice'.[45] Again we see the confidence in nature that Bunyan so suspected in Fowler: 'we are all naturally endowed with a strong appetite to know, to see, to pursue truth; and with a bashful abhorrency from being deceived, and entangled in mistake'.[46] Tell that to Adam and Eve, Milton might reply. It might be symptomatic that, in his first Court sermon, he clinches two pages of scripture reference with a page from Aristotle's *Ethics*. Barrow is not incapable of lyric flights or telling similes, but the basis of his preaching is moral propositions derived from scripture, with an emphasis on the heavenly rewards of obedience.

The political dimension of such an emphasis on obedience, which is not just Barrow's, is clear enough in the context of the Restoration, even when it is not political obedience that is being stressed. The tone of reasonableness is also a reaction to the heat of Civil War preaching; but it is a tone that depended for a long time on the active suppression of opposing views, not just on the force of argument.

Notes

1. *The English Poems of George Herbert*, ed. C.A. Patrides (1974), p. 85.

2. From *Pierce Penniless* (1592), in Thomas Nashe, *The Unfortunate Traveller and Other Works*, ed. J.B. Steane (Harmondsworth, 1972), p. 114.

3. First published as *For Lancelot Andrewes* (1928).

4. MS autobiography, quoted in Lancelot Andrewes, *Sermons*, ed. G.M. Story (Oxford, 1967), pp. xii–xiv. Alabaster was a Jesuit who also wrote analyses of the Bible using number symbolism; see *The Sonnets of William Alabaster*, ed G.M. Story and Helen Gardner (Oxford, 1965?) and J.W. Binns, *Intellectual Culture in Elizabethan and Jacobean England* (Leeds, 1990), pp. 308–9.

5. Story, p. 95.

6. *The Works of George Herbert*, ed. F.E. Hutchinson (Oxford, 1941), p. 235. Herbert's criticism is not specifically of Andrewes, but the method he made popular.

7. Story, p. 181.

8. Quoted in Paul A. Welsby, *Lancelot Andrewes, 1555–1626* (London, 1964), p. 195.

9. Lancelot Andrewes, *Works*, ed. J.P. Wilson and J. Bliss (Oxford, 1851–54), V, 14.

10. Ibid., p. 38.

11. For early Stuart Divine Right theory, see Ch. 1 of J.P. Sommerville, *Politics and*

Ideology in England, 1603–40 (Harlow, 1986); Saul is used as an example of a bad monarch a number of times in Milton's *The Tenure of Kings and Magistrates* (1649). Typological reading is very close to allegory; the appearance of Charles II as David in Dryden's *Absalom and Achitophel* shows how close they can get.

12. Andrewes, *Works*, IV, 160.

13. Ibid., p. 155.

14. Ibid., p. 163

15. Story, p. 50.

16. Story, p. 51.

17. Deborah Shuger, *Sacred Rhetoric: The Christian Grand Style in the Renaissance* (Princeton, 1988), p. 233.

18. R.C. Bald, *John Donne: A Life* (Oxford, 1970).

19. Donne had been made a Prebendary of the Cathedral as well as Dean, and preached on the five Psalms allotted to his Prebend, there being thirty in all to take up the 150 Psalms. See Janel M. Mueller (ed.), *Donne's Prebend Sermons* (Cambridge, Mass. 1971); the Introduction is also one of the best short accounts of Donne's preaching, and my discussion of the influence of Augustine is indebted to her account.

20. Mueller, p. 157.

21. John Donne, *Selected Prose*, ed. Neil Rhodes (Harmondsworth, 1987), p. 259.

22. There is a sensible summary of this, particularly on the literary meaning of 'baroque', in the first chapter of Joan Webber, *Contrary Music: the Prose Style of John Donne* (Madison, 1963); the art-historical analogy is more fruitfully dealt with in Murray Roston, *The Soul of Wit* (Oxford, 1974), where he argues for Mannerism rather than the Baroque.

23. *The Sermons of John Donne*, ed. G.R. Potter and E.M. Simpson (Berkeley and Los Angeles, 1953–62), III, 374.

24. *The Sermons of John Donne*, VI, 55.

25. *Selected Prose*, p. 326.

26. Stanley E. Fish, 'The Aesthetic of the Good Physician', in *Self-Consuming Artifacts: The Experience of Seventeenth Century Literature* (Berkeley, 1972).

27. *Selected Prose*, p. 313.

28. From a sermon preached to Queen Anne (1617); *Selected Prose*, pp. 145–6.

29. Horton Davies, *Like Angels from a Cloud: The English Metaphysical Preachers 1588–1645* (San Marino, 1986), pp. 49ff.

30. Richard Sibbes, *The Fountain Opened* (1638), in *Expositions of St Paul* (Edinburgh, 1977), p. 508. This is a reprint of Vol. 5 of Grosart's nineteenth-century edition of Sibbes.

31. Cited in Christopher Hill, *Society and Puritanism in Pre-Revolutionary England* (1969 edn), p. 63. The first two chapters contain much interesting material on the political ramifications of preaching in the period.

32. There is a useful discussion of Perkins and his influence in William Haller, *The Rise of Puritanism* (New York, 1938).

33. Perkins, *Works* (Cambridge, 1609), II, 736. *The Art* was translated from Perkins' Latin by Thomas Tuke.

34. Ibid., pp. 759, 762.

35. Contemporary sources cited by Perry Miller, *The New England Mind* (New York, 1939), I, 331.

36. *The Works of Thomas Adams* (1630), p. 428.

37. Ibid., p. 485.

38. Ibid., p. 22.

39. Ibid., p. 483.

40. The case for the Restoration Church settlement being essentially Laudian is found in R.S. Bosher, *The Making of the Restoration Settlement* (Westminster, 1951); this needs qualifying by more recent studies, notably Ronald Hutton, *The Restoration* (Oxford, 1985), and Hugh Trevor-Roper, 'The Great Tew Circle', in *Catholics, Anglicans and Puritans* (1987).

41. *A Defence of Justification, by Faith* (1672), in John Bunyan, *Miscellaneous Works* IV, ed. T.L. Underwood (Oxford, 1989), p. 27.

42. Ibid., p. 31.

43. Robert South, 'A Discourse against Long and Extempore Prayers: In Behalf of the Liturgy of the Church of England', in *The English Sermon, Vol. II: 1650–1750*, ed. C.H. Sisson (Cheadle, 1976), p. 108.

44. Ibid., p. 109.

45. Isaac Barrow, *Sermons Preached upon Several Occasions* (1678), p. 1. See Irène Simon, 'The Preacher', in *Before Newton: The Life and Times of Isaac Barrow*, ed. Mordechai Feingold (Cambridge, 1990), and her earlier *Three Restoration Divines: Barrow, South and Tillotson*, 2 vols (Paris, 1967), an anthology as well as a critical study.

46. Ibid., pp. 2–3.

Chapter 8
Devotions and Meditations

I am uneasy about the division between private and public religion implied by the heading of this and the following chapter. Much of the best Christian writing of the century proclaims a continuum between the two; it is part of the tragedy of the century that the perception was an integral part of the Civil War. One of the ways the two sides learned to live with each other after the Restoration was to agree on a distinction between private belief, 'liberty of conscience' being the Nonconformist slogan, and public duty. The Quaker word 'inwardness' would be another appropriate description for these genres, other than the sermon, which express the practice of spirituality for the individual. None the less, we must remember that many of the works discussed in the next section, on the various political dimensions of religion, are not therefore devoid of spirituality. 'My kingdom is not of this world', said Jesus; yet his disciples were described as the men who turned the world upside down.[1]

Meditation first. Bishop Joseph Hall, in *The Art of Divine Meditation* (1627), defined it as 'nothing else but a bending of the mind upon some spiritual object, through divers forms of discourse, until our thoughts come to an issue'. He attacks those who have confined the practice to their cells (monks and nuns) instead of leaving it for all Christians. Indeed, he suggests, we all meditate, but it's a question of which thoughts we meditate on, and how seriously we take the battle: 'by this do we ransack our deep and false hearts, find out our secret enemies, buckle with them, expel them, arm ourselves against their re-entrance'.[2] Hall's attempt to demystify meditation was popular; he is representative of widespread Protestant appropriation and adaptation of Catholic devotional practice in the period.[3]

John Donne spans both traditions, having been brought up in a Catholic family before switching his allegiance to the Church of England. His *Devotions upon Emergent Occasions, and several steps in my Sickness* (1624) was published while he was Dean of St Paul's. It was written during convalescence from an illness (possibly typhus or a relapsing fever) he had in November and December 1623. It takes us through the twenty-three stages of the illness, each investigated by a meditation, expostulation and prayer. On Good Friday Catholics meditate together on the 'stations of the Cross'; it is characteristic of Donne that he should take a personal experience and work out from it to spiritual significance and literary expression, each an analogy of the other. As he put it in a letter to the Duke of Buckingham: 'To make myself believe that our life is something, I use in my thoughts to compare it with something . . . . And, as in some styles there are open parentheses, sentences within sentences, so there are lives within our lives.'[4] The style of the *Devotions*, then, is part of the meaning, part of the effort to find the significance of what is happening in the illness. But we need to consider it as part of a vision of analogy.

If everything is analogous to something else, then creation is coherent. For it to be meaningful as well Donne needs a sense of proportion, and here, as so often in his work, egotism and humility battle it out on a cosmic, theologically defined stage. No one will need reminding of his 'No man is an island' thought (Meditation 17); even his thoughts of solidarity with the rest of humanity focus on himself – 'any man's death diminishes me'. Compare that with these thoughts in Meditation 4, developing from the commonplace of Man as a little world:

> Man consists of more pieces, more parts, than the world;
> than the world doth, nay than the world is . . . our creatures
> are our thoughts, creatures that are born giants: that reach
> from East to West, from earth to heaven, that do not only
> bestride all the sea, and land, but span the sun and firmament
> at once; my thoughts reach all, comprehend all. Inexplicable
> mystery; I their creator am in a close prison, in a sick bed,
> anywhere, and any one of my creatures, my thoughts, is
> with the sun, and beyond the sun . . . .[5]

The power of thought is held in check by his illness, but encouraged by his theology, where man is the summit of creation, not just another part of nature. The illness forms part of the discipline of meditation in its focusing and limiting power. But the analogical imagination is always breaking out again. Take Meditation 12, on the unlikely practice of applying pigeons to draw vapours from the head (pigeons, being hot and moist, were thought to conteract the cold humours of melancholy and phlegm). First he thinks of how small things can kill – like the presumably mythical mouse running up the trunk of an elephant – and so to the vapour, which is so like air, which we need to breathe to live, and then to the thought that it is self-produced, a kind of inadvertent suicide. 'They tell me it is my melancholy; did I infuse, did I drink in melancholy into my self? It is my thoughtfulness; was I not made to think? It is my study; doth not my calling call for that?'[6] The merest whiff of self-pity here is swept away as he moves on to a political analogy: 'That which is fume in us, is in a state, rumour.'

When we move to the expostulation and prayer, we note by contrast how secular, or based on nature, the meditations are. The expostulation (addressed to God) moves around a series of biblical texts, first on life as a passing vapour, then on the Holy Spirit (the pigeons accordingly become doves). It concludes with a parallel move to the meditation, on obedience, this time to God rather than the state: 'Let us draw down the vapours of our own pride, our own wits, our own wills, our own inventions, to the simplicity of thy sacraments, and the obedience of thy word.'[7] The prayer concludes the tripartite attempt at calm – the *Devotions* often betray the worry of illness. Even with the king's physician at hand, Donne's fear of death was not melodramatic. It begins with the awkward syntactic move, common in the Prayer Book, of putting the qualities of God that are appealed to in a relative clause; the main imperative verb is a long time coming:

> O eternal and most gracious God, who though thou have
> suffered us to destroy ourselves, and hast not given us the
> power of reparation in our selves, hast yet afforded us such
> means of reparation, as may easily, and familiarly be
> compassed by us, prosper I humbly beseech thee, this means
> of bodily assistance in this thy ordinary creature, and prosper
> thy means of spiritual assistance in thy holy ordinances.[8]

The prayers are the most restrained in personality and imagination, and yet the most syntactically complex, of the *Devotions*. Reading the more popular and accessible meditations without their expostulations and prayers misses out the dialectic, the rhythm of opening up and closing down. The *Devotions* show how inherently literary the practice of meditation in this period can be, encouraging expressiveness with discipline.

Such purposeful attentiveness can take many forms. The *Resolves* of Owen Felltham (1623, a second part in 1628) combine some of the discursive, aphoristic style of the essay with the moral and religious resolution implied by his title. The opening sentence gives the clue to the divided response:

> There is no spectacle more profitable, or more terrible, than
> the sight of a dying man, when he lies expiring his soul on

> his deathbed: to see how the ancient society of the body and
> the soul is divelled [torn; a neologism]; and yet to see how
> they struggle at the parting, being in some doubt what shall
> become of them after.[9]

'Profit' may be the end of the meditation, but the terror is clear enough. What is impressive about Felltham is the way he confronts in detail the experience of watching someone die before heading off to the sententiae and the commonplaces. His resolution against 'indulgiating' the flesh 'which I must one day yield to the worms' is Stoic more than Christian.

The *Religio Medici* ('the faith of a physician') of Sir Thomas Browne was written in the 1630s and published by the author in 1643 after a pirated edition of the manuscript the previous year. Like Donne, Browne starts with himself, but from a general sense of his temperament rather than a specific, historical sense of his life. This relaxed, eirenic quality is either celebrated as unusually tolerant (particularly in the rising temperature of the 1630s and 1640s) or attacked as complacent, snobbish and self-satisfied.[10]

In the historical context, it can be shown that Browne revised his text to respond to the mass action, particularly over the trials of Strafford and Laud, that prefigured the Civil War.[11] Such a sentiment as 'If there be any among those common objects of hatred I do condemn and laugh at, it is that great enemy of reason, virtue and religion, the multitude' may be a commonplace; in 1643 it is a political statement; coming two pages into a section on charity, it might also cause us to ask some other questions of Browne's sense of intellectual and social superiority.[12] His desire for peace has a Horatian, conservative cast to it. Views like 'a good cause needs not to be patroned by a passion' may seem like a relief if one comes to it straight from a tirade of Bastwick or Prynne; but it may not be true.[13]

Browne was educated in Europe, and spoke six languages. That may explain something of his approach to Catholic practice, using images or bells as triggers for his own devotion, without entirely agreeing with their aim or scorning them like his companions. A detached sympathy, proper to the traveller, in the English context might sound like qualified approval of Laudianism. The Church of England certainly commands his loyalty, even while his reason holds back a bit on inessentials. Browne's devotion, however, is most often displayed as private, meditative, intellectual. Some of the most successful moments in the book are where he leads us through such a process of thought to a conclusion:

> Now for these walls of flesh, wherein the soul doth seem to
> be immured before the Resurrection, it is nothing but an

elemental composition, and a fabric that must fall to ashes;
All flesh is grass, is not only metaphorically, but literally true,
for all those creatures we behold, are but the herbs of the
field, digested into flesh in them, or more remotely carnified
in our selves. Nay further, we are what we all abhor,
Anthropophagi and cannibals, devourers not only of men, but
of ourselves; and that not in an allegory, but in a positive
truth; for all this mass of flesh which we behold, came in at
our mouths: this frame we look upon, hath been upon our
trenchers; in brief, we have devoured our selves.[14]

This also shows what achieved performances of argument and
symmetry some of Browne's sentences are. The witty audacity of
merging levels of discourse combines with the symmetry, a mixture
that might properly be called 'baroque'. The occasional but prominent
Latinity of vocabulary is partly for emphasis, but also part of the tone
of educated urbanity that is integral to his self-portrait.

The two-part structure of the book, on faith and charity, has been
compared to the division in the Ten Commandments between love of
God and love of neighbour, and to the two-fold emphasis in the
Hippocratic oath on dedication to the art of medicine and sympathy for
the patient. That sympathy we have come to characterise as
'professional', implying a certain detachment, and Browne's sense of
others is certainly detached, usually betrayed by synecdoches like
'heads'.[15] The intimacy of his self-revelation, too, is conversational
rather than confessional; a marvellous performance.

The prose of Thomas Traherne (1637–74) was hardly known until
this century. His *Roman Forgeries*, an attack on the Catholic Church,
was the only book published in his lifetime; a year after his death
Christian Ethicks appeared. The manuscript of the *Centuries of Meditation*
was not discovered and published until this century; a number of prose
manuscripts discovered more recently still remain unpublished. The
Ethicks is not a book about conduct so much as the virtues, with the
emphasis on how to acquire them rather than how to exercise them.
He was much influenced by the 'Cambridge Platonists', a group of
academics led by Ralph Cudworth, Henry More and Benjamin
Whichcote, whose uniting of Platonism with Christianity tended to
argue away central Reformation tenets like total depravity and
predestination in favour of the wisdom of God and the reasonableness
of mankind.[16] Traherne's prose ignites this theology into a kind of
affirmative mysticism, promoting the love of God as a route to the
love of self which will overflow into the love of fellow-humans. 'That
pool must first be filled, that shall be made to overflow.'[17] He takes

Reformation and Counter-Reformation inwardness, meditative practice and attention to the signs of providence and refocuses them quite dramatically.

The steps are easiest to follow in the *Ethicks*: 'Above all, pray to be sensible to the excellency of the creation, for upon the due sense of its excellency the life of Felicity wholly dependeth.'[18] Felicity, a key concept, is defined as 'the perfect fruition of a perfect soul, acting in perfect life by perfect virtue'.[19] However, this is not a return to good deeds as the pathway to heaven; he is quite Pauline in his insistence on justification by faith, but stresses the need for 'evangelical righteousness' as the consequence.

We have become used to seeing self-knowledge as the path to repentance via anxiety in this period; for Traherne 'The knowledge of a man's self is highly conducive for his happiness, not only as it gives him power to rejoice in his excellencies, but as it shows him his end, for which he was created.'[20] Even vices become signs of the eternal; 'it is the glory of man, that his avarice is insatiable',[21] because any infinite desire leads to God. His text is punctuated, not by spiritual battles, but by raptures:

> My joy, my life, my crown, my glory; my exceeding great
> reward, my love, my soul, my idol, nay the GOD of my
> soul! My all in all! This is the language of love in its rapture.
> Seraphic love! It is altar, heart and sacrifice, angelical love! It
> is priest and temple: all service, freedom, duty, reward,
> desire, enjoyment, praise, adoration, thanksgiving, ecstasy,
> pleasure, bliss and happiness. It is all goodness and beauty,
> paradise, heaven; the life and soul of heaven![22]

And so on; well might we agree with Stanley Stewart, that 'repetition is the primary stylistic underpinning of Traherne's art'.[23] It is also integral to his spirituality of enjoyment. More means better.

'I have a mind to fill this with profitable wonders', wrote Traherne at the beginning of a notebook, known to us as *Centuries of Meditations*, which he addressed to his friend and patron, Susannah Hopton. He sees the bar to successful meditation as learned rather than inherent, custom rather than nature. The anticipations of Romanticism, at times Wordsworth, at times Blake, are critically seductive, particularly in the autobiographical *Third Century*, where he describes the innocent insight of his childhood – 'Certainly Adam in Paradise had not more sweet and curious apprehensions of the world, than I when I was a child.' Nature is suspended in a biblical eternity, like the Book of Revelations: 'The corn was orient and immortal wheat, which should never be reaped, nor was ever sown. I thought it had stood from everlasting to everlasting.'[24] But he is corrupted by the 'dirty devices of this world', which he has to unlearn, ironically by book-learning at university. Again, we might see a proto-Romantic divisIon here between utility and wonder: 'He that studies polity, men and manners, merely that he may know how to behave himself and get honour in this world has not that delight in his studies, as he that contemplates these things that he might see the ways of God among them.'[25] He retreats into the country, 'among silent trees' and relative poverty in order to study felicity in 'the most obvious and common things'. At the same time, in a very seventeenth-century manner, he finds a second voice for his contemplation in the Psalms of David; and in his unpublished notebook known as *The Church's Year Book* shows his attachment to celebrating Holy Days, and to the new tradition of Anglican spirituality in Andrewes, Herbert and Jeremy Taylor.[26] We might trace affiliations between his visionary theology and that of the Quakers, but he did not recognise them himself.

So far we have stressed Traherne as the prose-poet of simplicity and wonder, with a correspondingly straightforward aesthetic. Only occasionally, in the reference to King Charles the Martyr for example, do we see the imprint of a man who was educated at Oxford in the turbulent 1650s and Chaplain to the Lord Keeper of the Seal. Traherne's language of retreat, of innocence corrupted by the world, of the ultimate simplicity of Christian devotion, is most properly seen in the history of Christian mysticism. But it has specific historical reference, too; to a language of truthfulness and devotion in exile characteristic of the defeated Anglicanism of the 1650s, and as evidence of the considerable theological latitude that existed within the tight ring-fence of Anglican conformity to episcopacy and Prayer Book after 1660.

Finally, we should also beware of taking Traherne's simplicity as naivety. He can think. As he goes through his variations on the mutual indwelling of God and man, or on God's love, he is concerned with the subtleties of the reflexives that language about God always ends up with – along with the hiddenness, 'there being still something infinite in it behind'.[27] However plainly he writes 'God is love', there is still some more exploring to do.

Notes

1. John 18: 36; Acts 17: 6.
2. Joseph Hall, *Works* (1627), p. 105.

3. The key discussion here is Louis L. Martz, *The Poetry of Meditation* (2nd edn, New Haven, 1962); of the numerous modifications and revisions of his position, Barbara Lewalski, *Protestant Poetics and the Seventeenth Century Religious Lyric* (Princeton, 1979) is the most important.

4. Quoted in the Introduction to John Donne, *Devotions Upon Emergent Occasions*, ed. Anthony Raspa (New York and Oxford, 1987), p. xix.

5. Donne, *Devotions*, pp. 19–20.

6. Donne, *Devotions*, p. 63.

7. Donne, *Devotions*, p. 66.

8. Donne, *Devotions*, p. 66.

9. *The Seventeenth-Century Resolve: A Historical Anthology of a Literary Form*, ed. John L. Lievsay (Kentucky, 1980), p. 93.

10. The immediate contemporary responses of Kenelm Digby and Alexander Ross, as well as the tributes of Aubrey and Dryden, set the parameters of admiration and impatience; most modern studies are respectful, though the attack in Stanley Fish, *Self-Consuming Artifacts*, has prompted some useful rethinking, as in Jonathan Post, *Sir Thomas Browne* (Boston, 1987) and a number of pieces in C.A. Patrides (ed.), *Approaches to Sir Thomas Browne: the Ann Arbor Tercentenary Lectures and Essays* (Columbia, Missouri, 1982). Most judicious is Anne Drury Hall, 'Epistle, Meditation and Sir Thomas Browne's *Religio Medici*', *PMLA*, 94 (1979), pp. 234–46.

11. See '*Religio Medici* in the English Revolution' in Michael Wilding, *Dragons Teeth: Literature in the English Revolution* (Oxford, 1987).

12. Sir Thomas Browne, *The Major Works*, ed. C.A. Patrides (Harmondsworth, 1977), p. 134. Further references to *Religio Medici* are to this edition.

13. *Religio Medici*, p. 65.

14. *Religio Medici*, p. 107.

15. A point made by Joan Webber, *The Eloquent 'I'* (Madison, 1968), p. 165.

16. There is a useful anthology, *The Cambridge Platonists*, ed. C.A. Patrides (1969); see also Ch. 8 of Basil Willey, *The Seventeenth-Century Background* (1934). The term was a nineteenth-century invention; for the wider context, linking them with the 'latitude-men', see Ch. 2 of Isabel Rivers, *Reason, Grace, and Sentiment: A Study of the Language of Religion and Ethics in England, 1660–1780, vol. I, Whichcote to Wesley* (Cambridge, 1991).

17. Thomas Traherne, *Poems, Centuries, and Three Thanksgivings*, ed. Ann Ridler, p. 341, *Centuries*, IV. 55. All subsequent references to the *Centuries* are to this text, by section.

18. Thomas Traherne, *Christian Ethicks*, ed. Carol L. Marks and George Robert Guffey (Ithaca, 1968), p. 6.

19. *Christian Ethicks*, p. 19.

20. *Christian Ethicks*, p. 42.

21. *Christian Ethicks*, p. 54.

22. *Christian Ethicks*, p. 275.

23. Stanley Stewart, *The Expanded Voice: The Art of Thomas Traherne* (San Marino, 1970), p. 73.

24. *Centuries*, III. 1, 3.

25. *Centuries*, III. 41.

26. For the *Year Book*, see A.M. Allchin, 'The Sacrifice of Praise and Thanksgiving' in *Profitable Wonders* (Oxford, 1989), pp. 22–37, and Carol L. Marks, 'Traherne's Church's Year Book', *Papers of the Bibliographical Society of America*, 60 (1966), pp. 31–72. See also Julia J. Smith, 'Attitudes to Conformity and Nonconformity in Thomas Traherne', *Bunyan Studies* I (1988), 26–35.

27. *Centuries*, IV. 62. This is best discussed in Ch. 2 of A. Leigh Deneef, *Traherne in Dialogue: Heidegger, Lacan, and Derrida* (Durham, N.C., 1988).

Chapter 9
Politicised Religion

The history of Christianity in the seventeenth century is dominated by war. For thirty years what is now Germany was devastated by a war between Protestants and Catholics. The belief that religion ought to be enforced, in spite of, or perhaps because of, the increasing variation in beliefs and practices was widespread. In most of Europe, its success comes down to the efficiency of persecution. In England, it was a major contributory factor in the Civil War.[1] Oliver Cromwell wrote to his brother-in-law after the Battle of Marston Moor, July 1644, in these terms: 'Truly England and the Church of God hath had a great favour from the Lord, in this great victory given unto us, such as the like never was since this war began. It had all the evidences of an absolute victory obtained by the Lord's blessing upon the godly party principally.'[2] 'England and the Church of God' – such phrases could be matched by Royalists citing New Testament texts about the sinfulness of disobedience. The king had told his troops in 1642 that they would 'meet with no enemies but traitors, Brownists, Anabaptists and atheists, such who desire to destroy both church and state'.[3] The language of rebellion as well as the language of loyalty had to have a Christian construction. While neither the Thirty Years War nor the English Civil War were simply wars of religion, in a period where loyalty to the state and religious conformity were reckoned to be interdependent, it is difficult to disentangle reasons and motives. The problem is not a new one. Christ was crucified by the Roman Empire at the behest of religious authorities he had challenged; three centuries later, Christianity became the Empire's official religion. Christianity has always had a political dimension.

However, the European wars of religion, many of them, in effect, civil wars, came to an end in the seventeenth century. On the one hand it could be because the Reformation and its associated movements and counter-movements were running out of steam; perhaps those movements had to change in character because of their perceived destructiveness. A judicious mixture of toleration and repression served to deal with Dissent in this country. It is often argued that the main dissenting movement of the eighteenth century, Methodism, actually helped to avert a French-style revolution in England. Certainly the relationship between political and religious dissent changes after 1688. While religious toleration is not exactly a seventeenth-century invention, nor was it completely accepted by the end of the century, it is at least beginning to be possible to dissent quietly from the Church of England, either as a Catholic or a Nonconformist, even if that meant, effectively, having to abandon public life. At least imprisonment, torture, punitive fines and death were less likely than they were at the beginning of the century.

I have already suggested that the sixteenth and seventeenth centuries reinvented the first person singular, not least in the language of religious devotion. That more widely acceptable stress on the private and personal nature of religious belief merges with an incipient division between the public and private spheres generally to make toleration seem more appropriate. But for much of our period the 'confession' might well be exacted by a law court, or even a torture chamber, as much as by the individual conscience at work with God and pen alone in a study.

Such a history of the politics of religion can seem to owe too much to the Liberal tradition, a kind of hindsight which sees the seventeenth-century conflicts working towards the triumph of individual liberty over state tyranny. The usual criticism of this is that it is Whiggish, seeing history as a kind of steady escalator to the present moment of parliamentary democracy, which of course is the best of all possible worlds; in other words it is ascribing a, strictly, unhistorical motive to participants in past struggles. One way for the late twentieth-century reader to understand these conflicts is to reflect on those states in our world where 'fundamentalist' religion is in the ascendant – or even a rigorously enforced state atheism. The trials, repressions and inspirations of dissident religious writers in seventeenth-century England might then seem more comprehensible. But it is only a parallel, and is still susceptible to the charge that it is using liberal habits of mind like sympathy and the value of individual liberty. Two aspects of most people's thinking at this time need to be stressed. First, from the point of view of the authorities (or those who wanted to be authorities) a dissenting religious belief was dangerous. Secondly, a wilfully mistaken belief (even ignorance) meant that you went to Hell.

One of the peculiarities of a literary approach to such problems is that it will tend to seize on moments which may not be particularly significant in the history of Church government. Religious controversy can make dull reading, especially with the seventeenth-century habit of refuting a work (and its refutation) paragraph by paragraph, even word by word. However, when some alternative strategy is found, the result can sometimes leap off the page; but more than that, its very literary effectiveness may make it historically significant. For example, the Marprelate tracts are important because they developed a startlingly colloquial, irreverent and inventive style of controversy; but their success at catching the imagination of the reading public meant that the full apparatus of Church/state repression was brought to bear on them.

'Martin Marprelate'

All through Elizabeth's reign the Puritan party, at that stage still mainly a radical rather than a separatist movement within the Church of England, was proposing alternative methods of Church government to the episcopal. The main alternative was Presbyterian, proposed by Thomas Cartwright, in which the national Church would be governed by an assembly of representatives of individual congregations rather than bishops.[3] In 1587 John Bridges, the Dean of Salisbury, set out to answer some of the presbyterian arguments in *A Defence of the Government Established in the Church of England* . . . . He was answered, in part, by two Presbyterians, Dudley Fenner, pastor of an English church in the Netherlands, and Walter Travers. But they only nibbled at Bridges' book, which ran for 1,400 pages. Would the definitive Presbyterian refutation have to be similarly massive?

In October 1588 a rather different and more devastating attack appeared, usually referred to as *An Epistle*, because even the title page is a joke at the expense of Bridges and plodding seriousness. 'Oh read over D. John Bridges for it is a worthy work', it begins in small letters; then larger 'Or an epitome of the first book of that right worshipful volume', with praise and deference getting suspiciously extended – perhaps the author is making a bid for Bridges' patronage? But no, he is a gentleman, 'the reverend and worthy Martin Marprelate, gentleman', stealing the 'reverend' from clergymen, 'Martin' from Luther, and 'Marprelate' because he unremittingly attacks bishops and archbishops.

The Marprelate tracts (the longest of them runs to forty-eight pages) are a compendium of embarrassing stories, accusations, insults and biblical arguments against bishops, continuously referred to as 'petty popes and antichrists' (most Protestants then thought the Pope was the Antichrist of Revelation). The *Epistle* is so called because it turns out not to be an epitome at all – 'The Epitome is not yet published', announces the title page, the bishops will have to wait (normally writers had to wait, as the Bishops controlled the censorship) and in the meantime be content with an epistle to the 'terrible Priests of the Confocation house'. Marprelate often subtitutes 'f' for 'v' in unsubtle contexts ('Fycker' for 'Vicar').

How does Marprelate defend his style? Isn't it too indecorous for serious religious controversy? Martin argues that Bridges is such a dunce that comedy is the only possible style (I have preserved the unusual punctuation):

> Again/may it please you to give me leave to play the dunce
> for the nonce as well as he/otherwise dealing with master
> doctors book/I cannot keep *decorum personae*. And may it
> please you/if I be too absurd in any place (either in this
> Epistle/or that Epitome) to ride to Sarum [Salisbury] and
> thank his Deanship for it. Because I could not deal with his
> booke commendably according to order/unless I should be
> sometimes tediously dunsticall and absurd.[5]

Still, Bridges' stupidity can do no harm to the cause of reformation:

> But the patch can do the cause of sincerity no hurt. Nay/he
> hath in this book wonderfully graced the same by writing
> against it. For I have heard some say/that whosoever will
> read his book/shall as evidently see the goodness of the cause
> of reformation/and the poor poor/poor nakedness of your
> government/as almost in reading all master Cartwright's
> works.[6]

Marprelate's humour is fierce; he threatens the bishops that he will write against them further if they do not clean up their act – avoiding corrupt practices such as simony and non-residence, stopping using the Church courts oppressively, and making godly learning and preaching a priority instead of appointing dumb guides for the people. It is very close to the Puritan programme; in *Hay any Worke for Cooper* (an attack on Thomas Cooper, Bishop of Winchester, who had unwisely waded into the fray) he expresses mock surprise at it: 'When/when/but where have I been all this while. Ten to one among some of these puritans. Why Martin? Why Martin I say hast tow forgotten thy self? . . . never wink on me good fellow/for I will speak the truth/let the puritans do what they can.'[7] A Puritan using a gambling expression? The great Puritan preacher Richard Greenham criticised Martin as making sin ridiculous when it should appear odious.[8]

Martin is a curious mixture of the utterly clear and the elusive. No one could doubt his contempt for bishops, or his support for the alternative pattern of ministry derived from the Epistle to the Romans, of doctors (i.e. teachers), elders, pastors and deacons. But who is he? There is an elaborate game of double-bluff as he names his associates – defiance or cunning? Raymond Anselment suggests that the tracts are caught in increasing seriousness as the sequence continues, even as the commissioned replies became steadily jokier.[9]

The three main problems the Marprelate affair throws up are those of style, authorship and the political impact of writing at the time. They cannot easily be separated, because the conditions of publication affect all three. To begin with, the Marprelate style is not simply a matter of words on the page, or even of breaking the decorum of religious controversy (something Travers had complained of in Bridges). It is to do with books, using the apparatus of publishing as part of the satiric strategy. I have mentioned title pages; in the *Epitome*, the running heads augment the humour of the argument by their very brevity – 'Any thing in religion may be altered, by the bishops divinity', for example, or 'All beetleheaded ignorance, lieth not in M. Doctor.' The *Errata* at the end, instead of listing proof-reading errors, suggest another kind of 'fault' in what has gone before – 'There is nothing spoken at all/of that notable hypocrite Scambler/Bishop of Norwich. Take it for a great fault/ but unless he leave his close dealing against the truth/I'll bestow a whole booke of him. And let the rest of you hypocrites take heed of persecuting.' The series itself parodies different styles of religious controversy: *Certain Minerall and Meta-physicall Schoolpoints* is a broadside of debating points (like Luther's ninety-five Theses). *Theses Martinianae* is set out as Martin's ideas published by 'a pretty stripling of his, Martin Junior' in defiance of the censorship; a week later *The just censure and reproof of Martin Junior*, by his elder brother, 'son and heir unto the renowned Martin Mar-prelate the Great' appeared. It appears to be a telling off for the youngster's rashness, with mock encouragements for the Archbishop's pursuivants, who were harassing the printers, but ends up praising him for his plainness in naming the Archbishop's corruption. The last of the Marprelate tracts, *The Protestatyon of Martin Marprelat*, is a weary-sounding work. In the space of two years Martin has burst onto the scene, sired a couple of children, and entered old age, despairing because the bishops will never be cured. While the hired respondents like Nashe had picked up the original Marprelate style, best seen in the *Epistle* and *Hay any Worke for Cooper*, Martin has moved on stylistically, to a plainer confrontation with persecution and the possibility of martyrdom. Several of those suspected of association with Marprelate were racked and two were executed. For Martin, unanswered except with 'slanders, ribaldry, scurrility, reviling, imprisonment and torture', it was time to look 'more narrowly into my self, to see whether I be at peace with God or no'.[10] He concludes that his position is right, not least because the opposition is so inhuman. The rules of the Court of High Commission, where the bishops could compel self-accusation, against the practice of the rest of English law, 'savoreth so rankly of the Spanish inquisition, that it is flat contrary to all humanity'. Only at the end, with an anecdote of the Bishop of Lichfield calling his dog to him in the pulpit, is there a flash of the old bantering Martinist offensive. Otherwise, Martin falls silent on a solemn, even despairing note.

Who was he? Leland Carlson has argued convincingly that the most likely candidate is Job Throkmorton, a country gentleman from Haseley in Warwickshire who was an MP during 1586–87.[11] There are a few other candidates; and certainly the Marprelate enterprise was a collaboration between Throkmorton and a Welshman, John Penry, along with two printers, Robert Waldegrave and John Hodgkins, a number of others who lent houses for the printing presses to be set up, and John Field, who died early in 1588 but who left a useful collection of anti-episcopal stories. Penry is named as Martin by Nashe in his *An Almond for a Parrat* (1590), but Carlson suggests that Penry's usual style is too solemn, and he was more likely to have been the business manager of the enterprise.

The search for a single author does raise questions. The episcopal 'police' were obviously looking for an author as well as a printer to punish. Nowadays, the assumption is that, because the tracts have a distinctive style, there must be a single authorial origin for this; an assumption which needs arguing for an age where collaboration, especially in writing for the stage, was so common.[12]

Carlson's arguments, with their combination of verbal parallels (some more striking than others) and examination of the legal evidence, suggests that Throkmorton leaves his personal stylistic blueprint (e.g. double negatives, and words like 'something' used adverbially) on his acknowledged material as well as on the Marprelate tracts. When Throkmorton denied being Marprelate under examination, he was not necessarily equivocating; Marprelate was a fictional character from the beginning.

The Marprelate style is not a complete innovation. We need to keep the 'Martin' in mind; the scurrility may depart spectacularly from the Puritan controversial manner, but has some affinity with Luther's more rumbustious pronouncements. However, it does signal a change in pamphlet prose style generally. It has been argued that Nashe learns much of his extempore vein from his early brush with Marprelate and much of the satirical, freewheeling impetus of Dekker and Middleton can be traced to Marprelate as much as Nashe. The way in which Marprelate makes us aware, almost co-conspiratorially, of the acts of writing and printing as we read is not quite the same as the self-consciousness of the new, professional writer. There is a different kind of earnestness about it; Hill calls it moral urgency.[13] Certainly Marprelate's positives are more identifiable than, say, Nashe's, but they share a similar contradiction between aim and method. Nashe attacks Marprelate's name-calling of the bishops: 'Think you this merry mouthed mate a partaker of heavenly inspiration, that thus abounds in his uncharitable railings?' but does so in the midst of a similarly abusive text.[14] 'I speak plain English, and call thee a knave in thine own language' won't resolve the contradiction. Calling Penry Pen-ry (a pen going awry) is a weak response to calling Aylmer (the choleric Bishop of London) Elmar because he chopped down some elms in Fulham; and in the end supports the Martinist position that clowning is the only possible response to some of the episcopal goings-on.

It is more likely that 'Martin' fell silent under legal and personal rather than literary pressure. However, once the rising star of Richard Bancroft had commissioned such wits as Nashe and Lyly to answer his points, those points had been made. Not until the 1640s were the tracts reprinted; and more than that, they provided the Leveller Richard Overton with a means of attacking his ecclesiastical opponents – ironically, the Presbyterians (of which more later). First, we must look at another text in ecclesiastical politics which has been influential far beyond its immediate remit, and its relatively slight immediate popularity.

Richard Hooker: *Of The Laws of Ecclesiastical Polity*

Hooker's own life matched the 'law' and the 'ecclesiastical' parts of the title of his major work. After an early academic career in Oxford under the patronage of Bishop Jewel, one of the Marian exiles and a notable defendant of the Elizabethan Church settlement, he was made Master of the Temple, the church of the London law schools, in 1585. His deputy, Walter Travers, mentioned above as a chief apologist for the Presbyterian position, was something of a pain to him, refuting in his afternoon sermons what Hooker had declared in the morning. In 1591 he was made Subdean of Salisbury Cathedral, and in 1595, two years after the first four books of *The Laws* were published, presented by the

Queen to the living of Bishopsbourne in Kent. However, only the first
five books of *The Laws* were published before his death in 1600; Books
VI and VIII appeared in 1648, Book VII in 1661, and the scholarly
consensus is that these are drafts, even if Hooker had finished them in
manuscripts that have not survived.[15]

From one point of view it is a partisan work, a defence of the
organisation and power of the Church of England against Puritan
criticism. However, the kind of praise that Hooker receives suggests
something different; here is J.W. Allen in 1928, in the context of a (still
valuable) history of political thought:

> Not merely as controversialist but as a political thinker, he
> was incomparably the greatest Englishman of the sixteenth
> century and on the continent had few compeers. For breadth
> of view, combined with intellectual honesty and detachment,
> he had no serious rival save Bodin . . . . Among learned or
> controversial or philosophical books, no literary style is
> comparable in excellence to his, save the totally dissimilar
> style of Calvin.[16]

In the first place, the controversial battle that Hooker was engaged in
did not immediately die. In the 1590s it had become quite mild, with
the immediate threat of Spanish Catholic invasion lifted, and
Puritanism more a party within the state Church than a militantly
separatist movement. Presbyterianism, Hooker's main target, had
started to fall apart even before it was effectively repressed around the
time of the Marprelate controversy. However, the English Civil War
was in many ways fought around the issues that Hooker addresses
(hence, perhaps, the publication of 1648), and the later apologists for
the Restoration, such as Clarendon, were deeply indebted to his
work.[17] In the 1590s the *Ecclesiastical Polity* was not particularly
celebrated or influential. After the Restoration it became a kind of
touchstone of Anglicanism, as much for its tone and method as for its
content.

Hooker also addresses two crucial issues of seventeenth-century
political thought – natural law and the social contract. In a European
context he is not exactly innovative, but for many English debates his
work is inaugural. Locke, in particular, found Hooker important.

There is something more still; Robert Eccleshall describes it as 'the
most systematic and stylistically beautiful exploration in English of the
theme of a rationally ordered universe'.[18] A metaphysical justification
for the new Elizabethan Establishment? Or a new, post-Reformation
synthesis, the first notable work of English philosophy for centuries?

The organisation of *The Laws* is indicative of the steadiness ('judiciousness' is the usual, punning term of praise) of Hooker's approach; there is a strategy of deferral, of waiting until the theoretical foundations have been laid before making the specific, defining point. So, the first book discusses laws in general, and the second the role and authority of Scripture, before Book Three tackles the Puritan assertion 'That in Scripture there must be of necessity contained a Form of Church Polity, the Laws whereof may in no wise be altered.' Books IV and V contain a defence of the Church of England against accusations of Popery and superstition, which in the extensive Book V turns into a defence of all that was to become increasingly at issue in spirituality, liturgy and church building. Book VI is about ecclesiastical jurisdiction, Book VII bishops (this, incidentally, not as popular with the Restoration divines who otherwise beatified Hooker); and Book VIII on the position of the monarch as Head of the Church of England.

The Preface is not the best introduction to Hooker's characteristic tone; it is much more like the usual language of controversy (the pedestrian rather the Martinist sort). It shows Hooker's dislike of 'these last times, which for insolence, pride, and egregious contempt of all good order are the worst' against which his intellectual edifice defends the status quo. His principal target is the would-be importers of Calvin's Church polity (Calvin as a theologian and a biblical exegete is excepted; he held almost unchallenged intellectual sway over the Anglican establishment). But they merge with the Anabaptists, radical Protestants who were regarded as dangerous anarchists and generally used as bogeymen. Hooker's extended portrait and critique of them has a dismissive irony which is not usually associated with him, but it is a necessary adjunct to his Establishment 'judiciousness':

> When they and their Bibles were alone together, what
> strange fantastical opinion soever at any time entered into
> their heads, their use was to think the Spirit taught it them
> . . . . And forasmuch as they were of the same suit with
> those of whom the Apostle speaketh, saying, *They are still*
> *learning, but never attain to the knowledge of truth*, it was no
> marvel to see them every day broach some new thing, not
> heard before . . . . The differences amongst them grew by
> this mean in a manner infinite, so that scarcely was there
> found any one of them, the forge of whose brain was not
> possessed with some special mystery.[19]

The irony is not just that of the Renaissance intellectual mocking the mistakes of the half-learned. Hooker did have an intellectual disagreement with what we would nowadays call fundamentalism, because he regarded the exercise of reason as on a par with the biblical text, and as much a gift of God as that text. Some Puritans reckoned that human reason had been made worthless by the Fall. However, his main worry is that such private encounter with the Scriptures will produce endless division in Christendom, a series of privately inspired individuals and sects rather than the national unity of an interdependent Church and state. (Hooker had no time for the supranational unities of Catholicism or militant Protestantism.)

This fragile linkage, between political and religious peace, is what is threatened by Nonconformity; and who could say, after the English Civil War, that Hooker was wrong? 'Of peace and quietness there is not any way possible, unless the probable voice of every entire society or body politic overrule all private of like nature in the same body.'[20] Hooker's intellectual habits point backwards, then, too; against the increasingly important private sphere, as well as to the scholastic unity of Christianity with natural law that he derived principally from Aquinas.

Hooker had a sense of the universe as governed by law, and thus amenable to understanding by reason. This was before Newton, and the laws of physics as the way the universe ticked. It was more immediately theological; only God could voluntarily put himself under law; everything, everyone else was under law because it was limited, not infinite. 'See we not plainly that the obedience of creatures unto the law of nature is the stay of the whole world?'[21] For men under law it is different, because by nature they are rational (this is what distinguishes them) and so there has to be an element of will, 'appetite's controller' as he calls it at one point. This emphasis on reason and will, while not in so many words anti-Calvinist, does shift the ground away from the Calvinist, and indeed Lutheran, emphasis on the bondage of the will.

What are the political consequences of this position? Hooker is very keen on obedience to law, but it has to be a rational consent. In the terms of the period, he is more interested in mixed government, the queen in Parliament, rather than in absolutism. In Book VIII he picks up a Common Law saying, *lex facit Regem*, the law makes the king, as opposed to the absolutist view that the king makes the law. Hooker is not exactly a contractualist in his view of the beginnings of civil society, but he does posit a myth of origins which is more like that of later contractualists, such as Locke, and it is explicitly not a patriarchal myth:

> To take away all such mutual grievances, injuries, and
> wrongs, there was no way, but only by growing into
> composition and agreement amongst themselves, by
> ordaining some kind of government public, and by yielding
> themselves subject thereunto, that unto whom they granted

authority to rule and govern, by them the peace, tranquillity
and happy estate of the rest might be procured.[22]

'Composition and agreement': the best way of characterising this is
Cargill Thompson's, that it describes a theory of consent rather than
contract. The monarch's power may be derived from the people, but
that does not make him subject to popular control, only legal
control.[23] However, consent is important, because it implies a
conscious, reasoned acceptance of political rule, in which the antiquity
of institutions is to be a guide, though not an infallible one, to their
wisdom: 'Antiquity, Custom and Consent in the Church of God,
making with that which Law doth establish, are themselves most
sufficient reasons to uphold the same, unless some notable public
inconvenience inforce the contrary' (V. vii). The Church of England
was at most only sixty years old, after all; though Hooker stressed that
it was a reformed continuation of the Church of Rome. Here is
Anglicanism as a middle way between Rome and Geneva.[24]

Hooker's main political aim, particularly in Book VIII, was to
defend the queen as head of the Church of England. There was a
strong biblical argument, that the kings of Israel were both spiritual
and temporal leaders. At the same time, dismissing the Presbyterian
case, it was argued that the New Testament did not present one,
normative pattern of Church organisation, and therefore Christians
ought to obey whichever of the rational alternatives was in place.
Behind this is a desire for a peaceful unity without arguments over
inessentials, and, more profoundly, a state with a care for the spiritual
as well as material welfare of its members.

Hooker's spirituality comes out in Book V as an inclusive, if not
exactly ecumenical alternative to the discipline of the Puritan position.
A Church which included the whole country plainly could not enquire
too deeply into the inward state of its members – an enquiry which
was at once the strength and vice of the Puritan position. Could not,
and should not, argued Hooker, because it would replace the Last
Judgement with the judgement of men. However, what is original
about his sense of the Church in the 1590s is his opposition to the
simply word-centred spirituality which was not simply Puritan –
though their argument against the Establishment had always been that
it had failed to found a body of preaching clergy, and had in fact
silenced many of the same. To maintain 'that mutual inward hold
which Christ hath of us, and we of him' (V. lvi) Hooker stresses the
role of the sacraments: 'they serve as bonds of obedience to God, strict
obligations to the mutual exercise of Christian charity, provocations to
godliness, preservations from sin, memorials of the principal benefits
of Christ' (V. lvii). It is a Protestant version of the sacraments: just

Communion and Baptism, though the account is principally indebted to the Church Fathers. His defence of Church buildings is similarly based; his theology leads him to dismiss Puritan aesthetics along with their central emphasis on preaching.

If Hooker's thought is so much of a piece, what, finally, of his sentences? The quotations from *The Laws* ought to have demonstrated their basic clarity, but reading them is an unusual experience, because of the habit of qualification that extends them. 'For Hooker', argues George Edelen, 'the complex sentence is the reflection of rational process.'[25] Certainly it would be a mistake simply to analyse the purple passages, or the list-like summaries that conclude or clarify the steps in the argument as we go along. Here are the last two sentences of Book I:

> Thus we see how even one and the self-same thing is under divers considerations conveyed through many laws, and that to measure by one kind of law all the actions of men were to confound the admirable order, wherein God hath disposed all laws, each as in nature, so in degree distinct from other. Wherefore that here we may briefly end, of law there can be no less acknowledged, than that her seat is the bosom of God, her voice the harmony of the world, all things in heaven on earth do her homage, the very least as feeling her care, and the greatest as not exempted from her power, but Angels and men and creatures of what condition soever, though each in different sort and manner, yet all with uniform consent, admiring her as the mother of their peace and joy.[26]

The last sentence is an impressive formal peroration, constructed mainly out of a series of antitheses and parallels, leading to the climax of peace and joy. The previous sentence is also in praise of law and order, but in a different, we might say more intellectual, way. The first proposition is straightforward enough; but what is so characteristically Hooker in the rest of the sentence is to make us wait for the key word 'distinct'. It's almost a Latinate construction, except that in this instance the resolving word is not a main verb. One can multiply examples; it makes Hooker very different, and perhaps less immediately attractive, than, say, Donne or Bacon, who grip our attention with a startling or simply declarative opening. He is not incapable of short sentences. However, the main work of *The Laws* is carried on in those only temporarily elusive periods.

The recognition of Hooker's achievement was similarly suspended; even in the Restoration it was partisan and partial. In his defence of the status quo which virtually invented the nature of Anglicanism and yet provided a quarry for more radical political ideas than he would have recognised; and in his prophetic recognition of the nature of the implications of Puritan ideas (not to mention his anticipation of some of the key ideas of the Oxford Movement of the nineteenth century) there is a considerable achievement. The paradox is that the style of the man who tried to decentre an exclusively word-centred approach to Christianity should be remembered and admired long after that of the word-men, at least of his day.

John Milton

One of the key ideas within Max Weber's notion of the Protestant ethic is that the Reformation secularised the idea of vocation. 'Calling', in English, becomes a term for any kind of employment, not simply the divine summons to the priesthood. In Puritan writing it also denotes a stage in conversion (usually with 'effectual' in front of it); though the special calling to the preaching ministry remains of signal interest.[27] Milton's felt calling to be a Christian poet nestles somewhere between all those meanings, and no one should come to his writings underestimating his sense of divine mission. Immodest, maybe, but then he had something to be immodest about, and the inductions in *Paradise Lost* show an awareness of presumption as well as ambition.[28] Should we regard Milton's prose as an interruption of this calling? In *The Reason of Church-Government* (1642), the fourth of his anti-episcopal pamphlets, there is an extended self-defence and modesty topos which is often referred to. He argues that he entered the controversy out of conscience rather than envy or hunting for praise; and the subject itself, as well as the 'tumultuous times', do not lend themselves to 'all the curious touches of art'. Then: 'Lastly, I should not choose this manner of writing wherein knowing my self inferior to my self, led by the genial power of nature to another task, I have the use, as I may account it, but of my left hand.'[29] So, there is a collection of essays on Milton's prose called *Achievements of the Left Hand*, and a more pervasive assumption that Milton shelved his plans for Arthurian epic and Edenic tragedy for twenty years while he wrote prose, first in defence of his friends and his own ideas, then in the service of the Commonwealth. However, as James Grantham Turner has argued, the polarities that lie behind these assumptions – not just poetry/prose, but aesthetic/functional, literary/political and occasional/eternal – will not

lie still in Milton's own writing. After all, he was an engaged poet as
well as a prose polemicist who recognised that a sense of the eternal
might demand engagement with the present.[30] We also need to
recognise that many of these critical arguments are themselves political;
the hostility of Samuel Johnson, or T.S. Eliot to Milton's republican
Nonconformity is echoed in as much subsequent Milton criticism as
the desire to emphasise and appropriate it is in Blake or Christopher
Hill.[31]

An important way of reading Milton's prose is to see it as the
product of the Christian orator. *Areopagitica* presents itself on the title
page as a 'speech' to Parliament, but the pattern of the deliberative
oration is common to a number of the tracts. Furthermore, rhetoric
links both prose and poetic method in the Renaissance, and as a
defensive strategy was crucial to both Renaissance Italian ideas of
liberty as well as Christian Reformation preaching.[32] The ideal of the
orator, who linked in his person as well as his text the virtues he was
espousing is quite unlike the bohemian notion of the artist, who is
forgiven everything for the sake of his art. The ethical links were
perceived quite differently in the seventeenth century, and that is one
reason why many of the controversies that Milton was involved with
turned into matters of style and personality as much as ideas. These
were not perceived as dirty tricks, diverting attention from an
argument that cannot be won on fair grounds, but part of the basic test
of the truth of a position. Style was seen as the expression of the
rectitude of the speaker and thus of his position. In 1642 Milton
portrayed Christ as the perfect orator and teacher, not only in
matching life to words, but in his mastery of all three levels of style,
high, middle and low, just as Cicero had suggested:

> Our Saviour who had all gifts in him was Lord to express his
> indoctrinating power in what sort him seemed; sometimes
> by a mild and familiar converse, sometimes with plain and
> impartial home-speaking regardless of those whom the
> auditors might think he should have had in more respect;
> otherwhiles with bitter and ireful rebukes if not teaching let
> leaving excuseless those his wilful impugners.[33]

In Milton's prose, just as surely as the poetry, the radical energies of
Puritanism join forces with the Renaissance rediscovery of the classics
of republican Athens and Rome. Milton was a revolutionary, with all
the violent energy of the new movement convinced of its rightness.
His prose is exhilarating rather than comfortable.

Rather than attempt a survey of all of Milton's prose works, I shall
concentrate on four main areas: the early pamphlets against bishops,

the divorce tracts, *Areopagitica*, and finally, some of the tracts written in defence of the Republic after 1649. Though this strategy omits some major pieces, it does give us a representative sample of his various polemic modes, and it emphasises that many of Milton's pieces come as parts of series, developing arguments and varying styles and strategies according to the stage of the controversy.

Thomas Young, Milton's Cambridge tutor, was the immediate cause of Milton's first engagement in controversy. He was one of 'Smectymnuus' (from the initials of Stephen Marshall, Edmund Calamy, Thomas Young, Matthew Newcomen and William – double-U – Spurstowe), who had written an *Answer* to Bishop Joseph Hall's *Humble Remonstrance* in 1641. The state Church was in trouble; when Milton began writing, Archbishop Laud was already in prison as a result of the Long Parliament's attack on the regime of personal rule which Charles I had been attempting for over ten years. Why were the bishops so unpopular by 1641? Three reasons have already been mentioned in the Marprelate discussion: the arguments for Presbyterian Church government, multiple office-holding and profiteering, and the Church courts. The first moves into something more general, that the bishops were seen as the remnants of Catholicism, not just because of their resistance to more radically reformed ideas about Church government, but because they appeared to be cornering the 'managing of our salvation' (Milton's phrase) to the priesthood. But then there was Laud. As Kevin Sharpe argues, Laud ought to have had a lot in common with the Puritans – he wanted an educated clergy, he was ascetic, and he documented his personal devotional life and the impact of external events – 'providences' – in his diary. Nor was he pro-Catholic: his one work of theology is a defence of the Church of England against the Jesuit Fisher. But he was seen as a Papist sympathiser because of his sudden and vigorously enforced interest in ceremony and Church buildings, and his closeness to Charles, whose wife was Catholic and kept priests at court.[34] Hugh Trevor-Roper, the biographer and defender of Laud, suggests that he was betrayed by Charles, but that is another story.[35] It is enough to know that when Milton began his attack on the bishops, the Laud–Wentworth policy of 'Thorough' (enforcing the prerogatives of king and Church to the limit in the interests of Charles I's personal rule) was on the ropes, its main authors in prison. Wentworth was executed in May 1641, Laud not until 1645.

The first of the five books Milton published within a year was *Of Reformation Touching Church-Discipline in England* (1641). The framework of the argument is historical, indebted in particular to Foxe's history of Christian martyrdom. England had begun the Reformation, but fell behind, particularly in the matter of bishops. The problematic

relationship between Church and state, bishops and monarchy is traced
back to Constantine, the first Roman Emperor to convert to
Christianity. Christianity is about simplicity, but worldly, upper-class
politicians are liable to over-decorate it, 'to set a gloss upon the
simplicity, and plainness of Christianity which to the gorgeous
solemnities of Paganism, and the sense of the World's children seemed
but a homely and yeomanly religion, for the beauty of inward sanctity
was not within their prospect'.[36] At this stage Milton is not against
monarchy, arguing that the bishops of a political persuasion ('political',
here, probably implies 'devious' rather than simply 'unspiritual') are
the danger to monarchy. Whether Charles would have welcomed
Milton's definition of monarchy is unlikely, though: 'Monarchy is
made up of two parts, the Liberty of the subject, and the supremacy of
the King.'[37] Like Marprelate, Milton is purporting to defend his
monarch against the threat posed by the bishops. He attacks the
bishops' courts, and the Book of Sports, which encouraged rural
games on Sunday, but which Milton saw as an encouragement to
luxury (i.e., lechery) which would 'effeminate' the nation.[38] The
temperature rises at the end; Milton cannot resist consigning the
bishops to Hell in the peroration.

Of Prelatical Episcopacy, a reply to Ussher, Hall and others, is less
often discussed because, after the initial premise that there is nothing in
the Bible to suggest that bishop and presbyter (meaning servant rather
than priest) are different orders, the argument is largely a display of
scepticism of authorities that would say otherwise. Stanley Fish
describes it as a 'minimalist' enterprise designed to dismiss all but the
self-sufficient Scriptures, a strategy soon to be abandoned.[39]

Much more heated is the next, Animadversions upon the Remonstrants
Defence against Smectymnuus, (July 1641) an attack on Bishop Hall.
Milton usually gets a bad press for this one; 'scurrilous and distorting'
is his editor's verdict. He defends his 'rougher accent' as a plain way of
dealing with an enemy of truth 'that is conceited to have a voluble and
smart fluence of tongue'.[40] 'Answer a fool according to his folly', the
text from Proverbs which lies behind the Marprelate strategy, is
Milton's defence. Hall, Bishop of Norwich at the time, may well have
been a nice man, as his biographers have asserted. But he had been a
satirist – Milton mentions his Mundus Alter et Idem (1605), about an
imaginary commonwealth – and, as Thomas Kranidas points out, is no
slouch at the underhand sneer in the work in question.[41] Milton
pointedly contrasts the 'true pastor' with the tempting rewards of
prelatical office, and praises the preacher in terms which could also
admit his own ambition to be God's spokesman in other contexts,
other genres: 'certainly there is no employment more honourable,
more worthy to take up a great spirit, more requiring a generous and

free nature, than to be the messenger, and herald of heavenly truth from God to man'.[42] True eloquence, argues Milton later in the series, 'I find to be no more, but the serious and hearty love of truth.'[43] There is a straight line from this to saying that Hall is a bad man who proves it by writing badly.

Next in the series comes *The Reason of Church-Government urged against Prelaty* (January/February 1642). Formally, it is close to the Ciceronian classical oration, though it is disrupted by an extended digression. The digression is of particular interest because it signals his ambitions as a poet.

The Preface announces the book as a more gently persuasive, less aggressive than its predecessors. Once again Milton constructs the figure of the wise and virtuous orator as the touchstone, this time of the lawgiver:

> . . . such a one as is a true knower of himself, and himself in whom contemplation and practice, wit, prudence, fortitude and eloquence must be rarely met, both to comprehend the hidden causes of things, and span in his thoughts all the various effects that passion or complexion can work in man's nature; and hereto must his hand be at defiance with gain, and his heart in all virtues heroic.[44]

Milton will not leave such a picture without its negative, 'these wretched projectors of ours that bescrawl their pamphlets every day'.

This Renaissance Christian ideal is further amplified in Book II, as he slips into a discussion of his career as a writer. This is where we get the definition of prose as 'the cool element', the practice only of his 'left hand'.[45] His ambition goes beyond the immediate cause, to counter the 'libidinous and ignorant poetasters' of his day, a style of festival governed only by the Book of Sports, and, supremely, to write English, Christian poetry fit to stand with Homer and Virgil. Such an achievement will need solitude and study, the kind of self-preparation he had intended for the ministry of the Church until he saw its tyranny. In particular, it would have required him to take an oath 'which unless he took with a conscience that would retch, he must either straight perjure, or split his faith.' (He is probably referring to the notorious 'Etcetera Oath' of 1640, so called because it required subscription to the clause 'Nor will I ever give my consent to alter the government of the Church, by Archbishops, Bishops, Deans, and Archdeacons, etc.') So, 'Church-outed by the Prelates', he has a right to intervene in the matter of Church government.[46]

As so often, Milton is torn between a high ambition to match the importance of the task he sees for himself and the recognition that the first Christian virtue is humility. Tonally, he stays on the high side, but takes care that he is not stuck with its usual values. This anticipates his revaluation of epic heroism: 'It had been a small mastery for him [God] to have drawn out his legions into array, and flanked them with his thunder; therefore he sent foolishness, to confute wisdom, weakness to bind strength, despisedness to vanquish pride.'[47] 'Therefore' is the key word (not 'instead'); it's an argument from God's nature, that he does not do the easy thing, the pagan thing, he turns the usual power games on their heads. This sentence is also a good example of how Milton weds Ciceronian symmetries to Pauline paradoxes (with the echoes of I Corinthians 1: 25–8). The much-discussed Latinity of Milton's larger sentences is much better described as Miltonic; no one else, with the same Latin learning, does it quite this way, and, while you can sense the longer Latin sentences behind it, the syntax is only English.

Milton's final strike in the 1641–42 controversy was *An Apology against a Pamphlet call'd a Modest Confutation of the Animadversions upon the Remonstrant against Smectymnuus* (April 1642). Not a catchy title. It returns to the sharpness of his earlier attack on Hall, in reponse to a piece that may have been by one of Hall's sons. Structurally, it is a point-by-point refutation of the *Modest Confutation*, with some jolly jibes – 'This is a piece of sapience not worth the brain of a fruit-trencher', for example.[48] But abuse makes way for something of an altogether higher class of anger, reminiscent of the great attack on the bishops in 'Lycidas'. With a reproach that goes back to Marprelate, he accuses them of falling down on their duties, only to blame the people they have let down for the consequences: 'For while none think the people so void of knowledge as the prelates think them, none are so backward and malignant as they to bestow knowledge upon them . . . they who have put out the peoples' eyes reproach them of their blindness.'[49] This rises into a fine peroration against those who 'possess huge benefices for lazy performances, great promotions, only for the execution of a cruel disgospelling jurisdiction'.[50]

The anti-episcopal work shows Milton's grasp of history as well as theology, and the urgency of his patriotic sense of the Reformation in England getting under way again, even as he examines himself. The writing is exuberant, hostile rather than defensive in tone, though the pretext was defence. The next series of writings concern divorce, and show a more private aspect of his concern with liberty, but they are still consciously political, part of the same programme: 'Farewell all hope of true Reformation in the state, when such an evil as this lies undiscerned or unregarded in the house.'[51]

Much of Milton's income came from investments made by his father; including for example the interest on a debt incurred by Richard

Powell. In June 1642 Milton met and fell in love with Mary, Richard's eldest daughter. In July they got married; he was thirty-three, she seventeen, though such an age gap was common, sometimes even recommended at the time. In August Milton let her return to her family for a while, perhaps because she was homesick. She stayed away; the Powells were Royalists, and Charles had raised his standard in August, the start of the Civil War. It would have been difficult for her to return, had she wanted to; whether the Powells were scheming to get out of a debt, or whether she had hated the rather Spartan life at Milton's house, or what, we do not know. The four divorce pamphlets certainly spring from the trauma of that, although there is no direct allusion to his circumstances, and the obvious ground for him, desertion, is only mentioned in passing, hardly entering the argument.[52]

The Doctrine and Discipline of Divorce was published in August 1643, and revised six months later. The argument is a tricky one. The one clear statement on the subject made by Jesus in the Gospels (Matthew 5: 31–2) seems to forbid divorce except for adultery; Milton wants to make the case for incompatibility as a ground for divorce. To do that while maintaining the authority of scripture he tries to establish two points, the true aim of marriage and the nature of New Testament commandments, within a much more complex hermeneutics than he had used in the anti-episcopal tracts. It is less a question of citing proof-texts than of establishing principles from the Bible (particularly the contrast between Law and Gospel, Old Testament and New), trying to determine intention and context against 'leaden daggers of your literal decrees'.[53] It might sound merely cynical – after all, what argument that didn't have scriptural backing stood a chance of being accepted at the time? But it is more than that. Part of the distinct personal tone of the divorce tracts, its trapped eloquence, comes from disappointed idealism, from expecting much and getting nothing from marriage; and the ideal is derived from Scripture and Christian teaching as much as anything. 'What thing more instituted to the solace and delight of man than marriage, and yet the misinterpreting of some Scripture . . . hath changed the blessing of matrimony not seldom into a familiar and co-inhabiting mischief; at least into a drooping and disconsolate household captivity . . . .'[54]

What does marriage mean for Milton? The Prayer Book Service of Matrimony might stand for the received view at the time:

> First, it was ordained for the procreation of children . . . .
> Secondly, It was ordained for a remedy against sin, and to avoid fornication; that such persons as have not the gift of continency might marry . . . .

> Thirdly, It was ordained for the mutual society, help, and
> comfort, that the one ought to have of the other, both in
> prosperity and adversity.

Milton reversed the order, and in doing so transformed the analysis.
Many commentators have argued as to how far he was on his own in
his view of marriage, and how far he was innovating. John Halkett
finds a similar emphasis on the spiritual bond in Vives and Erasmus;
and the Hallers find the celebration of domestic intimacy a central
feature of Puritan social teaching. More recently, Mary Nyquist has
suggested that there are texts from earlier in the century that are more
committed to mutuality and equality than Milton.[55] Certainly Milton
was picking out a strand of Renaissance and Reformation thinking
about marriage that already existed; and his translation/summary *The
Judgement of Martin Bucer Concerning Divorce* (1644) brings in a
prominent German Reformer as a kind of character witness (Arnold
Williams's term) to show that Milton was not the anarchic libertine
that early outrage at *The Doctrine and Discipline* had assumed.
'Conversation' is a key word, meaning living together, society and
intimacy as well as talking; here is a sentence from the Preface which
pits it against mere sensual union:

> For although God in the first ordaining of marriage, taught
> us to what end he did it, in words expressly implying the apt
> and cheerful conversation of man with woman, to comfort
> and refresh him against the evil of solitary life, not
> mentioning the purpose of generation till afterwards, as
> being but a secondary end in dignity, though not in
> necessity; yet no, if any two be but once handed in the
> Church, and have tasted of any sort of the nuptial bed, let
> them find themselves never so mistaken in their dispositions
> though any error, concealment, or misadventure, that
> through their different tempers, thoughts, and constitutions,
> they can neither be to one another a remedy against
> loneliness, nor live in any union or contentment all their
> days, yet they shall, so they be but found suitably weaponed
> to the least possibility of sensual enjoyment, be made, spite
> of *antipathy* to fadge together [put up with each other], and
> combine as they may to their unspeakable wearisomeness
> and despair of all sociable delight in the ordinance which
> God established to that very end.[56]

Part of the argument, then, is that sensuality, normally reined in by
Christian ethics, has become, quite inappropriately, the sole ground of

judgement. Milton's language for physical sex in the tract is often suspiciously interesting: 'to grind in the mill of an undelighted and servile copulation',[57] for example, suggests a mixture of distaste for physical work and alarm at the disappointing nature of dutiful sex. 'Suggests' is all, of course; whether symptomatic reading or prurient speculation, such critical reactions show how much the voice of the offended party is woven into the text of the tracts whatever the relation between Milton's biography and his argument. As James Grantham Turner neatly puts it, 'Every proposal in these tracts is weighed by the standard of love, and every complaint issues from a wounded expectation of love.'[58]

You don't have to be a feminist (though it might help) to see Milton's plea for liberty of divorce to be distinctly one-sided. Chapter 15 of *The Doctrine and Discipline* dismisses the argument that the Mosaic permission for divorce might have existed to protect afflicted wives: 'Palpably uxorious', he says, woman was made for man, not vice versa. However, at one point in *Tetrachordon* (expositions of the Scriptures which deal with marriage, published in 1645) the logic of his reading of Genesis 1: 27 ('God created man in his own image . . . male and female created he them') leads him elsewhere. There the 'golden dependence of headship and subjection' can be broken by either party if the other is wicked or heretical – 'the wife . . . is not still bound to be the vassal of him, who is the bondslave of Satan'.[59] Certainly the kind of marriage of fit minds that Milton desires seems to need something very like equality.[60] Yet there seems to be no sensitivity to the problems of a divorced woman; and the downgrading of the sexual aspects of marriage also leads to a surprising silence on the fate of children after divorce.

The divorce sequence concludes with *Colasterion* (1645), a tetchy reply to an anonymous critic of *The Doctrine and Discipline of Divorce*. Reconciliation with Mary, and two other marriages after her death, intervene before *Paradise Lost* demonstrates that Milton's idealism about marriage, his suspicion of women, and his sense of the distance between paradisal and fallen sex are still in place; and shouldn't Adam have divorced Eve rather than sharing the fruit?

Back to 1644, and *Areopagitica*. The title appears to derive from the Athenian orator Isocrates, whose *Areopagiticus* of c. 355 BC was, like Milton's, a written oration to Parliament – though his purpose was virtually the reverse, urging it to take back the powers over education and censorship it had abandoned. Perhaps Milton also meant his audience to recall St Paul's sermon at the same location as the old Court of the Areopagus (Acts 17) which attacked pagan superstition while quoting from its sources.[61]

Part of the problem of interpreting *Areopagitica* is like that of *Hamlet*:

it is full of quotations – 'a good book is the precious life-blood of a master spirit', 'I cannot praise a fugitive and cloistered virtue', and so on. The difference is that everyone knows that *Hamlet* is endlessly reinterpretable; popular citations of *Areopagitica* assume it has one message, that censorship is wrong. But aren't, as John Illo has argued, 'the grand libertarian generalities' actually a distraction from the less than libertarian conclusions? And didn't Milton himself act as a censor for Parliament in 1649?[62] It has long been recognised that Roger Williams, *The Bloudy Tenent of Persecution* (also 1644), for example, advocates a more complete toleration than Milton; though he did so from the perspective of Rhode Island in New England.[63] Milton may have had tactical reasons; he could not have followed Williams in his essential prior move, the complete separation of Church and state, if he was trying to enlist the Erastian party's support in Parliament away from the Presbyterians, who had been behind the setting up of pre-publication censorship in May 1643.

Even the title page is defiant, listing no printer or publisher, as was required by the ordinance; and the quotation from Euripides can be seen in context as expressing a preference for republican democracy over tyranny.[64] The opening of the oration proper, after praise of Parliament, concedes the danger of books before the praise of their liveliness takes a more positive direction:

> I deny not, but that it is of greatest concernment in the
> Church and Commonwealth, to have a vigilant eye how
> books demean themselves, as well as men; and thereafter to
> confine, imprison, and do sharpest justice on them as
> malefactors: for books are not absolute dead things, but do
> contain a potency of life in them to be as active as that soul
> whose progeny they are; nay they do preserve as in a vial the
> purest efficacy and extraction of that lively intellect that bred
> them. I know they are as lively, and as vigorously
> productive, as those fabulous dragon's teeth; and being sown
> up and down, may chance to spring up armed men. And yet
> on the other hand unless wariness be used, as good almost
> kill a man as kill a good book; who kills a man kills a
> reasonable creature, God's image; but he who destroys a
> good book, kills reason itself, kills the image of God, as it
> were in the eye.[65]

The concession leaves plenty of space for government action; 'sharpest justice' is uncomfortably physical, like the floggings and cropped ears that Milton's contemporaries suffered for verbal offences like libel. The argument shifts a little with the dragon's teeth image; the Civil War was still being fought, and books are part of this conflict, dangerous, but also part of the dynamic. Looking back, it seems as though the pamphlet war of the 1640s was of parallel importance to Cromwell winning battles; we can see a revolutionary ideology being created, pushing as well as pulled by events. In civil wars people get killed, often with more contumely than in foreign wars, and Milton was not squeamish about violence. The process of thorough Reformation he saw as the key issue; it was the cause and effect of true liberty, which some see as the prior virtue. He never quite abandons the link between the two, but he finds increasing problems of implementation. *Areopagitica* traces a classic revolutionary problem, in fact. The English Revolution, as I think we must call it, dismantled some of the key institutions of state control in the name of liberty, but found the need to replace most of them with new ones. Milton celebrates the new liberty, sees the need of new institutions, but cannot find in the alliance which produced that liberty anyone who can be wholeheartedly trusted to set bounds to it. The presbyter will be turned into a prelate, just as the bishops have been overthrown; the independent congregations will be turned into conventicles, meeting to censor every week; the individual scholar with the learning and discrimination to be a censor will get so bored, or wearied, with the job as to ruin him as a scholar.

Milton's miniature history of censorship, which follows the quoted paragraph, is in part a direct response to the historical pretences of the Licensing Order, which made much of 'ancient custom' in the power it gave to the Stationers Company.[66] Elsewhere Milton pointedly uses the language of commerce, and in particular associating the Order with Charles I's much resented selling of monopolies, to criticise the Stationers' control. The main thrust of the history, though, is to suggest that censorship is unEnglish and unworthy of a republic. There is no English word for '*imprimatur*'. Neither Greece nor Rome banned satire, or criticism of the state; only the Popes after 800 started 'burning and prohibiting to be read, what they fancied not'.[67] The real sophistication in methods of suppressing books came in with the Council of Trent and the Spanish Inquisition (Milton misses out the growth of printing in the same century), and what reformer would want to imitate them?

Milton has a vision of London as the vanguard of Reformation, but his vision is not of pulpits, or soldiers, or Parliament, but a host of studies with their individual writers and readers:

> The shop of war hath not there more anvils and hammers
> waking, to fashion out the plates and instruments of armed
> Justice in defence of beleaguered Truth, than there be pens
> and heads there, sitting by their studious lamps, musing,

searching, revolving new notions and ideas wherewith to
present, as with their homage and their fealty the
approaching Reformation; others as fast reading, trying all
things, assenting to the force of reason and convincement.[68]

If the divorce tracts can be read as a commentary on a frustrated
romance of true love, *Areopagitica* at times reads like a romance of
revolution achieved through learning.

Parallels with a modern sense of 'revolution' are both illuminating
and misleading. Milton was republican – still, in 1644, a revolutionary
position – but hardly democratic in twentieth-century terms. He was
still a Calvinist at this stage, and the Calvinist notion of an elect is at
least structurally similar to Lenin's idea of the revolutionary avant-
garde which will lead rather than follow the mood of the masses.[69] The
Marxist model of revolution is often compared with the Christian
Messianic hope, the Second Coming of Christ. It is also true that
revolutions have a repressive as well as liberating tendency. What did
Milton want to repress, still?

The tract sends out different signals, not least because sometimes
Milton is discussing means, sometimes ends, and sometimes deferring
to his immediate audience. There is an ideal, that error is best
suppressed by truth, in the open:

> And though all the winds of doctrine were let loose to play
> upon the earth, so Truth be in the field, we do injuriously by
> licensing and prohibiting to misdoubt her strength. Let her
> and Falsehood grapple; who ever knew Truth put to the
> worse in a free and open encounter. Her confuting is the best
> and surest suppressing.[70]

That position links with the vision of the city full of writers and
readers collectively sifting the truth. But there are limits. First, the
potential suppressors should themselves be suppressed: 'I mean not
tolerated Popery, and open superstition, which as it extirpates all
religions and civil supremacies, so it self should be extirpate . . . .'[71]
(Milton had earlier mentioned his meeting with Galileo, imprisoned by
the Inquisition.) Then at least the printer's name needs to be registered;
and if the book is mischievous (plenty of scope here, though the word
did not have such playful connotations then) or libellous, then 'the fire
and the executioner' would come in. The executioner would burn
books – and he was also responsible for the associated corporal
punishment on printer and author. Finally there is self-censorship, the
most pervasive and the most elusive result of any kind of restriction on
press freedom. Milton clearly expects good behaviour in debate; the

provisional nature of civil liberty he asks Parliament for is predicated on the sobriety of English civil society as much as on the more exciting ground, that truth is liable to come from an unexpected, even despised direction.

So then, we must not be misled by the ringing sentences of liberty into thinking that *Areopagitica* is an uncompromisingly libertarian document. For the judicious reader – like Milton himself – anything is valuable, if only as a warning of the consequences of its erroneous position. However, for a revolutionary government, some things cannot be tolerated. Milton argued that they should tolerate a lot more than they did. In 1654, in the course of his *Defensio Secunda*, a Latin (and therefore European) defence of the English people as regicides, he remarked that *Areopagitica* was written 'that the determination of true and false, of what ought to be published and what suppressed, might not be in the hands of the few who may be charged with the inspection of books, men commonly without learning and of vulgar judgement'.[72] By then he had tried his hand at censorship, too. However, Milton's sense of the impracticalities and absurdities of censorship, as well as his embattled commitment to liberty against both old and new establishments, suggest that the libertarian reading of *Areopagitica* is less a misreading than a partial reading.

In 1649 Charles I was executed and Milton became a member of the republican government as Secretary for Foreign Tongues, in part a response to his defence of regicide in *The Tenure of Kings and Magistrates*, published only a fortnight after the execution. He was immediately pressed into service to write *Eikonoklastes*, a response to *Eikon Basilike*, supposedly written by Charles but in fact ghosted by John Gauden, and a great popular success inaugurating the cult of King Charles the Martyr. There were the two *Defences* of the English People in the 1650s; increasing blindness (and virtual retirement from the Council of State after 1655); and increasing disillusion.

Yet the last thing Milton wanted was the return of the monarchy. On the eve of the Restoration in 1660 he published *The Ready and Easy Way to Establish a Free Commonwealth*. Like all Milton's political work, it is an immediate response to a crisis, and was rewritten three months after first publication to take account of changes in the political situation.[73] To begin with, the tone matches the 'spare functionalism' which Thomas Corns has identified as the main feature of Milton's later prose style.[74] The sentences themselves haven't got any shorter; but, for example in the history of Charles's concessions in 1648, there is an almost breathless, shorthand quality to the account. The republican value words are not missing, either; it is not bare in that sense. The tone alternates between warning and lament. Like the prophet Jeremiah, Milton warns the chosen people of God against betraying their calling. The cost, spiritual and financial as well as political, of restoring the monarchy is enormous – 'people must needs be mad or strangely infatuated'.[75] Milton could hardly have been confident that the people he so despairs of should follow his advice; it is more an expression of despair that a people who had fought for liberty, and tasted it, should so ignominiously hand it back. Would one last rallying call, one last great sentence do it? The prophetic voice that had risen so impressively from so many in the 1650s is now like Jeremiah's, compelled to tell the truth still, courageously, to the perversely deaf. But he will not allow himself elegy or retirement yet; there might still be enough sensible men:

> . . . to some perhaps whom God may raise of these stones to
> become children of reviving liberty; and may reclaim,
> though they seem now choosing them a captain back for
> Egypt, to bethink themselves a little and consider whither
> they are rushing; to exhort this torrent also of the people,
> not to be so impetuous, but to keep their due channel; and at
> length recovering and uniting their better resolutions, now
> that they see already how open and unbounded the insolence
> and rage is of our common enemies, to stay these ruinous
> proceedings; justly and timely fearing to what a precipice of
> destruction the deluge of this epidemic madness would hurry
> us through the general defection of a misguided and abused
> multitude.[76]

It is never less than impressive, but it is a desperate sentence, moving off differently several times as Milton seems to recall the situation and how all the forces he appeals to are moving away from him. It confronts failure, but cannot, quite, name it as irrecoverable.

Radical religion

Events moved fast in the 1640s and 1650s, with most people's thinking limping along behind. With the fall of the bishops censorship relaxed; and though there was both the state censorship that Milton attacked, and the Blasphemy Law of 1650, triggered by Ranter activities and an extraordinary rash of self-proclaimed Messiahs, there was still an enormous outburst of writing about the area we are discussing, the relationship between religion and politics, which can truly be called radical.

Historians have marshalled some of this into order, though party labels are slippery and liable to be anachronistic, particularly if we are looking for denominations, or political parties in anything like the modern sense. Levellers and Diggers, for example, were names applied to enclosure rioters earlier in the century, before they settled to the quite specific, short-lived movements of the late 1640s.[77]

The Levellers were the best-known, the best organised, and, subsequently at least, the most influential. The three principal leaders, John Lilburne, Richard Overton and William Walwyn, were vigorous pampleteers for the cause in interestingly complementary ways. Lilburne survives the least well on the page; his writing (some eighty pamphlets) is most clearly an adjunct to his personal, dramatised, attack on episcopal, and then Parliamentary oppression. The engravings of Lilburne that accompany some of these, show him reading from Coke in his defence, or behind bars; his suffering is evidence of his integrity, as well as the tyranny of those who so brutally dealt with him. The pamphlets are often part of a wider campaign, a legal case for example, and read like a set of documents, including opponents' words as well as his own. At the same time, there is a recognisable series of motifs, of which 'Free-Men of England' is the key. 'Oh Englishmen! Where is [sic] your freedoms?' he asked in 1645, 'what is become of your liberties and privileges that you have been fighting for all this while, to the large expense of your bloods and estates, which was hoped would have procured your liberties and freedoms? but rather, as some great ones order it, ties you faster in bondage and slavery, than before'.[78]

Earlier, whipped through the streets because of his attacks on the bishops, he portrays his sufferings in the language of martyrology – but even then the physical pain is noted along with the providential strengthenings.[79] Later, the language modulates into a series of arguments and demands, the insistent questioning of Parliament, which held his hopes and created most of his disappointments. After his acquittal on charges of treason in 1653, he published *The Just Defence of John Lilburne against such as charge him with Turbulency of Spirit*, which gives his principled rationale for regarding himself as a representative of legal freedom, not just singularly awkward:

> I then contended also against close imprisonment as most
> illegal, being contrary to the known laws of the land, and by
> which tyrants and oppressors have broken the spirits of the
> English, and sometimes broken their very hearts: a cruelty

> few are sensible of, but such as have been sensible by
> suffering, but yet it concerns all men to oppose in
> whomsoever, for what is done to anyone may be done to
> everyone.[80]

The heroism of principle is again signalled, modestly but tellingly, in his own suffering. And, despite the awkwardness of the sentence as a whole, the phrases are often stirring, potential slogans – 'what is done to anyone may be done to everyone'.

A lot of Leveller writing is collaborative, and shows its committee origins. Richard Overton is probably the best of them at clear formulation, as well as an accomplished satirist. One of his defences of Lilburne, sent to the Tower by the Lords in 1646, *An Arrow against all Tyrants*, shows this rational clarity in an early formulation of natural rights:

> To every individual in nature, is given an individual
> property by nature, not to be invaded or usurped by any: for
> every one as he is himself, so he hath a self propriety, else he
> could not be himself, and on this no second may presume to
> deprive any of, without manifest violation and affront to the
> very principles of nature . . . .[81]

As Richard Tuck has noticed, the Levellers weren't the first to use the language of inalienable rights, but Overton's various formulations of 1646–47 provide the best statements of their adaptation of it against Parliament, the courts, and the grandees of the army.[82]

But that is only half of Overton the prose writer. The title page of *An Arrow* describes a spoof printer: 'Printed at the backside of the Cyclopian Mountains, by Martin Claw-Clergy, Printer to the Reverend Assembly of Divines, and are to be sold at the sign of the Subjects Liberty, right opposite to persecuting Court'. Yes, Marprelate is back. *Hay any work for Cooper* had been reprinted in 1642; Overton had already combined Marprelate's style of attack on the bishops with that of popular drama in *Canterbury his Change of Diet* (1641), described by Margot Heinemann as a 'revenge fantasy' in support of Prynne and others who had had their ears cropped for seditious libel.[83]

With *The Arraignement of Mr Persecution* (1645), the first of seven 'Marpriest' tracts of which *An Arrow* is the last, Overton has turned the weapon of the Presbyterians against them.[84] As with old Martin, every bit of the book gets turned on the target; there is a mock Epistle to the mostly Presbyterian Westminster Assembly (later associated with the Spanish Inquisition and the Court of High Commission, the latter one of old Martin's targets) and a mock reply from the Assembly, authorising them to print it 'as a divine hand'maid to the right understanding of the Directory' (the Assembly's Directory of Worship). Sir John Presbyter's attack on Liberty of Conscience is punctuated by sarcastic parenthetical summaries and counter-arguments.

The main part of the book is a dramatised trial, carried on in something between allegory and name-calling. With names like the Constable, Mr Reward-of-Tyranny, Mr State-Policy and Gaffar Christian, it is difficult to believe that Bunyan hadn't seen this book. 'Gaffar' is a term of respect for elders who are not of the status to be called 'Master'; this is rather like Bunyan's habit, particularly in Part One of *The Pilgrim's Progress*, of naming most of his heroes without prefixes, and many of their opponents 'Mr' and 'Lord'. Some of the figures are clearly personal: Sir John Presbyter gets most of his words from Thomas Edwards, and Mr Compassionate-Samaritan is doubtless Walwyn. There is plenty of play on titles – 'Dissembly', 'Priest Bitterall'.

The real achievement of *Mr Persecution* is to sustain a serious argument for liberty of conscience in a consistently entertaining satiric fashion. Even the extended speeches, though they owe something to sermon style, are enlivened by a mixture of mockery – 'give us this day our daily tithes' – and proverb, German in one case. Like Marprelate at his best, the anger is engaging because there is a genuine moral and religious feeling behind it:

> . . . no man knoweth but in part, and what we know, we
> receive it by degrees, now a little, and then a little; he that
> knows the most, was once as ignorant as he that knows the
> least . . . yet we see how common a thing it is, if we know
> not, nor believe so much as the multitude knoweth or
> believeth, or the doctrine of the Presbyterian Church
> requireth, we must be persecuted; and if our knowledge go
> beyond them, that we protest against their errors, and labour
> to inform them better, we must taste of the same sauce too
> . . .[85]

This gentleness in the midst of rumbustiousness is an important element in Leveller writing, and is most evident in William Walwyn; perhaps as a result, he was perceived as the most sinister of them by their opponents.

One of Walwyn's strategies is to lower the temperature of controversy; as in *A Whisper in the Ear of Mr Thomas Edwards* (March 1646), the author of *Gangraena*, an attack on the sects: 'In your 96. page, you have me in these uncharitable expressions, one Mr Walwyn a seeker, and a dangerous man, a strong head: truly in the mind you were in, when you wrote this *Gangreen*, I am heartily glad I appeared not worthy of your Commendations.'[86] In *A Prediction of Mr Edwards His Conversion and Recantation*, he suspects that Edwards's violence is now so great, that, like Saul on the way to Damascus, he must be heading for conversion. So he identifies the best aspects of the sects with their old hammer turned penitent ('wholly incorprate into the Family of Love', for example) and composes a recantation. It is a considerable achievement to find a mode of loving one's enemies, or at least projecting a better view of them than hell-bound, in the heated atmosphere of pamphlet warfare. It might be an elaborate form of mockery; but to my mind, it is better than insults, and incidentally a serious question-mark over those who have regarded Walwyn's approach as 'securely secular'.[87] He does quote Montaigne approvingly, but in an ecumenical rather than a rationalist spirit: 'Go to this honest Papist, or to these innocent cannibals, ye Independent churches, to learn civility, humanity, simplicity of heart; yea, charity and Christianity.'[88] He goes further down the road of toleration than Milton in *Areopagitica*, then; Catholics as well as Brownists (separatists from the Church of England). His first published pamphlet in favour of toleration (1641) was issued with two titles: *The Humble Petition of the Brownists* and *A New Petition of the Papists*; the body of the text is the same. He is prepared to believe the best of anyone, good practice for a Christian, though an inevitable prelude to political disappointment. From *The Humble Petition* to his most famous text in defence of liberty of conscience, *The Compassionate Samaritan*, the note is the same:

> There is no man that professeth a religion, but is in
> conscience persuaded that to be the best wherein to save his
> soul . . . his judgement is convinced, and therefore holds it
> unreasonable, to be forced to follow other men's judgements
> and not his own in a matter of so great importance as that of
> his salvation is, which is the only mark his tender soul aims
> at in his religion, and for which he reads the Word daily, and
> hourly sucking from thence sweet and holy doctrines as bees
> do honey from sweet flowers in the Spring time.[89]

After the collapse of the Leveller movement in 1649 Walwyn was arrested and remained silent, apart from a brief defence of the jury system. Later, he seems to have recognised the force of his own arguments against monopolies, and gave up being a merchant (which depended on monopoly conditions) for medicine. His rationality, charity and disprespect for tradition were all useful, and his last published works are popular medical treatises.

We do not know enough about Walwyn to suggest that canonisation would be appropriate; but his writings suggest that, for a model of plain prose, Christian rationality and tolerance in the mid-century, one might look to Walwyn before the rational but coercive disciples of the Great Tew circle like Clarendon, Hammond and Chillingworth.[90]

The Levellers were by no means the most radical. The title of *The True Levellers Standard Advanced* (1649), signed by Gerrard Winstanley and fourteen others, lays down a challenge, and goes further than the Leveller programme in the desire for common ownership of land. It is the manifesto for a community 'beginning to plant and manure the waste land upon George Hill' in Surrey. It begins by reworking Genesis: 'In the beginning of time, the great creator Reason made the earth to be a common treasury.'[91] Reason rather than God, the logos of John's Gospel perhaps; and a stress on the inwardness of the self, and of nature. The Fall is to neglect this inward light and start looking for teachers and rulers; covetousness and 'selfish imagination' together kill the spirit and bring man into bondage, 'and that earth, that is within this creation made a common storehouse for all, is bought and sold and kept in the hands of a few'.[92]

This inaugurates a number of themes and strategies in Winstanley's writing. It is private property that is the curse; inward illumination has to be pursued into outward, material freedom; the great biblical themes have to be reinterpreted, re-allegorised into a message resonant with the language of the Old Testament prophets. Nor is the spirit of prophecy just a work of reinterpretation; Winstanley adds prophetic voices from a trance to his Biblical texts. Most of the Digger tracts are addressed to the perceived oppressors – Lords of Manors, the Army and Parliament.

In political terms, Winstanley's ideas are also expressed in terms of opposition to the Norman Yoke, the laws of prerogative and property which he dated from the Conquest and linked with the Fall.[93] In the later work, *The Law of Freedom in a Platform* (1652), a detailed utopian programme written after the Diggers had been forcibly dispersed in 1650, he proposes a system of government that may look hierarchical, but at every stage it challenges current assumptions.[94] Economic security, whether of the younger son unable to inherit, or for anyone in need, is the first requisite. The main insurance against tyranny and bureaucracy is, by contrast, insecurity of tenure. There are numerous advanced ideas, like practical education; as well as regressive ones, like a system of temporary slavery. It does not have the millenarian confidence of the earlier declarations, but Winstanley had not lost his ideals, even if he had lost his prophetic tone. There is nothing quite as impressive as the wonderful directness of the opening of *A Declaration from the Poor Oppressed People of England* (1649):

> We whose names are subscribed do in the name of all the
> poor oppressed people in England declare unto you that call
> yourselves lords of manors and lords of the land that in
> regard the King of righteousness, our maker, hath
> enlightened our hearts so far as to see that the earth was not
> made purposely for you to be lords of it, and we to be your
> slaves, servants and beggars; but it was made to be a
> common livelihood to all, without respect of persons.[95]

Winstanley's theological ideas are best seen in *Fire in the Bush* (1650), a series of interpretations of elements from the Garden of Eden story. In his dramatisation of the two trees in the garden, for example, he envisions the world shot through with the presence of God, not so much pantheism as a tissue of analogies, images and messages. This links him less with the rational Levellers than with a range of radical religous writers, some of them loosely called Ranters or Seekers, voicing their sense of an inner light, a world and a Bible freed from the restraints of institutionalised interpretation.[96] At the time they were shocking; many of them found a home later in the Quakers, who shared their commitment to an inner light.

Abiezer Coppe (1619–72) will have to stand for them all; a prophetic voice soaked in the language of the Bible, so much so that his writing becomes a cento of biblical texts, who at one time seems to be speaking in code for the adepts, at another is unmistakably direct. His *Fiery Flying Roll* (1650) was condemned as blasphemous, and he was accused of sensational misdeeds. One suspects, with Richard Baxter, that it was his communism that people really disliked; he was another prophetic Leveller:

> Thus saith the Lord: Be wise now therefore, O ye rulers, &c.
> Be instructed, &c. Kiss the sun, &c. Yea, kiss beggars,
> prisoners, warm them, feed them, clothe them, money
> them, relieve them, release them, take them into your
> houses, don't serve them as dogs, without door, &c . . . .
>   Once more, I say, own them; they are your self, make
> them one with you, or else go howling into hell; howl for
> the miseries that are coming upon you, howl.
>   The very shadow of levelling, sword-levelling, man-
> levelling, frighted you, (and who, like your selves, can
> blame you, because it shook your kingdom?) but now the
> substantiality of levelling is coming.
>   The eternal God, the mighty Leveller is coming, yea
> come, even at the door; and what will you do in that day.[97]

The appeal is no longer to reason; he has appropriated the *persona* of Ezekiel, along with some of the more testing commands of the Gospels, and the expectation of an imminent Last Judgement which was widespread. Coppe is more radically antinomian than Walwyn, or even Winstanley, but his ethic of liberty from sin is no more the self-indulgence of the anti-Ranter propaganda than Fox's. Perhaps his language of 'male and female . . . all one in Christ' might have been misconstrued as indifference to sexual sin; more likely, 'I had as live hear a daughter, as a son prophesy', which follows it, would have worried the opponents of women preachers and prophets.[98]

True prophets are felt as threats; women prophets compound feelings of threat in all sorts of half-acknowledged ways. The Fifth Monarchist Anna Trapnel is a good example of a visionary who reported, and interpreted, her dreams as if they had the same authority as Joseph's in Genesis (e.g., *The Cry of a Stone*, 1654); this proves doubly unsettling when she has a command of law-court argument and quoting proof-texts at her accusers as well (*Anna Trapenel's Report and Plea*, also 1654).

The Authorised Version, then, spawned some very unauthorised thoughts. To what extent it generated, or simply provided a language for spiritual experience is impossible to say. What does seem clear is that the popular voice of dissent in the mid-century is biblical, and that produces not only a feeling of authority and justice in the face of repression, but also a flexible, readily learnable and impressive language which had nothing to do with Renaissance Latinity.

Notes

1. See, most recently, Conrad Russell, *The Causes of the English Civil War* (Oxford, 1990), Chs 3–5.

2. Cromwell to Colonel Valentine Walton, 5 July 1644, in W.C. Abbott (ed.), *Writings and Speeches of Oliver Cromwell* (Cambridge Mass., 1937), I, p. 287.

3. *The Causes of the English Civil War*, p. 58; Brownists wanted separation from the Church of England; Anabaptists was a general term applied, more strictly, to those who espoused believer's baptism; atheists was a still more general term of abuse for heterodoxy.

4. The 'Book of Discipline', published in 1644 as *Directory of Church Government*, but in circulation from c. 1587, attributed to Cartwright, but probably by Walter Travers, provides the best contemporary summary of Presbyterian

church government. See the reprint in *The Reformation of the Church*, ed. Iain Murray (1965).

5. *The Marprelate Tracts [1588–9]*, facsimile (Leeds, 1969). [The Epistle], p. 1.

6. [The Epistle], pp. 1–2.

7. *Hay Any Worke for Cooper* (1589), p. 30, in *Marprelate Tracts*.

8. J. Dover Wilson, 'The Marprelate Controversy', *Cambridge History of English Literature*, ed. A.W. Ward and A.R. Waller (1932), III, 374–98. Still one of the best introductions to the controversy.

9. Raymond A. Anselment, *Betwixt Jest and Earnest: Marprelate, Milton, Swift and the Decorum of Religious Ridicule*, (Toronto, 1979), pp. 49, 51.

10. *The Protestatyon*, pp. 13 and 3, in *Marprelate Tracts*.

11. Leland H. Carlson, *Martin Marprelate, Gentleman: Master Job Throkmorton Laid Open in his Colours* (San Marino, 1981).

12. The notion of the 'author' is under question, admittedly, in essays like Roland Barthes's 'The Death of the Author', in *The Rustle of Language*, trans. Richard Howard (Oxford, 1986).

13. Christopher Hill, 'From Marprelate to the Levellers', *Collected Essays*, I (Brighton, 1985), p. 77.

14. Thomas Nashe, 'An Almond for a Parrat' in *Works*, III, p. 347.

15. For a full account see *The Folger Library Edition of the Works of Richard Hooker*, ed. W. Speed Hill (1977–); Vol. III, ed. P.G. Stanwood (1981) contains Books VI–VIII.

16. J.W. Allen, *A History of Political Thought in the Sixteenth Century* (1928), p. 184.

17. See, e.g., Hugh Trevor-Roper, *Catholics, Anglicans and Puritans* (London, 1989), pp. 45, 191.

18. Robert Eccleshall, *Order and Reason in Politics* (Oxford, 1978), p. 126.

19. Richard Hooker, *Of the Laws of Ecclesiastical Polity, Preface and Books I and VIII*, ed. Arthur Stephen McGrade (Cambridge, 1989), p. 43.

20. Ibid., p. 32.

21. Ibid., p. 60.

22. Ibid., p. 89.

23. W.D.J. Cargill Thompson, 'The Philosopher of the "Politic Society": Richard Hooker as a Political Thinker' in *Studies in Richard Hooker*, ed. W. Speed Hill (Cleveland, 1972), pp. 41, 47.

24. See Peter Lake, *Anglicans and Puritans?* (1988) for a persuasive account of Hooker's originality in this and other respects.

25. George Edelen, 'Hooker's Style', *Studies in Richard Hooker*, p. 244.

26. McGrade, p. 127.

27. Max Weber, *The Protestant Ethic and the Spirit of Capitalism*, trans. Talcott Parsons (1930) Ch. 3; for the Puritan religious use see, e.g., William Perkins, *The Golden Chaine*; for the Puritan secular use, Richard Steele, *The Tradesman's Calling*, although late, is important as a key text in R.H. Tawney, *Religion and*

the Rise of Capitalism, which applies Weber's ideas to England. Bunyan uses 'calling' in the secular sense (e.g., p. 37), the summons to conversion (p. 24) and the call to the ministry (p. 82) in *Grace Abounding*.

28. Compare, e.g., *Paradise Lost*, I. 12–16 with VII. 12–20.

29. *Selected Prose*, ed. C.A. Patrides (Harmondsworth, 1974), pp. 53–4.

30. Turner, 'The Poetics of engagement' in David Loewenstein and James Grantham Turner (eds), *Politics, Poetics and Hermeneutics in Milton's Prose* (Cambridge, 1990), pp. 257–75.

31. A summary guide to these kinds of appropriations of what was felt to be Milton's politics may be found in Stevie Davies, *Images of Kingship in 'Paradise Lost'* (Columbia, Missouri, 1983), pp. 3–4.

32. For rhetoric and liberty in Renaissance Italy see Quentin Skinner, *The Foundations of Modern Political Thought* (Cambridge, 1978), I, pp. 41–8; for the Reformation generally as well as Milton, see Joseph Antony Wittreich, ' "The Crown of Eloquence": The Figure of the Orator in Milton's Prose Works' in Michael Lieb and John T. Shawcross (eds), *Achievements of the Left Hand: Essays on the Prose of John Milton* (Amherst, 1974) and James Egan, *The Inward Teacher: Milton's Rhetoric of Christian Liberty* (Pennsylvania, 1980).

33. *An Apology against a Pamphlet*, in *Collected Prose Works*, ed. Don M. Wolfe (New Haven, 1953–82) I, pp. 899–900. Hence abbreviated as *CPW*.

34. Kevin Sharpe, *Politics and Ideas in Early Stuart England* (1989), pp. 123–8.

35. See H.R. Trevor-Roper, *Archbishop Laud* (2nd edn London, 1965), pp. 435–6; and Ch. 2 of his *Catholics, Anglicans and Puritans* (London, 1987). The final chapter of this latter, 'Milton in Politics' is a swingeing attack on Milton, which forms an interesting contrast to more recently pro-revolutionary accounts of Milton; though, like Laud's career, its intemperance does scant justice to its supposedly Erasmian, tolerant premises.

36. *CPW*, 1, p. 556.

37. *CPW*, 1, p. 592.

38. *CPW*, 1, p. 588; and see the discussion in C. Hill, *Milton and the English Revolution* (1977), p. 80.

39. Stanley Fish, 'Wanting a supplement: the question of interpretation in Milton's early prose', in Loewenstein and Turner; see especially p. 52.

40. *CPW*, 1, p. 662; see also the defence in Ch. 7 of Joan Webber, *The Eloquent 'I'*.

41. Thomas Kranidas, 'Style and Rectitude in Seventeenth-Century Prose', *Huntington Library Quarterly*, 46 (1983), 237–69.

42. *CPW*, 1, p. 723.

43. *CPW*, 1, p. 949.

44. *CPW*, 1, p. 753.

45. *CPW*, 1, p. 808.

46. *CPW*, 1, p. 823.

47. *CPW*, 1, p. 824.

48. *CPW*, 1, p. 908.

49. *CPW*, 1, pp. 932–3.

50. *CPW*, 1, p. 952.

51. *CPW*, 2, pp. 229–30.

52. The point about desertion is made by W.R. Parker, *Milton: A Biography*, I, p. 240; the narrative is adapted from this source, though Hill, *Milton*, pp. 121–3, is more suspicious of the Powells.

53. *CPW*, 2, p. 333. The earliest usages of 'literalist' and 'literalism', according to *OED*, are in this tract.

54. *CPW*, 2, p. 235.

55. John Halkett, *Milton and the Idea of Matrimony* (New Haven, 1970); William and Mary Haller, 'The Puritan Art of Love', *HLQ*, 5 (1941–42), pp. 235–72. Mary Nyquist, 'The genesis of gendered subjectivity in the divorce tracts and *Paradise Lost*', in *Re–membering Milton*, ed. Nyquist and Margaret W. Ferguson (New York, 1987), pp. 99–127.

56. *CPW*, 2, pp. 235–6.

57. *CPW*, 2, p. 258

58. James Grantham Turner, *One Flesh: Paradisal Marriage and Sexual Relations in the Age of Milton* (Oxford, 1987), p. 209.

59. *CPW*, 2, p. 591.

60. See David Aers, Bob Hodge and Gunther Kress, *Literature, Language and Society in England 1580–1680*, p. 130.

61. *CPW*, 2, pp. 486, 508; and see Joseph Antony Wittreich, Jr, 'Milton's *Areopagitica*: Its Isocratic and Ironic Contexts', *Milton Studies* 4 (1972), 101–15.

62. John Illo, 'The Misreading of Milton', in *Radical Perspectives in the Arts*, ed. Lee Baxandall (Harmondsworth, 1972), pp. 178–92; Abbe Blum, 'The author's authority: *Areopagitica* and the labour of licensing', in *Re–membering Milton*, pp. 74–96, discusses the relation between *Areopagitica* and Milton's censoring activities.

63. Williams is most easily available in the extracts in *Puritanism and Liberty*, ed. A.S.P. Woodhouse (3rd edn 1986), pp. 266–92; see William Haller, *Liberty and Reformation in the Puritan Revolution* (New York, 1955), Ch. 5, and Edmund S. Morgan, *Roger Williams: The Church and the State* (1967). See also the remarks about toleration attributed to Walwyn, in particular.

64. The point about the epigraph can be seen by looking at the passage in context in *The Suppliants*; the more general point about Euripides being seen as a radical writer in the 1640s I owe to David Norbrook, in a paper delivered to the London Renaissance Seminar, July 1990.

65. *CPW*, 2, p. 492.

66. For a text of the Order see *CPW*, 2, pp. 797–9.

67. *CPW*, 2, p. 502.

68. *CPW*, 2, p. 554.

69. The general point is made, e.g., in Michael Walzer, *The Revolution of the Saints*.

70. *CPW*, 2, p. 561.

71. *CPW*, 2, p. 565

72. *Selected Prose*, p. 72.

73. For more detail, see Barbara K. Lewalski, 'Milton: Political Beliefs and Polemical Methods, 1659–60', *PMLA*, 74 (1959), 191–202.

74. Thomas N. Corns, *The Development of Milton's Prose Style* (Oxford, 1982), p. 102.

75. *CPW*, 7, p. 427; for the links with the jeremiad, see Laura Lunger Knoppers in Loewenstein and Turner, pp. 213–25.

76. *CPW*, 7, p. 463.

77. The best guide to these movements is undoubtedly Christopher Hill, *The World Turned Upside Down* (1972; repr. 1984). Joseph Frank, *The Levellers* (Cambridge, Mass. 1955) is still valuable, and Leveller ideas are important in C.B. Macpherson, *The Political Theory of Possessive Individualism* (Oxford, 1962). For the Ranters, Ch. 5 of J.F. McGregor and B. Reay (ed.) *Radical Religion in the English Revolution* (Oxford, 1984) is best, along with the introduction to *A Collection of Ranter Writings from the 17th century*, ed. Nigel Smith (1983) though some of the objections in J.C. Davis, *Fear, Myth and History: The Ranters and the Historians* (Cambridge, 1986), have some force. For the Diggers, see Hill, Aylmer in *Radical Religion in the English Revolution*, and the recent Bibliography in Gerrard Winstanley, *Selected Writings*, ed. Andrew Hopton (1989), pp. 116–17.

78. *Englands Birth Right Justified* (1645), p. 11; facsimile in *Tracts on Liberty in the Puritan Revolution*, ed. William Haller (New York, 1965), III.

79. See the discussion of *The Christian Mans Triall* (1638 and 1641) in Thomas N. Corns, 'The Freedom of Reader-response', *Freedom and the English Revolution*, ed. R.C. Richardson and G.M. Ridden (Manchester, 1986), especially pp. 104–8.

80. Extracts in *Divine Right and Democracy*, ed. David Wootton (1986), p. 147.

81. Richard Overton, *An Arrow against all Tyrants*, facsimile (Exeter, 1976), p. 3.

82. Richard Tuck, *Natural Rights Theories* (Cambridge, 1979); he identifies Henry Parker's *Observations* (1642) as the key text, though Parker's Erastianism is very different to Leveller toleration.

83. Margot Heinemann, *Puritanism and Theatre* (Cambridge, 1980), Ch. 13, 'From Popular Drama to Leveller Style'.

84. See Nigel Smith, 'Richard Overton's Marpriest Tracts', *Prose Studies*, 9: 2 (1986), 39–66.

85. Richard Overton, *The Araignment of Persecution* (1645), p. 24; facsimile in *Tracts on Liberty in the Puritan Revolution*, ed. William Haller (New York, 1965), III.

86. *The Writings of William Walwyn*, ed. Jack R. McMichael and Barbara Taft (Athens, Georgia 1989), p. 182.

87. The phrase is T.B. Tomlinson's, in 'Seventeenth-Century Political Prose: William Walwyn', *Critical Review*, 29 (1989), 25–41.

88. *The Writings of William Walwyn*, p. 400.

89. *The Writings of William Walwyn*, p. 57.

90. For Clarendon and Great Tew, see Part I, section 3, above; the values of the Great Tew circle are celebrated in Ch. 4 of L.C. Knights, *Public Voices: Literature and Politics with special reference to the Seventeenth Century* (1971) and Ch. 4 of Hugh Trevor–Roper, *Catholics, Anglicans and Puritans* (1987).

91. Winstanley, *The Law of Freedom and Other Writings*, ed. Christopher Hill (Harmondsworth, 1973), p. 73.

92. Winstanley, *Writings*, p. 78.

93. *The World Turned Upside Down*, p. 145; and see Hill's extended essay on the topic in *Puritanism and Revolution* (1958), Ch. 3.

94. See the discussion in J.C. Davis, *Utopia and the Ideal Society* (Cambridge, 1981), Ch. 7.

95. Winstanley, *Writings*, p. 99.

96. The best description of this world is Nigel Smith, *Perfection Proclaimed: Language and Literature in English Radical Religon 1640–1660* (Oxford, 1989). Ch. 6 is particularly useful in its comparisons of Winstanley with Salmon, Coppe and Clarkson.

97. Abiezer Coppe, *A Fiery Flying Roll*, in *Selected Writings*, ed. Andew Hopton (1987), p. 25.

98. Coppe, *Some Sweet Sips of Some Spiritual Wine* (1649) in *A Collection of Ranter Writings*, p. 66. For women prophets as a threat, see Christine Berg and Philippa Berry ' "Spiritual Whoredom": An Essay on Female Prophets in the Seventeenth Century' in *1642: Literature and Power in the Seventeenth Century*, ed. Francis Barker et al. (Essex, 1981), pp. 37–54; see also Elaine Hobby, *Virtue of Necessity* on women prophets. 'I had as live' means 'I had rather'.

Part Three
Essays and Cornucopian Texts

Chapter 10
The Essay

Etymology is often a dangerous road to definition, but somewhere between the French *'essai'*, an attempt, and the English 'assay', analysis, lies the nature of the essay. The term comes from the French; Montaigne was the first to use it in his *Essais* (1580). In England, Bacon's *Essays*, first published in 1597, inaugurated the use of the term, though both of them thought the idea of the essay was ancient. Bacon suggested that Seneca's *Epistles* were in fact essays; Montaigne, though rightly more assertive of his originality, finds a similar interest in Cicero's letters to Atticus, as well as referring constantly to Seneca. Two of his essays are couched as letters,[1] but do not stand out significantly from the others as a result.

A more significant clue to the nature of this new form is in the publishing history of Montaigne's and Bacon's essays. Montaigne's 1580 *Essais* were followed by a slightly revised 1582 edition, a much augmented 1588 edition, and a posthumous 1595 edition, with no new essays but much authorial revision.[2] Bacon's *Essays* were substantially augmented and revised in 1612 and 1625, and there is an intermediate manuscript stage as well, between 1607 and 1612. This kind of publishing history is not unique among Renaissance texts, but in both these cases it points to the authors' strong sense of the provisional in what they wrote. If the 'essay' on a subject could be attempted once, it could, even ought, to be attempted again. Even the most ringing, aphoristic, complete-sounding statement could be restated – or, indeed, worked for, arrived at, over a process of thinking and writing that could take years. It was not until the eighteenth century that the periodical essay redefined this quality in another way, as ephemeral, or provisional, because of the nature of publication. Then, perhaps, the subject might be returned to in another issue, or the essay revised for a more permanent life in a book. The essay should be seen as a function of publishing conditions as well as a new attitude to knowledge.

The essay is also characterised as a personal statement. Before it becomes institutionalised in the periodical, as a channel for private opinion to mould public opinion, it can be seen as an alternative among the new literary forms of confession.[3] The essay is inflected by the nature of educated conversation and letter-writing, much as the spiritual autobiographies of the seventeenth century are inflected by the discourse of public testimony in the Nonconformist sects. It inhabits that half-way house between the spontaneous and the finished. The essayist writes so as to approximate to conversation, but with the finish of the written, the printed – speaking from the desk, as it were. Again, this is not a unique feature among Renaissance texts, but a defining rather than an incidental characteristic.

Thirdly, the early essay is bookish. In his essays in particular, Bacon is concerned with the wisdom of the classics and the Bible, sifting, quoting, summarising. Montaigne is self-deprecating about his education – 'a smack of every thing in general, but nothing in particular' – though the great Scottish poet and political writer Buchanan was one of his tutors. Yet only a few lines later he writes of his constant debt to Plutarch and Seneca, his study of history and his delight in poetry.[4] If the experience of reading Bacon and Montaigne is of listening to a personal point of view, it is a personality interwoven with the voices of past masters.

Florio's Montaigne

In 1603 John Florio, a naturalised Italian who had worked for the French Embassy, translated the *Essays* of Michel, Sieur de Montaigne (1533–92) into English. His translation gives me the pretext for dealing with the work in the context of English prose. It was influential on more than the English essay genre – Shakespeare, we know, drew on it directly for *The Tempest*, and seems to have found its viewpoint generally congenial (Florio apparently borrows a phrase or two from Shakespeare, too).[5] Most discussions of the essay form seem to need both Montaigne and Bacon as the originals, as expressions of two tendencies; as Alexander Smith put it in the last century: 'Bacon is the greatest of the serious and stately essayists – Montaigne the greatest of the garrulous and communicative.'[6] Such polarities need to be treated with reserve, but there is no doubt that Montaigne is more openly personal, at a time when the importance of the individual, particularly the private, retired, individual, might still be assumed to have little claim on the attention. To press one more polarity: the plainness of Bacon, much admired by Ben Jonson and others since, is a plainness of style, stripped of ornamental accretions. In 'The Author to the Reader'

Montaigne also aspires to plainness, but it is the openness of his self more than the clarity of his precepts that he hopes to reveal: 'I desire therein to be delineated in mine own genuine, simple and ordinary fashion, without contention, art or study; for it is my self I portray.'[7] Yet he feels the need to apologise: 'my self am the groundwork of my book: it is then no reason thou shouldest employ thy time about so frivolous and vain a subject.'

This is a translated self, though. For a start, it is Florio's Montaigne. Florio, whose father had come to England to escape persecution for his Protestant principles, shared many of his views, which occasionally colour Montaigne's own rather different ones: for example, 'les erreurs de Wiclef' become 'Wyclif's opinions'.[8] Florio is less than Puritanical in his style, however, and often doubles the size of Montaigne's sentences by adding synonyms and parallel phrases, often to a Euphuistic effect which is quite different from Montaigne's often spare and restrained French. Despite this, Florio is not incapable of rendering short sentences epigrammatically. A whole series of them in 'That to Philosophy [sic] is to Learne How to Die' is not entirely free of doubling synonyms, but shows how he is responsive to a stylistic feature which is important to the content: short sentences about the shortness of life: 'Nothing can be grievous that is but once. Is it reason so long to fear a thing of so short time? Long life or short life is made all one by death.'[9]

On the evidence of some random sampling, it also appears that Florio embellished less the deeper he got into the text. Perhaps the earlier, more laconic essays of Book I in particular seemed to him to need expansion. The essays in Book III, often extended, and referring back to topics raised earlier, get a more literal, almost crib-like treatment, except where Montaigne cites a proverb. At this point, Florio, with his encyclopaedic knowledge of English proverbs, will supply an equivalent of similar meaning rather than a translation. 'Ill may the Kill call the Oven burnt Tail'[10] may raise the suspicion of translationese in modern readers used to the pot calling the kettle black, but that was the Elizabethan version that Florio had collected. At other times he is a little like Tyndale, responding to the foreignness of his text by deliberately coining new words or adapting older ones like 'conscientious', 'endear', 'tarnish' and 'facilitate'. In the earlier *First Fruites* (1578), an Italian–English textbook, he had scorned English as a language of multiple origins, 'a language confused, bepeesed [pieced together, or something ruder?] with many tongues'; for his Montaigne he decided to exploit the feature. There are some mistakes – 'poison' for 'poisson' is a classic howler – but equally, there are particular renderings that impress contemporary Montaigne scholars more than some more consistently reliable modern translations.[11]

Secondly, as is already apparent, the voice of Montaigne is interwoven with those of many others. Florio almost doubled this effect by getting Matthew Gwynne to help him with translating the poetry quotations – though this leaves to one side the allusions and paraphrases that scholars have discovered over the years. For Montaigne himself, it is an important issue. He writes surrounded by books, but is uneasy about his debt to them, as though it's cheating, the kind of empty scholarship he hates:

> I am ever here and there picking and culling, from this and
> that book, the sentences that please me, not to keep them
> (for I have no storehouse to reserve them in) but to transport
> them into this: where to say truth, they are no more mine,
> than in their first place: we are (in mine opinion) never wise,
> but by present learning, not by that which is past, and as
> little as that which is to come . . . . We can talk and prate,
> Cicero said thus, these are Plato's customs, these are the very
> words of Aristotle; but what say we ourselves? What do we?
> What judge we?[12]

As R.A. Sayce has pointed out, part of this could be just aristocratic disdain of being shown to be working too hard, or looking too learned. It might even be an aspect of Montaigne's originality, that he should be worried about originality in a literary culture which revered the past as a textual and conceptual quarry. It is sometimes a problem of reliability, or truth. In the essay 'Of Cannibals', which prizes those recently discovered societies which seem to be more under the law of nature than his own, he makes a great deal of the simplicity of witnesses as a guide to their reliability. However, the nature–art dichotomy is never stable, in the Romantic version of the inevitable superiority of nature; the Renaissance version, that an image of art is often needed to encapsulate nature, and a borrowed one at that, is more like it. He advises in a later essay, 'Of Physiognomy': 'If you know not how to die, take no care for it, Nature her self will fully and sufficiently teach you in the nick, she will exactly discharge that work for you; trouble not yourself with it.'[13] Yet he follows that advice with a supporting quotation from Catullus, and later with the death speech of Socrates, as an example of the 'natural' approach to death. Natural men can be found in the new French colonies, or even among the workers in Montaigne's own fields; but anecdotes about them seem to need buttressing with the exemplary man of classical learning. Even then, there is uncertainty, whether the reports of him are authentic. All the time, then, Montaigne seems to be worrying at dichotomies, between art or civilisation and nature, lived experience and bookish experience, certainty and doubt, which turn out not to be mutually exclusive. Rather (to use the word in its modern critical sense) they need to be negotiated and renegotiated. For example, Montaigne cannot simply 'assay' his art by nature, because that assaying process has to be done through the medium of art.

Right in the middle of the *Essays* comes an extended (200 pages in my edition) piece, 'An Apology of Raymond Sebond', which brings the debate about truth to a philosophical and religious crisis. It is a response to a fifteenth-century Latin work owned by his father: the *Theologia Naturalis*. It is odd to call it an 'apology' (i.e., defence), in that he appears to come to the opposite, sceptical conclusion to Sebond's defence of the rationality of Christian faith. It would also seem that the essay is more than just a response to Sebond; Montaigne had earlier read the second-century sceptic Sextus Empiricus, and had some of his precepts engraved on the beams of his study. Because, subsequently, both Christians and atheists in France have claimed this essay as support for their own position, it is important to remember that in this period scepticism was not opposed to belief. It called into question the status of the arguments meant to lead to faith. Instead, one had to believe to make the reasons valid, and then they would only function as secondary reinforcements of faith (the position is sometimes called fideism). This Pyrrhonian scepticism holds that there is insufficient knowledge to determine if knowledge (except what derives from basic sense data) is possible, so we must suspend judgement on such matters, and live undogmatically.[14] Such scepticism, though ancient in origin, had particular force at the time. The Reformation movement urged people to make faith their own, not to assume it as natural inheritance; humanism involved a critical, if still reverent, approach to ancient wisdom; and the new discoveries had accentuated a recognition, already present in Montaigne's beloved Pliny and Plutarch, that values, laws and customs were often culture-specific. Montaigne had seen wars of religion in his own country; his father was Catholic, his mother a Protestant converted from Judaism. The result is not a cool philosophic treatise. The 'Apology' is a miscellany of stories and arguments, driven by the sense that rational activity is arrogant and futile before the serious business of being wise and living well. At more than one stage it becomes a welter of stories of intelligent and sociable elephants, logical dogs and other animals which give the lie to man's claim to unique rationality and domination over nature. Why so many? There is the 'tortured' argument, that Montaigne wanted to hammer away until every corner of rational activity was brought into question; but it needs to be tempered by the recognition that Montaigne's crisis came in the midst of his books, and he worked it out through his books: there is an almost saving fascination with accumulating more elephant stories or whatever. There is a similar mixture of tensions and quirks in his religious discussion. He confesses his ignorance of scripture, and most of the argument about God and first causes is carried on in a fairly Aristotelian, scholastic fashion. Then, almost immediately after the disclaimer, comes the most concentrated series of quotations from Scripture in the whole of the *Essays*. It remains true that Plato on religion is used with equal, if not greater, prominence in those pages; but he, too, is adduced to the general point that knowledge is a disadvantage in belief and right living. The ancient voices are counselling caution in the most basic of theological assertions. This in turn links with Montaigne's constant preoccupation with the desirability of the state of nature in other civilisations, or individuals:

> Incivility, ignorance, simplicity and rudeness, are commonly joined with innocency; curiosity, subtlety, and knowledge, are ever followed with malice: humility, fear, obedience and honesty (which are the principal instruments for the preservation of human society) require a single docile soul and which presumeth little of her self: Christians have a peculiar knowledge, how curiosity is in a man a natural, and original infirmity.[15]

The destructive arguments and examples, then, still function in a broadly humanist direction. In another kind of Christian story, that of Luther or Bunyan, say, this kind of crisis would be a prelude to conversion to God, of the transcendent power of grace resolving the human dilemma; for Montaigne, the uncertainties lead him not so much beyond man as back to him. If there is a pattern akin to conversion, it is a secular one, of finding the self.[16]

In the end that self will be found amongst books and in his books. The essays are not yet critical essays in the modern literary sense, but the seeds are there in that special mode of 'internal commentary', as André Tournon puts it – even if he sees that as coming from Montaigne's experience with juridical commentary while he was still in the courts of Bordeaux, rather than from literary models.[17] The mode is questioning, eclectic, ultimately coming back to the self as arbitrator, though even that is not finally fixed or authoritative. As a mode of autobiography it seems limited to us, who are used to circumstantial detail to the point of prurience. We hear nothing of his wife or children; his friend La Boétie and his father, both dead, are the important personal reference points. Yet the idea of making the self the basis of such a discourse seemed audaciously original. It is still informed by the Renaissance belief that writing pleases in order to teach. The pronouns are a clue here, as he switches from first-person singular to first-person plural in asserting the changeability of mankind. Received ideas and discourses break against his personal experience or scepticism, and also against his age. The essays of the third book, written later and with a firmer though still discursive grasp of form, constantly refer to the inabilities of his aged body. 'Upon some verses of Vergil', which discusses why we speak of sex with shame when it is so natural and necessary, is a particularly poignant example, though it strenuously attempts to avoid self-pity. (Either Florio or Gwynne decided that some of the more risqué Latin verses should remain untranslated, which provides an odd counterpoint to Montaigne's theme.)

The essay also demonstrates another aspect of the originality of Montaigne, the way he can respond to texts, not just as precepts, but also as literature, in a critical fashion. In a comment on Lucretius he first points to the choice of words, and then takes off into a praise of good writing, with the strong Renaissance conviction that to write well is to think well. Like English writers of the same period, he remains anxious about the abilities of his native tongue against Latin – 'It commonly faileth and shrinketh under a pithy and powerful conception.'[18] Even when speaking of himself in his own book he is self-deprecatory; is it Montaigne we are seeing, or the last book he read, or the last strong impression that another person made on him? 'Speak I not so everywhere? Do I not lively display myself? That sufficeth: I have my will: all the world may know me by my book, and my book by me: but I am of an apish and imitating condition.'[19] We now know, wrote Roland Barthes in 'The Death of the Author':

> . . . that a text consists not of a line of words, releasing a
> single 'theological' meaning (the 'message' of the
> Author–God), but of a multi-dimensional space in which are
> married and contested several writings, none of which are
> original; the text is a fabric of quotations, resulting from a
> thousand sources of culture . . . [the writer's] sole power is
> to mingle writings, to counter some by others, so as never to
> rely on just one; if he seeks to *express himself*, at least he
> knows that the interior 'thing' he claims to 'translate' is itself
> no more than a ready-made lexicon, whose words can only
> be explained through other words . . . .[20]

Montaigne knew that, before Bouvard and Pecuchet, or Mallarmé. But he was more worried than them by its implications, and rightly so.

The essays of Francis Bacon

The modern reader in an academic library is most likely to pick up the first edition of Bacon's *Essays* (1597) in a small, slim, facsimile edition that contrasts markedly with the plumpness of Montaigne. Even the much expanded and extended essays of 1625 rarely stray above a couple of pages in length. There is a tightness of argument and a conciseness of sentence structure which demand an intellectual attentiveness comparable to poetry. Their opening sentences recall the opening lines of some of Donne's *Songs and Sonets* in their arresting clarity – 'What is truth, said jesting Pilate, and would not stay for an answer'; 'Men fear death as children fear to go into the dark'; 'Revenge is a kind of wild justice' – and I've missed only one out of the first four.[21] But once the comparison is made, the difference with Donne's dramatised egotism is manifest. The first-person singular, when it does make an appearance, is there to define terms rather than confide: 'I take goodness in this sense, the affecting of the weal of men.'[22] The opening of 'Of Atheism' is so unusual in offering a personal preference that one is led to suspect a particular warmth (or anxiety) in what follows: 'I had rather believe all the fables in the Legend, and the Talmud, and the Alcoran, than that this universal frame is without a maker.'[23] Bacon is so often the observer, arbitrator, rephraser and summer-up, that the intrusion is like the impartial judge suddenly revealing his prejudices at the end of the trial. The difference between this and a modern example which might cause a flutter in the newspapers is that this reinforces our sense of Bacon's judiciousness rather than raising questions about the selection of judges. Don't trust this man's engaging personality, trust his mind. It isn't going to be taken in by widely believed fictions.

Bacon was a lawyer, of course, so I've been cheating a bit. His essay idiom is the product of training for and in the law courts, but then so was the writing of half the intelligentsia of London. They hadn't all been Solicitor-General, Attorney-General and Lord Chancellor, though or, indeed, sacked on dubious charges of bribery. The alternative title to the *Essays*, 'Counsels, Civil and Moral', may be revealing here; this is the voice of the distinguished lawyer overlaid with the Renaissance mode of the scholar offering advice to princes, and anyone else who will listen, even if his merit has not been sufficiently appreciated. The essay 'Of Counsel' (which first appeared in 1612, after Bacon was on the political ladder) shows how seriously he took such a role, and how seriously he wished monarchs would:

> The greatest trust between man and man is the trust of
> giving counsel. For in other confidences men commit the

> parts of life; their lands, their goods, their children, their
> credit, some particular affair: but to such as they make their
> counsellors they commit the whole; by how much more
> they are obliged to all faith and integrity. The wisest princes
> need not think it any diminution to their greatness or
> derogation to their sufficiency to rely upon counsel.[24]

The contrast with Montaigne in retirement is instructive; even out of office, Bacon regards the public rather than the private sphere as the place of most importance, the place where a man can be complete. 'Of Friendship', the only essay to be completely rewritten rather than expanded and adapted, is also symptomatic here; there is no La Boétie to anchor the discussion in the particular. As John C. Briggs argues, there is an uneasy oscillation between the sentimental and the utilitarian in the earlier version.[25] Even in 1625 friendship sounds more like a necessity than a delight, painful, though less painful than the lack of it, 'without which the world is but a wilderness'.[26]

What does Bacon count as evidence, then? In a later chapter we will look at his project for a new kind of scientific knowledge, where what counts, and what must be discounted as authoritative, is of pivotal importance. The *Essays* are not directly a part of this 'Great Instauration', but there is a great deal of mutual indebtedness, particularly as his ideas developed over the thirty years between the first and last versions.[27] What they have in common is a suspicion of received ideas, and a sense that knowledge will only be advanced if these are tested against experience. In Bacon's scientific programme this is to be done by direct attention to the phenomena of nature. In the *Essays* it is experience that counts, and the experience recorded by history in particular. Personal experience – the kind of evidence nowadays dismissed as anecdotal – is implied more often than stated. In 'Of Cunning' he mentions a secretary he knew 'that never came to Queen Elizabeth of England with bills to sign, but he would always first put her into some discourse of estate [i.e. state politics], that she mought [might] the less mind the bills'.[28] But such titbits are rare. They may reveal things that Bacon knew because he was close to the centre of power, but they are immediately directed back into advice on wielding power. In that environment the self-regarding man is a positive hindrance: 'men that are great lovers of themselves waste the public'.[29] The *Essays* are not so much records of experience as acts of investigation and persuasion, the result of digested experience. Bacon is interested in changing other people's minds, rather than revealing the inwardness of his own.

Where did these minds start from, in this period? From books, mostly, regarded and studied in a particular way. Bacon, like most of his educated contemporaries, was a great collector of commonplaces. These were self-evident truths found in the classics, Scripture, and subsequent authors ('authorities' might be a better description). There are two intellectual operations involved here, recognition and classification. Recognition is a kind of cumulative, almost institutional process, most significantly for Bacon's development in the legal profession, where a continuing process of case law ('common law') would confirm and adapt the principles encoded in legal maxims. In Bacon's first legal work, a *Discourse on the Commission of Bridewell* (1587), he argues: 'The Maxims are the foundations of the Law, and the full and perfect conclusions of reason.'[30] All Renaissance students of rhetoric, not just lawyers, would have their commonplace books organised by subject, to enrich their discourse, and to round out their education with authoritative advice. There were ready-made compilations, too, like Erasmus's *Parabolae sive Similiae* (1514), which Bacon raided for his own stockpile.[31] Bacon, in turn, published his own, and there are other works of his which are simply assemblies of aphorisms. This is the filing system side of classification; the organisation of these into a coherent argument is another skill. It is not simply a matter of building up an impressive range of authorities in neat, quotable fragments, though such a habit of reading for the quotable bits is bound to produce a practice of writing for the commonplace books as well as out of them.

However, Bacon's fondness for the aphorism is more than a feature of his education and habits of study; it is a key to understanding his position generally, and one of the best ways into the *Essays*. It places him very firmly in a Renaissance intellectual framework – excited by the potential of old texts to reveal politically and socially useful knowledge. Study is the best preparation for power. Coupled with that is a certain scepticism about the received wisdom when it is not tested against the realities of political experience; here he is very close to Machiavelli, especially the author of the *Discourses*, which might be read as an extended test of political axioms, based on Livy's history of Rome, but also driven by his own experience of more recent Italian history. The essay 'Of the True Greatness of Kingdoms and Estates' is deeply indebted to Machiavelli, and contains one of the few direct allusions to contemporary politics in the *Essays* in its discussion of sea-power.

Bacon takes this testing a stage further. Aphorisms are useful because they allow growth, in a way that systematic 'method' does not. In Book One of *The Advancement of Learning* he argues:

> . . . as young men, when they knit and shape perfectly, do
> seldom grow to a further stature; so knowledge, while it is

> in aphorisms and observations, it is in growth: but when it
> once is comprehended in exact methods, it may perchance be
> further polished and illustrate and accommodated for use and
> practice; but it increaseth no more in bulk and substance.[32]

It is important to remember that in the same work he also criticises the
Scholastics for taking one maxim at a time, out of the context of a
whole work. Bacon is not hostile to intellectual system-building, but is
suspicious of its tendency to close off areas of knowledge from all but
limited enquiry. However, in this extract we can see how Bacon could
make the aphorism into a principal feature of the essay mode; both
forms aim for definitive statement, while admitting their provisionality.

In the *Essays* themselves, both aphorisms and essays can be
rearranged or modified. Even the order is a part of it. In 1597, 'Of
Studies' is the first essay, and might serve as an introduction, with the
advice 'Read not to contradict, not to believe, but to weigh and
consider', and the emphasis on experience as the chief supplement to
the essential disciplines of book learning. Bacon was not a young man
in 1597, but he was still falling short of serious office, and so the
preparatory nature of study is appropriate. In 1625, when he had
experience of public office, the essays begin with 'Of Truth', and 'Of
Studies' is relegated to a later position. Truth is a more comprehensive
aim, but a harder one. Writing out of the experience of power in a
sequence which is increasingly concerned with the public, political and
social, Bacon stresses less the usefulness, or desirability of truth than
the near impossibility of finding it. As with many of the essays of
1625, we could gloss the title 'Of the extreme difficulty of finding
anything remotely resembling . . . , especially in public life'. As Stanley
Fish has warned us, even words like 'certainly' and 'surely' usually
need to be modified by the surrounding 'buts', or other devices which
undermine the high-flown generalisations.[33]

As with Bacon's larger schemes for the reformation of knowledge,
these acts of unseating plausible errors are intended to be useful. They
might aid the reader's political survival, for example, or tell him where
to build a country house. Advice to the well-placed, then, even the
princely; how to avoid disaster, more than how to be successful. If
Bacon had begun in 1612 rather than 1597 we might have seen an even
closer link with James I, who liked to be compared with Solomon, the
biblical master of proverbial wisdom as well as the famously judicious
resolver of disputes. As it is, we have to see these *Essays* as being rather
more on the margins. The death of Prince Henry meant that the 1612
Essays had to lose their royal dedication; the dedication to Buckingham
(then Lord High Admiral, and James's favourite) in 1625 mentions that
he had dedicated the *Instauratio* to James and the Natural History to

Prince Charles. Though he hopes that, in Latin at least, they may 'last as long as books last', there is an inescapable sense that these have to come second to the major project; or even worse, cherished but powerless, like contemporary columnists read more attentively by the general public than those they purport to advise. Perhaps this is unfair to Bacon; but he has such a strong sense of the pitfalls in political life, along with its importance, that we have to attend to such hints as dedications as much as his giving the last word to the essay 'Of Vicissitude of Things'. Certainly his desire to fix things in a short, pithy statement is only matched by his sense that fixing things should only, can only, be provisional.

Cowley and Temple

The Restoration preference for the conversational had all sorts of literary consequences, from the nature of comedy to the style of political controversy. In the essay it meant that the amplitude of Montaigne became the dominant manner more than the terseness of Bacon – oddly in a way, in view of the success of Bacon's scientific enterprise fifty years after he had propounded it. Doubly odd in the case of Abraham Cowley, our first example, who was a great supporter of the new science; in 1661 he published *A Proposition for the Advancement of Experimental Philosophy*, and the following year became one of the founder members of the Royal Society. It may be a matter of intellectual weight – it is not difficult to patronise Cowley as derivative, second-rate, etc. – and it may be a matter of temperament, too, of being content with a modest but comfortable retirement. *A Proposition* takes the Baconian case virtually for granted, and homes in on the practical details of establishing a scientific college – less fun than *The New Atlantis*, but someone has to discuss academic salaries on the road from Utopia to reality. But even the crispness of practical considerations is absent from the *Essays*. The opening sentence of the 1668 *Several Discourses by Way of Essays*, 'Of Liberty' is a definition. Coming to it after Bacon makes it seem very relaxed, though not slack: 'The Liberty of a people consists in being governed by Laws which they have made themselves, under whatsoever form it be of Government. The Liberty of a private man in being Master of his own time and actions, as far as may consist with the laws of God and his country.'[34] However, the real difference with Bacon is marked by the political vocabulary. 'Liberty' is not a significant part of his monarchical lexicon. Cowley had lived through the Civil War, an exile in Paris with the Court of the future Charles II where he was Secretary to Queen Henrietta Maria, and there was a brief though probably mistaken imprisonment after the Royalist uprising of 1655. However, he prefaced his 1656 *Poems* with an admission that the Royalist cause was dead; in 1661, his *Vision concerning his late Pretended Highness Cromwell, the Wicked*, a mixture of verse and prose, suggests either that he was following in the footsteps of other literary turncoats like Dryden, or that the original accommodation with republicanism was half-hearted. 'Liberty' may have been one of the keywords of the Good Old Cause, but for Cowley its most important meaning is the opportunity for a quiet life, away from 'the slavery of greatness'. Only the Roman civil wars get mentioned in the essay, but this needs little decoding. The old classical ideal of retirement (Cowley quotes Horace) had a special attraction after the English Civil War. It is a favourite Royalist mode in the Interregnum. For an old Royalist exile in 1668 it might be construed as justifying disappointment – unless his accommodation to the Puritan state had gone a bit deeper than most people think. 'Of My Self', the last essay, says that quietness was his best hope of the Restoration, but then he calls his poem about it 'a shrewd prophecy against my self', which might suggest a little envy of those who made fortunes from the same event with no greater 'probabilities or pretences' than himself.[35] For an intellectual like Cowley it is difficult to decide; is this wisdom, or making the best of a bad job?

> The first Minister of State has not so much business in
> public, as a wise man has in private; if the one have little
> leisure to be alone, the other has less leisure to be in
> company; the one has but part of the affairs of one nation,
> the other all the works of God and Nature under his
> consideration.[36]

Fair enough, though in fact there is little direct observation of the works of God and Nature in these essays; they are almost always mediated through the Greek and Latin classics. The only point where Cowley's new scientific loyalties peek through is where he complains that the gentry invariably appoint dancing masters for their children, but never tutors in agriculture. However, he is not the sentimental townee; in 'The Dangers of an Honest Man in Much Company' he confesses that he had approached Chertsea (his rural retreat) as if it were full of Arcadian shepherds, 'but to confess the truth, I perceived quickly, by infallible demonstrations, that I was still in old England . . . if I could not content myself with any thing less than exact fidelity in human conversation, I had almost as good go back and seek for it in the Court, or the Exchange, or Westminster-Hall'.[37]

In the end, Cowley's achievement in the essay form is limited. There is some formal innovation in the mixing of prose and verse, with the division between them lightly policed by a notion of 'extravagance'. The antithetical, defining mode of thought of the early essay is still there, as in some of the sentences quoted above; but it has eased off in rigour. Bacon's posthumous amanuenses would not have reached for their commonplace books that often, though the constant citing of Virgil's *Georgics* shows the influence of Bacon's commitment to usefulness.

By contrast, the essays of Sir William Temple are not short of range. Indeed, he got his fingers burnt when straying into areas of knowledge such as classical literature which were becoming more professionalised. His career has a similar shape to Bacon's. After his marriage in 1654, he spent seven years in Ireland with his family, his garden and his books. After a spell in the Irish Parliament he embarked on a remarkably successful diplomatic career, the high point of which was the Triple Alliance between England, the Dutch Republic and Sweden.[38] This and other subsequent achievements were largely undermined by Charles II's undercover alliance with France. In 1681 his name was removed from the list of Privy Councillors, and until 1699 he lived in retirement.

Most of the essays (edited after his death by Swift, who had been his secretary) date from this last period. However, a series of untitled essays from his stay in Brussels in 1652 survive, as an interesting youthful stab at the mode of Montaigne. The self-revelation is obviously less mature; the lightness of the tone, and the focus on the self, often come out as garrulous party talk: 'I lose half my thoughts between my fancy and my tongue but tis well I do for otherwise I should be an unconscionable talker, perhaps I should find and utter them all if I spoke through my nose they being lost between my forehead and my mouth.'[39] There are some more serious pointers to the mature manner, though. Already he is drawing on his personal experience of travel, and contemporary events to make his points. He is also seriously concerned with the nature of pleasure, with a neat comparison between lechery and ambition. (The lecher looks happy before the fulfilment of his pleasure, the ambitious man afterwards.)

An Essay upon the Original and Nature of Government was published in the first volume of *Miscellanea* (1680), and is altogether more objective and considered. It shows just how varied the 'essay' could be, even by the same author. Like many political theories, it goes back to some imagined but totally undocumented origin of human society. It is generally characterised as an unoriginal defence of patriarchy against

social contract theory, and he does seem to regard monarchies as more
'natural' than republics; but he attempts to combine the two. Any
contract, he argues, must have been made by heads of families who
were already authoritative in the smaller unit. Nor should primogeniture be pushed if the eldest son is 'degenerate'. There is a strong sense
of the provisional position of the ruling class; beginning with the
Roman state, but moving quickly to modern examples, England in
1660 (a more tactful choice than 1649!) and the reversion to monarchy
from 'popular' government in the United Provinces in 1672. Temple's
thought does occasionally express itself in axioms – 'Authority arises
from the opinion of wisdom, goodness, and valour in the persons who
possess it'[40] – but the style is rarely magisterial, reflecting his
pragmatic, culturally relativist approach in its accumulation of
alternative models of government.

His other political writings, like the 1673 *Observations upon the
United Provinces* (i.e. the Dutch), are meant to influence policy, but
already he is moving away from the Renaissance 'advice to the Prince'
mode, not least because of his commitment to the mixed state, with a
strong role for Parliament. The role of intimate adviser to William of
Orange was probably open to him; the essays, when they do stray into
political matters, praise the peacemakers. Retirement at Moor Park
was, in a sense, what Temple's diplomacy was aiming for:

> The designs and effects of conquests are but the slaughter
> and ruin of mankind, the ravaging of countries, and defacing
> the world: those of wise and just governments are preserving
> and increasing the lives and generations of men, securing
> their possessions, encouraging their endeavours, and by
> peace and riches improving and adorning the several scenes
> of the world.[41]

Once again we are in Montaigne territory, ideologically as well as
temperamentally. It is the opposite of Bacon's Christian stoicism.
However, Temple is less nervous as well as less innovative than
Montaigne. It's a bit more pipes and slippers, such as when he quotes
Alphonsus the Wise in praise of 'old wood to burn, old wine to drink,
old friends to converse with, and old books to read'.[42] No sign of the
epistemological crisis of 'An Apology of Raymond Sebond'; more an
eclectic Epicureanism, characteristic of more rakish Restoration wits.[43]

Temple was a serious gardener; there is a good deal more substance
to his love for the country than we can find in Cowley. Bacon's essay
'Of Gardens' is unusually relaxed and positive about the 'purest of
human pleasures', though it is mainly concerned with siting and
planting. Temple's essay, 'Upon the Gardens of Epicurus; or, Of

Gardening, in the Year 1685' tells of his own garden. To begin with, it follows the Montaigne technique, of the subject as pretext. The pleasure of the garden leads into a more general treatment of pleasure, attempting to reconcile the best of Stoic and Epicurean, but always following the latter: 'The Epicureans were more intelligible in their notion and fortunate in their expression, when they placed a man's happiness in the tranquillity of mind and indolence of body; for while we are composed of both, I doubt both must have a share in the good or ill we feel.'[44] Temple may have got a bit lazy and gouty in his later years, but 'indolence' here probably means a state of rest, in neither pleasure nor pain.[45] By the end of the essay, though, Temple has gone even further than Bacon in giving useful directions to real gardeners. He was particularly fond of fruit, and comments on the appropriate varieties, with the best soils and other growing conditions.

Such a blend of philosophy, personality and utility, became characteristic of the discourse of the educated gentleman (or at least, the professional writer addressing him) in the eighteenth-century periodical essay. Add this to his early patronage of Swift, and Temple becomes more important for what he heralded than what he achieved. To enjoy Temple for his own sake you would probably have to leave the Rare Books Rooms where he is usually found, and sit down with a glass of port and a bowl of fruit in front of the fire. The discipline of English literature has gone in for more rigorous forms of *jouissance* lately; a Temple revival is unlikely.

Notes

1. 'Of the Institution and Education of Children; to the Lady Diana of Foix, Countess of Gurson'.

2. See Ch. 2 of R.A. Sayce, *The Essays of Montaigne* (1972).

3. I am taking off from a stimulating discussion by John Mowitt, 'The Essay as Instance of the Social Character of Private Experience', *Prose Studies*, 12 (1989), 274–84.

4. *The Essayes of Michael Lord of Montaigne,* trans. John Florio (1910), I, pp. 148–9, 'Of the Institution and Education of Children'. Further page references will be to this Everyman text, with titles of essays for those with other editions.

5. For *The Tempest*, see the modern editions by Frank Kermode or Stephen Orgel; still valuable on the general relationship is G.C. Taylor, *Shakespeare's debt to Montaigne* (1925), and for a more recent treatment see Tetsuo Anzai, *Shakespeare*

and Montaigne Reconsidered (Tokyo, 1986) which discusses *Hamlet* and *Lear* as well as *The Tempest.*

6. Quoted (with some scepticism) by Joel Hafner in 'Unfathering the Essay: Resistance and Intergenerality in the Essay Genre', *Prose Studies* 12 (1989), 259–73.

7. Montaigne, *Essayes*, I, p. 15, 'The Author to the Reader'.

8. For this and much else on Florio, see Frances Yates, *John Florio: The Life of an Italian in Shakespeare's England* (Cambridge, 1934).

9. Montaigne, *Essayes*, I, p. 86.

10. *Essayes*, III, v, p. 128

11. E.g., R.A. Sayce, *The Essays of Montaigne* (1972), p. 113.

12. Montaigne, *Essayes*, I, pp. 138–9, 'Of Pedantism'.

13. *Essayes*, III, p. 306. I am indebted to the discussion of this essay in Terence Cave, *The Cornucopian Text* (Oxford, 1979), pp. 302–12.

14. See Richard H. Popkin, *The History of Scepticism from Erasmus to Spinoza* (Berkeley, 1979), especially Preface and Ch. 3; the discussion is of exemplary clarity.

15. *Essayes*, II, xii, p. 199.

16. My argument here is indebted to Richard L. Regosin, *The Matter of my Book: Montaigne's Essais as the Book of the Self* (Berkeley, 1977), especially pp. 53 and 61.

17. André Tournon, 'Self-Interpretation in Montaigne's *Essais*', *Yale French Studies*, 64 (1983), 51–72.

18. *Essayes*, III. v, p. 102.

19. Ibid., p. 103

20. In Roland Barthes, *The Rustle of Language*, trans. Richard Howard (Oxford, 1986), pp. 52–3.

21. The comparison is Anne Righter's; see her 'Francis Bacon' in *Essential Articles for the Study of Francis Bacon*, ed. Brian Vickers (Hamden, Connecticut, 1968), pp. 300–21.

22. Bacon, *Essays*, ed. John Pitcher (Harmondsworth, 1985), p. 96, 'Of Goodness and Goodness in Nature'.

23. *Essays*, p. 108.

24. *Essays*, p. 120.

25. John C. Briggs, *Francis Bacon and the Rhetoric of Nature* (Cambridge, Mass., 1989), p. 223.

26. *Essays*, p. 138.

27. See Ronald S. Crane, 'The Relation of Bacon's *Essays* to his Program for the Advancement of Learning' (1923), most easily available in *Essential Articles for the Study of Francis Bacon*, pp. 272–92.

28. *Essays*, p. 126.

29. 'Of Wisdom for a Man's Self', *Essays*, p. 130.

30. *Works*, ed. Spedding, Ellis and Heath (1857–74), Vol. VII, p. 509. For this quotation, and this discussion generally, I am indebted to Ch. 3, 'The Aphorism', of Brian Vickers, *Francis Bacon and Renaissance Prose* (Cambridge, 1968).

31. See David K. Weiver, 'Bacon's Borrowed Imagery', *Review of English Studies*, n.s. 38 (1987), 315–24.

32. Francis Bacon, *The Advancement of Learning*, ed. G.W. Kitchin (1915), I. v. 4, p. 32.

33. Stanley E. Fish, 'Georgics of the Mind: The Experience of Bacon's Essays', in *Self–Consuming Artifacts* (Berkeley, 1972), pp. 78–155.

34. Abraham Cowley, *The Essays and Other Prose Writings*, ed. Alfred B. Gough (Oxford, 1915), p. 108. There is a new standard edition of Cowley in progress.

35. Cowley, *Essays*, p. 220.

36. Cowley, *Essays*, pp. 132–3, 'Of Solitude'.

37. Cowley, *Essays*, p. 203.

38. For a fascinating account of this episode, see K.H.D. Haley, *An English Diplomat in the Low Countries: Sir William Temple and John de Witt, 1665–1672* (Oxford, 1986), especially Ch. 6; Ch. 11 contains an important discussion of Temple's political writings, including his *Observations upon the United Provinces of the Netherlands*.

39. *The Early Essays and Romances of Sir William Temple*, ed. G.C. Moore Smith (Oxford, 1930).

40. Sir William Temple, *An Essay upon the Original and Nature of Government* (facsimile from 1680 *Miscellanea*), Introduction R.C. Steensma (Los Angeles, 1964), p. 55.

41. *Five Miscellaneous Essays by Sir William Temple*, ed. S.H. Monk (Ann Arbor, 1963), p. 172; the conclusion to 'Of Heroic Virtue'.

42. *Five Miscellaneous Essays*, p. 71; 'An Essay upon the Ancient and Modern Learning'.

43. For Restoration Epicureanism see Thomas Franklin Mayo, *Epicurus in England 1650–1725* (Dallas, 1934); the key English text is Walter Charleton, *Epicurus's Morals* (1656). Charleton was a member of the Royal Society, who also wrote fiction.

44. *Five Miscellaneous Essays*, p. 7.

45. *OED*, 2; in view of Swift's admiration of Temple, it is interesting that the *OED* gives an example of this meaning from Orrery's 1751 remarks on Swift, with very similar phrasing to Temple's.

Chapter 11
The Cornucopian Text

In the Renaissance, the text as cornucopia ('horn of plenty') is thought of in two related ways. The first is essentially a reading concept, that the classical text (Scripture as well as Homer or Virgil) is an inexhaustible source of ideas, of figures and stories. The second is compositional, an ambition to write a text that will overflow with meaning and invention. There is a tension here, that much of the richness is imitative, deriving from a notebook culled from wide reading; the old texts are honoured and raided as well as (potentially) displaced. Terence Cave describes it as a Utopian myth of dynamic productivity which 'will sooner or later begin to appear, in the post-lapsarian world, as an emptying out, or as mere flux or repetition'.[1] There is an anxiety as well as an exuberance about these writings. In Nashe the richness of utterance depicts physical poverty and wasting; the vast edifice of *The Anatomy of Melancholy* is a tribute to the power of depression; the rich variety of beliefs examined in *Pseudodoxia Epidemica* is a cornucopia of error.

There is an interesting parallel to this concept in Henry James's description of a certain kind of novel in his Preface to *The Tragic Muse*. They are not novels he really likes – *The Newcomes*, *The Three Musketeers* and *War and Peace*: 'What do such large, loose baggy monsters, with their queer elements of the accidental and the arbitrary, artistically mean? . . . I delight in a deep-breathing economy and the organic form.'[2] He does admit that these books have life, even if they don't follow his artistic ideals. In this chapter I want to look at those lively texts, part of whose life seems to derive from their spreading over the limits of the genre they appear to belong to – the essay, or the treatise, or the mock encomium. It is not that looseness in itself is admirable; but those features that James calls queer can, with the skill and panache of writers such as Nashe, Burton and Browne, turn into a constant source of life, of entertaining and persuasive dialogue with the reader.

At first, none of these books seem particularly novelistic. Their commitment to narrative of the beginning, middle and end sort ranges from the confusing through the minimal to the non-existent; but they often have narrators, or rather authorial devices similar to narrators in fiction. Again, the modern novelist often uses the narrative as a pretext for other kinds of discourse. Joseph Heller's *Picture This*, for example, ostensibly about Rembrandt painting Aristotle, becomes in large part an analysis of Greek history. The works I am discussing here have that kind of amplitude and inclusiveness, sometimes opportunistic, sometimes uneasy. Some of the ways that the contemporary novel, as well as thinking about the novel generally, is going, might make this older kind of writing easier to grasp and enjoy now. It is not just the matter of structures loosening towards inclusiveness; it is the notion of reading for a stylistic buzz, and the aesthetics of the amazing sentence, that characterise a certain strand of postmodern fiction.

Consider *Tristram Shandy*. In the old Pelican Guide, there is an essay suggesting that Burton's *Anatomy of Melancholy* provides a better generic comparison for Sterne's display of learned wit than Fielding or Richardson.[3] Then we come upon the argument of the Russian Formalist Victor Shklovsky, that *Tristram Shandy* was actually the typical novel, perfectly revealing the processes that delay narrative fulfilment and thus make the novel more than the first and last sentences of its synopsis. Both perceptions are true; the 'typical' novel is both a process of narrative events, or delays, and a discourse which brings together a range of other discourse. The seventeenth-century works I am putting together here have a similar relation to Renaissance rhetoric; their structure, and some of their devices, may owe something to the rhetorical tradition, but it is being stretched even beyond the Renaissance ambition of *copia* (richness and fullness in both language and invention)[4] to include an almost encyclopaedic range of stuff. The conception is similar to Bakhtin's influential characterisation of the novel as the discovery of multiple languages – though his template doesn't fit completely, it is important to remember that other forms than the novel in the seventeenth century were generically loose, full of 'heteroglossia', other voices.[5]

Finally, these works form a bridge between the essay and the rigours of the new philosophy, which Browne in particular anticipates. The essayist's sense of provisionality in his discourse, his bookishness, his relying on other texts to provide material even though testing them by experience, all appear in these larger forms. The self as the matter, or at least the authenticator of the discussion, is a more complex business, as it is projected by what a modern reader would recognise as quasi-narrative devices. But it is time to let the heterogeneity of these texts get the better of my generalisations.

Nashe: *Pierce Penniless his Supplication to the Devil* and *Nashe's Lenten Stuff*

You have to pronounce it properly – 'Purse Penniless' – and realise that *Piers Plowman*, though hardly the most influential Middle English text in the 1590s, was still current as providing a figure of the plain man as radical critic.[6] There may be a joke on 'Pierce'/*persona* as well as *per se* and purse. Certainly it became Nashe's nickname, the public face of the discontented scholar, poor but talented, with a sharp pen that neither satiric victim nor literary rival should underestimate.[7]

'This paper-monster'[8] is supposedly searching for the devil to conclude a Faustian pact; only here it is for money rather than power, and it's hard enough to find a postman, let alone a Mephistophilis, to deliver the note to the infernal pawnbroker. In the end he finds a 'Knight of the Post', a professional false witness, to deliver his letter. Wayne Booth's 'reliable narrator' thus finds his unreliable listener. This narrative/dramatic pretext, which itself arises out of a complaint against the poverty of writers and scholars, soon mutates into a parade of the seven deadly sins as seen in contemporary London (with foreign variations chauvinistically delineated), interspersed with defences of poetry and stage plays and attacks on the Harveys (rival writers; the controversy ran and ran), concluding with an excursus into demonology and a kind of epistle to the reader.

One of the things Nashe picked up from the Marprelate controversy was playing with printing conventions like title pages and dedications. (His early work, *An Almond for a Parrot*, was anti-Martinist but imitated its manner.) A dedication to a patron would have been the usual thing – two pounds was the standard tip expected for such a compliment – but poverty as a result of inadequate patronage prompts Nashe to defer the attempt, until later in the text he is forced to resort to the Devil. That also spoofs the vogue of the reformed prodigal (like Gascoigne in the preface to the *Posies*) presenting early, licentious work as a moral warning.[9]

The voice is modern, fascinated by the new but at a spiky distance from fashion. Only in the framework of the Seven Deadly Sins, and occasional devices like the Ship of Fools is there a vestige of the old-fashioned, which seems inescapable for any kind of moral tone to satire in the period. Whereas the anti-Court poets such as Ralegh reach for an archaic language to denounce its vanity, Nashe concocts new words, nicknames and a very modern restlessness of style to delineate the vices of high and low life at home and abroad.[10] The high-flown, rhetorically colourful and the undercutting specific detail exist side by side, in a constant flux of decorum: here is 'The Counterfeit Politician':

Some think to be counted are politicians and statesmen by being solitary; as who should say 'I am a wise man, a brave man, *Secreta mea mihi; Frustra sapit, qui sibi non sapit* [My secrets are mine; knowledge is useless to a man who does not know his own business], and there is no man worthy of my company or friendship; when, although he goes ungartered like a malcontent cut-purse, and wears his hat over his eyes like one of the cursed crew, yet cannot his stabbing dagger, or his nitty love-lock, keep him out of The Legend of Fantastical Coxcombs.[11]

Bathos is Nashe's ever-present weapon. His satire of human pretension almost invariably comes down to the telling physical detail, in tandem with some inventive name-calling. The squalor of bodily decay or dismemberment is his speciality:

I warrant we have old hacksters in this great grandmother of corporations, Madame Troynovant [London] that have not backbited any of their neighbours with the tooth of envy this twenty year, in the wrinkles of whose face ye may hide false dice, and play at cherry-pit in the dint of their cheeks: yet these aged mothers of iniquity will have their deformities new plastered over, and wear nosegays of yellow hair on their furies' foreheads, when age hath written, 'Ho, God be here', on their bald, burnt-parchment pates.[12]

There is something fascinated and disgusted in the excess of Nashe's physical description – the grotesquerie is more sermonic than carnival, exposure more than celebration.

The running theme of light-hearted diabolism may itself have a satiric edge, apart from any Marlowe reference. The tale of the foul-mouthed 'Friar Charles' of Chester, though told in the context of the sin of wrath, may have some reference to Charles Chester, a Catholic arrested and imprisoned by Cecil in 1592. Charles Nicholl argues that the 'great personage' taking his revenge for defeat in a contest of 'villainous words' with Charles was not Cecil, but Ralegh, himself in trouble that year for his secret marriage and, more significantly for the context, suspected atheism and occultism.[13]

It would also be nice to identify the stationary stationer (the joke is Lorna Hutson's) in the sloth section

. . . who, if a man come to his stall and ask him for a book, never stirs his head or looks upon him, but stands stone still

and speaks not a word; only with his little finger points
backwards to his boy, who must be his interpreter, and so all
the day, gaping like a dumb image, he sits without motion,
except when he goes to dinner or supper.[14]

The Stationers' Company had the monopoly of publishing, and its
members controlled particular privileges like printing prayer books;
when, in 1599, Nashe's works were banned along with other satires by
Archbishop Whitgift in his role as censor, the bonfire took place
outside the Stationers' Hall. (Ironically, Whitgift had been the man
who had first blooded Nashe as a commercial satirist, as one of the
wits employed by the Church of England in the Marprelate
controversy.) The sale of monopolies was a great source of Crown
revenue, and a chief source of economic exploitation, as even staples
like soap and salt were controlled in this way – not to mention Nashe's
own living.[15] His economic desperation was a feature of the general
set-up, not just personal bad luck. As we might expect of a penniless
persona, the moral categories are particularly stretched when it comes to
economics; if it comes down to the thrifty versus the gallant, choose
the gallant, because at least he provides employment for people. The
'Protestant ethic' combination of thrift and production will never result
in general wealth without some thriftless consumers.

Talking of Protestants, Nashe has sometimes been identified as a
closet Catholic; certainly the Italians get off a bit better than the Danes
and the Dutch in his conspectus of European styles of drunkenness,
and he defends plays against (presumably Puritan) moral attacks; but
that has to be set against his very Protestant connoisseurship of
sermons.

In 1593 the vein of repentance does find a text: *Christ's Tears Over
Jerusalem*. It is Nashe's most sustained attempt at serious religious
prose: high-flown, elaborate, inventive within a quite different moral
vein to *Piers Penniless*. It is haunted by death – the plague, the death of
his friends, the wormy physicality of it. Phrases like 'woe-infirmed
wit' and 'care-crazed' suggest a mind close to the edge; although *The
Unfortunate Traveller* appeared the following year, it had probably been
written earlier, and he seems to have left London as well as left writing
for a while. In 1597, the furore over the satirical play *The Isle of Dogs*
(co-written with Jonson, and one of the great literary losses of
Elizabethan censorship) drove him from London again, this time to
escape prison.

The last of his works to be published before Whitgift's ban was
Nashe's Lenten Stuff (1599), a praise of the red herring (fish was still a
staple foodstuff, for Lent).[16] It is also a history of Yarmouth, the town

next to Nashe's birthplace, and a major herring fishing port. To say the exuberance is back would be an understatement. We are used to dedications being high-flown in the period, and we have seen Nashe taking the rise out of them, but this opening sentence (to Humfrey King, author of *A Halfpenny-worth of Wit in a Pennyworth of Paper*, and the last in Nashe's lower-class 'patrons') is a long way ahead in self-mocking bravura:

> Most courteous, unlearned lover of poetry, and yet a poet
> thyself, of no less price than H.S. [unidentified], that in
> honour of Maid Marian gives sweet Margaret for his
> Empress and puts the sow most saucily upon some great
> personage, whatever she be, bidding her (as it goes in the old
> song) 'Go from my garden, go, for there no flowers for thee
> doth grow': these be to notify to your Diminutive
> Excelsitude and Compendiate Greatness what my zeal is
> towards you, that in no straiter bonds would be pounded
> [enclosed] and enlisted, than in an Epistle dedicatory.[17]

Is this code, an appeal to the readership as in-group? In effect, Nashe is first addressing his fellow-writers from a kind of exile, then his readership. The theme once again, or at least the pretext, is poverty, the lack of decent patronage and so Nashe's inventiveness, his richness, has to be spent on characterising poverty and the skinflint rich. Nashe's most commercially successful vein had been the praise of poverty; by 1599 it had become a reality for him again. He is creating a readership out of these prefatory squibs, people who will pay their debts, and, most importantly, won't be stupid – or, at least, will enjoy listening to other people being called stupid. The *Tom Nashe Book of Insults* would be a useful stocking-filler: 'ninnyhammer', 'greybeard huddle-duddle', or 'crusty cumtwangs', from *Lenten Stuff*, and the really cutting ones from the Harvey controversy, 'a case of tooth-pikes, or a lute-pin in a suit of apparel', 'thou arrant butter whore, thou cotquean and scrattop of scolds', not to mention his names for Gabriel, of which Gaffer Jobbernoule, Gamaliel Hobgoblin, Gilgilis Hobberdehoy and Infractissime Pistlepragmos are only my favourites from a vast selection.[18]

The two main features of the *Lenten Stuff* performance are a description and history of Great Yarmouth and a pageant in praise of the red herring (or kipper, as we would call it). Yarmouth is a town of well-organised bourgeois plenty; no profiteering in the market while foreign sailors are in town, and no shortages either, 'that, if all Her Majesty's fleet at once should put into their bay, within twelve days' warning with so much double beer, beef, fish and biscuit, they would bulk them as they could wallow away with'.[19] It's not a democracy –

Nashe's populism did not lean in that direction – but its riches are better spread than most towns:

> Not that it is sib or cater-cousins to any mongrel
> Democratia, in which one is all and all is one, but that in her,
> as they are not all one, so one or two there pockets not up all
> the pieces; there being two hundred in it worth three
> hundred pound apiece, with poundage and shillings to the
> lurched.[20]

'Lurch' can mean 'cheat' or 'engross' at this time, so perhaps the richer merchants of Yarmouth operated a commercial safety-net. It is these anonymous groups of city fathers that are the heroes of Yarmouth's history; not even the sailors.

Nashe abandons his antiquaries and worm-eaten parchments (he is always reminding us of the labour that produces his texts) for a more literary prelude to the praise of the red herring. It would have been a fitting climax to Nashe's career, to end it in praise of digression, but even the literal root of that figure of speech, its use to lay a false trail in hunting, first appears nearly a hundred years later. It is a climax of sorts, a mock climax of course, populist, chauvinist, above all a celebration of the consumable. The food of rich and poor, caught in small boats that bring back more, and kill less, than grander fleets; health-giving, drink-inducing; it would be mock epic, or mock encomium for the gap between style and subject, but Nashe is always more cutting in his put-downs than this. It is a Lenten carnival: 'City, town, country, Robin Hood and Little John, and who not, are industrious and careful to squire and safe conduct him in . . . . The red herring is a legate of peace.'[21] For a while; but being red, the colour of choler, it is good food for soldiers, 'enough to make the cravenest dastard proclaim fire and sword against Spain'.[22] Virtually the last plea to his readers Nashe makes before his peroration is to take up their swords in his quarrel. Peaceableness and delicacy are not useful attributes for the reader who would enjoy Nashe.

Burton: *The Anatomy of Melancholy* (1621–41)

The dates above are of the first and the posthumous sixth edition. Robert Burton (1577–1640) was not so much a careful reviser as a constant accumulator, an engaging scholarly obsessive. The first edition ran to some 350,000 words; the final edition takes it up to over 515,000.[23] The revisions range from sections to odd words, but they are always adding, rarely subtracting. Burton's rhetorical training would have taught him to argue both sides of a case, and he often does that in the *Anatomy*, so much so that we cannot be sure of his own opinion on a matter, or even whether he had one. It also means that, if he reports something new about a particular subject, it is unlikely to displace what is already there.

What kind of a book is it? There's lots of scholarly argument here, and we might take a Burtonian view that there are several possible answers which don't necessarily conflict. In the first place, it is a treatise on melancholy, arranged according to an elaborate sub-division of the subject. The word 'anatomy' in a literary sense is very fluid, somewhere between 'anatomising' in the modern, point-by-point sense, and an attempt at completeness, 'all you need to know about melancholy'. Or rather, all anyone could possibly know about melancholy. The encyclopaedic treatise is a notable late Renaissance genre, or tendency. Burton has other Renaissance humanist qualities, too: his bookishness, which is both antiquarian, respectful of the classics, and experimental, regarding the experience of the individual reader as a key to the text, rather than seeing its authority residing in its age or prestige. Burton was aware of new intellectual developments, and welcomed them. He also had a taste for popular literature, and collected playtexts and curious and sensationalist reports of odd happenings; hardly scientific, but evidence of a voracious curiosity. He had the advantage of being in at the birth of Oxford's libraries, the Bodleian and that of Christ Church, his own college, which together with his own collection, unusually if not uniquely large for a don, made such a compendious production as *The Anatomy* possible. It is a library book. Its vast bulk is, after all, about two-thirds either quotation or paraphrase. Such a performance is unthinkable without a library of printed sources ready to hand. Its mixture of intricate classification and digressive serendipity is exactly what a library would encourage – bringing a large collection to order, and yet finding things on the edge, or next on the shelf, that interrupt and enliven the work of classification. At times, for example in the digression on anatomy, Burton is condensing material for those without access to large libraries, or Latin.

Recent argument has put to one side the idea of the *Anatomy* being a treatise on melancholy in favour of it being a satire or a vast homily.[24] The trouble with such arguments lies in their search for an all-encompassing term, a setting of limits. Burton wanted to be all-encompassing, and that results in a kind of generically inclusive piece, like the (also much shorter) dramatic mixing of modes so popular in the same period. The fact that Renaissance writers were so sensitive to the nuances of genre means that they could mix them to particular effect. So, for example, mixing satire with a treatise on healing madness may suggest a point about the nature of satire as diagnosis which need not make one a subsidiary of the other.

The opening of the book offers a whole series of clues. The title page, the division of the subject, and the long satirical preface, 'Democritus Junior to the Reader', all suggest complementary ways of reading. The *Anatomy* veers between medical textbook, sermon and satire, sometimes mingling, often putting one or the other into the background for a while.

The three main divisions of the book aim to provide an exhaustive guide to the various manifestations of melancholy, and to suggest cures and therapies, both physical and spiritual. The complexity of Burton's plan reflects in part the (admittedly imprecise) complexity of psychological concepts in the period. Here the root metaphor of 'anatomy', the dissection, gives a clue to what the book might be, a teasing out of a single concept into its constituent parts.

The history of the book's expansion, though, suggests something closer to an intellectual squirrel than a surgeon. Burton is inclusive to an encyclopaedic degree; everything he read seemed to have something to do with the subject. This may be due to his admission that he is a victim as well as a would-be healer of melancholy. 'I write of Melancholy, by being busy to avoid Melancholy.'[25] In writing its anatomy he is sometimes writing a proxy autobiography, though he is not such a hypochondriac as to think he is suffering from every form of the disease.

The first-person singular of the book is, however, complicated. Easier in a way is the second person: 'Thou thy self art the subject of my discourse.'[26] The third person is present as well, but not so frequently as to dissipate the personal tone. Even when listing the various kinds of baths that might cure the melancholic (a dry humour needs moistening), the impression is of the author ranging through his sources, rather than the impersonal report. Paradoxically, one of the less useful features of impersonality is present: he doesn't decide between the options: plain baths, herbal baths, or even baths with a ram's head boiled in them. He is not always so distant, but sometimes organising and listing are felt to be enough.

Burton is one of the masters of the list, and the lists constitute one of the great pleasures of the book. In 'Democritus to the Reader' it is a central device for satirising the world; listing reduces everything to a similar level, 'A vast confusion of vows, wishes, actions, edicts, petitions, law-suits, pleas, laws, proclamations, complaints, grievances, are daily brought to our ears.'[27] Listing is a sure way of further confusing the already confused, and thus operates as a satiric counterweight to Burton's classification system. Or they can have a ferocious cumulative effect, steering close to overkill, as in the passage (too long to quote) where he attacks the madness of war by listing the casualties of famous battles. Most often, and most characteristically, Burton's lists demonstrate his pessimism and his fecundity simultaneously; there is something heartening about someone who can be so inventively fed up:

> . . . hard students are commonly troubled with gouts, cattarhs, rheums, cacexia, bradiopepsia, bad eyes, stone and colic, crudities, oppilations, vertigo, winds, cramps, consumptions, and all such diseases as come by overmuch sitting; they are most part lean, dry, ill coloured, spend their fortunes, loose their wits, and many times their lives, and all through immoderate pains, and extraordinary studies.[28]

Whether this comes from experience, observation, or quotation, the personal tone of this whole chapter, on the misery of scholars, is generally hard done by. There is occasionally a less attractive, sour tone, of complaint that scholarship is so little rewarded, by patrons, or the kind of Church preferment that came late to Burton himself, and then gave him more trouble than reward.

The list is the loosest form of ordering, and reflects the confusion and chaos that he sees in the world. Order can be imposed from the outside, rhetorically, but the tendency is for the chaos of the human world to repeat itself chaotically. Sometimes Burton's lists are organised with a certain amount of symmetry within a long but syntactically controlled sentence, but even here the sense remains that *copia* is spreading into excess:

> Because therefore it is a thing so difficult, impossible, and far beyond Hercules labours to be performed; let them be rude, stupid, ignorant, incult, *lapis super lapidem sedeat*, and as the Apologist will, *Resp. tussi & graveolentia laboret, munus vitio*, let them be barbarous as they are, let them tyrannize, Epicurize, oppress, luxuriate, consume themselves with factions, superstitions, lawsuits, wars and contentions, live in riot, poverty, want, misery, rebel, wallow as so many swine in their own dung, with Ulysses companions, *stultos jubeo esse libenter*.[29]

Burton's orchestration of the long sentence is also related to his Latinity. He complained that his stationers would not let him write the whole thing in Latin, though he might have been reconciled to it by its popular success, as opposed to the international scholarly reputation a Latin treatise might have given him. As it is, the text is studded with Latin, and very rarely Greek. Sometimes it is translated, often (as above) not. The modern reader with small Latin could always revert to the all-English text of Floyd Dell and Paul Jordan-Smith,[30] but that is a slightly different book from Burton's, useful as it is. Having the sense is better than a puzzle – they translate the Latin in the quotation as 'stone above stone', 'let the state suffer from coughing and short breath, the world from vice' and 'let them be fools, since that's their wish'. However, the smoothness of a single language pushes the style into a slightly misleading uniformity. Burton's actual method is more involved, leaving some of his sources on the page as raw material, working others into the syntax, and letting others still to be indistinguishable from his own flow. He says of his borrowing 'The matter is theirs most part, and yet mine'; and then, as if to demonstrate how often it happens, quotes a quoter (here he translates directly afterwards): 'I must usurp that of *Wecker é Terentio, nihil dictum quod non dictum prius, methodus sola artificum ostendit*, we can say nothing but what has been said, the composition is ours only, and shews a scholar.'[31] In displaying his borrowing, he is displaying a key part of his method.

The epigrammatic quality of Latin can also be exploited as a counter to Burton's English exuberance; and even by this stage, it was felt that English was still inferior to Latin for some intellectual purposes, so that some things might be said better in Latin than English. (Burton's surviving verse and drama, written for academic audiences, are in Latin.) His English is not Latinate, particularly by comparison with Browne or Milton. Burton is proud of his scholarship, but not obscurantist about it; the laws, he said, should be 'plainly put down, and in the mother tongue, that every man may understand'.[32]

The *persona* of Democritus Junior, the laughing philosopher, gives him a more ironic distance from the world with its inverted values. 'Democritus to the Reader' keeps a respectful distance from the Greek philosopher for much of the time, but Burton sees the parallel with his own career, a private man, a non-specialist who would occasionally 'walk down to the Haven, and laugh heartily at such variety of ridiculous objects, which there he saw'.[33] Most significantly, Democritus senior was a melancholic who anatomised melancholy – though his text was unfinished, and lost. So Burton picks up his project, and his stance. So much so that his monument in Christ Church Cathedral names him only as Democritus Junior, with another coded reference, the sign of Saturn, which induces melancholy, according to Burton's own astrological diagnosis from the date of his conception. (Who else in the self-regarding pantheon of English Literature records the date of his *conception*? Tristram Shandy, of course, in homage.) Democritus was already established for Burton's readership; in 1607 Samuel Rowlands, the satiric poet, had published *Democritus, or Doctor Merry-Man his Medicines, against Melancholy Humours*, and there is the example of the melancholy Hamlet's antic disposition from 1600, too.

The principal mode of Democritus, then, is satire. It begins, in the classical manner, with wide-ranging denunciation. of the madness of the world. However, as the criticism gets more political, he constructs a miniature utopia. Utopia is a complex tool for the satirist; it does enable him to sound a positive note, but this fictional ideal state should not necessarily be construed as a social programme. Burton's utopia is monarchical and hierarchical, in open contrast to More, Bacon and Campanella. All the same, he dislikes villages with one domineering house, and prefers cities where plebeians are not excluded from honour and where (of course) scholars are paid more than soldiers. There is little attempt to give it fictional life; the liveliness comes from the sceptical reining in of his speculations:

> If it were possible, I would have such priests as would
> imitate Christ, charitable lawyers should love their
> neighbours as themselves, temperate and modest physicians,
> politicians contemn the world, philosophers should know
> themselves, noblemen live honestly, tradesmen leave lying
> and cosening, magistrates corruptions etc. but this is
> unpossible, I must get such as I may.[34]

However, he is not just the traditional moralist. He felt that England was economically backward, and some of the cures are in his utopia: practical proposals for regulation, not just moral laments. For example, he recognises the need for efficient transport, with well-kept roads, and proposes something like a land register to enable available resources to be used more productively.[35]

What *is* melancholy, then? It is one of the four humours, or liquids, making up the human body according to classical medicine. In a balanced character, 'Melancholy, cold and dry, thick, black and sour, begotten of the more fæculent part of nourishment, and purged from the spleen, is a bridle to the other two hot humours, blood and choler.'[36] As a disease, 'Fear and sorrow are the true characters, and inseparable companions of most melancholy, not all, as *Her. de Saxonia, Tract. posthumo de Melancholia, cap.2.* well excepts, for to some it is most pleasant, as to such as laugh most part; some are bold again, and free from all manner of fear and grief.'[37] Not all pain, then. It was a fashionable affliction in the seventeenth century, particularly for the upper class; and it was prized for its association with creativity by such as the young John Donne. Delusions, fearfulness, sadness and love of solitude are the symptoms recognised by psychologists other than Burton.[38] But if this paradox about melancholy holds, that it is a disease that can delight, or be desirable, so too do Burton's paradoxes, or at least scepticism, about treatment. Study, for example, appears as both cause and cure. The whole of the Second Partition is devoted to cures, social and psychological as well as medical, but, particularly in view of the state of medicine at the time, Burton was probably right to end on this sceptical note: 'a good choice of receipts must needs ease, if not quite cure: not one but all, or most, as occasion serves'.[39]

The Second Partition is notable for its digressions, and the freedom they offer to the writer is a temporary freedom from melancholy, the subject and the affliction. The digression of the air is an imaginative escape, 'wherein I may freely expatiate and exercise my self, for my recreation a while rove, wander round about the world, mount aloft to those æthereal orbs and celestial spheres, and so descend to my former elements again'.[40] Burton's imaginative roaming in the steps of the new geography and cosmography is not at all melancholic; compared to Donne, say, he finds the new discoveries exhilarating rather than depressing and disordering. He reveals himself as a great reader of maps as well as discovery narratives, cheerfully willing to accept how much is yet unknown. It is as much of a 'change of air', as he calls it at the end, as you can get while staying in the library.

The speculation becomes giddy when he begins to enquire into the nature of God, and he quickly reins it back: 'my melancholy spaniel's quest, my game is sprung, and I must suddenly come down and follow'.[41] Burton was after all a minister of the Church of England, and while his analysis of the purpose of that ministry might seem to a cynical reader to be no more than an inadequate reward for scholarship, Burton does sometimes see the link between minister and healer. So, the satire by Democritus Junior of the world's madness is paralleled in the First Partition of the treatise proper by the comprehensive effects of the Fall of Adam. The principal religious interest of *The Anatomy*, though, is psychological; in the First Partition, where he considers God, as well as evil spirits, as causes of melancholy, and in the conclusion to the Third Partition, where he analyses religious melancholy as a special case of love melancholy. Though God may punish sin with madness, Burton's authorities see the actual humour of melancholy as 'the Devil's bath'; and 'of all other, melancholy persons are most subject to diabolical temptations, and illusions, and most apt to entertain them, and the Devil best able to work upon them'.[42] This is the darker side of melancholy's association with imagination and creativity; though Burton's examples show the fruit of his fascination with collections of strange occurrences, the 'believe it or not' side of his curiosity. They may seem fantastic to us, but his belief in the Devil's powers of illusion was not unusual at the time, and should not be seen as contradicting his attack on superstition.

Burton's analysis of religious melancholy as love-melancholy is altogether more extensive and original; and has a distinct focus on the troubles of his own time as well as a therapeutic aim: 'all the world again cannot afford so much matter of madness, so many stupend symptoms, as superstition, heresy, schism hath brought out'.[43] There is swingeing Anglican satire on the 'slavish superstition' of Roman Catholicism, and Nonconformity – 'where God hath a temple, the devil will have a chapel'.[44] False religion, often in the service of unscrupulous politicians (the word is used in its pejorative, Machiavellian sense), is a prime cause of religious melancholy. Christian heresy is bundled in characteristic fashion with pagan and Islamic practices. Burton's first aim seems to be satiric, despairing of a cure for those who are 'so refractory, self-conceited, obstinate, so firmly addicted to that religion in which they have been bred and brought up'.[45] The pastoral, healing note finishes the book, however, as he deals with guilt and despair, the final extreme of melancholy. Here Burton is most anxious to stress the extreme pain; and the possibility of healing, by a mixture of physical and spiritual means. Here he sounds most like a seventeenth-century preacher, assuring the desperate of God's mercy over and over again. Avoid over-scrupulous preachers, he says, and most of all, 'be not solitary, be not idle'.

Burton's own cure, scholarship, was in one sense solitary; in another sense, his text is thronged with other people, all contributing to what Michael O'Connell has finely characterised as 'the true therapy of humanism, the therapy of language'.[46]

Browne: *Pseudodoxia Epidemica, The Garden of Cyrus* and *Hydriotaphia*

Sir Thomas Browne (1605–82) provides some of the most splendid examples of 'art prose' in the century; but their Latinate intricacies rarely sound a hectoring note. Essayistic, personal, witty, they contrast with the public rhetoric of sermons and political tracts in the period. His Christian scepticism links with a kind of country cosmopolitanism to make him a voice of peace and reason in a period when the pressures were for taking sides. Peace and reason do, however, often have conservative tendencies, and Browne welcomed the Restoration. More than that, most of his major works were published during the Civil War and Interregnum, and, mostly by implication, offer an alternative to religious and political revolution. Browne's religious beliefs are best explored in his first book, *Religio Medici*, discussed in an earlier chapter.

As with Burton, the effect of reading Browne is of entering a cabinet of curiosities, though with Browne the cabinet is more than a library: his texts are full of objects as well as scholarly authorities.[47] When John Evelyn visited Browne in October 1671, he remarked 'his whole house and garden being a paradise and cabinet of rarities, and that of the best collection, especially medals, books, plants, natural things, did exceedingly refresh me'.[48] Browne, then, can be seen as a typical intellectual of the mid-century, still bookishly respectful of authority, but also committed to investigating the direct evidence of natural phenomena, with a bias to the extraordinary. Some of Browne's scholarly instincts are Baconian, as in *Pseudodoxia Epidemica* (1646), which actually answers to a call from Bacon to investigate popular errors as a preliminary to true knowledge. True scientific investigation needs to disencumber itself of errors, not just add to and classify the accumulated store of centuries. The style has a certain Baconian briskness, though its sheer size and range link it to the encyclopaedic ambitions shared by a whole range of late Renaissance writers less 'modern' than Bacon. If Bacon's main aim for empirical knowledge was to increase our control over the natural and social world, Browne saw 'intellectual endeavours as fulfilling a duty that man owed God for having been endowed with reason'.[49] Though both *The Advancement of Learning* and *Pseudodoxia* have an explicit theological base, Browne's is more extensive.

The book may be a catalogue of popular errors, but Browne's instincts are not to popularise. The people, in his view, 'being the most deceptible part of mankind, and ready with open arms to receive the encroachments of error'.[50] Their view of scripture is literal, without 'deuteroscopy', Browne's own coinage from Greek to mean the second intention of the words (as with Burton's Latin, a paraphrase follows, but the effect of an inner sanctum of learning remains). There are a number of hints like this, that Browne was impatient with the popularisation of the Reformation that was going on around him in Norfolk, a bastion of Puritanism despite the attentions of an aggressively Laudian bishop, Matthew Corbet. The first edition, we remember, is 1646, deep into the Civil War, though it wouldn't really have seemed like a popular uprising then . The twentieth-century perspective, that medical men are even more sceptical of lay learning than theologians, may be anachronistic, but Browne's lofty tone in these opening remarks is still unmistakable. We might expect the follower of Bacon to be clear and simple. In his crucial study of Browne's styles, Austin Warren regards the *Pseudodoxia* as the prime example of his low style, as opposed to the high style of *Urn Burial* and *The Garden of Cyrus*, and the middle style of *Religio Medici*.[51] So how are we to judge? The relative grandness of style in Browne is as much an attitude as a matter of cadence, which is Warren's emphasis. Once he gets down to examples, he sounds less like Coriolanus; the tone is businesslike, briskly making discriminations. So, in Book III, he swiftly summarises the authorities for and against the existence of griffins and dismisses the evidence for as hearsay, derivative, or symbolic rather than descriptive, all in a matter of two or three pages. The Latinity of Browne's vocabulary is of striking, but secondary importance to this focused, critical conciseness – the kind of shrewd snap judgements that the practice of medicine requires. He may have been a polymath, but keeping the picture of Browne the physician in the back of one's mind is often an aid to reading him.

The loftiness of tone insists on the space between the educated, inquisitive intellect of the author and its confused, vulgar subject. Many of the 'vulgar' errors are from more elevated sources than folklore, though; errors from the classics and the Church Fathers come in for regular debunking. The *Pseudodoxia* is more respectful of modern than ancient learning, though there are moments when the loyalties are mixed. In the chapter on the badger he writes:

> That a brock or badger hath the legs of one side shorter than
> of the other, though an opinion perhaps not very ancient, is
> yet very general, received not only by theorists and
> unexperienced believers, but assented unto by most who
> have the opportunity to behold and hunt them daily; which
> notwithstanding upon enquiry I find repugnant unto the
> three determinators of truth, Authority, Sense and Reason.[52]

The rest of the chapter, after citing the medieval sceptic Albertus Magnus and the seventeenth-century zoologist Aldrovandus, argues against the belief from general observation of four-legged animals, 'as is determined by Aristotle'. He grants the unequal length of lobster claws, but says they are not strictly legs but for seizing prey; his principal strategy is to stress the irrationality of the belief by thinking about it – an obvious alternative, of unevenness diagonally, is more likely to produce movement because the legs of the same length will be on the ground at the same time. So here he is appealing to authority (Aristotle, no less), rationality in thinking through the consequences, and a certain amount of observation, but no direct evidence of his own or others on badgers themselves. By contrast, the final chapter of Book III, a compendium of assorted beliefs about animals, cites William Harvey's work on animal reproduction, published in 1651, to the praise of only two pillars of truth. The context is the fertilisation of hen's eggs:

> . . . how in the cicatricula or little pale circle formation first beginneth, how the grando or treadle [sperm], are but the poles and establishing particles of the tender membranes, firmly conserving the floating parts, in their proper places, with many other observables, that ocular philosopher, and singular discloser of truth, Dr Harvey hath discovered, in that excellent discourse of generation; so strongly erected upon the two great pillars of truth, experience and solid reason.
>   That the sex is discernible from the figure of eggs, or that cocks and hens proceed from long or round ones, as many contend, experiment will easily frustrate.[53]

This first appeared in the 1658 edition, and indicates either that Browne was willing to make use of reliable 'ocular' evidence when it was available, whether from an admired scientist like Harvey, or, as the second paragraph suggests, from his own experience; or that he was increasingly persuaded of the primary need for experimental evidence, in response to his own experience and the increase in scientific activity in the country in the 1650s. Browne was watching eagerly from the sidelines as science progressed in Europe as well as England; the contents of his own library testify to that, though it was his son rather than he who joined the Royal Society.

The style is essayistic in its wide-ranging associativeness, but the first-person singular is rare – 'we' is preferred. Browne is halfway to the impersonal essay form increasingly favoured from the Restoration as most appropriate for scientific reports.[54] The organisation into seven books, with 'Of Man' as the fourth, central one, derives from a number symbolism which belongs to what we now think of as a separate tradition of knowledge to science. Even this gets sceptical attention in his chapter 'Of the great climacterical year, that is, sixty-three': 'whatever is observable in any, falls under the account of some number; which notwithstanding cannot be denominated the cause of those events'.[55] The more detailed arrangement of sections within the books owes more to Bacon's categories than magic.[56] The range of his curiosity is enormous: if you want a seventeenth-century discussion of whether Adam and Eve had navels, or why Jews are supposed to stink, or the horn of unicorns, this is the book. Browne steadily added to it over several editions until 1672, and the final compilation is one of the last great Renaissance encyclopaedic treatises. Its increasing commitment to the evidence of the senses more than the authority of books makes it also an important text in the history of science. He is also aware that such projects are more suited to 'co-operating advancers' rather than the solitary scholar in his library, and that, too is a sign of the intellectual times.

As with all Browne's books, there is the strong note of elegy. Here it is in the farewell to exotic and fascinating beliefs as well as the stupid ones which can be summarily dismissed; as he says to the reader, in the second sentence of the book, 'what is worse, knowledge is made by oblivion; and to purchase a clear and warrantable body of truth we must forget and part with much we know'.[57]

Hydriotaphia, Urn-Burial, or, A Discourse of the Sepulchral Urns lately found in Norfolk was first published with *The Garden of Cyrus, or the Quincuncial, Lozenge, or Network Plantations of the Ancients, Artificially, Naturally, Mystically Considered* in 1658. Compared to the massive scope of the *Pseudodoxia* they are no more than extended essays, but they both range widely. The Norfolk urns of *Hydriotaphia*, some of which Browne himself had come across in Walsingham and Caister in Norfolk (he was a doctor in Norwich at the time) are really no more than pretexts for the discussion of burial customs, and thus human attitudes to death and immortality, but they do give an archaeological substance to the discussion which is often a combination of ancient and modern scholarship. If you would look, 'The treasures of time lie high, in urns, coins, and monuments, scarce below the roots of some vegetables.'[58] The plangent tone, the note of elegy which is seldom absent from the work, needs the 'vegetables'. It is a reminder of the ordinariness of death, that heroic monuments lie in ordinary earth.

Browne picks up a tone and a message from Ecclesiastes in the Old Testament, as well as an occasional quotation:

> Ægyptian ingenuity was more unsatisfied, contriving their
> bodies in sweet consistencies, to attend the return of their
> souls. But all was vanity, feeding the wind, and folly. The
> Ægyptian mummies, which Cambises or time hath spared,
> avarice now consumeth. Mummy is become merchandise,
> Mizraim cures wounds, and Pharaoh is sold for balsams.[59]

Browne himself notes in the margin that the second sentence in this quotation is Ecclesiastes 1: 14. His message, that burial customs which seek to preserve immortality without reference to 'Christian immortality' are folly, fits with a Christian use of this dark Old Testament book, and so does the plangency. But Browne's curiosity mixes the dismissiveness with a certain respect, rather like the famous paradox that 'man is a noble animal, splendid in ashes, and pompous in the grave'. Finish that last sentence as Browne does, 'in the infamy of his nature', and the paradox is resolved. What may begin as high elegiac phrases often end as rejections of paganism from a secure Christian orthodoxy.

If *Hydriotaphia* is Browne's Ecclesiastes, argues Frank L. Huntley, then *The Garden of Cyrus* is his Song of Solomon, his celebration of human work imitating nature and nature imitating God.[60] The way Browne puts it in the dedicatory letter suggests not only his sense of the connection between the two works, but why, like Bacon and Temple, he valued gardens:

> That we conjoin these parts of different subjects, or that this
> should succeed the other; your judgement will admit
> without impute of incongruity; since the delightful world
> comes after death, and paradise succeeds the grave. Since the
> verdant state of things is the symbol of the resurrection, and
> to flourish in the state of glory, we must first be sown in
> corruption. Beside the ancient practice of noble persons, to
> conclude in garden-graves, and urns themselves of old, to be
> wrapped up in flowers and garlands.[61]

The approach is nonetheless antiquarian, almost occult (his term is 'mystic') in the way he discovers the quincunx (an arrangement of five points, four at the corners of a rectangle and one in the middle) at every level from plantation to the mind of God. To begin with, the network of lozenge shapes, what you get from stringing Xs together, is simply the principal mode of planting and building of the ancients, from the hanging gardens of Babylon onwards. This is a pattern that is imitated from nature to assist in the cultivation of nature. The evidence is before us – roses had, originally, five leaves, and leaves themselves are often five-sided. Browne appeals to 'the eyes of signal discerners' here, not books, and then, as if to prove he is not completely obsessed by fives, describes the six-sided cells of the bee. The book, like its twin, is divided into five chapters.

The way that Browne's analysis veers between history and observation, art and nature, reminds us that the Enlightenment and Romantic versions of those polarities will not do for Browne. His universe is held together by analogy still, and that admits a numerological, or geometrical, or hieroglyphic series of correspondences which illuminate matters as much as Newton's laws of physics would for subsequent generations. That may suggest something overly firm – the tone is speculative and questioning, and perhaps, in the end, comic. Samuel Johnson, whose 'Life of Sir Thomas Browne' is still critically interesting, suggests an affinity with mock epic, those productions (mostly lost) of classical authors which trained great learning and disproportionate stylishness on trivial objects. The concluding paragraphs are not those of a treatise, or a victim of occult obsession; but of a diversion, a bedside book. The dream of paradise garden fades in the dullness of sleep, 'and though in the bed of Cleopatra, can hardly with any delight raise up the ghost of a rose'.[62] Browne's supreme skill at the prose cadence is not just to lull his reader good night, but also to remind him of the resurrection: 'who can be drowsy at that hour which freed us from everlasting sleep? or have slumbering thoughts at that time, when sleep itself must end, and as some conjecture all shall awake again?'[63] 'Conjecture' had to have almost the last word in this treatise. As Jonathan Post remarks of *Hydriotaphia*, it is entirely and uniquely characteristic of Browne to contain grand Christian truth and the drive to personal contentment with many an outlandish piece of learning.[64] He is enough of a scientist to introduce a sceptical note in such moments, too.

Notes

1. Terence Cave, *The Cornucopian Text* (Oxford, 1979), p. 183.

2. James E. Miller, ed., *Theory of Fiction: Henry James* (Lincoln, Nebraska 1972), p. 262.

3. D.W. Jefferson, '*Tristram Shandy* and its Tradition', *From Dryden to Johnson*, The Pelican Guide to English Literature, Vol. 4, ed. Boris Ford (Harmondsworth, 1957), pp. 333–45.

4. For a helpful discussion of the sixteenth-century theories of *copia* see Cave, *The Cornucopian Text*, Ch. 1.

5. See 'Epic and Novel' in M.M. Bakhtin, *The Dialogic Imagination*, ed. Michael Holquist (Austin, 1981).

6. See David Norbrook, *Poetry and Politics in the English Renaissance* (1984), especially pp. 43–90.

7. See Charles Nicholl, *A Cup of News: The Life of Thomas Nashe* (1984), p. 99.

8. Thomas Nashe, *The Unfortunate Traveller and Other Works*, ed. J.B. Steane (Harmondsworth, 1972), p. 57.

9. The last point is made by Lorna Hutson, *Thomas Nashe in Context* (Oxford, 1989); her chapter on *Pierce* (pp. 172–96) is of considerable interest.

10. Compare the discussion of 'archaic moralism' in the more oppositional court

poetry of the sixteenth century (the phrase is used of Ralegh) in Gary Waller, *English Poetry of the Sixteenth Century* (Harlow, 1986), Ch. 4.

11. Nashe, p. 65

12. Nashe, p. 78

13. Nicholl, pp. 103–8.

14. Nashe, p. 109.

15. For some examples of the working of patents of monopoly, see Joan Thirsk, *Economic Policy and Projects: The Development of a Consumer Society in Early Modern England*, (Oxford, 1978) pp. 59–66.

16. For the survival of fasts and feasts in the period, see Keith Thomas, *Religion and the Decline of Magic* (paper edn, Harmondsworth, 1973), pp. 738–43.

17. Nashe, p. 372.

18. The main anti-Harvey pamphlet is *Have with You To Saffron Walden*; for the complete text see McKerrow's edition.

19. Nashe, p. 383.

20. Nashe, p. 394.

21. Nashe, pp. 414–16.

22. Nashe, p. 420.

23. For the precise figures for each edition, see the Textual Introduction to Vol. I of Robert Burton, *The Anatomy of Melancholy*, ed. Thomas C. Faulkner, Nicholas K. Kiessling and Rhonda L. Blair (Oxford, 1989–), p. xxxvii.

24. For satire, see Bud Korkowski, 'Genre and Satiric Strategy in Burton's *Anatomy of Melancholy*', *Genre*, 8 (1975), 74–87; for homily, E. Patricia Vicari, *The View from Minerva's Tower: Learning and Imagination in The Anatomy of Melancholy* (Toronto, 1989).

25. Burton, *Anatomy*, I, p. 6.

26. Ibid., I, p. 1.

27. Ibid., I, p. 5.

28. Ibid., I, p. 304.

29. Ibid., I, p. 85.

30. *The Anatomy of Melancholy*, ed. Floyd Dell and Paul Jordan-Smith (New York, 1948).

31. Burton, *Anatomy*, I, p. 11.

32. Burton, *Anatomy*, I, p. 90.

33. Burton, *Anatomy*, I, p. 3.

34. Burton, *Anatomy*, I, p. 91.

35. See J.C. Davis, *Utopia and the Ideal Society* (Cambridge, 1981), Ch. 4.

36. Burton, *Anatomy*, I, p. 141

37. Burton, *Anatomy*, I, p. 163.

38. See the fascinating study of Richard Napier and his patients in this period, Michael Macdonald, *Mystical Bedlam: Madness, Anxiety and Healing in Seventeenth-Century England* (Cambridge, 1981); pp. 150–60 concentrate on melancholy.

39. Burton, *Anatomy*, II, p. 266.

40. Burton, *Anatomy*, II, p. 33.

41. Burton, *Anatomy*, II, p. 58.

42. Burton, *Anatomy*, I, p. 194.

43. Burton, *Anatomy*, ed. Holbrook Jackson (1932), III, pp. 312–13. (The Oxford edition of the Third Partition was not published when I wrote this section; so all references to the Third Partition are to the earlier edition.)

44. Burton, *Anatomy*, III, p. 321.

45. Burton, *Anatomy*, III, p. 375.

46. Michael O'Connell, *Robert Burton* (Boston, 1986), p. 67.

47. For the relationship between the cabinet of curiosities and late Renaissance texts (Browne is mentioned, but Shakespeare is a more prominent example), see Steven Mullaney, 'Strange Things, Gross Terms, Curious Customs: The Rehearsal of Cultures in the Late Renaissance' in *Representing the Renaissance*, ed. Stephen Greenblatt (Berkeley, 1988), pp. 65–92.

48. *The Diary of John Evelyn*, ed. John Bowle (Oxford, 1985), p. 241.

49. Leonard Nathanson, 'Sir Thomas Browne and the Ethics of Knowledge', in *Approaches to Sir Thomas Browne: The Ann Arbor Tercentenary Lectures and Essays*, ed. C.A. Patrides (Columbia, Miss., 1982), pp. 12–18.

50. *Pseudodoxia Epidemica*, ed. Robin Robbins (Oxford, 1981), I, p. 15.

51. Austin Warren, 'The Styles of Sir Thomas Browne', in *Seventeenth-Century Prose*, ed. Stanley E. Fish (New York, 1971), pp. 413–23.

52. *Pseudodoxia Epidemica*, I, p. 176.

53. *Pseudodoxia Epidemica*, 1, p. 288, and see Robbins' notes in II, p. 895.

54. See Ted-Larry Pebworth, 'Wandering in the America of Truth: *Pseudodoxia Epidemica* and the Essay Tradition', in *Approaches to Sir Thomas Browne*, ed. C.A. Patrides (Columbia, Missouri, 1982), pp. 166–77.

55. *Pseudodoxia Epidemica*, I, p. 342.

56. See *Pseudodoxia Epidemica*, I, p. xxxi.

57. *Pseudodoxia Epidemica*, I, p. 1.

58. Sir Thomas Browne, *The Major Works*, ed. C.A. Patrides (Harmondsworth, 1977), p. 267.

59. Ibid., p. 312.

60. Frank L. Huntley, 'Sir Thomas Browne: The Relationship of *Urne Burial* and *The Garden of Cyrus*', in *Seventeenth-Century Prose: Modern Essays in Criticism*, ed. Stanley E. Fish (New York, 1971), pp. 424–39.

61. Browne, *Major Works*, p. 321.

62. Ibid., p. 387.
63. Ibid., pp. 387–8.
64. Jonathan F.S. Post, *Sir Thomas Browne* (Boston, 1987), p. 157.

Part Four
The Discourse of Modernity: New Idioms in Science and Politics

Introduction

Almost every period in English history has its emergent discourse, an approach to describing the world which, by hindsight, is the one that will dominate people's perceptions in the following period. It is then presented as a growth in knowledge (which it usually is) and a loss of past wholeness. This latter perecption is more likely to be a mixture of truth and nostalgia. Thomas Kuhns' theory of paradigm change in scientific revolutions, whether applicable to other kinds of change or not, does remind us that old schemes of knowledge are very resilient, because people are wary of change, and they can absorb a lot of adaptations and new information before they actually displace the whole framework.

In retrospect, we can see a number of changes in the prose literature of the seventeenth century which signal paradigm shifts in their society's perception of the world. I group many of them together in this chapter, not least because they all result in a different kind of prose being written. Some of them – the new sense of the self, for example – have already been treated, and will only reappear in a subordinate role.

Chapter 12
The Great Instauration and the Royal Society

Francis Bacon

The changes that science has brought on the way we live and think about the world have made it almost coterminous with modernity. The changes would be impossible without the institutional structure to network information and research, and the process of technological and industrial exploitation to ensure that the discoveries make some impact beyond the laboratory. The seventeenth-century pioneers were important in their institutional innovations as much as the experimental science they did, or their philosophical ground-clearing.

Francis Bacon was not a great scientist, but he had a very clear sense of what was needed for science to flourish. He was a formidable legal rhetorician who recognised the intellectual limits of rhetoric; and enough of a politician to see that a new development of the scope he wanted needed an institutional base. He suggested as early as 1594 that Elizabeth should spend some money on a laboratory – a decidedly optimistic suggestion in view of her usual aversion to parting with money.

His first substantial intervention was the 1605 *Advancement of Learning*. The first part begins with a praise of James I, which to a modern reader may sound fulsome, but it was astute. James had some pretence to learning – the later discussion of Solomon picks up his favourite self-image – and the project Bacon had in mind needed considerable resources. What we would now call 'science', with all its claims of usefulness and objectivity, had an eccentric if not suspicious reputation at the time. Jonson's *The Alchemist* (1610) gives one verdict on its practice – high-sounding nonsense mixed with greed – while other critics suspected atheism or occult involvement. Ralegh's circle had been investigated for atheism, and Ralegh had an alchemical laboratory set up in the Tower. Admittedly, the fact that one of his products, the Great Cordial, was administered to the ailing Prince Henry in 1612, stretches all kinds of assumptions, not just about the legitimacy of alchemy but about the status of a convicted traitor. Royal patronage would mean respectability, and might attract intelligent men to join the project.

The main thrust of Part One, though, was to survey the limitations and criticisms of the current state of knowledge. The originality of Bacon's approach is apparent even in this, with its assumption that knowledge is cumulative. In a culture which educated its élite almost entirely in the substance and method of ancient texts, it was close to iconoclasm. Bacon wasn't completely revolutionary, though; *The Advancement* is studded with arguments from scripture, Aristotle and Plato, and he did not regard every branch of knowledge as operating in the same way:

> And as for the overmuch credit that hath been given unto authors in sciences, in making them dictators, that their words should stand, and not counsellors to give advice; the damage is infinite that sciences have received thereby, as the principal cause that hath kept them low at a stay without growth or advancement. For hence it hath come, that in arts mechanical the first deviser comes shortest, and time addeth, and perfecteth; but in sciences the first author goeth farthest, and time leeseth and corrupteth.[1]

The terms need a bit of glossing: 'author' is closer to our 'authority'; 'arts mechanical' include things like artillery and printing; 'sciences' include philosophy as well as geometry. Bacon is here stating the facts as they would have appeared in 1605: clearly navigation, say, had improved, but philosophy hadn't got further than Aristotle, partly because it hadn't allowed itself to. Bacon wanted advance in all areas, and in Part Two identifies some of the branches of knowledge where work might start. ('Branches' is no dead metaphor, incidentally; his work is full of organic metaphors for the interlinking of knowledge.)

If we compare *The Advancement* with the appeals of modern educationalists for cash and respect, we notice a similar plea for usefulness, though economics is not so high on Bacon's agenda. Political usefulness is prominent; an educated government results in peaceful times, he argues, though learned men are not above externally directed warmongering, and they are better at strategy. Where a traditional liberal position might argue for the disinterested pursuit of learning, Bacon argues from Scripture that it is part of the purpose of creation for human beings to enquire and experiment. We might also hesitate at the masculine assumptions, as in the description of Queen

Elizabeth 'endued with learning in her sex singular, and great even amongst masculine princes'.[2]

The student of Bacon's prose is likely to see a tension between his programme and its expression. The organisation and expression of *The Advancement* is that of a reformed Renaissance rhetorical document. It is an argument for a position, and he marshals his authorities, stories and metaphors to make it as persuasive as possible. However, as Lisa Jardine has argued, he was bound to see these arts as parasitic 'because he is so deeply preoccupied with *discovery* as the primary mode of human experience'.[3] He identifies 'the first distemper of learning, when men study words and not matter . . . for words are but the images of matter; and except they have life of reason and invention, to fall in love with them is all one as to fall in love with a picture'.[4] Such a view was bound, in the end, to topple rhetoric and dialectic from its primary position in education. But there is a problem, because words are not simply 'the images of matter', however much one would like to get, say, the medical lecturer away from expounding Galen and into the dissection room with his students. His later advice, always to start with definitions, is more helpful; words get their meaning from human agreement rather than from some symbiosis with matter.

A literary interest in Bacon's scientific works runs the risk of seeming skewed, stressing the stylistic implications of his project more than the institutional or philosophic aspects. However, Bacon realised that such a revolutionary programme had to advance on all fronts. The culture of argument which he was aiming to replace was a literary one, and had to be faced in its own terms, at the level of language and method. This was particularly true because he did not place mathematics at the centre of his scientific programme, and that might have fulfilled some of the roles of his reformed logic and language. The paradox is that his attack on decadent learning is still in the terms of Renaissance rhetoric. Bacon thus offers a good example of the game of spot the metaphor used in the attack on excess metaphor, a game of particular delight to students of Restoration prose. But we should beware of stretching this too far. Bacon is not so much attacking humanism with its own weapons as drawing out one of its most liberating tendencies, the return to origins rather than relying on the encrusted commentaries of the ages. Where someone like Erasmus was doing this with classical and biblical texts, Bacon was proposing this with nature as well. In this he was close to humanistic learning on the Continent, which was already ahead in such areas as anatomy and astronomy.

We can see Bacon's programme more explicitly set out in *The Great Instauration* of 1611, published in Latin, towards 'a total reconstruction of sciences, arts, and all human knowledge, raised upon the proper foundations'.[5] A grand scheme, and one with different aims to the education and much of the scholarship of his time:

> For the end which this science of mine proposes is the invention not of arguments but of arts; not of things in accordance with principles, but of principles themselves; not of probable reasons, but of designations and directions for works. And as the intention is different, so accordingly is the effect; the effect of the one being to overcome an opponent in argument, of the other to command nature in action.[6]

Bacon still has plenty of arguments to win before this can happen, which is why so much of his work is rhetorical in the old sense. Commanding nature, though, is a new centre, a strongly modernising ambition. (I am using modernity here in an extra-literary sense; nothing to do with Modernism as an artistic movement, but close to what a Third World country today might think of as 'modernisation', exploiting natural resources for human benefit.) A few pages later he remarks that man is only a servant and interpreter of nature, which may seem contradictory, but could be taken as a further pointer to his attempt to refocus scholarly interest on nature before texts about nature. The six-part project is outlined as follows, with those works of Bacon which might be taken as part of the project in parentheses:

(1) The Divisons of the Sciences [*Great Instauration, Advancement of Learning/De Augmentis*]
(2) The New Organon; or Directions concerning the Interpretation of Nature [*Novum Organum*]
(3) The Phenomena of the Universe; or a Natural and Experimental History for the foundation of Philosophy [*Sylva Sylvarum*]
(4) The Ladder of the Intellect
(5) The Forerunners; or Anticipations of the New Philosophy
(6) The New Philosophy.[7]

The fourth section is really a series of exercises and examples from section two, to prepare the mind for the new way of investigation; section five describes the observations and speculations that are published on the way to the certainties of the new philosophy. Bacon was always wary of being too certain too soon.

What was Bacon's method?[8] We have emphasised the ground-clearing side of his project, the rejection or suspension of received ideas and procedures, to which we must add his project for training the mind so that it does not leap to conclusions on the evidence of the senses which can itself be deceptive – here he sees the value of instruments, though, with his usual mathematical blind spot, does not stress their ability to give precise numerical values. On the positive side is his concept of induction, of piling up reliable experimental data until a general conclusion from them is inescapable. It is cumulative, but also eliminative, recognising the power of the negative instance to dislodge a hypothesis.

Bacon's brilliant theoretical and institutional proposals made him the patron saint of the Royal Society when it was founded in 1660. Notoriously, though, he missed some of the best science that was going on around him – William Harvey was his personal physician, but he discounted his discovery of the circulation of the blood (hailed as Copernican in its implications by Thomas Browne – but then Bacon didn't rate Copernicus either). He dismissed Gilbert's work on magnetism as occult fantasy, whereas the usual view is that it was the best combination of observation and theory in English science before the 1660s. He may have regarded himself as a bell to call the wits together, but that only happened posthumously. Money may have been as much a problem as his perception of who the best scientists were; his bequest of lectureships to Oxford and Cambridge foundered because he died in debt.

Bacon's proposals are sometimes criticised for being overly technological, of not leaving enough space for the imagination in science. This may seem odd, as Bacon has survived more than anything as a literary figure, but it may be part of the Bacon-as-cold-fish syndrome which also affects appreciation of the *Essays*. There are a number of answers to this, but let two suffice, *The New Atlantis* and his use of metaphor.

New Atlantis was published posthumously, unfinished, a fragment of some forty pages. It is a scientific Utopia, with nods to More's example as well as the travel literature of the period. The island of Bensalem is discovered by some sailors between Peru and China. To begin with, this fictional frame mixes description of the island and its inhabitants with satire of the society the explorers have left behind in the classic utopian manner. The inhabitants are clever enough to operate a quarantine system – many New World populations had been decimated by influenza and similar Western imports. They also refuse presents, describing salaried officials who do so as 'twice paid', a clear reference to the kind of corruption of which Bacon himself had been accused. The keynotes of Bensalem society, then, are honesty and applied scientific knowledge. Honesty in the seventeenth-century sense, too – chastity: 'there is not under the heavens so chaste a nation as this of Bensalem; nor so free from all pollution or foulness. It is the virgin of the world.'[9] This comes in the description of the Feast of the Family, a ceremony to celebrate a father with thirty 'descended of his body alive together'. Such a patriarchy could only have a monarchy at its heart, and that is virtually all we hear of its political institutions, and many judicial functions seem to be devolved onto the family as well.

The main focus of the unfinished text is the description of Salomon's House, 'dedicated to the study of the works and creatures of God', and, in terms parallel to the Instauration, for 'the knowledge of causes, and secret motions of things; and the enlarging of the bounds of humane empire, to the effecting of all things possible'.[10] There is a strong emphasis on the practical benefits, improving medicine and cultivation in particular. The college has an impressive array of laboratories, caves, towers, lakes, wells and so on. The fellows of this 'college' have responsibility for particular tasks, ranging from the collection or compilation of information to 'three that raise the former discoveries by experiments into greater observations, axioms, and aphorisms. These we call Interpreters of Nature'.[11]

The 'Father' of the house that the traveller meets, who tells him all this, is much honoured. The procession that carries him is described in rich, emblematic detail (rather like the Temple of Solomon in the Old Testament), and he carries a crosier and a pastoral staff like a bishop, 'and had an aspect as if he pitied men'.[12] That last phrase manages to imply scholarly detachment, and humane, or even Godlike concern at the same time.

The link with the Old Testament Solomon would, ten years earlier, have suggested the favourite self-image of James I; whether Bacon was still dreaming of a Royal Society *avant la lettre* is unlikely. It does reinforce our sense that Bacon conceived his scientific project in Christian terms, and while some critics have detected elements of Masonic ritual in the description of the Father of Salomon's House (and the oath of secrecy they all take), none of Bacon's publishing or experimental behaviour suggest occultism. There is a thesis, associated with Frances Yates in particular, that the road from medieval to modern science in the Renaissance goes through Renaissance hermeticism, but Bacon seems to have been wary of it. Indeed, if Charles Webster is right, one reason why Bacon's work was taken up by the Puritan scientists of the 1640s and 1650s was its resolutely Christian, progressive, and thus potentially millenarian cast.[13] Certainly Bensalem is a society based on revealed Christianity (through an ark containing the scriptures cast on the water by one of the apostles).

Bensalem has managed to acquire the essence of European wisdom, then, first by revelation and then by scientific research. What they have avoided is Aristotle; they have a long tradition of empirical research instead dating back to Salomon, their pre-Christian founder of the arts and sciences.

One of the most interesting of the research jobs in Salomon's House is the Merchant of Light. The trading expeditions of Bensalem are for knowledge rather than commodities; they leave three behind, *incognito*,

> whose errand was only to give us knowledge of the affairs
> and state of those countries to which they were designed,
> and especially of the sciences, arts, manufactures, and
> inventions of all the world; and withal to bring to us books,
> instruments, and patterns in every kind . . . thus you see we
> maintain a trade, not for gold, silver, or jewels; nor for silks;
> nor for spices; nor any other commodity of matter; but only
> for God's first creature, which was Light: to have light (I
> say) of the growth of all parts of the world.[14]

In embryo, Bacon is describing the project of Enlightenment, though out of Genesis 1, rather than the secularisation of knowledge. By this means (it would be industrial espionage if it were not the whole of Bensalem's trading ambition) they manage to acquire the wisdom of the world without being corrupted by it. *New Atlantis* thus becomes a powerful comment on the experience of colonialisation – the fact that they speak Spanish reflects the success of the Spanish empire at this stage. The country is described as a virgin, like Ralegh's Virginia or Guiana, but it does not share in the cultural youthfulness of America.[15] The emphasis on chastity suggests that neither is it likely to be ravished by colonial exploitation. It absorbs its visitors by its generosity, and thus remains hidden. The fictional problem of how to get the message out is not tackled – the work was left unfinished at Bacon's death, with the scientific programme clear but with the social and political structures only sketched. Bacon directed that it should be published with *Sylva Sylvarum*, the major collection of his scientific experiments, showing where he had decided to put the remainder of his energies.

So, Bacon was enough of an innovator for us to think of much of the growth of science in the century as the growth of the Baconian tradition, yet he made no major discoveries and formulated no new scientific laws. His literary bequest to science was crucial in helping to free it from the need to expound the ancient texts. But no one reading Bacon could think that the plainness of his style is to do with the absence of metaphor.[16] His demolition of unproductive practices is unthinkable without his incisive choice of imagery. His major organising descriptions of what is wrong with learning – 'distempers', or diseases, and 'idols', false objects of worship – have a precise range of implication beyond their immediate satiric force, suggesting the organic nature of learning (if one part is infected, the rest is affected) and the proper reverence involved in studying creation. The role of images in the detail of Bacon's polemic is best illustrated by the two linked pictures in this passage from the first book of the *Advancement*:

> Surely, like as many substances in nature which are solid do putrify and corrupt into worms; so it is the property of good and sound knowledge to putrify and dissolve into a number of subtle, idle, unwholesome, and, as I may term them, vermiculate questions, which have indeed a kind of quickness and life of spirit, but no soundness of matter or goodness of quality. This kind of degenerate learning did chiefly reign amongst the Schoolmen: who having sharp and strong wits, and abundance of leisure, and small variety of reading, but their wits being shut up in the cells of a few authors (chiefly Aristotle their dictator) as their persons were shut up in the cells of monasteries and colleges, and knowing little history, either of nature or time, did out of no great quantity of matter and infinite agitation of wit spin out unto those laborious webs of learning which are extant in their books. For the wit and mind of man, if it work upon matter, which is the contemplation of the creatures of God, worketh according to the stuff, and is limited thereby; but if it work upon itself, as the spider worketh his web, then it is endless, and brings forth indeed cobwebs of learning, admirable for the fineness of thread and work, but of no substance or profit.[17]

In such an extended quotation we can see how the images are woven into the argument, and provide a clinching as well as an illustration of it. The passage demonstrates not only Bacon's hostility to scholasticism and its descendants, but the shift from 'matter' as the subject or topic of a discourse to something much more material, things, the works of creation.[18] Bacon's own strategy of belittling weaves images and their associations with devastating skill. First, putrefaction produces worms – bookworms, or the ones you find on corpses. That image is clinched by 'vermiculate', according to OED Bacon's own coinage (from the Latin for 'worm'), and in itself the kind of 'inkhorn term' that the English Renaissance had variously spawned, or tried to avoid. However, the word appears to have passed into general usage. Bacon was no enemy of Latin as the international scholarly language, but there is a difference between writing in Latin, and writing English as if it were Latin, and Bacon is rarely Latinate in that sense, except for special effects such as this. From the worms of learning, with entirely parasitic liveliness, we pass to the cells in which they are created, isolated from the world and thus the reality of things. The mention of monasticism discredits it further by association with the dreaded Catholicism. 'Knowing little history, either of nature or time' shows where Bacon's source, and test, of real knowledge is to be found; 'Natural History' is still a current term, and putting it next to our other sense of History shows that their retirement is doubly fruitless. Instead they are spinning cobwebs, the proverbial sign of an unswept room. This implication of the image remains in the background as Bacon works out his conceit, picking up the sense of 'subtle' from the previous sentence (then almost entirely pejorative). The spider is particularly apt because its web is generated out of its own substance, but thin; intricate, but of no great strength. Such a comprehensive use of the image comes from that precise contemplation of nature which Bacon is advocating. It is not everywhere in Bacon that one can adopt close reading techniques to show the complexly useful nature of his imagery, but they are often there when his argument needs to be most forceful. Both construction and demolition modes show a rich imagination.

During the thirty years between Bacon's death and the foundation of the Royal Society a number of groups as well as individuals took the idea of collaborative, experimental science on, though, as with Bacon, there was more scheming than achievement. A number of groups were active. Gresham College in London, which had been founded in the late Elizabethan period, had a distinguished record in mathematics and its application to navigational problems, but was not at its peak during this period; its importance as a meeting place was revived when the Royal Society met on its premises. The '1645 group', so called by historians after the date of their first meeting, consisted of a group of mathematicians who happened to be parliamentarians; and a group of physicians, mostly followers of Harvey, with an interest in experimental science, with Royalist sympathies. They avoided discussing theology and politics! They later split into groups based in London and Oxford, whose membership overlaps with the early Royal Society. Then there was the crucial influence of the emigrés, Hartlib, Comenius and Haak, who imported continental models of co-operative research as well as European contacts.[19] The atmosphere, the millenarian excitement of the Commonwealth encouraged science; but in such a way that it was never so linked to Cromwell's regime as to be anathema after 1660. On the contrary, it became fashionable. The Royal Society's first heyday, of the 1660s and 1670s, is one demonstration of the intellectual continuity of the mid-century.

The foundation of the Royal Society does not mark anything as revolutionary as the birth of modern science, or its professionalisation, but it comes close at times. It was a corporate, public body, with salaried officials, and with the important privilege of publication independent of censorship. However, it depended on the subscriptions of individuals rather than public funds – though that is often true of learned societies today. It had no premises of its own until 1710. A glance at their early membership, or the *Philosophical Transactions*, first issued in 1665 and edited by Henry Oldenburg, shows something much more amateur than the work of a modern academic science department or research institute, if taken as a whole. Some of the activities are recognisably those of modern science – the collection of new and reliable experimental instruments, such as Boyle's air-pump, or the presentation of new data. There is a strong interest in technology, applying science to manufacture, agriculture, or the defence of the realm. Equally, there are the curiosities, the amazingly tall man, or the strange varieties of shells; somewhere between the collection of rare specimens and the *Guinness Book of Records*.

The membership ranged from those such as Pepys, or the bishops, whose interest in science was genuine but incidental to their main work, to the Boyles, Ray and Hooke, whose scientific work seems to have been the focus of their working lives. As the century progresses we see an increasing tension between the wide-ranging and inclusive intellectual ambitions of the Society and its resources in an age which generated an information explosion; 'the difficulties of trying to reform the whole of knowledge about the natural world through the part-time activities of volunteers' caused insurmountable organisational problems.[20]

We should also beware of thinking that Restoration science was confined to the activities of the Royal Society, ignoring the groups, individuals and universities working outside.[21] The work of the College of Physicians in particular is representative of another tradition of experimental usefulness; William Harvey's discovery of the circulation of the blood, one of the most remarkable as well as useful scientific achievements of the century, is in this rather than the Baconian tradition.

Thomas Sprat and John Wilkins

An account of science in a history of prose is bound to take a sideways approach, but there are several points of contact of importance to both activities. First is the Royal Society's reforming programme for English prose, expressed most vigorously in Thomas Sprat's commissioned *History* of 1667. Linked with that are the universal or philosophical language experiments of the period, most notably Wilkins's *Essay* which was printed by the Society in 1668. These answer to the Baconian project, not just against that 'distemper of learning' which elevates words over things, but also the desire to encompass learning within a new, comprehensive scheme. The other side of Bacon, the aphoristic, provisional statement of knowledge in process, can be seen in the accounts of experiments in the period, and their relationship to the essay and narrative. Finally, we must consider two riders to the scientific project after 1660: the extent to which it was linked with a new temper in the Church of England, particularly the Latitudinarian movement, and its role in the Ancients versus Moderns controversy.

A brief semantic preliminary is necessary. I have been using 'science' in its modern sense, and there is some seventeenth-century usage which corresponds, though more usually it simply means 'knowledge', or the branches of knowledge without the modern overtones of a particular 'scientific' approach. However, the more usual term is 'philosophy', which includes some of what we would call philosophy as well as all that we would call science. 'New philosophy', a phrase used more than once by Donne in the earlier part of the century, usually refers to the astronomy of Copernicus and his successors such as Kepler and Galileo. In the Restoration, 'natural philosophy', and, more pointedly, 'experimental philosophy', are the terms by which the new science is usually recognised.

Thomas Sprat's *History of the Royal Society* was published in 1667, so early in the Society's history that one suspects less history than promotion, and its manner is 'not altogether in the way of a plain history, but sometimes of an apology [i.e., defence]' as he admits in the 'Advertisement to the Reader'. In fact it should have come out in 1664, but the writer's delays, and the Plague and the Great Fire, pushed it back. Only the second part is, strictly, the story of how the Society was founded; the first part surveys science from the Babylonians and Greeks through to the present day, and the third part is a more general defence of 'Experimental Knowledge', though with the emphasis on the Society's role. It was commissioned by the Society, printed by it, and supervised by its secretary, John Wilkins, who had been Sprat's mentor at Oxford.

The early, promotional status of the book means that we need to see it as a statement of intent for a wider audience rather than a description of its actual practice. A recent study of its institutional and political purpose argues that 'by a combination of subtle misrepresentation and selective exposition, Sprat portrayed a method which would further the aims of social and ecclesiastical stability and material prosperity'.[22] Certainly there are whole sections where Sprat is performing a characteristic Restoration task, of appropriating the millenarian and nationalist rhetoric of the Commonwealth period for the new establishment. There is a lot about the special English genius for plain practicality. The scientific activity of the Commonwealth is seen as a relief from the tensions of Civil War in contemplating Nature, and the scientific discipline as a less disputatious, and thus more politically eirenic philosophy than scholasticism: 'the unfeigned and laborious philosophy gives no countenance to the vain dotage of private politicians: that bends its disciples to regard the benefit of mankind, and not the disquiet: that by the moderation it prescribes to our thoughts about natural things, will also take away all sharpness and violence about civil . . .'.[23] Sprat is also anxious to demonstrate that the new science is not anti-religious in its attention to the material world. This was a common focus of attack, and one that particularly engaged Joseph Glanvill, another vigorous apologist for the young society. Both of them emphasise the rationality of science and religion, in contrast (sometimes implicit) to the disruptive enthusiasm of the Commonwealth sects, and to occult and alchemical tendencies within science.[24] The Baconian emphasis on separating 'the knowledge of nature from the colours of rhetoric, the devices of fancy, or the delightful deceit of fables'[25] has acquired more targets than scholasticism on its journey through the seventeenth century.

Sprat's account of the society's respectability precedes his praise of its method of working, the weekly meetings, the experiments, the international contacts through correspondence and the 'noble and inquisitive genius' of merchants; finally, he praises their manner of discourse and their methodical keeping of registers. The 'luxury and redundance of speech . . . this superfluity of talking' have already corrupted most other arts and professions, so much that 'eloquence ought to be banished out of all civil societies, as a thing fatal to peace and good manners' if that would not leave innocence exposed to 'armed malice'.[26] So he won't abandon rhetoric for the right purposes. The Royal Society will correct its 'excesses' in Natural Philosophy:

> They have therefore been most rigorous in putting in
> execution, the only remedy, that can be found for this
> extravagance: and that has been, a constant resolution, to
> reject all the amplifications, digressions, and swellings of
> style: to return back to the primitive purity, and shortness,
> when men delivered so many things, almost in an equal
> number of words. They have exacted from all their

members, a close, naked, natural way of speaking; positive
expressions; clear senses; a native easiness; bringing all things
as near the mathematical plainness, as they can: and
preferring the language of Artisans, countrymen, and
merchants, before that, of wits, or scholars.[27]

This paragraph is itself not free of rhetorical devices, but that is not a
disabling criticism. The statement needs testing against the Society's
practice, too, which we will do later. We need to note here the
ideological markers: that this is a return to primitive purity, as the sects
promised and as Anglicanism claimed, not 'progress'; the appeal to
'nature', next to 'naked' and close to 'things', as the source of what is
good in language; and the anti-scholastic appeal to artisans, countrymen
and merchants, which may at first seem at odds with Sprat's bid for
respectability, but in fact chimes happily with his description of the
Society as composed largely of gentlemen, and thus with landed
interests, as well as his foregrounding of the usefulness of the Society's
work for economic activity.

There is also a tension between the theory of words as being close to
things, and the 'mathematical plainness', which is the plainness of
abstraction. The first theory, taken literally, can seem absurd, as Swift
noted in Book III of *Gulliver's Travels*, where he has his language
reformers carry a sack of objects round with them, with which they
carry on conversation. Nouns stand for classes of things, but can be
used to indicate particular things; the habit of generalisation is thus
built into language, however much the Baconian programme might
resist it. As we have noted, mathematics is the blind spot in Baconian
science, but the most important innovators of the Royal Society, most
particularly Newton, made their chief contribution by allying the
abstracting power of mathematics with precise observation.

Appreciating this relationship might also solve the problem of the
apparent antagonism between Royal Scoiety plainness and the kind of
generalisation that we associate with the Augustan mode in literature
coming into being in parallel. William Youngren has rightly stressed
the continuity between Renaissance and Restoration critical theory;
Sidney, Dryden and Pope all stress the power of poetry as opposed to
philosophy in providing examples.[28] The increasing prestige of abstract
nouns comes, not just from the philosophy of Hobbes and Locke
stressing the connection of words and ideas, but from the new science's
achievements in building a series of predictive 'laws' of nature. So,
while the poetic theory continues to stress examples and truth to
nature, the diction, and the sense of what nature is, is changing.[29]
Sprat's *History* is one of the important markers of that change, but it is
a statement of intent, angled by all sorts of institutional and political

pressures, rather than the statement of achievement that he has persuaded many to read it as.

The year following Sprat's *History* saw his patron and adviser John Wilkins's *Essay Towards a Real Character, and a Philosophical Language*, though it had been in preparation for much longer, and was delayed further by the first printing being lost in the Great Fire of London. Wilkins had published earlier work on language, with the aim of clarifying communication. *Mercury* is an early attempt at an international script based on Hebrew characters; *Ecclesiastes* is a manual on preaching, with the emphasis on 'the most easy perspicuous phrase that may be' in expounding scripture.[30] *An Essay* is a comprehensive attempt to construct a language in which every symbol corresponds precisely to a category of reality – 'a real universal character, that should not signify words, but things and notions, and consequently might be legible by any nation in their own tongue'. He says that it derives from a wish of Galen for a representation of 'things by such peculiar signs and names as should express their natures'.[31] In other words, learning the character would involve learning the nature of things at the same time; the language is not just a more precise tool than English or Latin for representing knowledge, it *is* knowledge.

Although Wilkins was very perceptive about the nature of language, particularly the role of custom and the way language changes, the vast majority of *An Essay* is not about linguistics but the classification of knowledge. For 400 folio pages things and notions are classified under forty principal genera. In addition there is a class of conceptions, 'transcendentals' – kinds, causes, differences, modes, and so on – which function as a means of discussion and manipulation of the categories. Behind it is not just the desire to collect and classify real, observable knowledge, though Wilkins was very conscientious here, and collaborated with other members of the Royal Society, notably Ray on the botanical material, and Pepys on naval matters, to get the categories right. It is the sense that such classification can name real essences – in other words, it is still not emancipated from a central Aristotelian concept.

The drive to taxonomy which this represents is well suited to certain life sciences, such as botany and zoology. The new mechanical philosophy, as exemplified in the chemistry of Boyle and the physics of Newton, was different, more concerned with relations and probabilities than fixed essences. Wilkins's project was of no real use to them. The biologists of the period did need a more precise language, but their scientific jargon was more indebted to that older international language, Latin, than 'philosophical' languages, even if Latin took forty times longer to learn, on Wilkins's estimate. Ray himself had reservations about the restrictiveness of Wilkins's categories during their collaboration. There were some attempts to carry on the language even after Wilkins's death – some correspondence in it survives – but it turned out to be the conclusion as well as the culmination of the seventeenth century's universal language experiments as far as science was concerned. The next stage for scientific language was mathematical, even if the artificial languages lived on where they had begun, in shorthand, cryptography and the imaginary and utopian societies of fiction.[32]

Two institutional footnotes. Wilkins's scheme was originally suggested to him by Seth Ward, when he was Savilian Professor of Astronomy at Oxford in the 1650s. *An Essay* is as much a result of the Oxford scientific circle as the Royal Society which published it, and shows that the universities, though often recidivist about the new science, especially in their undergraduate syllabus, were nonetheless important homes for discussion.[33] Secondly, Wilkins's 'Epistle Dedicatory' shows that the Royal Society might have gone on to fulfil a similar language monitoring role to the Academie Française or the Italian Academy if these early manifestoes had succeeded; but they needed an international as well as a national remit to succeed. His language is typical of the Baconian ambitiousness of the early Royal Society, as well as a classic example of a stylistically elegant attack on stylistic elegance:

> Now if these famous assemblies, consisting of the great wits
> of their age and nations, did judge this work of dictionary-
> making, for the polishing of their language, worthy of their
> united labour and studies; certainly then, the design here
> proposed, ought not to be thought unworthy of such
> assistance; it being as much to be preferred before that, as
> things are better than words, as real knowledge is beyond
> elegance of speech, as the general good of mankind, is
> beyond that of any particular country or nation.[34]

From grand schemes we turn to experiments. The accounts of experiments show most clearly the workings of utilitarian prose, together with the strengths and some of the weaknesses of the Bacon-inspired approach to science. What are experiments for? Are they for testing hypotheses, which is the standard procedure for much modern science? Or are they to provide a base of reliable information from which more general statements may be inferred? The opposition to premature theorising which Bacon erected into a scientific principle meant that the second option was more usual in the early years of the society.

William Harvey, Robert Boyle and John Evelyn

Before looking at some representative experimental work from the Royal Society it will be useful to look at William Harvey's *Anatomical Exercises . . . Concerning the Motion of the Heart and Blood*, because it offers one of the most gripping narrative accounts of scientific discovery in the century. It was first published in Latin, in Leiden (one of the top European medical centres) in 1628; and, though Harvey was King Charles's physician, did not appear in England or in English until 1653, ironically with the dedication to King Charles intact.

Harvey begins his work in dialogue with the experiments on arteries of Galen, 'a divine man, father of physicians'. Thinking through Galen's conclusions, he comes to an opposite view, and begins experimenting himself, mostly on dogs, but with doves and fish for comparison. He concludes that the effect of the systole and diastole are precisely the opposite of what was thought: 'the arteries are filled and distended, by reason of the immission and intrusion of blood made by the constriction of the ventricles of the heart, as likewise that the arteries are stretched, because they are not filled like bags or satchels, and are not filled because they are blown up like bellows'.[35] It is noticeable that the old model, that the heart worked simply to infuse vital spirits into the artery, is described in slightly scornful imagery, whereas the new discovery is presented in precise, slightly Latinate terms.

Harvey's book is notable because we can see the processes of thought and experiment working in concert to produce an intellectual narrative of the discovery. We follow the steps of his thought and the phases of the experimental dissections until we get to Chapter 8, where the main proposition, that blood circulates through the body, becomes inescapable. He is well aware of the opposition to the novelty of it – 'so much does custom and doctrine once received and deeply rooted (as if it were another Nature) prevail with every one' – but argues that by 'reasons and ocular experiments' combined the alternatives to circulation of the blood are so absurd that his theory has to be right. He even suggests a little experiment on constricting the flow of blood to the reader's own arm that will demonstrate the truth of his discovery.[36]

The intellectual narrative has, of course, a constructed wholeness, and its conventions are not simply those of narrative realism. Chapter 8 comes in the middle of the book, and the crucial proposition is the fifth of nine points within the chapter itself – the great moment of recognition is thus numerologically marked. As far as we can deduce from Harvey's biography, the process of thought and experimentation took place over a number of years, which his narrative, free of any extraneous circumstantial detail, foreshortens.[37] The deference to Galen at the beginning plays down the revolutionary impact that Harvey's work would have, effectively demolishing the Galenic system of physic. The tone is modest rather than polemic, except for the brief, almost Baconian, strictures against the power of custom. The key formal feature, though, is in method; the process is from hypothesis, through experimental testing of that hypothesis to conclusion. It is more complex than that simple model, because there are a series of hypotheses to be tested on the way to the central one, and a number of reflections and *a posteriori* reinforcements of the argument as well. None the less, this is one of the earliest English examples of a recognisably modern scientific method.

He concludes with some thoughts about the mind–body connection in the light of this discovery, in a more expansive, speculative style:

> For every passion of the mind which troubles men's spirits,
> either with grief, joy, hope or anxiety, and gets access to the
> *heart*, there makes it to change from its natural constitution,
> by distemperature, pulsation and the rest, that infecting all
> the nourishment, and weakening the strength; it ought not at
> all to seem wonderful if it afterwards begets all sorts of
> incurable diseases.[38]

We remember that professional physicians had a humanist education before their medical training, so Harvey's turning to the more extended, meditative period is not surprising, any more than his skill at turning a witty conceit in the dedication to King Charles. To put it no higher, it gave him the ability to compose his work in Latin in the first place. We should not expect scientists of this period to be wedded to a single stylistic register, even if their manifestoes do cry up the plain style virtually to the exclusion of others.

This is particularly noticeable in the work of the Hon. Robert Boyle (1627–91). Boyle's courtly skills are particularly prominent in his youthful romance, *The Martyrdom of Theodora and of Didymus* (not published until 1687), which combines the story of a saint's life in the persecution of the Roman Empire with some wonderfully circumlocutory courtly dialogue. As we have seen, his work on the style of the Scriptures is strongly in favour of preserving the rhetoric of the original. When it came to science, Boyle had some early experiences with alchemy, which, even allowing for Jonson's satiric exaggerations, was well known for its deliberately mysterious and elaborate language. Boyle, Newton and Locke, of all people, exchanged alchemical secrets well into the Restoration.[39] When we consider that plainness meant openness as well as lack of adornment in the period, the commitment to plain discourse in the Royal Society's manifestoes gains further significance as an ideological commitment – not just against 'enthusiasm' as a code for all that went wrong with political and religious language during the Civil Wars, but against another 'enthusiasm', of seeing spirituality in matter. Boyle's principal attack on the alchemists, and in particular the Paracelsian reformers, *The Sceptical Chemist* (1661, drafted in the late 1650s), can be seen in this light. Towards the end of this dialogue, Carneades, the Boyle mouthpiece, says:

> And indeed, when in the writing of Paracelsus I meet with
> such fantastic and unintelligible discourses as that writer
> often puzzles and tires his reader with, fathered upon such
> excellent experiments, as though he seldom clearly teaches I
> often find he knew; methinks the chemists, in their searches
> after truth, are not unlike the navigators of Solomon's
> Tarshish fleet, who brought home from their long and
> tedious voyages, not only gold, and silver, and ivory, but
> apes and peacocks too; for so the writings of several (for I
> say not, all) of your hermetic philosophers present us,
> together with divers substantial and noble experiments,
> theories, which either like peacocks' feathers make a great
> show, but are neither solid nor useful; or else like apes, if
> they have some appearance of being rational, are blemished
> with some absurdity or other, that when they are attentively
> considered, make them appear ridiculous.[40]

The irrational and purely decorative elements of the Paracelsian writings are largely attributed to their theorising; strip them of that, and you have useful experiments well worth admitting to the new scientific community. Stylistic acceptability is thus related to intellectual acceptability.

Boyle provides a further gloss on the question of 'enthusiasm' by his own active, apologetic piety. For example, his *A Free Enquiry into the Vulgarly Received Notion of Nature*, written in 1666 but not published until 1685, attacks the habit of ascribing to Nature what should be ascribed directly to God and the laws of motion. The precisely mechanical view of the universe that results is clear from his comparison between the universe and the great clock at Strasbourg (which did all sorts of things besides tell the time) and this:

> . . . as it more recommends the skill of an engineer, to
> contrive an elaborate engine . . . so it more sets off the

wisdom of God in the fabric of the universe, that he can
make so vast a machine, perform all those many things
which he designed it should, by the mere contrivance of
brute matter, managed by certain laws of local motion, and
upheld by his ordinary and general concourse; than if he
employed from time to time an intelligent overseer, such as
Nature is fancied to be . . . .[41]

Then follows an investigation of the ambiguities of the word 'nature',
an important bit of ground-clearing of scholastic and Paracelsian
notions; his point is that 'nature' is not useful, because it encourages a
purely verbal mode of explanation. Part of Boyle's aim, then, was to
restructure chemistry as a mode of discourse. The Paracelsians had
already attacked the cult of chemical secretiveness, particularly
regarding medical remedies; Boyle wanted to go further, to see how
experimentally-gained knowledge might be placed within a theoretical
model derived from the new mechanics, even if he never really got as
far as a new model of chemistry.[42] So, we should not discuss Boyle's
style without recognising its aims: to persuade, certainly, but to
attempt explanations which are not just verbal rearrangements of the
problem, and to describe the experimental processes which point
towards those explanations as clearly as possible – so clearly that you
can repeat them yourself. One reason for the popularity of his writings
was that they were crammed with accounts of experiments.

One piece of Boyle's apparatus, the air-pump, became emblematic
of the new experimental science, appearing in the background of the
frontispiece of Sprat's *History* along with a telescope and various
smaller scientific instruments. It was also a focus of satiric attacks –
'weighing air' was a common jibe against the uselessness of the new
science. The air-pump was essentially a large glass sphere with a pump
designed to evacuate it of air; the point was to create a vacuum which
could be experimentally described and worked in. Creating a 'vacuum'
might have been constructed as an intervention in the argument
between those who thought that nature abhorred a vacuum – and
Boyle was hostile to any description involving such a lively view of
'nature'. However, he deliberately sidesteps the question of 'whether or
no, in our engine the exsuction of that air do prove the place deserted
by the air sucked out to be truly empty, that is, devoid of all corporeal
substance'.[43] The controversy surrounding these experiments did
prompt him to formulate what is now known as Boyle's Law, that at
constant temperature gas volume and pressure are inversely propor-
tional. The accounts themselves are all resolutely pre-theoretical, in the
Baconian tradition.

Their form is narrative, with the kind of appeal to truth that is akin to literary realism – in particular, the weight of circumstantial detail, including failures as well as successes. There is also an appeal to a legal model of truthfulness, with the experiments being performed before reliable witnesses.[44] He often called them essays, to distinguish them from system-building: 'this great conveniency of essays, that as in them the reader needs not to be clogged with tedious repetitions of what others have said already'.[45] This is very different from the moral essay of the early part of the century, with its eclectic mix of what others have said already.

The style, he says, is 'philosophical' because 'our design is only to inform readers, not to delight or persuade them', then a page later he worries 'that it disgust not his reader by its flatness', confesses his over-long periods and occasional use of 'exotic words', by which he means technical terms. Like many of his contemporaries, Boyle reached for Latin derivations when he wanted precision, or its appearance: 'subjacent' for 'underlying', 'fuliginous' for 'sooty' seem unnecessary, though 'electuary', a medicine in which dry matter is mixed with syrup, seems reasonable once one admits the necessity of technical terms to avoid repeating wordy descriptions. Listing such words is misleading, anyway; the frequency of such terms is not obfuscatingly high. If we compare the experimental work with some of his other, non-scientific writing, it becomes clearer that he is reining in his language for the purpose.

Before turning to Newton, the other unquestionably great scientist of the early Royal Society, I want to look at John Evelyn, whose scientific writing represents something different from the great law-makers, or the great observers and taxonomists like Hooke and Ray, who are excluded for reasons of space. Evelyn's *Sylva, or a discourse of Forest-Trees* was first published in 1664 and a great success. The third edition of 1679 is notable for a long introduction defending the Royal Society's 'accurate experiments, and public endeavours, in order to the production of real and useful theories . . .'; the stress on utility is important. Trees were of strategic importance to the navy, engaged in war with the Dutch during much of the 1660s and 1670s. Evelyn also stresses their other public projects, like advising on the rebuilding of London after the Fire. He is on the defensive against scoffing, but retorts with an alternative model of the gentleman, who does not leave planting to his servants in order to become one of 'those magnificent fops, whose talents reach but to the adjusting of their perruques, courting a Miss, or at the farthest writing a smutty, or scurrillous libel.'

The practical advice he gives is a mixture of the modern and the old-fashioned in presentation and content. There are diagrams of

machines, like the winch for grubbing up roots. There are quotations
from Virgil's *Georgics*, not just any old classical allusion, but implying
a particular ideology of nature ordered to be useful. There is a core
textbook on the propagation and uses of trees (not just for timber), and
it depends in part on the laborious information-gathering which
stretched the Society's resources during this period. There is unlikely
herbalist advice, too; on walnuts, he claims 'the distillation of its leaves
with honey and urine, makes hair spring on bald-heads'.[46]

Evelyn's work, then, is representative of another strand of the
Society's programme, for economically useful knowledge, and it was a
bestseller. It was criticised by some for its literary embellishments and
difficult vocabulary, though, which indicates how sensitive the stylistic
issue was at this stage.[47] He does include a glossary of words, some of
which demonstrate his fondness for Latin and Greek coinages; even
Browne's quincunx makes an appearance. But many of them seem
unremarkable now – 'compost' for 'dung', even 'espalieres' for 'wall-
fruit-trees' would not be overly precious in a modern garden centre.
Perhaps the explanation lies in his desire to persuade the gentry to take
a more direct interest in estate management instead of just cutting a
fashionable figure in London. So entertaining, persuasive prose, which
would not necessarily be understood by the less educated estate
workers would work better than the Anglo-Saxon vocabulary of utility
prose. This also fits with Sprat's picture of the Royal Society as being
largely composed of gentlemen; though his emphasis is more on their
leisure to contemplate Nature, Evelyn's is on working it.

The third edition of *Sylva* also contains *A Philosophical Discourse of
Earth*, presented to the Royal Society on 29 April 1675; despite the title,
it is less 'scientific' than useful, full of advice about making earth more
fertile. There are some reported experiments with pulverising earth,
and examining washed samples under a microscope, but these do not
function as a systematic examination of a hypothesis. Clearly,
experiment was expected in such presentations, and the appeal to direct
evidence as well as collected hearsay (the method of *Sylva*) forms a
large part of a cheerfully expansive discourse. However, the chemical
model of explanation that Evelyn brings to his observations is still
recognisably Paracelsan (the allusion to salt, one of the three major
constituents of the Paracelsan or Spagyrist chemistry is the giveaway),
and so there is a sense of the inherent liveliness of matter which is
different from the more 'mechanical' view of nature which, looking
back, we see as the dominant thinking of the major late seventeenth-
century scientists. For example, he explains the increased fruitfulness of
pulverised earth as follows: 'For the earth, especially if fresh, has a
certain magnetism in it, by which it attracts salt, power, or virtue (call
it either) which gives it life, and is the logic of all the labour and stir we

keep about it, to sustain us . . .'[48] We should not, then, dismiss Evelyn as one of the gentlemen-amateurs of the early Royal Society. He demonstrates a number of strands in the Society's activities – the desire to improve useful trades and set projects in motion, the reformation of the gentry from fashionable excess, the survival of older models of science, and the commitment to experiment. As with Boyle, the sheer variety of his aims means that his prose would be more than a reporter's plainness.

Isaac Newton

Isaac Newton is different. There is a mathematical austerity about much of Newton's scientific prose. Even more than with Harvey, the simple conceptual and narrative lines of his experimental reports are gained through excluding false starts and all but a minimum of circumstantial detail. Newton was an adept at other discourses – his interest in alchemy and the apocalyptic books of the Bible has been well documented recently – so we are not talking about personal style as much as a selected style.[49] We must stress, too, that scientific plainness was as much concerned with openness as lack of decoration. Here is a sample of the occult text *The Emerald Tablet*, as translated by Newton in the 1690s: 'The sun is its father, the moon its mother, the wind hath carried it in its belly, the earth is its nurse. The father of all perfection on the whole earth is here. Its force or power is entire if it be converted into earth.'[50] The reason this is obscure is not stylistic, but hermeneutic. The dream of spiritual power is clear enough, but the text demands a key, a practice of reading of a very different interpretative community than the Royal Society. There is a link; both are trying to delve into the 'secrets' of matter, but from opposite ends. Hermetic philosophy goes 'top down', from the One to the phenomena; the Royal Society, Baconian approach is from the phenomena to theory. Newton, as the ablest mathematician and theorist, probably of the century, is aware of the power of abstract models like mathematics; and, like Boyle, was running up against the limitations of experimental demonstration when the basic unit of the 'corpuscular' or (roughly) molecular theory was too small to be observed, even by the new instruments. (Newton's election to the Society resulted from his improved telescope.)

Newton's major work on mathematics, the *Principia*, was published in Latin, his *Optics* in 1704. One convenient way of approaching his

work within the confines of this study would be to look at his
celebrated letter of 1672 'concerning his new theory about light and
colours', published in *Philosophical Transactions*, and so edited by
Oldenburg. The form and the location is the first thing to notice. We
have already seen the affinity of the new essay form and the letter;
essays and letters are the new first stage of scientific communication.
Newton did not avoid systematic, book-length exposition, but he
approached it gradually. In presenting his findings to the Royal
Society, and to a wider audience through the *Transactions*, he was
submitting his findings to debate, opening an inquiry of a potentially
collaborative nature. In subsequent issues Robert Hooke commented
on his findings, mostly favourably, but questioning whether Newton's
observations actually proved his theory. The vituperative tone of
Newton's reply, and the fact that he only published the *Optics* after
Hooke's death, suggests that, whatever the contribution of Newton's
particular personality, sensitivity to criticism or whatever, the spirit of
seventeenth-century controversy was not dead in the Royal Society,
however much it might attempt to provide a new, calmer way of
dealing with disagreement.[51] Newton did adapt his theory in response
to Huygens's criticisms in particular, which suggests he was listening
receptively as well as apoplectically to the debate.[52]

Newton had been working on optics since at least 1664, and the
letter begins with an experiment with a triangular prism in 1666. The
experiment, of letting a small beam of light in an otherwise darkened
room strike the prism, and thus produce a rainbow effect, had been
done a number of times. Newton's variation was to catch the resulting
spectrum at a much greater distance than previously, which meant it
was considerably elongated, though still with faded, semicircular
edges. By precise measurement and calculation Newton was able to
show that current explanations of spectrum effects, basically modifica-
tion theories which suggested that, for example, disturbance at the
edges would account for colour variations, would not account for his
experimental results. It is here, the combination of the disciplines of
mathematics and experimental observation, that Newton is the real
innovator. The subsequent experiments, including the crucial one with
two prisms (he describes it as *experimentum crucis*, a term Boyle adapted
from Bacon) are prompted by this mathematically as well as
experimentally induced doubt of current theories. He still has a
'corpuscular' rather than a wave theory of light, which can equally well
account for his central conclusion that light 'is a heterogeneous mixture
of differently refrangible rays'.[53]

The shape of the letter is a narrative of a series of experiments,
culminating in that single proposition, followed by thirteen other
'doctrines' about the relationship of colours and the consequences for

telescope and microscope construction, then finally suggestions for further experiments, which displace and thus stress the provisional character of the conclusions. The descriptions are first-person, which with the dates link the new genre of the written-up experiment with the conventions of the letter, and distinguish it from the more impersonal form of the modern scientific report. Newton is more selective in his reporting than Boyle, with fewer personal and decoratively rhetorical touches. Boyle tended to theorise only under pressure; it was Newton's way of proceeding, though of course based on observation. More than one observer has commented that his mathematical and theoretical commitments lead to an imaginative 'idealisation' of his experimental results, because he recognises what they might signify.[54]

Newton, then, is still importantly filiated to Bacon's enterprise, in his commitment to observation before system. However, he does go further than the older notion of experiment, much closer to our word 'experience', whose aim is not so much thought as accurate reporting. The accounts of curiosities that fill up *Philosophical Transactions*, even more under Hans Sloane at the end of the century, show that simple commitment continuing, for all its satire-prone inability to sift out the trivial.[55] The Royal Society genres, gossipy descriptions and experimental report, microscopic observations and schemes for new languages or better cultivation, all point to the conclusion that new or revised intellectual ambitions tend to result in a new prose. Svetlana Alpers glosses Bacon's remark that 'the nature of things betrays itself more readily under the vexations of art than in its natural freedom' as follows: 'Art does not simply imitate nature, nor is it a play of the imagination, but rather it is the *techne* or craft that enables us, through constraint, to grasp nature.'[56] The achievements as much as the ambitious programmes of Royal Society discourse show how strikingly constraint can be both an art and a tool of perception. Not just the microscope and the air pump, but the prose style and the attitude to systematising were the vital tools of the change in science.

Notes

1. Francis Bacon, *The Advancement of Learning*, ed. G.W. Kitchin (1915), I. iv. 12, p. 30.

2. Ibid., VII. vi. 9, p. 47.

3. Lisa Jardine, *Francis Bacon: Discovery and the Art of Discourse* (Cambridge, 1974), p. 170.

4. Bacon, *Advancement*, I. iv. 3, pp. 24–5.

5. Bacon, *Works*, ed. Spedding, Ellis and Heath, IV, p. 8.

6. Bacon, *Works*, IV, p. 24.

7. Bacon, *Works*, IV, p. 22.

8. There is a useful discussion in Ch. 7 of Anthony Quinton, *Bacon* (Oxford, 1980).

9. Bacon, *Works*, III, p. 152.

10. Bacon, *Works*, III, pp. 145, 156.

11. Bacon, *Works*, III, p. 165.

12. Bacon, *Works*, III, p. 154.

13. Charles Webster, *The Great Instauration: Science, Medicine and Reform 1626–1660* (1975).

14. Bacon, *Works*, III, pp. 146–7.

15. I am indebted to an unpublished paper by Craig Rustici for prompting many of these ideas about the relation of this text to early British colonial discourse. J.C. Davis's chapter on Bacon in *Utopia and the Ideal Society* (Cambridge, 1981) remains the best published account.

16. For a discussion of the organising power of metaphor in Bacon, see Chs 5 and 6 of Brian Vickers, *Francis Bacon and Renaissance Prose* (Cambridge, 1968), the best literary study of Bacon.

17. Bacon, *Advancement of Learning*, I. iv. 5, pp. 25–6.

18. For the general move from *res* as topic to thing in this century, see the chapter on '*Res et Verba*' in W.S. Howell, *Logic and Rhetoric in England, 1500–1700* (Princeton, 1956).

19. See Webster, *The Great Instauration*.

20. Michael Hunter, *Establishing the New Science: The Experience of the Early Royal Society* (Woodbridge, 1989), p. 25.

21. See the discussion in Michael Hunter, *Science and Society in Restoration England* (Cambridge, 1981), especially Ch. 2.

22. P.B. Wood, 'Methodology and Apologetics: Thomas Sprat's *History of the Royal Society*', *British Journal for the History of Science* 13 (1980), pp. 1–21; see also Ch. 2 of Michael Hunter, *Establishing the New Science: The Experience of the Early Royal Society* (Woodbridge, 1989).

23. Thomas Sprat, *History of the Royal Society*, ed. Jackson I. Cope and Harold Whitmore Jones (St Louis, 1959), p. 429 (the text is a facsimile).

24. The argument of Brian Vickers, 'The Royal Society and English Prose Style: A Reassessment' in Vickers and Struever, *Rhetoric and the Pursuit of Truth* (Los Angeles, 1985), pp. 1–76, is particularly illuminating in this respect.

25. Sprat, *History*, p. 62.

26. Sprat, *History*, p. 111.

27. Sprat, *History*, p. 113.

28. William H. Youngren, 'Generality, Science and Poetic Language in the Restoration', *ELH*, 35 (1968), 158–87

29. The classic discussion of this as it affects Glanvill and Cowley is R.F. Jones, 'Science and English Prose Style in the Third Quarter of the Seventeenth Century', *The Seventeenth Century* (Stanford, 1951), pp. 75–110; however, the argument is weakened by his taking Sprat too much on trust, as Vickers, in 'The Royal Society and English Prose Style: A Reassessment', points out.

30. John Wilkins, *Ecclesiastes*, 2nd edn (1646), p. 12.

31. John Wilkins, *An Essay Towards A Real Character, and a Philosophical Language* (Menston, 1968: facsimile of 1668 edn), p. 13.

32. I have drawn on the following for my discussion of *An Essay*: James Knowlson, *Universal Language Schemes in England and France, 1660–1800* (Toronto, 1975); several pieces in Vivian Salmon, *The Study of Language in Seventeenth Century England* (Amsterdam, 1979); and M.M. Slaughter, *Universal Languages and Scientific Taxonomy in the Seventeenth Century* (Cambridge, 1982).

33. See Webster, *The Great Instauration*; and, for a Europe-wide perspective, John Gascoigne, 'A reappraisal of the role of the universities in the scientific revolution', in *Reappraisals of the Scientific Revolution*, ed. David C. Lindberg and Robert S. Westman (Cambridge, 1990).

34. Wilkins, *An Essay*, 'Epistle Dedicatory to the Royal Society'.

35. *The Anatomical Exercises of Dr William Harvey, Professor of Physick, and Physician Concerning the Motion of the Heart and Blood* (1653), p. 10.

36. *Anatomical Exercises*, pp. 44, 80.

37. See Gweneth Whitteridge, *Thomas Harvey and the Circulation of the Blood* (1971).

38. *Anatomical Exercises*, p. 84.

39. See Richard S. Westfall, 'Newton and Alchemy' in *Occult and Scientific Mentalities in the Renaissance*, ed. Brian Vickers (Cambridge, 1984), pp. 315–35.

40. Robert Boyle, *The Sceptical Chemist*, ed. M.M. Pattison Muir (n.d., Everyman; based on the 1680 edn), p. 227; see Steven Shapin and Simon Schaffer, *Leviathan and the Air-Pump: Hobbes, Boyle, and the Experimental Life* (Princeton, 1985), pp. 70–2. Their book as a whole is of great interest.

41. Robert Boyle, *A Free Enquiry into the Vulgarly Received Notion of Nature* (1685), pp. 7–8.

42. See the important discussion of Jan V. Golinski, 'Chemistry in the Scientific Revolution: Problems of language and communication', in *Reappraisals of the Scientific Revolution*, ed. David C. Lindberg and Robert S. Westman (Cambridge, 1990), pp. 397–436, which quotes from contemporaries who wished Boyle had been more systematic.

43. Boyle, *New Experiments Physico-Mechanical* (1660), Experiment XVII, in *English Science, Bacon to Newton*, ed. Brian Vickers (Cambridge, 1987), p. 62.

44. See Shapin and Scaeffer, *Leviathan and the Air-Pump*, pp. 55–60; and Barbara J. Shapiro, *Probability and Certainty in Seventeenth-Century England* (Princeton, 1983), especially Ch. 2.

45. Boyle, *Certain Physiological Essays* (1661), p. 9.

46. Evelyn, *Sylva*, 3rd edn (1679), p. 52. I confess I have not submitted this to ocular proof.

47. Michael Hunter, *Science and Society in Restoration England*, p. 101 and refs.

48. Evelyn, *Sylva*, p. 302.

49. See Arthur Quinn, 'Reading Newton Apocalyptically', in *Millenarianism and Messianism in English Thought and Literature, 1650–1800*, ed. Richard H. Popkin (Leiden, 1988), B.J.T. Dobbs, 'Newton's *Commentary* on the *Emerald Tablet* of Hermes Trismegistus: Its Scientific and Theological Significance' in *Hermeticism and the Renaissance: Intellectual History and the Occult in Early Modern Europe*, ed. Ingrid Merkel and Allen G. Debus (Washington, 1988); and, supremely, R.S. Westfall, *Never at Rest: A Biography of Isaac Newton* (Cambridge, 1980), Ch. 8.

50. Modernised from Dobbs's transcription of the MS, 'Newton's *Commentary*', p. 183.

51. See Thomas Kuhn, 'Newton's Optical Papers', in *Isaac Newton's Papers and Letters on Natural Philosophy*, ed. I. Bernard Cohen, 2nd edn (Cambridge, Mass., 1978). This contains facsimiles of the original edition of the letter (which, incidentally, shows what a miscellany *Philosophical Transactions* was) as well as Hooke's reply.

52. See Alan E. Shapiro, 'The Evolving Structure of Newton's Theory of White Light and Color', *Isis*, 71 (1980), 211–35.

53. 'A Letter of Mr Isaac Newton . . .' in *English Science, Bacon to Newton*, ed. Brian Vickers (Cambridge, 1987), p. 203.

54. The word is Kuhn's; and see R.S. Westfall, *Never at Rest*, pp. 164ff.

55. See, eg, William King's *The Transactioneer* (1700); and, of course, Book III of *Gulliver's Travels*.

56. Svetlana Alpers, *The Art of Describing: Dutch Art in the Seventeenth Century* (1983), pp. 103–4.

Chapter 13
Power and Idiom in Politics

England could never be the same after 1642. A civil war of any length and seriousness divides the country long after it has finished, and continues to be appropriated in different political circumstances. One of the features of English literary criticism of the seventeenth century is that two of its most influential founders, Samuel Johnson and T.S. Eliot, continued to fight on the Royalist side, and there are many contemporary Parliamentarians, too. The execution of King Charles is both the unacknowledged symbol of the 'dissociation of sensibility', and the high point of English republicanism.

In this section I want to consider some of the major changes in political idiom after King Charles's execution in 1649. One central feature is a drift towards secularisation. It seemed appropriate to discuss the major political texts of the first half of the century in the chapter on religious prose. The link between religious and political duty was not dissolved by Charles's execution, not least because his accusers felt themselves to be performing a religious as well as a legal and political duty. As we have seen, the Restoration bishops and court preachers emphasised the duty of obedience, virtually redefining the nature of reformed Christian belief in doing so. Religious allegiance also defined the nature of a subject's civil rights – after 1662 Nonconformists and Catholics were variously restricted, though the change was as much in the greatly increased number of those regarded as Nonconformists compared to the period before the Civil War as in the nature of the restrictions.

Thomas Hobbes

The dominant political thinker of the period is Thomas Hobbes, whose great work *Leviathan* (1651) arose from his alarm at the English Civil

War and the numerous wars on the Continent, and yet was characterised as 'atheist' as well as anti-Royalist by virtually all his seventeenth-century commentators.[1] In a way Hobbes holds a similar position to Machiavelli in the previous century, whose own political ideas of order were formed out of an experience of devastation; contemporaries spoke of him as a devil, but also took his advice, or at least found themselves arguing on his terms.

Those terms were a mixture of old and new, in both philosophical and literary senses. Apart from politics, Hobbes had two great intellectual passions, language and science. His earlier publications include translated and summarised versions of the classics, such as Thucydides and Aristotle, his last translations of Homer. To that extent his training and talent was that of a Renaissance humanist. His interest in science was fuelled by continental visits, where he met Galileo, the Mersenne circle in Paris and, eventually, Descartes. So he stands more in the continental tradition, with its emphasis on mathematical or logical certainty, than in the English experimental tradition. *Leviathan* is both a Renaissance rhetorical performance and an essay in iconoclastic philosophical rigour; though principally it is an attempt to find a basis for civil society ('common-wealth' is his term) which will avoid the conflicts that had beset Europe in his lifetime.

Hobbes summarised Aristotle's *Rhetoric* for his pupils in the 1630s; the emphasis is on rhetoric as a discipline of argument, to do with proofs, inferences and syllogisms.[2] He does concern himself with style, elocution and disposition once the proofs have been grasped, and particularly with metaphor: 'in a metaphor alone there is perspicuity, novity and sweetness'.[3] This may help to explain why the chapter 'On Speech' in *Leviathan* registers metaphor as one of the four abuses of speech as 'when they use words metaphorically; that is, in other sense than that they are ordained for; and thereby deceive others',[4] and yet the work itself is full of the most impressive images. Hobbes regards metaphor as misleading when constructing arguments, but not in persuading others of their desirability. It's not an easy boundary to draw, though. The title and concept of *Leviathan* itself demonstrate as much. A better description than metaphor in this kind of argument might be *model*; the development of political thought in the second half of the century is mapped by changes in the model of society and its power relations.

In the Introduction to *Leviathan* Hobbes takes the old metaphor of society as a body and reworks it by means of a different approach to nature. Early versions of the 'body politic' topos, like Menenius on the belly and the members in *Coriolanus*, suggest the naturalness of power relations: aristocrats are to plebeians as belly to limbs, and any injustice in the basic arrangement is illusory, because a body operates like an organism. Hobbes demystifies this, though not in the cause of liberalism, as we shall see. His body politic is artificial, a man-made creation:

> For by art is created that great Leviathan called a
> Commonwealth, or State (in Latin Civitas) which is but an
> artificial man; though of greater stature and strength than the
> natural, for whose protection and defence it was intended;
> and in which, the sovereignty is an artificial soul, as giving
> life and motion to the whole body; the magistrates, and
> other officers of judicature and execution, artificial joints;
> reward and punishment (by which fastened to the seat of the
> sovereignty, every joint and member is moved to perform
> his duty) are the nerves, that do the same in the body
> natural; the wealth and riches of all the particular members,
> are the strength; *salus populi* (the people's safety) its business;
> counsellors, by whom all things needful for it to know, are
> suggested unto it, are the memory; equity and laws, an
> artificial reason and will; concord, health; sedition, sickness;
> and civil war, death. Lastly, the pacts and covenants, by
> which the parts of this body politic were at first made, set
> together, and united, resemble that *fiat*, or the *let us make*
> *man*, pronounced by God in the creation.[5]

The model retains some of the advantages of the organic concept, particularly the interlinking of various functions and interests in society, and sees the ultimate disasters as sedition and civil war. However, it is an artificial, man-made creation, put together for a particular purpose – the people's safety. It is formed by contract.

One reason why Hobbes was regarded as an atheist by his contemporaries was that this model of society had no need of God, even though he constantly refers to God and devotes a vast section of the book to the discussion of a Christian commonwealth. One view is that Hobbes had a minimalist view of God, as first cause of the universe and thus author of the laws of nature, but not much else of significance that is knowable (a position similar to that of deism or unitarianism in the eighteenth century). Another is that Hobbes did not share the contemporary horror of atheists as threats to the state because they did not fear supernatural sanctions. Like Paolo Sarpi, whose ideas he encountered in Venice, and like Bacon in the essay 'Of Superstition', he regarded an atheist state as perfectly workable, simply on the basis of the pressures of social life on earth.[6]

Chapter 43 of *Leviathan*, which deals with the dilemma of obeying

God when his commands (or what seem to be his commands) conflict with those of the sovereign, says that there is only one necessary belief, that Jesus is the Christ, and does not find any instance where this conflicts with obedience to a Christian or infidel sovereign. At this point he disarms both Papist and radical by denying that civil action now affects salvation in the future.[7] Moreover, the laws of God when it comes to civil obedience are the same as the laws of nature.[8] As we have seen in the discussion of Boyle's science, some seventeenth-century Christians regarded this emphasis on nature as God's intermediary as a weakening of his sovereignty, though some influential Anglican thinking went along with it, particularly after the Restoration. The laws of nature are discovered by reason rather than revelation, really out of the need for survival – 'A Law of Nature (*Lex Naturalis*) is a precept, or general rule, found out by reason, by which a man is forbidden to do, that, which is destructive of his own life, or taketh away the means of preserving the same; and to omit, that, by which he thinketh it may be best preserved.'[9] The first section in particular of *Leviathan* is full of definitions like this; part of Hobbes's intellectual rigour stems from his policing the boundaries of his own concepts. These definitions formed the starting point of certainty on which strict philosophical argument could produce undeniable truth.

The laws of nature (or 'natural law', to use the more common modern formulation) thus bulked large for Hobbes the political scientist: central to his view of civil society as a contractual arrangement for everyone's safety is his concept of the state of nature. Here we must turn to the famous Chapter 13, 'Of the Natural Condition of Mankind as concerning their Felicity and Misery'. There is not much about felicity in it. Men without law are constantly quarrelling, whether out of competition, self-defence (diffidence) or the desire for glory. Not only is there no pleasure in keeping company 'where there is no power to overawe them all', they are effectively at war with each other: 'Out of civil states, there is always war of every one against every one.'[10] The climax of this argument is an example of Hobbes's relentless rhetorical force – and, incidentally, a list of the things he found most valuable about civilisation, or those that would appeal to Englishmen of the 1650s:

> In such condition, there is no place for industry; because the fruit thereof is uncertain: and consequently no culture of the earth; no navigation, nor use of the commodities that may be imported by sea; no instruments of moving, and removing of things as require much force; no knowledge of the face of the earth; no account of time; no arts; no letters; no society; and which is worst of all, continual fear, and danger of

> violent death; and the life of man, solitary, poor, nasty,
> brutish, and short.[11]

The last four words of the climax have had a life of their own, but this ought not to obscure Hobbes's skill in orchestrating his two lists, whittling down his descriptions of both civilisation and its opposites from expansive phrases to single words, like the descent from complex society to atomistic anarchy. The tone might be characterised as prophetic, but as no less a critic than Clarendon remarked, Hobbes's myth is not biblical, with a fall from an original paradise; mankind's primitive state is savagery. His appeal, like any good rhetorician's, is to the heart as well as the mind. If anyone doubts that nature is so dissociative:

> Let him therefore consider with himself, when taking a
> journey, he arms himself, and seeks to go well accompanied;
> when going to sleep, he locks his doors; when even in his
> house he locks his chests; and this when he knows there be
> laws, and public officers, armed, to revenge all injuries shall
> be done him . . . . Does he not there as much accuse
> mankind by his actions, as I do by my words?[12]

The cumulative sentence structure is there again, but the tone is less elevated, more intimate. The range is important to the effect; Hobbes is incorporating all the rhetorical powers of address into an argumentative structure that is in large part developed from his earlier formulations in the *Elements of Law* (1640) and *De Cive* (1642).

Why should Hobbes have adapted his writing to the kind of discipline he regarded as criminal? In *The Elements* he drew a distinction between the *mathematici*, the measurers, the scientists in the modern sense, whose contribution to civilisation is unquestioned and who never get caught in controversy, and the *dogmatici*, who multiply rather than reduce controversy and 'with passion press to have their opinions pass everywhere for truth, without any evident demonstration either from experience, or from places of Scripture of uncontroverted interpretation'.[13] The ideal method of knowledge and reasoning for Hobbes was mathematical, but he also reckoned in the same chapter 'commonly truth is on the side of the few, rather than of the multitude'. So how are the multitude to be persuaded of the truth, particularly when it comes to the central question for English civil society in the 1650s, obedience to sovereign power? By force? It didn't work for Charles I, not least because he no longer controlled his own armies. In his dialogues on the Civil War, *Behemoth, or the Long Parliament* (first authorised printing 1682, written by 1668), Hobbes argues that Charles's failure was due to the seducers of people's minds, Papists, Presbyterians, educated classical republicans and so on; because in the end, 'the power of the mighty hath no foundation but in the opinion and belief of the people'.[14] Rhetoric may be intellectually suspect, but strategically invaluable.[15] So a paragraph such as the following may seem self-defeating, using a simile to condemn metaphors; Hobbes might have answered that truth needed all the arts of persuasion in the age of the seditious pulpit:

> The light of humane minds is perspicuous words, but by
> exact definitions first snuffed, and purged from ambiguity;
> reason is the pace; increase of science, the way; and the
> benefit of mankind, the end. And on the contrary,
> metaphors, and senseless and ambiguous words, are like
> *ignes fatui* [will o'the wisps]; and reasoning upon them, is
> wandering amongst innumerable absurdities; and their end,
> contention, and sedition, or contempt.[16]

One of the aims of classical rhetoric is perspicuity, of course. Just as one can find rhetorical techniques in every denial of, or warning against rhetoric, so one can find exhortations to clarity in the best rhetorical sources. (Clarity is one of the four virtues of style Cicero derived from Theophrastus.) There is also a local argument, that here Hobbes is using a simile, which proclaims likeness rather than identity, and so is more modest, less deceptive, than the total claim of identity made by metaphor. It might work here and elsewhere, though not with the master-trope of *Leviathan*.

Hobbes's emphasis on opinion reflects the dilemma of the mid-century political theorist, looking for an alternative to Divine Right which, while not dead as an appeal to loyalty, had suffered a severe blow at the hands of Puritan preaching. One key issue was the interpretation of Scripture, which occupies a key position in the third and fourth sections of *Leviathan*. Both Part III, 'Of A Christian Commonwealth', and Part IV, 'Of the Kingdom of Darkness', begin with the problem of authority in interpreting Scripture. Here Hobbes sounds most like his opponents in the Parliamentarian camp, because he is discussing Scripture. Having derived so much from 'the principles of Nature only', Hobbes moves uneasily into the supernatural and the prophetic, retaining as much of his structure of definition as the basis of argument as he can. Essentially, he is trying to get back to the principles of the Henrician Reformation, 'in every Christian Commonwealth, the civil sovereign is the supreme pastor'.[17] In such a state, neither clergy nor private person has the supreme right of interpretation. They can have a go – after all, Hobbes is doing so himself.

However, from a viewpoint which begins an account of the Kingdom of Darkness (Part Four of *Leviathan*) with the misinterpretation of Scripture, some source of authoritative interpretation is needed. The Church cannot be trusted, so the Christian sovereign controls meaning. He might be wrong, but who can judge? The Christian is still bound in conscience to obey. Furthermore, if we accept the description that Hobbes's view of faith is essentially historical, based on authoritative transmission of the texts, whereas his view of power is ahistorical, that is, based on rational deduction from the laws of nature, we might even think that he has reversed the usual order of transcendence: the state is the transcendent entity, faith is vulnerable to the process of transmission.

Coming from an exile in France with Charles in 1651, this might easily be read as a plea for the return of the Stuart monarchy with its absolutist ambitions realised, French style. Hobbes was, briefly, one of Charles's tutors in Paris, and was a supporter of the Restoration. However, recent work on Hobbes suggests that he might equally have been recommending allegiance to the *de facto* government of the Commonwealth, in terms of the Engagement, or oath of loyalty, of 1650.[18] However, it is difficult to read *Leviathan* as anything but a recommendation of absolute monarchy, even if Chapter 18 refers to a 'man, or assembly of men' as alternative versions of sovereign power; one of the most revealing *lacunae* in his account of a civil society contracting with a sovereign for security is an account of that assembly. Why the omission? Too like Parliament – and thus admitting too much power to that assembly, even though its main purpose was to give it up? Historically speculative, and thus against the whole, scientific thrust of the book? Or does it reveal a contradiction in Hobbes's originary myth of the state, that it is difficult to imagine how such a violent, anarchic lot as Hobbesian men in a state of nature could have agreed for long enough to draw up a contract?

Whatever problems they leave for philosophy, the questions show what an interesting mix the writing is in *Leviathan*. 'There is nothing I distrust more than my elocution [i.e. style]; which nevertheless I am confident . . . is not obscure', he writes in the conclusion.[19] His long defence of his omitting quotations from the classics shows how much he wanted a new style of political treatise, preferring reason before authority (though Scripture has an important, if in the end restricted role). For all Hobbes's quarrels with the Royal Society, his loyalties are with scientific method. A civil science involves deducing the laws of nature as they affect the formation and dissolution of states, and much of *Leviathan* can be read in this way.[20] Yet there is a constant tug from the need to persuade, which results in some brilliantly effective metaphors as well as 'its apparently seamless reasoning in propounding truths and exposing errors, its irony and imperturbable self-confidence'.[21] At times, Hobbes seems to regard this as a potential contradiction in his project, at times a necessity. At the heart of the argument, though, is a fiction, man in the state of nature and the covenant, or contract that begins civil society. Perhaps readers remember it most because stories are easier to remember – more persuasive? – than the most elegant of arguments. A more likely explanation is that it is the moment in the text where Hobbes chooses to stir up the emotions of his readers, where cool evaluation has to give way to a recognition of the horrors of the state of nature that rationality and self-interest – the cooler courts of appeal for most of the text – have to combine to eradicate. The contract is similarly fictitious; it may have explanatory value, but no claims are made for its historical existence, for example as a document or a datable event in a particular location.

The seventeenth century was particularly concerned with myths of origin. The early chapters of Genesis were repeatedly scrutinised and expanded on; it was in this century that Archbishop Ussher calculated the date of the creation at 4004 BC. The greatest English poem of the century, *Paradise Lost*, gets much of its intellectual power (in the context, we ought to add 'political') from its profound engagement with how humanity started. The origin of biblical monarchy in Samuel's anointing of Saul is a major focus of disagreement between Royalist and republican theorists. There were other, more radical returns to Genesis, often referring to the Peasants' Revolt tag, 'When Adam delved and Eve span/Who was then the gentleman?'[22] Here is Winstanley's version, from 1650, suggesting that the Parliamentarians opposed to the Diggers are not radical enough because they do not go back far enough, to the true original purpose of creation:

> In the beginning, universal love appeared to be the father of
> all things (though self-love in our experience rules in man
> first) and as he made mankind to be the Lord of the Earth, so
> he made the earth to be a common treasury of livelihood to
> whole mankind without respect of persons . . . .

> This is your very inward principle, O ye present powers of
> England, you do not study how to advance universal love; if
> you did, it would appear in action; but imagination and self-
> love mightily disquiets your mind, and makes you call up all
> the powers of darkness to come forth and help set the crown
> upon the head of self, which is that kingly power you have
> vowed against, and yet uphold it in your hands.[23]

According to this account, politics before the Fall were communist.

Power, property and rank are a consequence of self-love and part of the kingdom of darkness; kings, preachers, lawyers, merchants, are all false saviours. The contrast in tone to Hobbes is striking: a consistent second-person address, with a prophetic, denunciatory voice directed towards a highly specified target. The argumentative strategy involving the originary myth is a mirror image of Hobbes's use of his picture of the state of nature; the state of love is what we have fallen from, and the people's political practice needs to recover that. Executing the king is no escape from that kind of power: 'the way to cast out kingly power again, is not to cast them out by the sword, for this doth but set him in more power, and removes him from a weaker to a stronger hand: but the only way to cast him out is for the people to leave him to himself, to forsake fighting and all oppression, and to live in love towards one another'.[24] In a curious way Hobbes and Winstanley intersect in their overriding desire for peaceful civil society; the difference is that Winstanley sees Hobbes's solution as part of the problem. It is also different to work from an agreed depiction of the first society, as Genesis was in the period, than to construct a new explanatory model. While Hobbes never says that Scripture is not authoritative, he is critical; he was one of the first to suggest that Moses was not the author of the Pentateuch (which includes Genesis).[25] The modernity lies not just in the critical approach, but also in the process which systematically demotes the spiritual in religion, leaving God as the first cause of the universe and (properly understood) as the guarantor of civil obedience from conscientious Christians.

Filmer and Locke

A parallel work of political modernisation occurs in the work of John Locke (1632–1704). *The Two Treatises of Government* are first of all a reply to Sir Robert Filmer's *Patriarcha*, and we can at least begin by seeing them as a response to Filmer's interpretation-of-cum-extrapolation-from Genesis, still sustained in the characteristic Reformation way as an argument about the meaning of the biblical text – in this case, how we might read the stories of Adam and Noah for political purposes. There is also an implied answer to Hobbes as he produces another fiction about the state of nature leading to another kind of social contract. The full title of the second treatise is 'An Essay concerning the True Original, Extent and End of Civil Government';

as with Hobbes, the origins of government are used as an explanation of the purpose of human society, aimed towards dealing with the revolutionary question – when can a ruler be disobeyed to the point of overthrowing him?

Filmer's work was printed in 1680, but had been circulating for forty years or more in manuscript (he died in 1653). His arguments relate to the 1640s rather than the 1680s, but their re-emergence does demonstrate the continuity in pro-Stuart arguments about monarchy either side of 1649. Like Hobbes's *Behemoth*, *Patriarcha* also shows that the principal perceived enemy, intellectually and perhaps politically too, was Catholicism rather than radical Protestantism. The seventeenth-century revolution may be written as Anglican vs. Puritan, because that is how the armies lined up in 1642. However, the anxieties of the monarchists, particularly after 1660, were as much fixed on the Catholics. The Popish Plot caused more popular hysteria than the Fifth Monarchist uprising in the 1660s and 1670s. In the same period John Bunyan shared his prison with Catholics and Quakers, not with members of his own congregation. Filmer's first target is Cardinal Bellarmine, for his 'pestilent and dangerous conclusion' that the people may change the kingdom into an aristocracy or democracy.[26] Only in the second half of the book does he turn his fire on 'popular' government and its parliamentary apologists, as being more violent than tyranny. (The accusation is repeated in his 1652 *Observations concerning the Original of Government*, which comments on Hobbes, Milton and Grotius.) The historical examples are from classical Rome, but the ideas in contest are those of the Parliamentary common lawyers.

Filmer's argument is that, from Adam and the Old Testament patriarchs on, the power of the father as head of the household is the origin of regal power:

> . . . subjection of children is the fountain of all regal
> authority, by the ordination of God himself . . . which quite
> takes away that new and common distinction which refers
> only power universal as absolute to God, but power
> respective in regard of the special form of government to the
> choice of the people. Nor leaves it any place for such
> imaginary pactions [contracts] between Kings and their
> people as many dream of.[27]

The agreed history of human origins, then, says that kingly power is (not just is like) patriarchal power. Although kings are not the natural fathers of their subjects 'they all either are, or are to be reputed, as the next heirs to those progenitors who were at first the natural parents of the 'whole people, and in their right succeed to the exercise of supreme jurisdiction'.[28] A lot hinges on 'reputed', and it is a point where Filmer's claim for the naturalness of kingly/patriarchal power might break under examination. Why should the Stuarts in particular be obeyed because of their descent from Adam, or Noah? He rejects any sense of development in political institutions; for example, if Parliament began in 1215 by being summoned by the king, then it must still remain only a privilege, not a right developed out of custom.[29]

As Genesis was generally regarded as historical, then Filmer's argument would not be based on a 'dream' such as contract theory (or an affront to God's creation, as he regarded Hobbes's state of nature). Just as surely as Hobbes, he derived it from a view of 'nature', of natural relations, though more obviously sanctioned by Scripture from the outset. (Goering is supposed to have said that when anyone mentioned 'culture' he wanted to reach for his gun; reading the political arguments of the seventeenth century, we might feel like reaching for our guns when anyone mentions the word 'nature'. We may regard this, too, as an index of modernity; contests over what is 'natural' form one important basis of political theory for at least a hundred years.)

In the 1640s we might see the argument as being between absolutist and mixed models of government, characterised in contemporary Europe (as the English saw it) by France and Venice respectively.[30] Charles I's own position, as drafted for him by Falkland and Colepepper in 1642, even began to suggest that the English constitution was a balanced mixture of monarchy, aristocracy and democracy, explicitly rejecting 'absolute monarchy'.[31] In the 1680s, when *Patriarcha* was printed for the first time, the logical conclusion from this tripartite model, that the king could be overruled by the other two, was excoriated. The reason was the Exclusion Crisis, occasioned by the possibility that a Catholic (James, King Charles's brother) might succeed to the throne. An unsuccessful negotiating position from forty years earlier might have been less attractive to Stuart supporters than Filmer's uncompromising model – Filmer's was not the only tract from the 1640s to be reprinted in the new context. Jonathan Clark argues that Parliament after 1660 was not interested in placing limitations on the monarchy, but in withdrawing into a critical and advisory role.[32] On that reading, late Stuart and Orange monarchs alike theorise themselves as part of a mixed government, but Lords and Commons are happy to retreat from executive responsibility, leaving government to a group of increasingly powerful central institutions, of which the monarchy is the centre. 1642 becomes a rebellion rather than a revolution, 1688 a change of dynasties from Catholic to Protestant, not a democratic watershed. A history of the English prose which formed part of the ideological battle of the seventeenth century is not quite the place to join the historiographical argument, but it cannot be ignored. When we turn to Locke as the climax of seventeenth-century political theory are we not just repeating the Whiggish error of seeing secular liberalism as the goal of politics from the Renaissance on, and foisting an unhistorical aim on past thinkers?

Putting aside the questions of audience and influence for a moment, let us see if we can answer three questions from Locke's text germane to this dispute. Does he attempt to displace patriarchy with contract, and thus absolute with limited monarchy? Does he see ultimate power as deriving from God or people – that is, is he thinking within a predominantly Christian or secular mind-set? Finally, is Locke's refutation of Filmer in any sense revolutionary?

Locke's main strategy against Filmer's view of patriarchal authority is to make distinctions in the place of identifications. This analytic method is, of course, one reason why Locke was so influential philosophically. The first treatise is in large part a refutation of the scriptural basis of Filmer's case. We might invert our comment on *Leviathan*; if the second half of that book centres so much on biblical interpretation as to make it seem much less 'modern' than the first half, so does Locke's first treatise compared with the second. The relative weight of modern commentary on these different halves of the two texts reinforces the point.

Locke's tone in much of this is urbane and witty, redolent of a certain post-Restoration tone which was trying to establish a less strenuous mode of controversy than that which led up to the Civil War. At the time, discussion of the causes of the war often involved blaming either the bishops or the Puritans for whipping up emotion, being over-strenuous in their rhetoric of denunciation, being absolute (not necessarily as in 'absolute monarchy'). It started with the restored Royalists blaming the Puritans; but people with Nonconformist or anti-Court sympathies responded to that in a tone more like Restoration wit than Puritan earnestness. In line with this, Locke pricks Filmer's certainty by arguing that his use of scripture is less erroneous than fanciful, even if the appeal is still to Scripture. Here is a passage where Locke is wondering why the father, and not the mother, is reckoned to have absolute power over the child:

> . . . the Mother cannot be denied an equal share in the
> begetting of the child, and so the absolute authority of the
> father will not arise from hence. Our A- [author] indeed is of
> another mind; for he says, *We know that God at the creation
> gave the sovereignty to the man over the woman, and that for this*

reason, because he is the nobler and principal agent in generation. I remember not this in my Bible, and when the place is brought where God at the creation gave the sovereignty to man over the woman, and that for this reason, because he is the nobler and principal agent in generation, it will be time enough to consider and answer it: but it is no new thing for our A- to tell us his own fancies for certain and divine truths, though there be often a great deal of difference between his and the divine revelation: for God in the scripture says, *his father and his mother that begot him.*[33]

A late twentieth-century reader is likely to see something more here than questions of royal prerogative. Doesn't the discourse of patriarchy demand a gendered reading? In particular, isn't the dominance of father over mother historically and logically prior to that of father over child? According to Carole Pateman, classic patriarchy (by which she means Filmer and others who identify patriarchal with political power) 'declares women to be procreatively and politically irrelevant'.[34]

Locke also makes two important concessions to patriarchy. The first concerns small, primitive societies, where he reckons that the father of the extended family was the most likely to be the ruler; and where there were slightly larger societies, it was families rather than individuals that made the initial agreement. However, even these tribal societies (his example is America before the conquests) would pass over a weak heir to find the best ruler.[35] This is also an implicit denial of Hobbes's apparently irreversible contract. In the context of the Exclusion Crisis the idea was particularly potent: the people's choice comes into play at the moment of succession, not at some safely remote or mythical moment. The other is contained within Locke's most far-reaching manoeuvre, the separation of a civil society constituted by a bonding of free, and at least formally equal individuals from a private, family world still constituted by the 'natural' subjection of wife and children. To use more modern terminology, Locke's public sphere may be contractual, but the private sphere remained patriarchal.

Locke's description of society remains wedded (I use the term advisedly) to family metaphors. Whether an early commonwealth was one family grown up into it, or a uniting of several families:

> . . . which ever of these it was, that at first put the rule into
> the hands of a single person, certain it is that no body was
> ever intrusted with it but for the public good and safety, and
> to those ends in the infancies of commonwealths those who
> had it, commonly used it: and unless they had done so,
> young societies could not have subsisted: without such

> nursing fathers tender and careful of the public weal, all
> governments would have sunk under the weakness and
> infirmities of their infancy; and the prince and the people had
> soon perished together.[36]

The public sphere remains patriarchal, not in Filmer's sense, but in a more general sense, that political society emerges from males giving birth.[37] A phrase like 'nursing fathers' demonstrates how potent the family model of society still was for Locke. This survival of patriarchy argument is only one way of putting it, though; there is another, thin end of the wedge type of argument, which recognises that Locke is opening up avenues for the critique of patriarchy even if he didn't think of going down them. So, once one elision of the mother from the picture has been noticed, others can be too. Mary Astell's *Some Reflections on Marriage* (first published 1700) asked why, if all men were born free (as they were in Locke's state of nature), 'how is it that all women are born slaves?' Again, his famous declaration that everyone has property ('propriety' in its usual seventeenth-century meaning) in their own bodies, and in what they have added labour to out of nature (e.g., by gathering, or killing), or that marriage is a 'voluntary compact' at least gives the potential for female independence, even if his own arguments do not follow that through.

Locke's denial of patriarchy, then, is limited. However, the revolutionary part of his thinking about political society is in his view of power. His vote may have been for 'moderated monarchy' at the time, but 'the people' is where supreme power lays in his general theory. Men may give up some personal liberty for the general good of society, but it is a rational calculation. The state of nature may have been so dreadful to Hobbes that residual liberty hardly enters his thinking; for Locke the question is, why give up liberty? Liberty often gets subsumed under property, because he has such an inclusive notion of property; the enemy of both is arbitrary power:

> Absolute arbitrary power, or governing without settled
> standing laws, can neither of them consist with the ends of
> society and government, which men would not quit the
> freedom of the state of nature for, and tie themselves up
> under, were it not to preserve their lives, liberties and
> fortunes; and by stated rules of right and property to secure
> their peace and quiet.[38]

The rules make the society, not the monarch; and the people control the lawmakers. In the abstract, that means everyone with an interest in society having a vote; in practice, in that period, the emphasis falls on men with property and trading interests. Contract, after all, is crucial to trade; a society which keeps its contracts is much better to trade in than one where a single leader can change the rules by right. In practice, some measure of consent is necessary for the most arbitrary of rulers to survive, but the British monarchy had some serious consent problems in the century, as did the increasingly oligarchic Cromwellian Republic. As a metaphor for English society at the end of the century, contract might be described as over-determined. A society increasingly dependent on overseas trade, and more likely to go to war for trade than religion, and a society which twice ejected its reigning monarch for transgressing what its elected body saw as the rules is ripe for a revised version of its self-understanding. Contract and consent did not have an immediate victory in the English official mind at the end of the seventeenth century, but their diplomatic cousin compromise did.

Thus, the picture of Locke as the ideologue of the rising merchant classes needs to be complemented with a picture of Locke the revolutionary. There are several strands to this, by no means confined to Exclusion Crisis and 'Glorious Revolution' politics. For example, his sustained attack on primogeniture in the first *Treatise* is not simply about controlling continuity in government, but at a local level would undermine the larger landed estates. This might lead to a more intense cultivation, and thus an 'industrialisation' of land. It was also part of the Levellers' programme.[39] Again, his assertions of freedom and equality among men in the state of nature can be found in the more radical voices in the Putney Debates between the Parliamentary army officers in 1647.[40]

Now we can rephrase our earlier questions about Locke's revolutionary and religious stance by examining his fictional/mythic state of nature. It is first of all a state of equality – a position he finds in Hooker, which was a more persuasive source for his opponents than Milton or the Levellers who had more recently articulated the same thing. He puts a similar emphasis on natural law, guaranteed less by 'Nature' as an independent construct than by an omnipotent and purposeful creator who restrained them from destroying each other. This is a clear rebuke to the Hobbesian position from a consciously Christian standpoint. Throughout his works Locke seems to value God principally as the author of rationality, which makes even the state of nature to be tolerable. Less 'convenient' than civil government (the word has a stronger moral component than now), perhaps; but because the problem with justice in the state of nature is that it is likely to be imposed selfishly, one form of civil government is no better:

Absolute Monarchs are but men, and if government is to be
the remedy of those evils, which necessarily follow from
mens being judges in their own cases, and the state of nature
is therefore not to be endured, I desire to know what kind of
government that is, and how much better it is than the state
of nature, where one man commanding a multitude, has the
liberty to be judge in his own case, and may do to all his
subjects whatever he pleases, without the least liberty to any
one to question or control those who execute his pleasure?
And in whatsoever he doth, whether led by reason, mistake
or passion, must be submitted to?[41]

Locke's rhetoric is raised against both Hobbes and patriarchy; as in
Leviathan, the arguments from the state of nature seem to raise the
temperature of the text – parallelism, climax and the vehemence of the
adjectives all combining. Why? In this period, if you have a definitive
version of the state of nature, and thus the origin of government, the
argument is won.

Almost. One problem with Filmer's patriarchal argument was the
gap in genealogy from Adam to the Stuarts; a resolutely ahistorical
myth such as Hobbes's did not stand or fall on continuity. Locke's
history of government, too, is discontinuous, with choices, or
covenants being made at every turn. One agreement seems particularly
momentous in the creation of modern society, the introduction of
money, 'that a little piece of yellow metal, which would keep without
wasting or decay, should be worth a great heap of flesh, or a whole
heap of corn'.[42] Locke does not regard this as a fall from golden age
equality; rather, it is a further incentive to labour and thus increasing
the benefit that nature can give to humanity. It is also the moment
when absolute monarchy becomes inappropriate; the social relations of
the market economy demand a society that will protect property
without giving one figure control over the market.[43]

These arguments also demonstrate how Locke is bringing to a fine
art a tendency we see in post-Restoration debate as a whole, whether in
sermons, science, or political treatises. The procedure is to start from a
datum – the text to be preached, but more usually a physical
phenomenon or a historical assertion – and from it to deduce, logically,
the rest of the argument. If the Renaissance and Reformation combined
to send people back to the original texts, rather than the accretion of
commentary on them, the Restoration period was even more radical
(and sometimes inventive) in its search for origins, assuming that once
you had got far enough back, then deduction, in a universe founded on
law and rationality, would get you the rest of the way.

Harrington's *Oceana*

The political arguments of the Commonwealth period were often carried on in a religious idiom. The years 1649–60 were notable for a great eruption of prophecy, exegesis and experiment as God's Englishmen came to terms with their achievement (or their mistake, depending on your viewpoint). It is debatable whether this great flowering of political theory was a significant contribution to political change or more a reaction to it. Alongside the prophetic, or biblical modes of argument, and the achievement of Hobbes, which mixes a philosophic argument from first principles with an explicit attempt to co-opt the power of Christian loyalties, there was a further idiom, now known as classical republicanism. In Milton it coexists with his prophetic Puritanism. In *Behemoth*, Hobbes places the republicans as a separate group in Parliament, after Papists, Presbyterians and Independents in his list of the seducers of the people in the Civil War period, 'as that in their youth having read the books written by famous men of the ancient Grecian and Roman commonwealths concerning their polity and great actions; in which books the popular government was extolled by the glorious name of liberty, and monarchy disgraced by the name of tyranny; they became thereby in love with their forms of government'.[44] Hobbes himself had translated Thucydides in the 1630s, though not with republican intention. To his analysis of classical influence we need to add that of the contemporary Italian republics, Venice and Florence in particular, and their principal apologists, Machiavelli, Guiccardini, Gianotti and Sarpi.[45] It was not an invention of the 1640s; to take obvious examples, the essays of Bacon and the Roman history plays of Shakespeare both engage with classical and Renaissance republican ideas.

Engagement, or borrowing, however, is quite different from wholesale approval. While the precise definition of tyranny, and when it was right to overthrow a tyrant, had been a live issue in England for many years, it is difficult to find republicanism as a systematic programme before the 1640s. One obvious explanation is that it would have been regarded as treason. It is more like a discourse, or a component of a discourse, which stressed the virtues of mixed government (monarchy, oligarchy and democracy) as against the prerogatives of monarchy.

For example, it would be an exaggeration to characterise James Harrington (1611–77) as a thorough-going republican in the 1640s, although the stories of his close personal devotion to Charles I need tempering; he attended him during part of his imprisonment as a consequence of his membership of a Parliamentary Commission of 1646, and it seems that Charles found him a congenial Parliamentarian, rather than a member of his court he could hang onto.[46] Blitzer describes him as 'torn between his intellectual commitment to republicanism and his emotional commitment to the person of the King', frustrated by his inability to persuade Charles to compromise.[47] Harrington's republicanism had been born of the study and European experience – principally a visit to the Venetian Republic, though he had served in a volunteer regiment in the Netherlands during the Thirty Years War, and became the English agent of the Protestant Elector Palatine.

His major work of political theory, *The Commonwealth of Oceana*, was published in 1656. At that stage, its arguments for a republic would have seemed more an intervention in the dispute about the increasing personal power of Oliver Cromwell, rather than a polemic against Stuart monarchy.

Oceana is not exactly a Utopia; its relationship to the real, historical Britain is too close. A lot of the time only the names have been changed: so, Scotland appears as Marpesia, 'the dry nurse of a populous and hardy people', Ireland as Panopea, 'the soft mother of a slothful and pusillanimous people' whose problems might be better solved by planting with Jews (a proposal to readmit Jews to England, banned since 1270, was being debated at the time).[48] Few of the devices of fiction are even attempted; much of the narrative element of the book comes from his retelling of Italian and English history.

The hero of the founding of the Commonwealth, Lord Archon, is clearly Cromwell, the dedicatee of *Oceana*. At the end of the book he dies, in the fiftieth year of the commonwealth; the device of the book, then, is a retrospective, showing how he managed to set up a constitution for the British republic which would last. The 'Corollary', the final section, is a brief history of the commonwealth, though it contains very little incident but a lot of detailed schemes. For example, there is an account of how to pay for the army without raising taxation, with tables of figures. Harrington was very fond of the precision of numbers. It is his equivalent of Hobbes's intellectual debt to geometrical theorems. The vast majority of the book, 'The Model of the Commonwealth of Oceana', is an attempt to provide a detailed written constitution, and, particularly in his descriptions of the numerous local and national ballots, gets down to arithmetical detail a lot. The elective structure is pyramidical, which means elections at each stage up, from the parish to the senate. The reform of agrarian law is another heavily statistical section. Such precision – whether it works or not – can be seen as part of the obsession with detail characteristic of utopian thinking, or equally as evidence of an obsessional desire for fixity and stability.[49] It may also be, like the evidence from Venice, a strategy to get an ideal, paper vision taken seriously.

In the nineteenth century, notably with Bagehot, and in our own, the unwritten 'constitution' of Britain is regarded as an arcanum, while the meaning and amendability of the American Constitution is a central feature of political debate. The very fact of Harrington's attempt to provide a written constitution might explain why *Oceana* is regarded as an important source of American constitutionalism a century later, while it was received with derision by many of his English contemporaries. The foundation principles are balance – following Venice, the One, the Few and the Many are a mutually corrective source of rule. The dangers of isolated monarchy (whose recent dissolution 'was as natural as the death of a man') and party are equal – 'they of all the rest are the most dangerous who, holding that the saints must govern, go about to reduce the commonwealth to a party'.[50] However, the centre of Harrington's government is law, in particular the laws of property and protection. The first is controlled by the agrarian law 'by the balance of domination preserving equality in the root'; by abolishing primogeniture it would gradually cut down the largest estates.

For a popular ballot to work, the voters would have to be educated, and Harrington proposed an extensive programme of free, compulsory state education (for boys). But faith in the people coexisted with a suspicion of them; in a 1659 tract, *A Discourse upon this saying: the Spirit of the Nation is not yet to be trusted with liberty; lest it introduce monarchy, or invade the liberty of conscience* (which is pretty much what happened), Harrington again emphasises that workable popular government depends on a well-designed framework, one that would dissolve parties. In this passage he displays the authentic utopian, or millenarian tone: 'If your commonwealth be rightly instituted, seven years will not pass ere your clutches of parties, civil and religious, vanish, not through any force, as when cold weather kills flies, but by the rising of greater light, as when the sun puts out candles.'[51] As with his account of the fall of Charles, we notice how free of violence his language and vision are. Just before that peroration, though, a rather more authoritarian fable of the constitution state is told, from a Shrovetide pageant in Italy:

> . . . at Rome, I saw one which represented a kitchen, with
> all the proper utensils in use and action. The cooks were all
> cats and kitlings, set in such frames, so tied and so ordered,
> that the poor creatures could make no motion to get loose,
> but the same caused one to turn the spit, another to baste the
> meat, a third to skim the pot and a fourth to make green

> sauce. If the frame of your commonwealth be not such as
> causeth everyone to perform his certain function as
> necessarily as this did the cat to make green sauce, it is not
> right.[52]

Liberty is not very high on the list of Harrington's political desiderata. Debate, regular ballotting, and the rotation of offices (not a virtue during the Commonwealth) are. For a brief, somewhat unreal period at the end of the Commonwealth his way of doing things was influential. The Rota club, which he founded in November 1659, was a forum for coffee-house debate, concluded by a ballot, which contemporaries found more interesting than Parliament, and which numbered in its regular membership both influential figures of the Commonwealth, such as Maximilian Petty, and those such as Pepys, Aubrey, and Sir John Hoskyns (later President of the Royal Society) whose influence was ahead of them. With the recalling of the Long Parliament, and the increasing desire for a return to monarchy, the Rota faded and Harrington started to fix his hopes on a further horizon. Aubrey records that he said at the time, 'Well, the King will come in. Let him come in, and call a parliament of the greatest Cavaliers in England, so they be men of estates, and let them set but seven years, and they will all turn Common-wealth's men.'[53] It was an underestimate.

Banter and balance: Marvell and Halifax

The main emerging idiom of Restoration argument is dedicated to a new way of deciding disputes, a desire to avoid arguing one's way into a civil war again. This extends from serious works of science, political philosophy and theology through to texts of a more ephemeral, or satiric nature. It sits uneasily with a more authoritarian, repressive attitude – dissent is dangerous, and cannot be allowed a voice.

After 1662 we have often seen in arguments against Nonconformists that it was the strenuousness, violence and obscurity of their discourse that was largely responsible for the past troubles. The Nonconformists couldn't win with protestations of loyalty either, because the Long Parliament had claimed to be loyal. Sir Roger L'Estrange, Surveyor of the Press from 1662, was particularly convinced that any expression of dissent was subversive – and he had power to effect his opinions, by seizing opposition presses as well as publishing against them. His idiom and actions were rarely eirenic. In his *An Account of the Growth of Knavery*, a reply to Marvell's *Account of the Growth of Popery*, he says: 'This is not the first time we have heard of words smoother than oil, which yet are very swords. It is the very style that brought the late King to the block; and the Saviour of the world was betray'd by a "Hail Master", and a kiss.'[54]

Andrew Marvell MP (1621–78), an associate of Milton, a praiser of Cromwell who had not, like Dryden, recanted, was a particularly awkward customer when it came to controversy. If, as Coleridge suggests, 'a free and easy style was considered as a test of loyalty, or at all events, as a badge of the Cavalier party' after the Restoration, Marvell wore it while defending John Owen, a leading Nonconformist, against Samuel Parker, a defender of the episcopacy, and later a bishop himself. In 1669 Parker had written *A Discourse of Ecclesiastical Polity, wherein the authority of the Civil Magistrate over the Consciences of Subjects in matters of Religion is asserted; the Mischiefs and Inconveniences of Toleration are represented, and all Pretenses pleaded in behalf of Liberty of Conscience are fully answered.* The title is a good sample of the tone as well as a summary of the argument. Various replies ensued, including John Owen's *Truth and Innocence Vindicated.* These were vociferously answered in *A Defence and Continuation of the Ecclesiastical Polity* (1671) and the arguments extended in his 1672 Preface to Bishop Bramhall's *Vindication of himself and the Episcopal Clergy from the Presbyterian Charge of Popery. The Rehearsal Transpros'd* joined the argument, anonymously, in 1672 but changed its tone; it brought numerous replies in a similar vein, as well as Parker's *Reproof* of 1673, to which Marvell replied with a Second Part, this time published under his own name.

The witty manner, as well as the loyal stance, of the two parts brought him the approval of Charles II, no great reader of anything, let alone of religious controversy. That might sound like the Marvell of T.S. Eliot's essay, the poet of wit as 'equipoise', holding different positions together.[55] The view of the Restoration Marvell is less elusive; it is difficult to maintain that the attacks on 'French slavery' and 'Roman idolatry' in his later *Account of the Growth of Popery* are those of 'a balance and proportion of tones'.[56] Cowley's contemporaneous ode may give us a better starting-point for understanding Marvell's wit in these prose pieces:

> In a true piece of wit all things must be
> Yet all things there agree
> As in the ark, joined without force and strife
> All creatures dwelt.[57]

This is wit being conservative, or at least peacemaking; holding things together, whether ideas or people, in an age when they tended to fly apart. Now, Marvell's purpose, especially in *The Rehearsal Transpros'd* and *Mr Smirke; or, the Divine in Mode* (1676) is certainly eirenic, using wit and a bantering tone to calm down the argument. However, his desire for liberty of conscience was a specifically Nonconformist aim at the time; the toleration rather than the quashing of dissent goes against the exclusive tendency of the ecclesiastical legislation of the 1660s. One of Marvell's central worries about the public power Parker would like for king and bishops is the extent to which it would make uncontrolled dissenting belief and expression illegal, whether in the public or private sphere. What are loosely called absolutist theories – Marvell calls Parker more Hobbist than the self-confessed Hobbists – would make the public sphere of government and political argument effectively monologic, as well as leaving no private space marked 'conscience'.

There was an older English concept of a public sphere of argument, deriving from the Common Law and the various precedents of liberties that it celebrated, defined against the operation of crown prerogative. Yet it is possible to argue this even from something like an absolutist position, by suggesting that all these liberties derive from royal generosity rather than 'rights', say – 'co-ordinate sovereignty' is Pocock's suggestive description in his discussion of the opposition idiom.[58] This might give us a clue to Marvell's different strategies in 1672–73 and 1677. In *The Rehearsal Transpros'd* he argued that King Charles II was much more in favour of 'liberty of conscience' than the hawks and promotion-seekers in the ecclesiastical hierarchy. In *An Account of the Growth of Popery and Arbitrary Government* he is still blaming the bishops, but argues the more traditional opposition view that the king is subject to the rule of law. With the Exclusion Crisis looming, and the increasing evidence of Charles's collusion with France, both sides were seeing conspiracies, and Charles (not to mention his successor) seemed less and less reliable.[59]

The political question in the Restoration – will granting liberty of conscience (not to mention liberty of expression) lead to another civil war? – is paralleled by an artistic question about the function of wit. Can apparent opposites be held together, or is there room for only one voice, one notion of 'true wit'? Writing of Dryden, George Williamson argues that the problem left him by the Interregnum discussions of Davenant and Hobbes as well as Cowley was 'the regulation of wit'.[60] In particular, how is a writer to steer a course between the 'wild and lawless imagination' or the 'wrestling and torturing a word' and the dull plainness which results from no imagination at all? Dryden's solution, he argues, is to go back to *mimesis*, to promote lively description rather than the intellectual play of metaphysical wit. Dryden praises Donne for 'deep thoughts in common language' as opposed to Cleveland's 'common thoughts in abstruse words', so he does have a place for intellectual as well as mimetic wit, but he also has the characteristic Augustan tendency to merge the desirability of truthful representation with the desirability of a particular political or religious truth (the particularity of which is often elided). For example, in his 'Life of Plutarch' (1683) he says: 'I have ever thought that the wise men in all ages, have not much differed in their opinions of religion, I mean as it is grounded on human reason. For reason, as far as it is right, must be the same in all men, and truth being but one, they must consequently think in the same train.'[61] Dissent, therefore, must be irrational. In a similar way, in 'His Majesty's Declaration Defended' (1681), Dryden cannot conceive of disagreement between the king and the people being anything but the fault of the latter's representatives; in his monistic view of truth, their interests must be one. Regulation of wit thus shades into the regulation of political thought and loyalty.

Marvell displays the new witty manner but he does not subscribe to this new theory of regulating wit. Rather, he goes back to the older concept of regulating wit, decorum. In Part One of *The Rehearsal Transpros'd*, he suggests that Parker's praise of Bramhall is inappropriate: 'Beside that it is the highest indecorum for a divine to write in such a style as this [part play-book and part romance] concerning a reverend bishop; these improbable elegies too are of the greatest disservice to their own design, and do in effect diminish always the person whom they pretend to magnify.'[62] Similarly, in The Second Part, he argues that his jesting style is necessary, not just because Parker himself is so ham-fisted stylistically, but because it is the only appropriate style to answer such a clown. In effect, *decorum personae* (the style appropriate to the character) is necessary to show what Parker is to himself, let alone others:

> In conclusion, this is that man who insists so much and
> stirrups himself upon the gravity of his profession, and the
> civility of his education: which if he had in the least observed
> in respect either to himself or others, I should, I could never
> have made so bold with him. And nevertheless, it being so
> necessary to represent him in his own likeness that it may
> appear what he is to others, and to himself, if possibly he
> might at last correct his indecencies, I have not committed
> any fault of style, nor even this tediousness, but in his
> imitation.[63]

He accuses Parker of breaking out of decorum in all directions – comic theatricality instead of sober divinity, romance hero-worship instead of moderate recommendation, and yelling and barking like a wolf instead of using the gentle tones of the shepherd/pastor that he ought to be.

Parker is being characterised as a particular kind of fool in Restoration comedy, the would-be wit. These can ape most of the verbal habits but not the judgement of the true wits.[64] We have to be careful here; the common pushing off-centre of the romance plot by the triumph of true wit over would-bes, as in *The Man of Mode* or *The Country Wife*, for example, is hardly a moral triumph. Marvell as a loyal Christian true wit has to ensure that he does not simply appear as a successful deceiver in the Horner or Dorimant mode. His allusion to *Volpone* is interesting here. In that play Sir Politick Would-Be, the incompetent English Machiavel in Venice, is exposed by Peregrine, the truth-teller, rather than Volpone, whose method of exposing the hypocrisy of others involves a series of con-tricks of his own. Marvell needs to be a Peregrine rather than a Volpone. The allusion comes in a passage which suggests that Parker is part of an ambitious minority, one far more dangerous and inflammatory than the Nonconformists – 'They are the Politick Would-Bes of the clergy. Not bishops, but men that have a mind to be bishops, and that will do anything in the world to compass it.'[65] His attack then modulates into a characteristically Reformed opposition of Law and Gospel within a Christian Humanist frame, an opposition increasingly absent from Restoration Anglican theology:

> You would think the same day that they took up divinity
> they divested themselves of humanity, and so they may
> procure and execute a law against the Nonconformists, that
> they had forgot the gospel . . . . The former Civil War
> cannot make them wise, nor his Majesty's happy return,
> good natured; but they are still for running things up to the
> same extremes.[66]

The unspoken villain here is Laud, of course; so why are his successors so unwilling to learn from his mistaken extremism? 'The softness of the Universities where they have been bred, the gentleness of Christianity in which they have been nurtured, hath but exasperated their nature.' The answer is immaturity. They are still resentful schoolboys who want to wield the cane themselves – 'they seem to have contracted no idea of wisdom, but what they learnt at school, the pedantry of whipping'. That final exposure is far more serious, even Jonsonian, than we get in most Restoration comedy.

Marvell's chief dramatic original was the Duke of Buckingham's *The Rehearsal* (1672, revised 1675). This is a burlesque of serious heroic drama, Dryden's in particular.[67] Bishop Burnet, a contemporary admirer of Marvell and certainly not of Parker, suggested that Drawcansir, the fustian fighter of *The Rehearsal*, contributes as much to the characterisation of Parker as Bayes, the Dryden figure.[68] Marvell thinks that Parker has mistakenly transferred these qualities to Bishop Bramhall as well:

> By the language he seems to transcribe out of the *Grand-Cyrus* and *Cassandra* [romances translated in the 1650s] but the exploits borrowed out of the *Knight of the Sun* and *King Arthur*. For in a luscious and effeminate style he gives him such a termagant character as must either fright or turn the stomach of any reader.[69]

Parker's lust for persecution is exposed by this ridiculously ferocious style. Bayes is also alarmingly and absurdly inventive in the play, concocting ideas for plays or scenes which amount to aborted conceits, like the two kings who fall out because they are *not* in love with the same woman. Marvell picks up this device when he summarises Parker's thought in six 'Aphorisms and Hypotheses', which later turn into titles for plays, like *The Unlimited Magistrate*, *The Public Conscience*, or *Debauchery Tolerated*. They are not expanded in a theatrical or even a narrative manner, but *Debauchery Tolerated* in particular is given an amusing re-run in the Second Part, where Marvell sets it out typographically as a mock royal declaration, flat contrary to the real king's 'Declaration of Indulgence to Tender Consciences and Proclamation against Debauchery' (1672, but withdrawn under pressure in 1673; though it may have been intended to benefit Catholics more than Nonconformists, the incident gives Marvell a further opportunity for the Nonconformists to suggest they are more friendly to the king than the supposedly loyal Anglicans).

The dramatic allusions in *The Rehearsal Transpros'd* are not the primary satiric strategy, more a running joke. Here the named author of the Second Part (the first was anonymous) comments on the anonymous author of the *Ecclesiastical Politie*:

> . . . if men were obliged to leave that anonymous and skulking method both of writing and licensing, they would certainly grow more careful what opinions they vented, what expressions they used, and we might have missed many books that have of late come out by the same authority contrary to all good manners, and even to the doctrine of the church under which they take protection. Had there been no other cause than this, it might have sufficed, and when *Ecclesiastical Politie* marched incognito,

and theology went on mumming, it was no less allowable
for anyone to use the licence of masquerade to show him,
and the rest of 'em the consequence of such practice.[70]

The literary incognito becomes a mumming mask, which in turn
licenses a more general masquerade. 'Licence' is a point of contention,
Parker wanting to deny it to Nonconformists, Marvell arguing that he
is allowing it to debauchees rather than loyal and sober citizens. Then,
out of a 'beside this', comes the discovery that there is a new company
of comedians, the divines with their 'dramatic and scenical way of
scribbling'. Remember there were only two theatrical companies in
London at the time, unless you count the trainees under Killegrew,
which he does shortly to the 'new' company's further disadvantage.
While they will probably get hissed and pelted off the stage by the
audience in the pit, Marvell, sitting quietly up to then, decides to use
the liberty of the house 'and revenging the expense of my time and
money, by representing the author of the comedy called *The
Ecclesiastical Politie* in that farce of mine own *The Rehearsal Transpros'd*'.[71]
From farce he descends into street theatre, suggesting that Parker's
arrogance is like a mountebank's 'scaffold pageantry', decrying all
others in a panegyric of his own balsam. Then he's off again, into
images of piracy and highway robbery. Like the true wit of
Restoration comedy, Marvell presents himself as the judicious audience
of another comedy, as well as writing and acting in his own. He is
doing so in perhaps the most honourable comic role the true wit has,
ridiculing and undermining 'unspeakable arrogance', not just for his
own satisfaction, but in defence of his friends.

There is a parallel point in *Mr Smirke, or the Divine in Mode* (1676),
where 'Andreas Rivetus', Marvell's *persona*, suggests that 'Jocular
Divinity' is the best way to promotion these days, and ironically
proposes an investigation into the 'dignity of the Church's jester' along
with the enquiries into the Nonconformists. A Church jester needs
sense, modesty and truth (and thus Marvell appropriates the very terms
that Parker, Simon Patrick and others were employing against the
language of Nonconformity); 'And lastly, it were not amiss that they
give some account too of their Christianity; for the world has always
hitherto been so uncivil as to expect something of that from the
clergy.'[72] 'Uncivil' is a beautifully precise dig at those who have sought
social advancement before Christian charity.

Not content with turning the new sense and style of wit to his
advantage, Marvell also turns to the older meaning, of wit as intellect
and learning. He deflates Parker with superior scholarship, for example
in exposing his ignorance of Julian the Apostate. It is not just
ignorance, but malice that informs Parker's misreading, he suggests; by

leaving out the conclusion of the Roman historian Marcellinus, Parker understates the viciousness of Julian's persecution. If only he had bothered to look at the Christian authors of the period – Augustine, Gregory of Nazianzus, or John Chrysostom, all of them prominent Church Fathers – he would have realised his mistake. But then he seems to have more sympathy with pagan authors and pagan persecutors than with Christians. It is passages like these that remind us of the serious religious purpose behind Marvell's attack; not just liberty of conscience for liberty's sake, but liberty for the standard-bearers of Reformation Christianity.

We might even extend our discussion of Marvell's wit to include his plain dealing, that side of Restoration true wit represented by Manly rather than Horner. Marvell needed to find a tone that would combine generosity with truth-telling, moderation with satire. The generosity is as much Charles II's as his, like the Emperor Constantine's in *Mr Smirke*, and abused or ignored by the Church hierarchy in both.

Plain dealing with Parker involves more than telling the truth against his erroneous ideas; it involves exposing him, not least to himself. 'Never man certainly was so unacquainted with himself', he suggests.[73] The cack-handed pomposity of the opening sentences of Parker's *Preface* to Bramhall is what gives the immediate impetus to Marvell's attack. What is this man? he wonders. An astrologer? A publisher? A fastidious stylist? An enthusiast (quite the worst insult, of course)? Parker's tonal uncertainty as well as his anonymity leaves him wide open. Later, his multiple holdings of Church benefices prompt similar enquiries – archdeacon? Rector? The 'Muster-roll of your self' is the phrase, reminiscent of a similar line of attack in the Marprelate tracts.[74]

The controversy as a whole is peculiarly self-conscious about style. Parker attacked his opponents by denigrating their language, Owen's 'peculiar uncouthness and obscurity of style', for example.[75] *Ecclesiastical Politie* is prefaced by suggestions that 'our dissenting zealots' will only be able to object to 'the vehemence and severity of its style', not its ideas; and there is that extraordinary proposal for an Act of Parliament 'to abridge preachers the use of fulsome and luscious metaphors' which, he argues, were one of the major causes of the Civil War.[76] Interestingly it is John Owen rather than Marvell who picks up on the metaphor question, arguing that they are 'Scriptural expressions of gospel mysteries', and part of a spiritual wisdom which Parker would reduce to mere obedience.[77]

Parker is vulnerable sometimes because he has not thought through these larger implications of style on his own part, even if the link between his opponents' errors and their style is clear to him. The Preface to *The Reproof to the Reherasal Transpros'd* (1673) openly dithers between the desire to be 'pleasant' and the stylistic claims of truth and reason. At one point his version of the plain dealer is a satirist, sharply exposing the zealots; at another point he is opposing the use of metaphors as religious imposture, and thus setting himself a far more austere standard than he can follow. Parker was a member of the Royal Society, like many Restoration divines. There is a link between the new scientific style and the new theological plainness, both set up as conscious correctives to the deceptive power of language. For Marvell, Parker's link with science is further proof of his stupidity; his 'projects' are like his trivial and incoherent arguments. The allusion is to a glass-works project:

> One burnt the weed, another calcined the flint, a third
> melted down that mixture; but he himself fashioned all with
> his breath, and polished with his style till out of a mere jelly
> of sand and ashes, he had furnished a whole cupboard of
> things so brittle and incoherent that the least touch would
> break them again in pieces, so transparent that every man
> might see through them.[78]

Marvell may display a Swiftian scepticism of the new science, but he remains close to Bacon, its precursor-hero. He cites Bacon's argument for moderation in religious controversy in The Second Part; and half-way through Mr Smirke, he moves from satiric banter to history, a mode continued in An Account of the Growth of Popery and Arbitrary Government. Annabel Patterson has argued that this is a Baconian move, assembling eye-witness accounts (Marvell was an MP and thus a witness himself) as an essential preparation to true history.[79] There is, though, as she recognises, more to An Account than this 'naked narrative' (Marvell's own term). Once again, the styles of the writer and his opponents are used as indications of political standards of truth and deceit. So the declaration of war with the Dutch, part of Charles's pro-French policy, is in 'a style so far from being most Christian, that nothing but some vain French Romance can parallel or justify the expression'.[80] In contrast, the defiance of the Test Oath produces a genuine heroism which transcends rhetoric: 'never was there a clearer demonstration how dull a thing is human eloquence, and greatness, how little, when the bright truth discovers all things in their proper colours and dimensions, and shining shoots its beams through all their fallacies'.[81] It is not unusual, even this late in the century, to find an assertion of the plainness of truth and the inadequacy of rhetoric cast in such rhetorical and metaphorical terms. Marvell's later, increasingly Baconian, emphasis on history, on the empirical, the anti-romance, as well as his distinctively Restoration commitment to a quieter tone of controversy, should not obscure his abilities at Renaissance rhetorical performance, nor his loyalty to Reformation theology.

It is an uneasy position, though; all his prose pieces contain declarations of loyalty to the king. This is not just to head off accusations of rebelliousness. For much of Charles II's reign he must have seemed a better bet for liberty for the Nonconformists than Parliament. But Marvell betrays increasing distrust, especially in *An Account*; and it is probably not a coincidence that this corresponds with his move from Restoration banter to the plain language of liberty, an idiom more indebted to the 1640s and 1650s, but which came into vogue again, much adapted, during the Exclusion Crisis and the Revolution of 1688.

George Savile, Marquis of Halifax (1633–95), was much closer to the centre of power than Marvell, but went through more than one period of disillusion with it. His political career carries paradox almost into principle. It seems that most of the time he went into office he was at least intellectually in opposition. His greatest political achievement, persuading the Lords to reject the Exclusion Bill that would have prevented James from succeeding to the throne, resulted in the succession of a man he (rightly) thought incompetent and stubborn. Nor was he a closet Catholic; he seems to have been as much of an atheist as respectability would allow, except when he was ill. Perhaps he feared that James would not go quietly, and so would precipitate another Civil War; or that the evidence from the Netherlands was that William of Orange was just as much of an absolutist.[82] However, when James abandoned the throne in 1688, Halifax was instrumental in sorting out a peaceful succession. Once again he had the ear of the king, and one who was more likely than his Stuart predecessors to take note of what he said; but he retired in 1690, stung by the attacks on him. As J.R. Jones suggests, it was paradoxical for such a sensitive person to play an active role in times of maximum tension, when the risks and unpopularity were greatest, only to retire in times of political peace.[83]

Through his writings we can see something more coherent, a political philosophy, or at least a consistent strategy, for which the term he made his own, 'trimming', is the neatest description. *The Character of a Trimmer* circulated anonymously in manuscript in 1685, and Halifax only admitted authorship after 1688. Like most of his published political writing, it had a specific, topical reference, but the tone and arguments are quite general. We are in at the establishment of party politics, where in the heat of the Exclusion Crisis, Whigs and Tories became much more organised.[84] 'Whig' was a term originally applied to the Scottish Presbyterian Covenanters in the Civil War, and gradually attached to the opposition to James's succession; 'Tory' was their pejorative term for their opponents, deriving from Irish Catholic bandits. Given a choice, we would have to call Halifax a moderate Tory; but *The Character of a Trimmer* describes party name-calling as a snowball fight, when stability would be a better aim. At the time, the gap between Whigs and Tories was starting to look as wide as those between the combatants in the Civil War; the Trimmer, he argues, is trying to keep the state even:

> This innocent word Trimmer signifieth no more than this,
> that if men are together in a boat, and one part of the
> company would weigh it down on one side, another would
> make it lean as much to the contrary, it happeneth there is a
> third opinion, of those who conceive it would do as well, if
> the boat went even, without endangering the passengers.[85]

'Innocent' is defensive; 'Trimmer' was just as aggressively pejorative a term at the time as Whig or Tory. An anonymous broadside of 1683, 'The Character of a Trimmer' is typical:

> A twisted brute, the satyr in the story,
> That blows up the Whig heat and cools the Tory;
> A state hermaphrodite, whose doubtful lust
> Salutes all parties with an equal gust.[86]

The real source for the trimmer perceived as villain, though, is the *Observator* of Roger L'Estrange, a periodical in dialogue form dedicated to political polarisation.[87] The anti-trimmer campaign began late in 1682; the following sample shows how different L'Estrange's tone is from Halifax's, as well as the reasons for his suspicion of trimming:

> . . . your downright-stark-staring-Whig is much more
> tolerable in a state, than your temporizing, fleering, and
> glozing Trimmer. The one's an open, and a professed
> enemy; the other a spy, and a conspirator both in one. The
> one murders his prince in a battle; the other, in a covenant.
> And prithee tell me, which was the more criminal, the
> soldier with his spear, or Judas with his kiss?[88]

Even L'Estrange has difficulties attacking moderation as such, but if the Trimmers can be labelled as an opposition party, not just a point of view, doing Whig work under cover (opposition was as good as treason to L'Estrange), then it would fail the loyalty test. It may seem a paranoid form of politics, and a strategy to weaken rather than broaden the Tory power base. L'Estrange's gamble was that mockery, repression, and the fear of another civil war would push the waverers into silence, or unconditional support for the government. Halifax, as a moderate Tory, favoured a more inclusive approach to opposition.

In the first two sections of *The Character of a Trimmer*, on laws and government, and on religion, Halifax identifies moderation and compromise as the principal virtue of civilisation, and English civilisation in particular. It might be thought that the mystique of the British 'constitution', with its concomitant pity for the benighted nations without it, is a creation of Walter Bagehot and Victorian Imperialism. Not a bit of it. Halifax's witty, aristocratic, slightly disdainful tone is an attempt to celebrate the mixed nature of British government at a moment of deep crisis. The balanced, antithetical phrases are in themselves an attempt at cooling controversy, resolving differences with a syntactic middle way; the image of the contending lovers is a deflation of political passion:

> The dispute, which is the greater beauty, a monarchy or a
> commonwealth, hath lasted long between their contending
> lovers; and they have behaved themselves so like lovers, who
> in good manners must be out of their wits, used such figures
> to exalt their own idol on either side, and such angry
> aggravations to reproach one another in the contest, that
> moderate men have in all times smiled upon this eagerness,
> and thought it differed very little from a downright frenzy.
>
> We in England, by a happy use of this controversy,
> conclude them both in the wrong, and reject them from
> being our pattern, taking the words in the utmost extent;
> which is, that monarchy is a thing which leaveth men no
> liberty, and a commonwealth such a one as alloweth them
> no quiet. We think that a wise mean between these
> barbarous extremes, is that which self-preservation ought to
> dictate to our wishes, and we may say, we have attained this
> mean in a greater measure, than any nation now in being,
> and perhaps than any we read of, though never so much
> celebrated for the wisdom or felicity of their constitution.[89]

'Barbarous extremes' – in phrases like this, Halifax reinforces his thesis that moderation is the mark of civilisation. He takes a similar line with differences in religion. Religion itself seems to exist for him principally as the 'foundation of government' (which of course means the existing form of government), but this does not turn into the usual Anglican aggression towards religious dissent which assumes it is a cover for political dissent. Rather, he suggests the Anglican clergy should be more inviting to dissenters and more gently converting towards

Catholics. Trimming in the religious sphere seems to be less the middle way between doctrinal or ecclesiastical extremes than good manners, and socially cohesive behaviour:

> No man doth less approve the ill bred methods of some of
> the dissenters in rebuking authority, who behave themselves
> as if they thought ill manners necessary to salvation; yet he
> cannot but distinguish and desire a mean between the
> sauciness of some of the Scotch apostles, and the undecent
> courtship of some silken divines, who one would think did
> practice to bow at the altar, only to learn to make the better
> legs at court.[90]

L.C. Knights's remark, that Halifax, for all his virtues, lacks the awareness of the potentially tragic nature of conflict, does have some force here.[91] Unless the Civil War was mostly a failure of political tone, or the Reformation a lapse in manners, his prescription of toleration for the tolerable would not work. However, if it is mass hysteria rather than tragedy you want to avoid, then Halifax would seem to be your model – except that during the Popish plot he rode the hysteria to get rid of Danby.[92]

The third section of *The Character of a Trimmer*, 'Things Abroad', suggests where his ultimate loyalties lay. In dealing with foreign policy, he reveals the one virtue where he is absolutist – patriotism: 'he would rather die than see a spire of English grass trampled upon by a foreign trespasser'.[93] 'Spire' is an interesting word, suggesting the crushing of Anglicanism by Catholicism; it fits with his earlier link of 'transubstantiation' with pro-French views. There are plenty of open and snide remarks about the French and their system of absolute monarchy, which he finds distasteful as well as dangerous; it is difficult to believe that he did not have his suspicions of Charles's covert pro-French policies. Certainly his posthumously published *Character of Charles II* has a separate section on 'His Dissimulation' – though, characteristically, he finds it a general fault: 'No King can be so little inclined to dissemble but he must needs learn it from his subjects, who every day give him such lessons of it.'[94] The conclusion to the section, though, is not so much generous as wary. Like other courtiers, Halifax has been bitten:

> When he thought fit to be angry, he had a very peevish
> memory; there was hardly a blot that escaped him. At the
> same time that this showed the strength of his dissimulation,
> it gave a warning too; it fitted his present purpose, but it
> made a discovery that put men more upon their guard

> against him. Only self-flattery furnisheth perpetual
> arguments to trust again: the comfortable opinion men have
> of themselves keepeth up human society, which would be
> more than half destroyed without it.[95]

That last reflection is not as witty, or as acidic, as some: notably, 'He lived with his ministers as he did with his mistresses; he used them, but he was not in love with them.'[96] But then Halifax is rarely as sharp as that; his prose would lose the taste of moderation if he was. K.G. Hamilton argues that the taste for antithesis, so central to earlier seventeenth-century prose, lingers in Halifax without the rigidity of the 'conscious stylists' such as Hooker and Browne.[97] There is some weight to this view of Halifax's modernity; though to say it is a more 'natural'-sounding version of antithetical style is to remark on his skill rather his naturalness. From another angle, we can see his style as a development from the essayistic, aphoristic style of Bacon, in itself a 'modern' style in the early part of the century, and with considerable influence on the modern learning of the Restoration. But Halifax is lighter, less bookish. He is resisting the intensity of the intellectual as well as the intensity of L'Estrange's vehemence. The range of qualities he celebrates at the end of *The Character of a Trimmer* – 'nature, religion, liberty, prudence, humanity, and common sense' – sounds like a roll-call of the enlightened eighteenth century's desiderata. It is his view of civil society as much as his urbanity and dislike of extremes that constitutes his modernity. His wit is as Augustan as Pope's; not as skilful, but better-tempered.

Both Marvell and Halifax represent a rising tendency in English prose, not more typical than L'Estrange's lampooning violence, but recognisably innovative in their defence of toleration and compromise. This marks no simple line of progress or emancipation, though. Marvell's *Rehearsal* prose is dense with allusion – my description of it is an attempt to do justice to its mingling of Restoration banter with the Reformation and Renaissance habit of answering text with text at every level – style, substance, intention, allusion, often sentence by sentence. It is an intervention in the history of wit as well as a defence of Nonconformist liberties. Its language of liberty is not as innovative or as perspicuous as Walwyn's or Winstanley's; in the circumstances, it could not be.

Even Halifax reminds us that seventeenth-century prose remains throughout its history committed to the stylishness of antithetical structures. The grand, cumulative effects of Lyly, or Donne, or some of Browne, are vanished, but the effect of control gained by syntactic parallels and antitheses is never abandoned. Indeed, as other effects are eschewed, it becomes even more noticeable. Even Locke, who must take the prize for the seventeenth-century attack on rhetoric which contains the fewest rhetorical figures, is still recognisably the product of a rhetorical education. His polemic thus turns into a display of its virtues in shaping a sentence as well as an attack on its vices:

> 'Tis evident how much men love to deceive, and be
> deceived, since Rhetoric, that powerful instrument of error
> and deceit, has its established Professors, is publicly taught,
> and has always been had in great reputation: and, I doubt
> not, but it will be thought great boldness, if not brutality in
> me, to have said thus much against it. Eloquence, like the
> fair sex, has too prevailing beauties in it, to suffer itself ever
> to be spoken against. And 'tis in vain to find faults with
> those arts of deceiving, wherein men find pleasure to be
> deceived.[98]

Even Locke is seduced into simile as he warms to the attack, and the turn on 'deceiving' and 'deceived' is still identifiably the rhetorical figure polyptoton. His remarks remind us that the later seventeenth century actually saw a great increase in the number of rhetorics published, increasingly in English, a sign that a desire for eloquence was spreading down the social scale. But the austerity of argument is winning out at an influential level. In the following chapter he launches into a programme to remedy the abuses of words in the line of Bacon, Wilkins and Sprat; and probably had more success than they did. The reality fell short of the programme, but the programmes had their cumulative effect. The prose tools inherited by Swift and Defoe, Berkeley and Shaftesbury, may have been shorn of some their grandest effects, and the growing suspicion of grandiloquence is culturally profound; but there were enough generic and stylistic options left to dispel any picture of dissociation of sensibility, or imaginative drought, at the end of the seventeenth century. The virtues of prosaic transparency did not banish the possibilities for performance.

Notes

1. See Samuel I. Mintz, *The Hunting of Leviathan* (Cambridge, 1962) for seventeenth-century reactions to Hobbes.

2. Thomas Hobbes, 'The Art of Rhetoric', in *Tracts* (1681), p. 2.

3. *Tracts*, p. 104.

4. Thomas Hobbes, *Leviathan*, ed. C.B. Macpherson (Harmondsworth, 1968), I. 4, p. 102.

5. *Leviathan*, pp. 81–2.

6. See Richard Tuck, *Hobbes*, p. 10.

7. Part of the argument of J.G.A. Pocock, 'Time, History and Eschatology in the Thought of Thomas Hobbes', in *Politics, Language and Time* (1972), pp. 148–201.

8. *Leviathan*, III. 43, pp. 615, 625. See Jean Hampton, *Hobbes and the Social Contract Tradition* (Cambridge, 1986), pp. 94–6.

9. *Leviathan*, I. 14, p. 189.

10. *Leviathan*, I. 13, p. 185.

11. *Leviathan*, I. 13, p. 186.

12. *Leviathan*, I. 13, pp. 186–7.

13. Hobbes, *The Elements of Law*, ed. F. Tönnies (1889), I. 13, p. 67.

14. Hobbes, *Behemoth*, ed. Tönnies, Introduction Stephen Holmes (Chicago, 1990), p. 16.

15. The argument here is indebted to David Johnston, *The Rhetoric of Leviathan* (Princeton, 1986), especially Ch. 3, and a paper by Quentin Skinner, '*Leviathan* as a Renaissance Rhetorical Performance' delivered to the London Renaissance seminar, July 1990.

16. *Leviathan*, I. 5, pp. 116–17.

17. *Leviathan*, III. 42, pp. 568–9.

18. Quentin Skinner, 'Conquest and Consent: Thomas Hobbes and the Engagement Controversy', in *The Interregnum*, ed. G.E. Aylmer (1972); though see the warnings by Kenneth Minogue in *Meaning and Context: Quentin Skinner and his critics*, ed. James Tully (Princeton, 1988), pp. 179–80. Pocock, 'Time, History and Eschatology', points out Hobbes's affinities with the Leveller Richard Overton's mortalism and the Digger Gerrard Winstanley's millenarianism.

19. *Leviathan*, p. 726.

20. See Tom Sorell, 'The Science in Hobbes' Politics', in *Perspectives on Thomas Hobbes*, ed. G.A.J. Rogers and Alan Ryan (Oxford, 1988), pp. 67–80.

21. Perez Zagorin, 'Hobbes on Our Mind', *Journal of the History of Ideas*, 51 (1990), 317–35.

22. For the frequency of this in popular uprisings in the period, see Annabel Patterson, *Shakespeare and the Popular Voice* (Oxford, 1989).

23. Gerrard Winstanley, 'A New Years Gift to the Parliament and Army', in *Selected Writings*, ed. Andrew Hopton (1989), pp. 82, 85.

24. Winstanley, p. 90.

25. See Arrigo Pacchi, 'Hobbes and the Problem of God', in *Perspectives on Thomas Hobbes*, p. 186n.; the chapter as a whole is one of the few convincing treatments of the role of theology in Hobbes's writing.

26. Sir Robert Filmer, *Patriarcha and Other Writings*, ed. Johann P. Sommerville (Cambridge, 1991), p. 6.

27. Filmer, p. 7.

28. Filmer, p. 10.

29. See his *The Freeholder's Grand Inquest Touching Our Soveraigne Lord the King and His Parliament* (1648), an expansion of the last chapters of *Patriarcha*, often attributed to Sir Robert Holborne, but printed in collected editions of Filmer from the seventeenth century. See Gordon Schochet, *Patriarchalism in Political Thought* (Oxford, 1975), especially p. 117.

30. Whether they were right about these countries is another matter; for France, see the comparative analyses of John Miller, e.g. in 'The Potential for "Absolutism" in Later Stuart England', *History*, 69 (1984), 187–207.

31. Charles I, *His Majesties Answer to the Nineteen Propositions of Both Houses of Parliament* (1642), extract in *Divine Right and Democracy*, ed. David Wootton (Harmondsworth, 1986), pp. 171–4. This also contains extracts from Philip Hunton's 1643 *Treatise of Monarchy*, which Filmer attacked.

32. J.C.D. Clark, *Revolution and Rebellion: State and society in England in the seventeenth and eighteenth centuries* (Cambridge, 1986), Ch. 5. This is part of a controversial 'revisionist' case which shifts the 'defeat' of monarchy, aristocracy and Church from the seventeenth century to 1828–32.

33. John Locke, *Two Treatises of Government*, ed. Peter Laslett (Cambridge, 1963), I. vi. 56.

34. Carole Pateman, *The Sexual Contract* (Oxford, 1988), p. 87.

35. Locke, *Two Treatises*, II. viii. 105.

36. Locke, *Two Treatises*, II. viii. 110.

37. See Pateman, *Sexual Contract*, p. 89; and cf. J.B. Elshtain, *Public Man, Private Woman: Women in Social and Political Thought* (Princeton, 1981). Laslett, in his notes to §105, draws attention to Locke's 'concessions' to patriarchalism in the context of contemporary formulations.

38. Locke, *Two Treatises*, II. xi. 137.

39. Richard Ashcraft, *Revolutionary Politics and Locke's Two Treatises of Government* (Princeton, 1986), p. 283.

40. E.g. Col. Thomas Rainborough, in *Puritanism and Liberty*, ed. A.S.P. Woodhouse (1986 edn), pp. 53, 56; his argument with Ireton here is partly due to different ideas of the Law of Nature.

41. Locke, *Two Treatises*, II. ii. 13.

42. Locke, *Two Treatises*, II. v. 37.

43. See the discussion by Carole Pateman, *The Problems of Political Obligation: A Critique of Liberal Theory* (Oxford, 1985 edn), pp. 66–8.

44. Hobbes, *Behemoth*, p. 3.

45. The pioneer work is Zera S. Fink, *The Classical Republicans* (Evanston, 1945); but see especially the work of J.G.A. Pocock, notably in his edition of Harrington, and in *The Machiavellian Moment* (Princeton, 1975).

46. See J.G.A. Pocock (ed.), *The Political Works of James Harrington* (Cambridge, 1977), pp. 3–4.

47. Charles Blitzer, *An Immortal Commonwealth: The Political Thought of James Harrington* (New Haven, 1960), p. 23

48. Harrington, *Political Works*, p. 159; for the Jews see Peter Toon, 'The Question of Jewish Immigration' in *Puritans, the Millenium and the Future of Israel*, ed. Toon (Cambridge, 1970), pp. 115–25.

49. For the first view, see J.C. Davis, *Utopia and the Ideal Society* (Cambridge, 1981), p. 235; for the second, Blitzer, *Immortal Commonwealth*, p. 219.

50. Harrington, *Political Works*, pp. 203–4.

51. Harrington, *Political Works*, p. 745.

52. Harrington, *Political Works*, p. 744.

53. *Aubrey's Brief Lives*, ed. Oliver Lawson Dick (1987 edn), p. 209.

54. Roger L'Estrange, *An Account of the Growth of Knavery* (1678), pp. 13–14.

55. T.S. Eliot, 'Andrew Marvell', *Selected Essays* (1975), pp. 292–304.

56. Andrew Marvell, *An Account of the Growth of Popery and Arbitrary Government in England* (Amsterdam, 1677; facsimile 1971), p. 14.

57. Abraham Cowley, *Works* (1905), p. 17.

58. J.G.A. Pocock, *The Ancient Constitution and the Feudal Law: A Reissue with a Retrospect* (Cambridge, 1987), p. 343.

59. For a brief account of the circumstances, including Charles's two contradictory policies at this time, with some attention to Marvell's position, see J.R. Jones, *Country and Court* (1978), Ch. 9.

60. George Williamson, *The Proper Wit of Poetry* (1961), pp. 84–5.

61. *The Works of John Dryden*, Vol. XVII, ed. S.H. Monk and A.E. Wallace Maurer (Berkeley, 1971), p. 250.

62. Andrew Marvell, *The Rehearsal Transpros'd and The Rehearsal Transpros'd, The Second Part*, ed. D.I.B. Smith (Oxford, 1971), p. 12.

63. *The Rehearsal Transpros'd*, p. 185; see John Coolidge, 'Martin Marprelate, Marvell, and *Decorum Personae* as a Satirical Theme', *PMLA*, 74 (1959), 526–32, and the discussion of decorum in Annabel M. Patterson, *Marvell and the Civic Crown* (Princeton, 1978), pp. 178ff.

64. Harold F. Brooks, 'Principal Conflicts in the Restoration Comedy of Manners: The Battle of Sex, and Truewits versus Witwouds and Lackwits', *Durham University Journal*, 80 (1988), 201–12.

65. *The Rehearsal Transpros'd*, p. 106.

66. *The Rehearsal Transpros'd*, pp. 106–7.

67. There is a modern edition by D.E.L. Crane (Durham, 1976); it is interesting that Dryden put on his last heroic play in 1675, though he had the satirist's revenge in the portrait of Buckingham in *Absalom and Achitophel*.

68. See *Andrew Marvell: The Critical Heritage*, ed. Elizabeth Story Donno (1978), p. 50.

69. *The Rehearsal Transpros'd*, p. 11.

70. *The Rehearsal Transpros'd*, p. 166.

71. *The Rehearsal Transpros'd*, p. 167.

72. Andrew Marvell, *Mr Smirke: or, the Divine in Mode* (1676), p. 3.

73. *The Rehearsal Transpros'd*, p. 7.

74. *The Rehearsal Transpros'd*, p. 286; Marvell acknowledges the Marprelate accusation on p. 294.

75. *Bishop Bramhall's Vindication of Himself and the Episcopal Clergy* (1672), Preface, sig. 23v.

76. Samuel Parker, *A Discourse of Ecclesiastical Politie* (1670), p. 76.

77. John Owen, *Truth and Innocence Vindicated* (1676), p. 20.

78. *The Rehearsal Transpros'd*, p. 172

79. Annabel Patterson, *Marvell and the Civic Crown* (Princeton, 1978), pp. 225–6.

80. Andrew Marvell, *An Account of the Growth of Popery and Arbitrary Government in England* (Amsterdam, 1677; facsimile reprint 1971), p. 44.

81. Ibid., p. 61.

82. These are the suggestions of J.P. Kenyon, in his introduction to Halifax, *Complete Works* (Harmondsworth, 1969), p. 14.

83. J.R. Jones, *Country and Court* (1978), p. 19.

84. The party politics of the late seventeenth century is a matter for hot and continuing debate among historians. See, most recently, J.C.D. Clark, *Revolution and Rebellion* (Cambridge, 1986), pp. 144ff.

85. *The Works of George Savile Marquis of Halifax*, ed. Mark N. Brown (Oxford, 1989), I, 179.

86. *Poems on Affairs of State vol.3: 1682–1685*, ed. Howard H. Schless (New Haven, 1968), p. 448.

87. See Mark N. Brown, 'Trimmers and Moderates in the Reign of Charles II', *HLQ*, 37 (1974), 311–36. For L'Estrange in general, see George Kitchin, *Sir Roger L'Estrange: a Contribution to the History of the Press in the Seventeenth Century* (1913); for his attacks on the Nonconformists see N.H. Keeble, *The Literary Culture of Nonconformity in later Seventeenth-Century England* (Leicester, 1987), pp. 102–10; for his polarising strategy see Robert Willman, 'The Origins of "Whig" and "Tory" in English Political Language', *Historical Journal* 17 (1974), 247–64.

88. *Observator*, 266 (1 Jan. 1683); quoted in Brown, 'Trimmers and Moderates', p. 316.

89. Halifax, *Works*, I, p. 184.

90. Halifax, *Works*, I, p. 207.

91. L.C. Knights, *Public Voices* (1971), p. 103.

92. Halifax, *Works*, I, p. 8 (Brown's introduction); cf. H.C. Foxcroft, *A Character of the Trimmer* (Cambridge, 1946), Ch. 6, which traces some elements of

'trimming' in his behaviour at the time, while belying the subtle
constitutionalism that Macaulay ascribed to him.

93. Halifax, *Works*, I, p. 237.

94. Halifax, *Works*, II, p. 489.

95. Halifax, *Works*, II, p. 490.

96. Halifax, *Works*, II, p. 493.

97. 'Two Restoration Prose Writers: Burnet and Halifax', in *Restoration Literature: Critical Approaches*, ed. Harold Love (1972), pp. 205–23.

98. John Locke, *An Essay Concerning Human Understanding*, ed. Peter H. Nidditch (Oxford, 1975), III. x. 34, p. 508.

Chronology

The dates for drama are for first performance, as far as is known; the rest are for publication, some much later than composition.

DATE	PROSE WORKS	OTHER WORKS	HISTORICAL AND CULTURAL EVENTS
1589	Marprelate tracts Greene *Menaphon* Nashe *Anatomy of Absurdity* Puttenham *Art of English Poesie*		
1590	Lodge *Rosalynde* Sidney *Arcadia*	Spenser *Faerie Queene, I–III*	
1591	Greene *Notable Discovery of Couzenage* Ralegh *Report about the Fight of the Isles of Azores*	Sidney *Astrophil and Stella* Southwell *Mary Magdalen's Tears*	Trinity College, Dublin founded
1592	Nashe *Pierce Pennilesse*	Daniel *Delia* Harvey *Four Letters and Certain Sonnets*	Elizabeth recalls Essex to Court Rose Theatre opens

DATE	PROSE WORKS	OTHER WORKS	HISTORICAL AND CULTURAL EVENTS
		Marlowe *Edward II* (?)	
		Shakespeare *Richard III*	
1593	Nashe *Christ's Tears over Jerusalem* Harvey *Pierce's Supererogation*	Drayton *Idea*	Plague in London
1594	Hooker *Ecclesiastical Polity, I–IV* Nashe *Unfortunate Traveller*	Shakespeare *Rape of Lucrece* *Titus Andronicus* *Taming of the Shrew* *Two Gentlemen of Verona* *Love's Labours Lost*	
1595	Montaigne *Essais* (final edn in French Sidney *Apology for Poetry*	Chapman *Ovid's Banquet of Sense* Spenser *Amoretti*	Southwell executed Death of Drake and Hawkins
1596	Nashe *Have With You to Saffron Walden* Lodge *A Margarite of America* Ralegh *Discovery of Guiana*	Spenser *Faerie Queene, IV–VI* Shakespeare *Romeo and Juliet* *Merchant of Venice*	Essex storms Cadiz
1597	Bacon *Essays* Deloney *John Winchcomb (Jack of Newbury)* James VI of Scotland *Demonology*	Dowland *First Book of Songs* Shakespeare *1 & 2 Henry IV* *Henry V*	Second Spanish Armada dispersed by bad weather

DATE	PROSE WORKS	OTHER WORKS	HISTORICAL AND CULTURAL EVENTS
1598		Chapman/Marlowe *Hero and Leander*	
		Jonson *Every Man in His Humour*	
		Marston *Scourge of Villainy*	
		Shakespeare *Much Ado about Nothing*	
1599	James VI *Basilicon Doron*	Shakespeare *As You Like It* *Julius Caesar*	Globe theatre built
	Nashe *Nashe's Lenten Stuff*		
1600	Cornwallis *Essays*	*England's Helicon*	Gilbert, *De Magnete*
		Jonson *Cynthia's Revels*	
		Shakespeare *Hamlet*	
1601	Dent *Plain Man's Pathway to Heaven*	Morley *Triumphs of Oriana*	Essex rebellion and execution
		Shakespeare *Twelfth Night*	Poor Law enacted
1602	Campion *Observations in the Art of English Poesie*	Middleton *Family of Love*	Bodleian Library opens
		Shakespeare *Troilus and Cressida*	
1603	Dekker *Wonderful Year*	Jonson *Sejanus*	Elizabeth I died; succeeded by James I
	Florio *Essays of Montaigne*	Marston *Dutch Courtesan*	Ralegh imprisoned Conquest of Ireland by Mountjoy
1604	James I *Counterblast to Tobacco*	Chapman *Bussy D'Ambois*	Hampton Court Conference Peace with Spain

DATE	PROSE WORKS	OTHER WORKS	HISTORICAL AND CULTURAL EVENTS
	Middleton *Father Hubbard's Tales* *Black Book*	Marston *Malcontent* Shakespeare *Measure for Measure* *Othello*	
1605	Bacon *Advancement of* *Learning* Hall *Meditations and Vows* *Mundus Alter et Idem*	Chapman, Jonson and Marston *Eastward Ho* Drayton *Poems* Jonson *Masque of Blackness* Middleton *Trick to Catch the Old* *One* Shakespeare *King Lear* Sylvester *Divine Weeks and Days* (trans. of Du Bartas)	Gunpowder plot Some Puritan clergy ejected
1606	Dekker *Seven Deadly Sins of* *London*	*Revenger's Tragedy* Jonson *Volpone* Shakespeare *Macbeth*	Charter for Virginia
1607	Markham *English Arcadia*	Beaumont *Knight of the Burning* *Pestle* Shakespeare *Antony and Cleopatra*	King forces bishops on Scotland
1608	Dekker *Bellman of London,* *Lanthorn and* *Candlelight* Hall *Characters of Virtues* *and Vices*	Jonson *Masque of Beauty* Shakespeare *Coriolanus*	League with Dutch Separatist congregation moves to Holland

DATE	PROSE WORKS	OTHER WORKS	HISTORICAL AND CULTURAL EVENTS
	Smith *True Relation of Virginia*		
1609	Bacon *De Sapientia Veterum* Dekker *Gull's Hornbook*	Daniel *Civil Wars* Shakespeare *Sonnets*	
1610	Douai (RC) trans. of Old Testament Donne *Pseudo-Martyr* Camden *Britannia* (trans. Holland) Jourdain *Discovery of the Bermudas*	Fletcher *Christ's Victory and Triumph* Jonson *Alchemist* Shakespeare *Winter's Tale* (?)	Petition of Right Assassination of Henri IV Galileo *Siderius Nuncius*
1611	King James Bible Donne *Ignatius His Conclave* Florio *Queen Anna's New World of Words* Speed *History of Great Britain*	Byrd *Psalms, Songs and Sonnets* Donne *Anatomy of the World* Jonson *Catiline, Oberon* Middleton *Chaste Maid in Cheapside* Shakespeare *Tempest*	Abbot made Archbishop Sale of baronetcies
1612	Bacon *Essays* (2nd edn) Bayley *Practice of Piety* Cervantes *Don Quixote* (trans. Shelton) Heywood *Apology for Actors*	Donne *Second Anniversary* Drayton *Poly-Olbion* Webster *White Devil*	Prince Henry d. Alliance with German Protestant princes

DATE	PROSE WORKS	OTHER WORKS	HISTORICAL AND CULTURAL EVENTS
1613	Purchas *Purchas his Pilgrimage*	Browne *Britannia's Pastorals* Shakespeare and Fletcher *Henry VIII, Two Noble Kinsmen*	Princess Elizabeth married Frederick, Elector Palatine
1614	Overbury *Characters* Ralegh *History of the World*	Jonson *Bartholomew Fair* Webster *Duchess of Malfi*	Addled Parliament Napier invents logarithms
1615	Adams *Mystical Bedlam*	Chapman *Odyssey* Harington *Epigrams* Jonson *Golden Age Restor'd*	
1616	Theophrastus *Characters* (trans. Healey) King James *Works*	Chapman *Whole Works of Homer* Jonson *Works*	Trial of Somerset Coke dismissed Inigo Jones begins Queen's House, Greenwich
1617	Moryson *Itinerary*		Ralegh's voyage to Guyana Pocahontas presented at Court
1618		Burton *Philosophaster* Jonson *Pleasure Reconciled to Virtue*	Thirty Years War begins Declaration of Sports Execution of Ralegh Bacon Lord Chancellor
1619	Bacon *Wisdom of the Ancients*		Queen Anne d. Synod of Dort Frederick chosen king of Bohemia

DATE	PROSE WORKS	OTHER WORKS	HISTORICAL AND CULTURAL EVENTS
1620	Bacon *Novum Organum* Cervantas *Don Quixote II* (trans. Shelton)	Jonson *News from the New World* *Pan's Anniversary*	Voyage of *Mayflower* George Herbert Orator at Cambridge
1621	First Newsbooks in London Burton *Anatomy of Melancholy* Wroth *Urania*		Bacon impeached Donne Dean of St Paul's First Parliament since 1614
1622	Bacon *Henry VII* Peacham *Complete Gentleman*	Massinger *New Way to Pay Old Debts* Middleton and Rowley *Changeling*	Parliament dissolved King restricts preaching Whitehall Banqueting House completed
1623	Drummond *Cypress Grove* Felltham *Resolves* (?) Bacon *De Augmentis*	Daniel *Whole Works* Shakespeare First Folio	
1624	Donne *Devotions* Lord Herbert *De Veritate*	Middleton *Game at Chess*	New Parliament cancels treaties with Spain
1625	Bacon *Essays* (final edn)	Jonson *Fortunate Isles*	James I d. Accession of Charles I; married Henrietta Maria Ferrar retires to Little Gidding

DATE	PROSE WORKS	OTHER WORKS	HISTORICAL AND CULTURAL EVENTS
1626	Bacon *Sylva Sylvarum* Bernard *Isle of Man* Donne *Five Sermons*	Jonson *Staple of News* Massinger *Roman Actor* Shirley *Wedding* Sandys (trans.) *Ovids Metamorphoses*	Parliament attempts to impeach Buckingham War with France
1627	Mead *Clavis Apocalyptica*	Drayton *Battle of Agincourt*	Ile de Rhé expedition Abbot suspended Sibthorp and Mainwaring on passive obedience
1628	Coke *Institutes* Earle *Microcosmography* Ralegh *Prerogative of Parliaments* Harvey *De Motu Cordis*	Ford *Lover's Melancholy*	Petition of Right becomes law Buckingham assassinated Laud Bishop of London
1629	Andrewes *XCVI Sermons* Adams *Works* Hobbes (trans.) *Thucydides*	Jonson *New Inn*	Parliament dissolved Laudian censorship of press Massachusetts Bay Company chartered
1630	Sibbes *Bruised Reed*	Quarles *Divine Poems*	Plague Peace with Spain Massive emigration to America
1631		Ford *'Tis Pity She's A Whore* *The Broken Heart* (?)	Famine: Commission for Poor Relief

DATE	PROSE WORKS	OTHER WORKS	HISTORICAL AND CULTURAL EVENTS
		Wither *Psalms of David*	
1632	Donne *Death's Duel* Ralegh *Instructions to His Son*	Massinger *City Madam*	Van Dyck settles in England
1633	Prynne *Histriomastix* Spenser *View of the Present State of Ireland*	Donne *Poems* Greville *Works* Herbert *Temple*	Laud Archbishop
1634	Donne *Six Sermons*	Carew *Coelum Britannicum* Milton *Mask (Comus)* Wither *Emblems* Shirley *Triumph of Peace*	Ship Money introduced Witch trials in Lancashire
1635		Quarles *Emblems*	
1636			Plague
1637	Chillingworth *Religion of Protestants*		Descartes *Discours sur la Mèthode* Trial of Hampden Star Chamber sentences Prynne, Bastwick and Burton
1638	Godwin *Man in the Moon*	*Justa Edouardo King* (including 'Lycidas')	Scottish Covenant

DATE	PROSE WORKS	OTHER WORKS	HISTORICAL AND CULTURAL EVENTS
	Lilburne *Christian Man's Trial* Wilkins *Discovery of a World in the Moon*	Randolph *Poems*	
1639	Fuller *Holy War* Laud *Conference with Fisher*		First Bishops' War against Scotland
1640	Donne *LXXX Sermons* Jonson *Timber* *English Grammar* Machiavelli *Prince* (trans. Dacres)	Carew *Poems* Davenant *Salmacida Spolia*	Short Parliament; Long Parliament impeaches Strafford and Laud Root and Branch Petition Second Bishops' War
1641	Milton *Of Reformation* *Prelatical* *Episcopacy* *Animadversions*	Shirley *Cardinal*	Laud imprisoned Strafford executed Irish rising Grand Remonstrance Suckling and Hobbes to France
1642	Hartlib *Reformation of Schools* Hobbes *De Cive* Milton *Reason of Church Government* *Apology for Smectymnuus*	Denham *Cooper's Hill*	King raises standard – Civil War Battle of Edgehill Theatres closed
1643	*Mercurius Aulicus, Mercurius Britanicus* and *Mercurius Civicus* (newsbooks) began	Cowley *The Puritan and the Papist*	Bishops abolished Battle of Newbury Westminster Assembly of Divines Solemn League and Covenant

DATE	PROSE WORKS	OTHER WORKS	HISTORICAL AND CULTURAL EVENTS
	Browne *Religio Medici* Milton *Doctrine and Discipline of Divorce* Overton *Man's Mortality* Walwyn *Power of Love*		Ordinance for licensing the press
1644	Milton *Areopagitica* *Of Education* Walwyn *Compassionate Samaritan* Williams *Bloody Tenent of Persecution*		Battle of Marston Moor
1645	Lilburne *England's Birthright* Milton *Tetrachordon* *Colasterion* Overton *Araignment of Mr Persecution*	Milton *Poems* Waller *Poems*	Prayer Book abolished Laud executed New Model Army Battle of Naseby
1646	Browne *Pseudodoxia Epidemica* Donne *Biathanatos* Edwards *Gangraena* Lilburne *London's Liberty* Saltmarsh *Smoke in the Temple* Wilkins *Ecclesiastes*	Crashaw *Steps to the Temple* Shirley *Poems* Vaughan *Poems*	Virtual end of war, Charles surrenders to Scots Presbyterian/ Independent friction

DATE	PROSE WORKS	OTHER WORKS	HISTORICAL AND CULTURAL EVENTS
1647	Andrewes *Private Devotions*	Cleveland *Poems* More *Philosophical Poems*	Charles given up to Parliament Army seizes king; king escapes Putney Debates
1648	Hooker *Ecclesiastical Polity, VI, VII*	Herrick *Hesperides* *Noble Numbers*	Second Civil War Leveller petition Pride's Purge End of Thirty Years War
1649	Coppe *Fiery Flying Roll* Donne *Fifty Sermons* Gauden *Eikon Basilike* Lilburne *Englands New Chains Discovered* Milton *Tenure of Kings and Magistrates* *Eikonoclastes* Winstanley *True Levellers' Standard Advanced*	Lovelace *Lucasta: Epodes*	Trial and execution of Charles I Rump proclaims Commonwealth Levellers suppressed Diggers Lilburne acquitted Milton Secretary of Foreign Tongues to Council of State
1650	*Mercurius Politicus* (–1660) Baxter *Saints Everlasting Rest* Taylor *Holy Living*	Bradstreet *Tenth Muse* Vaughan *Silex Scintillans I*	Cromwell succeeds Fairfax as Lord General Battle of Dunbar Acts on Sunday observance, swearing and blasphemy
1651	Donne *Essays in Divinity* Hobbes *Leviathan*	Cleveland *Poems* Davenant *Gondibert*	Charles crowned at Scone Battle of Worcester Charles a fugitive

DATE	PROSE WORKS	OTHER WORKS	HISTORICAL AND CULTURAL EVENTS
	Milton *Pro populo Anglicano Defensio* Taylor *Holy Dying*	Vaughan *Olor Iscanus*	
1652	Donne *Paradoxes* *Problems* Filmer *Original of Government* Greville *Life of Sidney* Herbert *Remains* Winstanley *Law of Freedom*	Crashaw *Carmen Deo Nostro* Benlowes *Theophila*	Proposed national Church with toleration End of Irish campaign Dutch War
1653	Duchess of Newcastle *Philosophical Fancies* Rabelais *Gargantua and Pantagruel* (trans. Urquhart) Walton *Complete Angler*	Duchess of Newcastle *Poems and Fancies*	Lilburne tried and acquitted Parliament expelled by Cromwell; nominated 'Barebones' Parliament Cromwell declared Protector Dutch defeated
1654	Milton *Defensia Secunda* Ward and Wilkins *Vindiciae Academiarum*		Peace with Holland
1655	Fuller *Church History of England* Hobbes *De Corpore Politico* Taylor *Golden Grove*	Denham *Cooper's Hill* Marvell *First Anniversary* Waller *Panegyric to My Lord Protector*	Rule of Major-Generals War with Spain Jamaica captured Cleveland and Cowley in prison Several newspapers suppressed

DATE	PROSE WORKS	OTHER WORKS	HISTORICAL AND CULTURAL EVENTS
1656	Bunyan *Some Gospel-Truths Opened* Charleton *Epicurus' Morals* Harrington *Oceana*	Cowley *Poems*	Jews readmitted to England
1657			Cromwell refuses kingship New charter for East India Company
1658	Browne *Hydriotaphia* and *Garden of Cyrus* Bunyan *Sighs from Hell*		Death of Cromwell
1659	Milton *Likeliest Means to Remove Hirelings*	Suckling *Last Remains*	Collapse of Richard Cromwell's Protectorate; Rump restored Rota Club
1660	Boyle *New Experiments* Milton *Ready and Easy Way*	Dryden *Astraea Redux* Lovelace *Lucasta: Posthume Poems*	Restoration of monarchy, Lords and Bishops Royal Society organised Theatres reopen Pepys begins diary Bunyan imprisoned
1661	Boyle *Sceptical Chemist* Glanvill *Vanity of Dogmatizing*	Cowley *Cutter of Coleman Street*	Fifth Monarchy Rising Cavalier Parliament Savoy Conference

DATE	PROSE WORKS	OTHER WORKS	HISTORICAL AND CULTURAL EVENTS
1662	Revised *Book of Common Prayer* Fuller *Worthies*	Butler *Hudibras I*	Act of Uniformity 1,200 Nonconformist clergy lose livings Licensing Act Charles II married Catherine of Braganza
1663	Boyle *Some Considerations*	Butler *Hudibras II* Dryden *Wild Gallant*	Sheldon Archbishop Declaration of Indulgence withdrawn
1664	Evelyn *Sylva*	Dryden *Indian Queen*	Conventicle Act New York occupied
1665	*Philosophical Transactions* begins Hooke *Micrographia* Walton *Life of Hooker*	Dryden *Indian Emperor* Marvell *Character of Holland*	Plague Five Mile Act Second Dutch War
1666	Bunyan *Grace Abounding*	Waller *Instructions to a Painter*	Fire of London
1667	Sprat *History of Royal Society* Duchess of Newcastle *Life* of husband	Dryden *Annus Mirabilis* Marvell *Last Instructions to a Painter* Milton *Paradise Lost*	Dutch burn ships in the Medway Clarendon impeached and exiled
1668	Cowley *Works* (including *Essays*) Dryden *Of Dramatic Poesy* Wilkins *Real Character*	Denham *Poems and Translations* Etherege *She Would if she Could*	Triple Alliance Dryden Poet Laureate

DATE	PROSE WORKS	OTHER WORKS	HISTORICAL AND CULTURAL EVENTS
1669		Dryden *Tyrannic Love*	Parliament prorogued
1670	Milton *History of Britain* Parker *Ecclesiastical Polity* Walton *Lives*	Behn *Forced Marriage* Dryden *Conquest of Granada I*	Cabal formed Treaty of Dover
1671		Buckingham et al. *Rehearsal* Milton *Paradise Regained and Samson Agonistes* Wycherley *Love in a Wood*	
1672	Marvell *Rehearsal Transpros'd* Temple *Observations upon the Netherlands*	Wycherley *Gentleman Dancing-Master* Dryden *Marriage à la mode*	Declaration of Indulgence; Bunyan freed Third Dutch War
1673	Marvell *Rehearsal Transpros'd II*		Declaration of Indulgence withdrawn; Test Act
1674			Cabal collapses
1675		Dryden *Aurung-Zebe* Wycherley *Country Wife*	Greenwich Observatory opened
1676	Cotton *Complete Angler II* Glanvill *Essays*	Etherege *Man of Mode* Wycherley *Plain Dealer*	King secret pensioner of Louis XIV

DATE	PROSE WORKS	OTHER WORKS	HISTORICAL AND CULTURAL EVENTS
1677	Marvell *Account of the Growth of Popery*	Behn *Rover* Dryden *All for Love*	
1678	Barrow *Sermons* Bunyan *Pilgrim's Progress I* Cudworth *True Intellectual System* L'Estrange *Account of the Growth of Knavery*	Butler *Hudibras III* Vaughan *Thalia Rediviva*	Popish Plot Danby impeached Treaty of Nijmegen
1679	Burnet *History of the Reformation I* South *Sermons*		Exclusion Crisis begins
1680	Bunyan *Mr Badman* Burnet *Life and Death of Rochester* L'Estrange *Citt and Bumpkin, trans. of Erasmus* Temple *Miscellanea I*	Rochester *Poems*	
1681	*Observator* and *Heraclitus Ridens* Baxter *Breviate Life of Margaret* Dryden *His Majesty's Declaration Defended* Hobbes *Behemoth*	Cotton *Wonders of the Peak* Dryden *Absalom and Achitophel* Marvell *Miscellaneous Poems* Oldham *Satires*	New Exclusion Bill Shaftesbury acquitted of treason

DATE	PROSE WORKS	OTHER WORKS	HISTORICAL AND CULTURAL EVENTS
1682	Bunyan *Holy War*	Dryden *The Medal* *Religio Laici* Otway *Venice Preserv'd*	
1683			Rye House Plot
1684	Behn *Love Letters between* *a Nobleman and his* *Sister* Bunyan *Pilgrim's Progress II* Burnet *Sacred Theory of the* *Earth*		
1685			Death of Charles II; accession of James II Monmouth rebellion put down at Sedgemoor; Bloody Assizes
1686		Bunyan *Book for Boys and Girls* Killigrew *Poems*	
1687	Newton *Principia Mathematica*	Dryden *Hind and the Panther*	
1688	Behn *Oroonoko* Halifax *Character of a Trimmer*		William of Orange lands; James flees
1689	Locke *Letter concerning* *Toleration*		Crown offered to William and Mary

DATE	PROSE WORKS	OTHER WORKS	HISTORICAL AND CULTURAL EVENTS
1690	Locke *Essay concerning Human Understanding* *Two Treatises of Government* Temple *Miscellanea II* Pepys *Memoirs of the Navy*		Battle of the Boyne
1691	Congreve *Incognita* Ray *Wisdom of God* Wood *Athenae Oxonienses*	Dryden/Purcell *King Arthur*	Tillotson Archbishop
1692	Bunyan *Works* L'Estrange *Fables of Aesop*	Dryden/Purcell *Fairy Queen*	Massacre at Glencoe
1693	Locke *Thoughts concerning Education* Rymer *Short View of Tragedy*	Congreve *Double Dealer*	
1694	Fox *Journal* Wotton *Reflections upon Ancient and Modern Learning*	Dryden *Love Triumphant*	Queen Mary d. Bank of England founded
1695	Locke *Reasonableness of Christianity* Tillotson *Works*	Congreve *Love for Love*	Whig Junto Licensing Act not renewed; growth of newspapers

DATE	PROSE WORKS	OTHER WORKS	HISTORICAL AND CULTURAL EVENTS
1696	Aubrey *Miscellanies* Baxter *Reliquiae Baxterianae*	Tate and Brady *Psalms* Vanbrugh *The Relapse*	Window tax
1697	Defoe *Essays on Projects*	*Poems on Affairs of State I and II* Vanbrugh *The Provoked Wife*	
1698	Behn *Histories and Novels* Collier *Short View of the Profanity and Immorality of the English Stage* Sidney *Discourses Concerning Government*		
1699		Farquhar *The Constant Couple*	Whig Junto breaks up
1700	Halifax *Miscellanies* Harrington *Works*	Dryden *Fables Ancient and Modern* *Secular Masque*	

General Bibliographies

(i) Historical and contextual studies
(ii) General studies of the prose
(iii) Other relevant literary criticism
(iv) Anthologies
(v) The English Bible

Note: Each section is arranged alphabetically. Place of publication is London, unless otherwise stated.

(i) Historical and contextual studies

Coward, B.
: *The Stuart Age*, Harlow, 1980 (mainly narrative history).

Davis, J.C.
: *Utopia and the Ideal Society: A Study of English Utopian Writing 1516–1700*, Cambridge, 1981 (chapters on Bacon, Burton, Winstanley and Harrington).

Hill, C.
: *Intellectual Origins of the English Revolution*, Oxford, 1965 (includes discussion of Bacon, Ralegh, Coke, and science and medicine).

Hill, C.
: *The World Turned Upside Down: Radical Ideas During the English Revolution*, 1972.

Kroll, R.W.F.
: *The Material Word: Literate Culture in the Restoration and Early Eighteenth Century*, Baltimore, 1991.

Miller, J.
: *Bourbon and Stuart: Kings and Kingship in France and England in the Seventeenth Century*, 1987 (readable and astute comparative study).

Parry, G.
: *The Seventeenth Century: The Intellectual and Cultural Context of English Literature, 1603–1700*, Harlow, 1989 (the companion volume in this series; discusses many of the same authors and issues).

Richardson, R.C, and Ridden, G.M.
: *Freedom and the English Revolution: Essays in history and literature*, Manchester, 1986 (essays on Marvell, Lilburne, Winstanley and Milton, along with the history).

Rivers, I.   *Reason, Grace, and Sentiment: A Study of the Language of Religion and Ethics in England, 1660–1780. Vol. I, Whichcote to Wesley*, Cambridge, 1991.

Shapiro, B.J.   *Probability and Certainty in Seventeenth-Century England*, Princeton, 1983 (science, religion, history, law and literature).

Trevor-Roper, H.   *Catholics, Anglicans and Puritans: Seventeenth-Century Essays*, 1987.

Wrightson, K.   *English Society 1580–1680*, 1982 (subtle and reliable analysis of social structure and conditions).

(ii) General studies of the prose

Adolph, R.   *The Rise of Modern Prose Style*, Cambridge, Mass. 1968 (useful corrective to Croll and Williamson; an extension of Jones's thesis).

Carey, J.   'Sixteenth and Seventeenth Century Prose', in C. Ricks (ed.), *English Poetry and Prose 1540–1674*, 1970, pp. 339–429 (lively, sometimes idiosyncratic survey).

Corns, T.M. (ed.)   *The Literature of Controversy: Polemical Strategy from Milton to Junius*, 1986: special issue of *Prose Studies*, 9: 2 (material on Milton, Overton, Hobbes, Marvell and Baxter).

Croll, M.W., ed. J. M. Patrick et al.   *'Attic' and Baroque Prose Style*, Princeton, 1969 (influential essays on the Latin models for style in the century; starting to show their age, and oddly light on close analysis, but still influential).

Fish, S.E. (ed.)   *Seventeenth-Century Prose: Modern Essays in Criticism*, New York, 1971.

Gordon, I.A.   *The Movement of English Prose*, 1966 (a brief survey, but suggestive on the seventeenth century).

Jones, R.F. et al.   *The Seventeenth Century: Studies in the History of English Thought and Literature from Bacon to Pope*, Stanford, 1951 (contains five seminal essays by Jones on science and pulpit language in the second half of the century).

McKeon, M.   *The Origins of the English Novel, 1600–1740*, Baltimore, 1987 (important exploration of concepts).

Mitchell, W.F.   *English Pulpit Oratory from Andrewes to Tillotson*, 1932.

Salzman, P.   *English Prose Fiction 1558–1700*, Oxford, 1985 (detailed survey).

Spufford, M.   *Small Books and Pleasant Histories: Popular Fiction and its Readership in Seventeenth-Century England*, 1981 (on the chapbooks).

Todd, J.   *The Sign of Angellica: Women, Writing and Fiction, 1660–1800,* 1989 (good material on Cavendish and Behn).

Webber, J.   *The Eloquent 'I': Style and Self in Seventeenth-Century Prose,* Madison, 1968 (outstanding essays: a good place to start).

Williamson, G. *The Senecan Amble: Prose Form from Bacon to Collier,* 1951 (extends Croll's questionable theories).

(iii) Other relevant literary criticism

Barker, F. et al. (eds) *1642: Literature and Power in the Seventeenth Century,* Essex, 1981 (useful pieces on women's writing, colonial discourse and Milton).

Bloom, Clive (ed.) *Jacobean Poetry and Prose: Rhetoric, Representation and the Popular Imagination,* 1988 (chapters on popular romance, Nashe and the Prayer Book).

Bush, D.   *English Literature in the Earlier Seventeenth Century, 1600–1660,* Oxford, 1962 (excellent on Milton, and useful on minor writers not treated in this study).

Fish, S.E.   *Self-Consuming Artifacts,* Berkeley, 1972 (nails a number of major authors to a theory of reading).

Howell, W.S. *Logic and Rhetoric in England, 1500–1700,* Princeton, 1956.

Keeble, N.H. *The Literary Culture of Nonconformity in Later Seventeenth-Century England,* Leicester, 1987 (formidably learned and detailed approach by topic more than author).

Smith, N.   *Perfection Proclaimed: Language and Literature in English Radical Religion 1640–1660,* Oxford, 1989.

Sutherland, J. *English Literature of the Late Seventeenth Century,* Oxford, 1969 (good on Restoration prose).

(iv) Anthologies

Edwards, P. (ed.) *Last Voyages: Cavendish, Hudson, Ralegh. The Original Narratives,* Oxford, 1988.

Erskine-Hill, H. and G. Storey (eds)	*Revolutionary Prose of the English Civil War*, Cambridge, 1983.
Graham, E., et al. (eds)	*Her Own Life: Autobiographical Writings by Seventeenth-Century Englishwomen*, 1989.
Harris, V. and I. Husain (eds)	*English Prose 1600–1660*, New York, 1965.
Lievsay, J.L. (ed.)	*The Seventeenth-Century Resolve: A Historical Anthology of a Literary Form*, Lexington, 1980.
Salgado, G. (ed.)	*Cony-Catchers and Bawdy Baskets*, Harmondsworth, 1972 (a collection of Elizabethan pamphlets about cozening rogues and their language).
Salzman, P. (ed.)	*An Anthology of Elizabethan Prose Fiction*, Oxford, 1987 (Gascoigne, Lyly, Greene, Nashe, Deloney).
Salzman, P. (ed.)	*An Anthology of Seventeenth-Century Fiction*, Oxford, 1991 (Wroth, Percy Herbert, Cavendish, Dangerfield, Bunyan, Congreve, Behn).
Seymour-Smith, M. (ed.)	*The English Sermon vol. I: 1550–1650*, Cheadle, 1976.
Sisson, C.H. (ed.)	*The English Sermon vol. II: 1650–1750*, Cheadle, 1976.
Smith, N. (ed.)	*A Collection of Ranter Writings*, 1983.
Vickers, B. (ed.)	*Seventeenth-Century Prose*, 1969.
Vickers, B. (ed.)	*English Science, Bacon to Newton*, Cambridge, 1987.
Wootton, D. (ed.)	*Divine Right and Democracy: An Anthology of Political Writing in Stuart England*, Harmondsworth, 1986.

(v) The English Bible

Butterfield, C.C.	*Literary Lineage of the English Bible*, Philadelphia, 1941.
Hammond, G.	*The Making of the English Bible*, Manchester, 1982 (from Tyndale to the Authorised Version; the best literary study).
Lawton, D.	*Faith, Text and History: The Bible in English*, Hemel Hempstead, 1990.
Pollard, A.W.	*Records of the English Bible*, Oxford, 1911.

Individual Authors

Notes on biography, editions and further reading

ANDREWES, Lancelot (1555–1626) From an ordinary London trading family to an academic career, Merchant Taylor's School, Pembroke Hall, Cambridge, where he became Master in 1589, as well as Vicar of St Giles', Cripplegate where his large London parish included two theatres. Chairman of one of the Authorised Version translating panels; considerable patristic and linguistic learning. Bishop of Chichester 1605, Ely 1609, Winchester 1619. Regular Court preacher. Perhaps too ascetic and eirenic to be interested in politics, though close to the centre of power. Arminian in theology, sermons edited posthumously by Laud.

> *Works*, ed. J. Bliss, Library of Anglo-Catholic Theology, 1851–54.
> *Sermons*, ed. G.M. Story, Oxford, 1967 (a selection of his Jacobean Court sermons).

> See: Eliot, T.S., 'For Lancelot Andrewes', 1928, in *Selected Essays*.
> Horton Davies, *Like Angels from a Cloud: the English Metaphysical Preachers*, San Marino, 1986 (critical discussion of Andrewes and some of his protégés).
> Welsby, P., *Lancelot Andrewes, 1555–1626*, 1958 (biography).

AUBREY, John (1626–97) Born Easton-Piers, Wiltshire; educated at Blandford School, Dorset and Trinity College, Oxford. In 1646 enrolled at Middle Temple. In 1656 began *Natural History of Wiltshire*. Fellow of Royal Society 1663. Friend of Hobbes, of whom he planned a biography. Ruined by lawsuits and marriage negotiations; lived on friends after 1671. Assembled biographical material with Anthony Wood, posthumously published as *Brief Lives*. Numerous other uncompleted projects – British antiquities (*Monumentum Britannicum*), chronology of British architecture, education, survey of Surrey. Only speculative *Miscellanea* (1696) published in his lifetime.

> *Brief Lives*, ed. A. Clark, 2 vols, Oxford, 1898 (complete edn).
> *Brief Lives*, ed. O.L. Dick, 1949 (good introduction and selection, available in paper).
> *Three Prose Works*, ed. J. Buchanan-Brown, 1972 (contains *Miscellanies, Remaines of Gentilisme and Judaisme, Observation*).

Aubrey on Education, ed. J.E. Stephens, 1972.
A Natural History of Wiltshire, Newton Abbot, 1969.
Monumentum Britannicum, ed. J. Fowles and R. Legg, 2 vols, 1980.
A Perambulation of the County of Surrey, 5 vols, Dorking, 1975.

See: Hunter, M., *John Aubrey and the Realm of Learning*, 1975.
Powell, A., *John Aubrey and his Friends*, 1948.

BACON, Francis (1561–1626) Educated at Trinity College, Cambridge and Gray's
Inn. MP for various constituencies 1584–1618. Associated with Essex (though
one of his prosecutors after the rebellion), unpopular with Queen Elizabeth.
Solicitor-General 1607, Attorney-General 1613, Lord Keeper (his father's
post) 1617, created Viscount St Albans 1621; in the same year fined by the
Lords and dismissed from office of Chancellor for taking bribes. Retired, and
died in debt. *Essays* first published 1597 with *Colours of Good and Evil* and
Meditationes Sacrae, revised and expanded 1612 and 1625. Published a series of
works proposing a new foundation for learning: *The Advancement of Learning*
(1605; expanded Latin version, *De Augmentis Scientarum*, 1623), *Novum
Organum* and plan for *Instauratio Magna* (1620) , *New Atlantis* (1624). *De
Sapientia Veterum* ('Of the Wisdom of the Ancients', 1609) was very popular,
he wrote a *History of Henry VII* (1622), and numerous legal and other
treatises.

Works, ed. J. Spedding, R.L. Ellis and D.D. Heath, 14 vols, 1857–74 (the
standard edn until the new Cambridge edn becomes available).
The Essayes, ed. M. Kiernan, Oxford, 1985.
The Essays, ed. J. Pitcher. Harmondsworth, 1985.

See: J.C. Briggs, *Francis Bacon and the Rhetoric of Nature*, Cambridge, Mass.,
1989.
L. Jardine, *Francis Bacon: Discovery and the Art of Discourse*, Cambridge,
1974 (quite technical but rewarding on dialectic, rhetoric and Bacon's
programme, as well as the *Essays*).
A. Quinton, *Bacon*, 1980 (brief, emphasises the philosophy).
B. Vickers (ed.), *Essential Articles for the Study of Francis Bacon*, Hamden,
1968.
B. Vickers, *Francis Bacon and Renaissance Prose*, Cambridge, 1968 (the
best sustained case for Bacon's literary stature).

BEHN, Aphra (1640–89) Little reliable information; probably born Johnson in Wye
to barber's family; moved to Canterbury. Went with them to Surinam
1663–64; married a Dutch or German, probably widowed; by 1666 a spy in
Flanders for Arlington. Returned to London 1667, moved in Court and
theatrical circles. Writing poetry and plays professionally; *The Forc'd Marriage*
staged 1670, about twenty others, most famously *The Rover* (1677).
Translated French novels, wrote Tory political satire. *Love Letters between a
Nobleman and his Sister* (three parts, 1684–87), *Oroonoko* (1688); other short
fiction published posthumously.

Works, ed. M. Summers, 1915 (unreliable; a new edn by Janet Todd is
forthcoming).
Love Letters between a Nobleman and his Sister, ed. Duffy, 1987.
Oroonoko and other stories, ed. Duffy, 1986.

See: M. Duffy, *The Passionate Shepherdess*, 1987 (biography).
A. Goreau, *Reconstructing Aphra*, Oxford, 1980.

S. Heller Mendelson, *The Mental World of Stuart Women*, Brighton, 1987 (Ch. 3 is the best biography).

M.A. O'Donnell, *Aphra Behn: An Annotated Bibliography*, New York, 1986.

BOYLE, Hon. Robert (1627–91) Son of first Earl of Cork. Educated at Eton, visited Geneva and Italy. Moved to Oxford 1654–55, set up laboratory and joined group of scientists round John Wilkins. Early and continuing interest in alchemy, but *Sceptical Chemist* (1661) and other essays crucial in modernising chemistry, away from Aristotelian theory. Formulated 'Boyle's Law' in *The Spring and Weight of the Air* (1662). Active in Royal Society from the beginning; wrote theology, and an early romance as well as many scientific treatises.

Works, ed. T. Birch (1744), 5 vols; rev. edn (1772), 6 vols.
Selected Philosophical Papers, ed. M.A. Stewart (Manchester, 1979).
The Sceptical Chemist, ed. E.A. Moelwyn Hughes (1964).

See: M.B. Hall *Robert Boyle and Seventeenth-Century Chemistry*, Cambridge, 1958.
J.R. Jacob, *Robert Boyle and the English Revolution*, New York, 1977.
S. Schaffer and S. Shapin, *Leviathan and the Air-pump: Hobbes, Boyle and the Experimental Life*, Princeton, 1985.

BROWNE, Sir Thomas (1605–82) Educated Winchester and Oxford; studied medicine at Montpelier, Padua and Leiden, then at the forefront of medical knowledge. Settled in medical practice in Norwich 1637; married Dorothy Mileham 1641, twelve children. First authorised edition of *Religio Medici* appeared 1643, after pirated versions in 1642. First of five editions in his life of *Pseudodoxia Epidemica* (1646). *Hydriotaphia* and *The Garden of Cyrus* (1658). Elected Fellow of Royal College of Physicians 1664, and testified at a witch trial in the same year. Knighted 1671. Posthumous works include *Certain Miscellany Tracts* (1684), *A Letter to a Friend* (1690) and *Christian Morals* (1716).

The Works of Sir Thomas Browne, 4 vols, ed. Geoffrey Keynes, 1964.
The Major Works, ed. C.A. Patrides, Harmondsworth, 1977 (the best student text, with a massive bibliography).
Pseudodoxia Epidemica, 2 vols, ed. R.H. Robbins, Oxford, 1981.
Religio Medici and Other Works, ed. L.C. Martin, Oxford, 1964.

See: J. Bennett, *Sir Thomas Browne*, Cambridge, 1962.
D.C. Donovan, M. G. Hartley Herman and A.E. Imbrie, *Sir Thomas Browne and Robert Burton: a Reference Guide*, Boston, 1981 (annotated bibliography).
F.L. Huntley, *Sir Thomas Browne: A Biographical and Critical Study*, Ann Arbor, 1962.
C.A. Patrides (ed.), *Approaches to Sir Thomas Browne: the Ann Arbor Tercentenary Lectures and Essays*, Columbia, Missouri, 1982.
J.F.S. Post, *Sir Thomas Browne*, Boston, 1987 (the best introduction).

BUNYAN, John (1628–88) Born Elstow, Bedfordshire of humble parents; basic schooling. Joined Parliamentary Army 1644. Married 1649. Received in Bedford congregation 1655. First book, against the Quakers, 1656. Second marriage, 1659. Imprisoned for preaching, 1660–72, and again 1676–77;

appointed pastor of Bedford Congregational Church. Sixty books of controversy, evangelism, doctrine, poetry and *Grace Abounding to the Chief of Sinners* (1666), *The Pilgrim's Progress* (Part 1 1678, Part 2 1684–85), *The Life and Death of Mr Badman* (1680) and *The Holy War* (1682).

> *The Pilgrim's Progress*, ed. J.B. Wharey, rev. R. Sharrock, Oxford, 1960.
> *Grace Abounding*, ed. R. Sharrock, Oxford, 1962.
> *The Holy War*, ed. R. Sharrock and J.F. Forrest, Oxford, 1980.
> *The Life and Death of Mr Badman*, ed. J.F. Forrest and R. Sharrock, Oxford, 1988.
> *Miscellaneous Works*, gen. ed. R. Sharrock, 13 vols, in progress, Oxford, 1976–.

> See: C. Hill, *A Turbulent, Seditious and Factious People: John Bunyan and his Church*, Oxford, 1988.
> N.H. Keeble (ed.), *John Bunyan, Conventicle and Parnassus: Tercentenary Essays*, Oxford, 1988.
> A. Laurence, W.R. Owens and S. Sim (eds), *John Bunyan and his England 1628–88*, 1990.
> V. Newey (ed.), *The Pilgrim's Progress: Critical and Historical Views*, Liverpool, 1980.
> R. Sharrock, *John Bunyan*, rev. edn, 1968.

BURTON, Robert (1577–1640) Son of Leicestershire gentleman. School at Sutton Coldfield and Nuneaton; lists tyrannical schoolmasters as a cause of melancholy. Brasenose College, Oxford, from 1593; moved to Christ Church in 1599, where he spent the rest of his life. Some Latin poems; contributed to *Alba*, a play for King James's visit in 1605; *Philosophaster*, another Latin comedy, 1617. First edition of *The Anatomy of Melancholy* 1621; subsequent, expanded editions in 1624, 1628, 1632, 1638 and 1651. Considerable popular success. Vicar of St Thomas's near Oxford; High Church sympathies.

> *The Anatomy of Melancholy*, ed. T.C. Faulkner et al., 5 vols, Oxford, 1989–.
> *The Anatomy of Melancholy*, ed. H. Jackson, 1932.

> See: D.C. Donovan, M.G. Hartley Herman and A. E.Imbrie, *Sir Thomas Browne and Robert Burton: a Reference Guide*, Boston, 1981 (annotated bibliography).
> B.G. Lyons, *Voices of Melancholy*, 1972.
> M. O'Connell, *Robert Burton*, Boston, 1986 (the best introduction).
> E.P. Vicari, *The View from Minerva's Tower: Learning and Imagination in The Anatomy of Melancholy*, Toronto, 1989.

CLARENDON, Edward Hyde, First Earl of (1609–74) Born near Salisbury; father MP. Educated Magdalen Hall, Oxford, 1622; Middle Temple 1629. Married Ann Ayloffe 1629, Frances Aylesbury 1632. Elected MP 1640, supported Pym until late 1641; soon became adviser to Charles I. In exile with him 1646; began *History of the Rebellion*. Returned as Lord Chancellor in 1660, effectively chief minister until impeachment in 1667; fled to France, where he completed the *History* and *His Life*.

> *The History of the Rebellion and Civil Wars in England*, ed. W.D. Macray, Oxford, 1888, 6 vols.
> *Selections* ed. G. Huehns, Oxford, 1955.

See: Fogle, F.R. and Trevor-Roper, H.R., *Milton and Clarendon*, Los Angeles, 1965.

R.W. Harris, *Clarendon and the English Revolution*, 1983.

B.H.C. Wormald, *Clarendon*, Cambridge, 1951.

COPPE, Abiezer (1619–72) Born in Warwick; educated Merton College, Oxford in 1630s; 1640s a Baptist preacher in Warwickshire, with a congregation. Broke with formal religion 1649; imprisoned in 1650 for blasphemy, connected with *A Fiery Flying Roll*. Released 1651; a sort of recantation in *Copp's Return*. In London during 1650s; *Divine Fireworks* (1657) a return to the old style. Changed his name to Higham and preached and practiced medicine in Barnes.

> *Selected Writings*, ed. A. Hopton, 1987.
> *A Collection of Ranter Writings*, ed. N. Smith, 1983.

> See: J.C. Davis *Fear, Myth and History: The Ranters and the Historians*, Cambridge, 1986.
> N. Smith *Perfection Proclaimed: Language and Literature in English Radical Religion 1640–1660*, Oxford, 1989.

DELONEY, Thomas (?1560–1600) Reliable information sparse. He may have been born in Norwich; by 1586 he was in London. He began as a writer of topical ballads. In 1595 he joined with his fellow-weavers to complain about immigrants breaking the apprenticeship rules; initially imprisoned, then released. His prose fictions were written after he went underground to escape the censoring attentions of the Mayor of London in 1597 – *Jack of Newbury*, the two parts of *The Gentle Craft*, and *Thomas of Reading*.

> *Works*, ed. F.O. Mann, Oxford, 1912.
> *Novels*, ed. M.E. Lawlis, Bloomington, 1961.

> See: M.E. Lawlis, *Apology for the Middle Class: The Dramatic Novels of Thomas Deloney*, Bloomington, 1960.
> L.C. Stevenson, *Praise and Paradox: Merchants and Craftsmen in Elizabethan Popular Literature*, Cambridge, 1984.

DONNE, John (1572–1631) Born into a Catholic family, studied at Oxford, probably Cambridge, and Lincoln's Inn. Renounced Catholicism in 1598, became Secretary to Egerton, Lord Keeper of the Seal, lost job as a result of his marriage to Ann More in 1602. MP in the 'Addled' Parliament of 1614. Ordained 1615, became Royal Chaplain, Dean of St Paul's in 1621. Early prose includes *Paradoxes and Problems*, *Biathanatos* (on suicide), *Pseudo-Martyr*, and *Ignatius His Conclave*. Of his 160 extant sermons, 145 were published in the seventeenth century. His *Devotions upon Emergent Occasions* (1624) record the progress of an illness. Few poems printed during his life; a collection in 1633.

> *Sermons*, ed. G.R. Potter and E.M. Simpson, 10 vols, Berkeley, 1953–62.
> *Donne's Prebend Sermons*, ed. J.M. Mueller, Cambridge, Mass., 1971.
> *Selected Prose*, ed. N. Rhodes, Harmondsworth, 1987.
> *Essays in Divinity*, ed. E.M. Simpson, Oxford, 1952.

> See: J. Carey, *John Donne, Life, Mind and Art*, London, 1981.
> E.M. Simpson, *A Study of the Prose Works of John Donne*, Oxford, 1948.
> J. Webber, *Contrary Music: The Prose Style of John Donne*, Madison, 1963.

EVELYN, John (1620–1706) Born into gentry family, early life in Sussex. Attended Balliol College, Oxford, 1637; death of father in 1640 interrupted education. Long travels through Europe for most of 1641–52; 1647 married Mary Browne, daughter of Royalist ambassador in Paris. Early and active in Royal Society; public servant from 1670s. *Sylva* (1664), and various books on architecture, navigation and coins.

> *Diary*, ed. E.S. de Beer, Oxford, 1955, 6 vols.
> *Diary*, ed. John Bowle, Oxford, 1985.

> See: J. Bowle, *Evelyn and His World*, 1981.

FILMER, Sir Robert (1588–1653) Born into a gentry family in Kent, educated Trinity College, Cambridge and Lincoln's Inn. Married Ann Heton (daughter of Bishop of Ely) 1618; lived in Lodge of Westminster Abbey. Supported king in Civil War, imprisoned 1643. Began publishing his ideas during 1647; including *The Anarchy of a Mixed or Limited Monarchy* (1648), *Observations concerning the Original of Government* (1652) and (authorship disputed) *The Free-Holders Grand Inquest* (1648). His most influential book, *Patriarcha*, not published until 1680, during the Exclusion Crisis, when it drew replies from Algernon Sidney, James Tyrell and John Locke.

> *Patriarcha and Other Writings*, ed. J.P. Sommerville, Cambridge, 1991 (supersedes Laslett's 1949 edn).

> See: J. Daly, *Sir Robert Filmer and English Political Thought*, Toronto, 1979.
> P. Laslett, 'Sir Robert Filmer: the Man versus the Whig Myth', *William and Mary Quarterly*, 5 (1948), 523–46.
> G.J. Schochet, *Patriarchalism and Political Thought*, Oxford, 1975.

FLORIO, John (1553–1625) Born in London of exiled Italian Protestant parents, perhaps educated in Tübingen as well as Oxford. Wrote two textbooks of Italian, *First Fruits* (1578) and *Second Fruits* (1591), and an Italian/English dictionary, *A World of Wordes* (first published 1598, much expanded as *Queen Anna's New World of Words*, 1611). Translated Montaigne's *Essais* (1603). Married Samuel Daniel's sister, patronised by Southampton at the same time as Shakespeare, and numerous other literary connections. Part of Queen Anne's Court from 1604, but died in poverty six years after her death.

> *The Essayes of Michael, Lord of Montaigne*, ed. A.R. Waller, 1910 and reprints; other works available in modern facsimiles.

> See: F.A. Yates, *John Florio*, Cambridge, 1934 (biography and criticism).

FOX, George (1624–91) Son of Puritan weaver, Fenny Drayton, Leicestershire. Limited education, left home 1643. First revelation 1647; first preached indwelling light to separatists 1648. 'Quaker' movement begins with Fox's visits to Yorkshire and Westmoreland 1651–52. Imprisoned eight times during Commonwealth and Restoration. Undoubted leader of Quakers by 1660s. Married Margaret Fell, another leader, 1669. 1670–73 visited Quakers in West Indies and America. *Journal* first edited and published 1694.

> *Journal*, ed. J.L. Nickalls, Cambridge, 1952.

GREVILLE, Fulke, Lord Brooke (1554–1628) Born in Warwickshire, started Shrewsbury School with Philip Sidney, whose friendship remained of greatest importance to him. Entered Jesus College, Cambridge 1568. A longstanding courtier. Treasurer of the Navy 1598–1604, Chancellor and Under-Treasurer of the Exchequer 1614–21. Poetry includes *Caelica*, a sequence of short poems, various treatises and two tragedies. His life of Sidney probably written c. 1610, but unpublished until 1652. Killed by a servant who believed he had been left out of his will.

> *The Prose Works*, ed. J. Gouws, Oxford, 1986.

> See: R. Rebholz, *The Life of Fulke Greville*, Oxford, 1971 (much useful critical material).
> J. Rees, *Fulke Greville, Lord Brooke*, 1971 (less detailed, but also good critical material).

HALIFAX, George Savile, Marquess of (1633–95) Born in Thronhill, Yorkshire, son of a baronet who was nephew to Strafford. Educated Shrewsbury School. Travelled in France and Italy from1647; implicated in Royalist uprising in 1655. Peerage 1668. Went over to the opposition in 1670s, but a loyal supporter of Charles in the Exclusion crisis. Lord Privy Seal 1682. A prime negotiator of the 'Revolution' of 1688, but left government 1690. Wrote a series of political pamphlets, of which *The Character of a Trimmer* (MS 1685, printed 1688) the best known, as well as unpublished maxims and characters.

> *Complete Works*, ed. J.P. Kenyon, Harmondsworth, 1969 (convenient, but not as complete as Brown).
> *Works*, ed. M.N. Brown, 3 vols, Oxford, 1989 (the standard edn, with a long biographical and contextual introduction).

HARRINGTON, James (1611–77) Born Upton, Northamptonshire, to a declining noble family. Educated Trinity College, Oxford, 1629, Middle Temple 1631 (briefly), continental travel and service with Elector Palatine. Friendship with Charles I, supporter of Parliament in 1640s. Some fruitless attempts at reconciliation 1647–48. Flurry of political writing in 1650s – principally *The Commonwealth of Oceana* (1656), *The Prerogative of Popular Government* (1657), *The Art of Lawgiving* (1659) – as well as essays on Virgil, a few poems. Founded the Rota Club for political discussion in 1659–60. In the Tower 1661–62; released without trial.

> *The Political Works of James Harrington*, ed. J.G.A. Pocock, Cambridge, 1977.

> See: C. Blitzer, *An Immortal Commonwealth: The Political Thought of James Harrington*, New Haven, 1960.
> J.C. Davis, *Utopia and the Ideal Society*, Cambridge, 1981, Chs 8 and 9.
> J.G.A. Pocock, *The Machiavellian Moment*, Princeton, 1975, Part 3.

HARVEY, William (1578–1657) Born in Folkestone, educated King's School, Canterbury, Gonville and Caius College, Cambridge and Padua (then the best medical education in Europe). Admitted to College of Physicians 1604, and married Elizabeth Browne. Began practising at St Bartholomew's Hospital in 1609. Attended James I on his deathbed; physician to Charles I, following him to Oxford during the Civil War. *De Motu Cordis* (Frankfurt, 1628, English trans. 1653) his most original work, on the circulation of the blood. *De Generatione Animalium* (1651), on animal reproduction.

Anatomical Exercises, ed. G. Keynes, 1928.
Anatomical Lectures, ed. and trans. G. Whitteridge, Edinburgh, 1964.

See: G. Keynes, The Life of William Harvey, Oxford, 1966.
W. Pagel, William Harvey's Biological Ideas, Basel, 1967.
G. Whitteridge, William Harvey and the Circulation of the Blood, 1971.

HERBERT of Cherbury, Edward, Lord (1582–1648) Born Eyton, Shropshire. Brief
education at Oxford interrupted by his father's death; married Mary Herbert,
1598. Extensive travels abroad 1608–16 (with periods at home). Twice
ambassador to France, twice recalled. Created Lord Herbert 1629. Retired to
Montgomery in 1642. Wrote a number of philosophical works, De Veritate
(1624), De Religione Laici and De Causis Errorum (1645), a history, The Life
and Raigne of King Henry VIII (1649) and his own Life, not printed until 1764.

De Religione Laici, ed. and trans. H.R. Hutcheson, 1944.
De Veritate, ed. and trans. M.H. Carre, 1937.
The Life of Edward, First Lord Herbery of Cherbury, ed. J.M. Shuttleworth,
1976.

See: R.D. Bedford, The Defence of Truth, Manchester, 1979.
M. Bottrall, Every Man a Phoenix, 1958 (long chapter on the
Autobiography).

HOBBES, Thomas (1588–1679) Born at Malmesbury; father a half-educated
clergyman. Studied at Magdalen Hall, Oxford, 1603–08; became tutor to the
Cavendish family, with whom he had life-long connections. Accompanied
his pupils on Grand Tours of Europe 1610–15, 1630 and 1634–36, during
which he met many of the major intellectuals of Europe, including Galileo.
Translations of Thucydides and other classics; great interest in the new
science and geometry. Fled to France 1640–1651/2, where he was briefly tutor
to the future Charles II. Drafted Elements of Law in 1640, revised into De Cive
(1642), and Leviathan (1651); published little more on politics after it was
threatened with official sanctions, though his later works include an attack
on Boyle's scientific method (Dialogus Physicus, 1661) Behemoth, or the Long
Parliament (written 1668, published 1682) and a Latin verse autobiography.

The English Works of Thomas Hobbes, ed. Sir W. Molesworth, 11 vols,
1839–45.
Thomae Hobbes . . . opera philosophica, ed. Molesworth, 5 vols, 1839–45
(the Latin works).
De Cive, ed. H. Warrender, 2 vols, Oxford, 1983 (the first of the new
Oxford edition of Hobbes; the English version, though contem-
porary, is not by Hobbes).
Elements of Law, ed. F. Tönnies, rev. Goldsmith, 1969.
Leviathan, ed. C.B. Macpherson, Harmondsworth, 1968.
Behemoth, or the Long Parliament, ed. Tönnies, intro. Holmes, Chicago,
1990.

See: K.C. Brown (ed), Hobbes Studies, Oxford, 1965.
D. Johnston, The Rhetoric of Leviathan, Princeton, 1986.
G.A.J. Rogers and A. Ryan (eds), Perspectives on Thomas Hobbes,
Oxford, 1988.
R. Tuck, Hobbes, Oxford, 1989 (the best introduction).

HOOKER, Richard (1554–1600) Born in Exeter; studied and taught at Oxford under the patronage of Bishop Jewel, one of the earliest apologists for the Elizabethan Church settlement. Master of the Temple in London 1585–91, which he gave up to write *Of the Laws of Ecclesiastical Polity*, his major work. The Preface and Books I–IV published 1593, Book V in 1597; the versions of VI and VIII published in 1648 are unfinished; Book VII appeared in 1661.

> *The Folger Library Edition of the Works of Richard Hooker*, general ed. W. Speed Hill, 6 vols, Cambridge, Mass. 1977–.
> *Of the Laws of Ecclesiastical Polity*, (Preface, Vols I and VIII), ed. A. S. McGrade, Cambridge, 1989.

> See: R. Eccleshall, *Order and Reason in Politics*, Oxford, 1978 (Ch. 5).
> W. Speed Hill (ed.), *Studies in Richard Hooker*, Cleveland, 1972 (includes an important chapter on Hooker's style).
> P. Lake, *Anglicans and Puritans? Presbyterianism and English Conformist Thought from Whitgift to Hooker*, London, 1988 (an important new case for Hooker's originality).

LOCKE, John (1632–1704) Born in Somerset to Puritan family; educated Westminster School and Christ Church, Oxford, then student for fifteen years. Joined the household of Ashley (later Shaftesbury) in 1667. Fled in 1683 to Holland; returned 1689. *Letter on Toleration, Two Treatises of Government, Essay Concerning Human Understanding* (1689). Involved with monetary reform at the Board of Trade. *Some Thoughts concerning Education* (1693), *The Reasonableness of Christianity* (1695).

> *An Essay Concerning Human Understanding*, ed. P.H. Nidditch, Oxford, 1975.
> *Two Treatises of Government*, ed. P. Laslett, Cambridge, 1960.

> See: R. Ashcraft, *Locke's Two Treatises of Government* (1987) and *Revolutionary Politics and Locke's Two Treatises of Government*, Princeton, 1986.
> J. Dunn, *Locke*, Oxford, 1984.
> G. Parry, *Locke*, 1978 (on the politics).
> J.W. Yolton, ed., *John Locke: Problems and Perspectives*, Cambridge, 1969.

MARPRELATE, Martin (fl.1588–89) Pseudonymous author(s) of a series of anti-episcopal pamphlets: *Oh read over D. Iohn Bridges* (The Epistle), *Oh read over D. Iohn Bridges* (The Epitome), (both 1588), *Certaine Minerall and Metaphysical Schoolpoints, Hay any worker for Cooper, Theses Martinianae, The iust censure and reproofe of Martin Iunior* and *The Protestatyon of Martin Marprelat* (all 1589), which inspired some notable replies. Probably Job Throkmorton, a Warwickshire gentleman, though some have argued for the Welshman John Penry and there have been several other candidates.

> *The Marprelate Tracts [1588–9]*, Menston, 1967 (facsimiles).

> See: W. Pierce, *An Historical Introduction to the Marprelate Tracts*, 1911 (still important for bibliographical as well as historical details).
> R.A. Anselment, *Betwixt Jest and Earnest: Marprelate, Milton, Marvell, Swift and the Decorum of Religious Ridicule*, Toronto, 1979.
> L. Carlson, *Martin Marprelate, Gentleman: Master Job Throkmorton Laid Open in His Colours*, San Marino, 1981 (the case for Throkmorton's authorship and much more).
> R.D. Kendall, *The Drama of Dissent: The Radical Poetics of Nonconformity,*

1380–1590, Chapel Hill, 1986 (Ch. 5 is a mixture of the interesting and the wrong-headed on Marprelate).

MARVELL, Andrew (1621–78) Son of a 'facetious, yet Calvinistical' clergyman, educated at Hull and Trinity College, Cambridge. A brief Catholic phase. Travelled in Europe 1642–46. Tutor to Lord Fairfax's daughter 1651–52; to a ward of Cromwell's 1653–56. During 1657–59 colleague of Milton's in Secretaryship of Foreign Tongues. From 1659 until his death MP for Hull. His later satirical poems published anonymously; the great earlier ones not until 1681. Controversial prose on the side of Nonconformity or opposition: *The Rehearsal Transpros'd* (1672; Second Part 1673), *Mr Smirke, or, The Divine in Mode* (1676) and *An Account of the Growth of Popery and Arbitrary Government* (1677).

> *Poems and Letters*, ed. H.M. Margoliouth, 3rd edn rev. Legouis and Duncan-Jones, 2 vols, Oxford, 1971.
> *The Rehearsal Transpros'd*, ed. D.I.B. Smith, Oxford, 1971.

See: W. Chernaik, *The Poet's Time*, Cambridge, 1983.
> P. Legouis, *Andrew Marvell*, Oxford, 1965.
> A. Patterson, *Marvell and the Civic Crown*, New Jersey, 1978 (contains the best account of the prose in its historical context).

MILTON, John (1608–74) Son of a musical London scrivener. Educated St Paul's School 1620; 1625 Christ's College, Cambridge; 1632–38 programme of private study at Hammersmith and Horsham. *A Mask* (*Comus*) performed 1634, 'Lycidas' published 1638. Travelled in 1638–39 to Italy, where he met Galileo and various men of letters. During 1641–42 published series of five prose attacks on the bishops. Married Mary Powell 1642; they soon separated. *The Doctrine and Discipline of Divorce* (1643), first of a series arguing for freer divorce. Letter to Hartlib *Of Education* (1644); *Areopagitica*, on freedom of press, same year. Pre-war *Poems* (1645). Defended the execution of Charles I in 1649 in *The Tenure of Kings and Magistrates*; became Secretary for Foreign Tongues for Council of State, wrote *Eikonoclastes* to counter *Eikon Basilike*. Two Latin defences of the English people (1651, 1654) addressed to Europe. Becoming blind 1652. Remarried 1656. *Treatise of Civil Power* and *The Likeliest Way to Remove Hirelings* (1659) and *The Ready and Easy Way to Establish a Free Commonwealth* (1660) against the break-up of the republic and the imminent Restoration. Only imprisoned briefly at Restoration. Wrote a *History of Britain* (1670) and the major poems: *Paradise Lost* (1667), *Paradise Regained* and *Samson Agonistes* (1671).

> *Complete Prose Works of John Milton*, ed. D.M. Wolfe, New Haven, 1953–82.
> *Selected Prose*, ed. C.A. Patrides, Harmondsworth, 1974.

See: T.M. Corns, *The Development of Milton's Prose Style*, Oxford, 1982 (a computer-based exercise in historical stylistics).
> C. Hill, *Milton and the English Revolution*, London, 1977.
> M. Lieb and J. T.Shawcross (eds), *Achievements of the Left Hand: Essays on the Prose of John Milton*, Amherst, 1974 (prose in the light of the poetry).
> D. Loewenstein and J. G. Turner (eds), *Politics, Poetics and Hermeneutics in Milton's prose*, Cambridge, 1990 (the most comprehensive treatment).

K.W. Staveley, *The Politics of Milton's Prose Style*, New Haven, 1975.
J.G. Turner, *One Flesh: Paradisal Marriage and Sexual Relations in the Age of Milton*, Oxford, 1987 (Important chapter on divorce tracts).

MONTAIGNE, Michel Eyquem, sieur de (1533–92) Born near Bordeaux, tutored by George Buchanan among others, magistrate at Perigeux, married Françoise de la Chassaigne, 1566. Retired from public life 1571. Books I and II of the *Essais* published 1580; Mayor of Bordeaux until 1585; added third book of *Essais* in 1588.

> *Les Essais*, ed. F. Strowski, F. Gebelin and P. Villey, 5 vols, Bordeaux, 1906–33 (standard edn).
> *Les Essais*, ed. P. Villey, rev. V.-L. Saulnier, 2 vols, Paris, 3rd edn, 1978.
> *The Essayes of Michael, Lord of Montaigne*, trans. John Florio, ed. A.R. Waller, 1910 and reprints.
> *The Complete Works of Montaigne*, trans. Donald M. Frame, 1958.

See: P. Burke, *Montaigne*, Oxford, 1981.
> T. Cave, *The Cornucopian Text: Problem of Writing in the French Renaissance*, Oxford, 1979.
> R.A. Sayce, *The Essays of Montaigne*, 1972.
> M.A. Screech, *Montaigne and Melancholy*, 1983.

NASHE, Thomas (1567–?1601) Born Lowestoft, son of minister. Educated St John's, Cambridge, 1581–88. From then mostly professional writer in London. Contributed *An Almond for a Parrat* to the Marprelate controversy (1590); popular success with *Pierce Penniless* (1592); picaresque narrative *The Unfortunate Traveller* (1594); quarrel with the Harveys which produced *Have with You to Saffron Walden* (1596); last publication *Nashe's Lenten Stuff* (1599). Only *Summer's Last Will and Testament* (1592) survives of his drama, apart from possible contributions to Marlowe's *Dido*. Escaped imprisonment for *Isle of Dogs* (1597), co-written with Jonson. All his books banned by Archbishop Whitgift's 1599 edict against satire.

> *The Works of Thomas Nashe*, ed. R.B. McKerrow, rev. F.P. Wilson, 5 vols, Oxford, 1958.
> *Thomas Nashe*, ed. S. Wells (1964) (a selection).
> *The Unfortunate Traveller and Other Works*, ed. J.B. Steane, Harmondsworth, 1972.

See: J.V. Crewe, *Unredeemed Rhetoric: Thomas Nashe and the Scandal of Authorship*, Baltimore, 1983 (on themelessness; poststructuralist).
> G.R. Hibbard, *Thomas Nashe, A Critical Introduction*, 1962.
> L. Hutson, *Thomas Nashe in Context*, Oxford, 1989 (economic context, largely; critically valuable).
> C. Nicholl, *A Cup of News: The Life of Thomas Nashe*, London, 1984 (lively and acute).
> N. Rhodes, *Elizabethan Grotesque*, 1980 (indispensable on N's style).

OVERTON, Richard (fl.1631–64) May have been the son of a Midlands clergyman, and taken refuge in a Baptist congregation in the Netherlands 1615–16. Matriculated Queens College, Cambridge, 1631, and may have been a professional actor. During 1640–42 wrote a number of tracts against Laud, the bishops, Catholicism, the legal system and monopolies. Married 1643, may have gone to Amsterdam. *Mans Mortalitie* (1644) argues that soul is not immortal between death and resurrection (Hobbes and Milton agreed). During 1645–46 wrote six 'Marpriest' tracts against the Presbyterians, notably *The Araignment of Mr Persecution*. Several imprisonments; joined Leveller cause as apologist and organiser. After crushing of Levellers in 1649 only occasional activity or writing. He may have been arrested as part of a republican plot in 1663.

> *An Arrow against all Tyrants* (facsimile, Exeter, 1976).
> *Mans Mortalitie*, ed. H. Fisch, Liverpool, 1968.

(The anthologies of Leveller writings ed. by William Haller, Don M. Wolfe and G.E. Aylmer all contain material by Overton.)

> See: J. Frank, *The Levellers*, Harvard, 1955.
> M. Gimelfarb-Brack, *Liberté, Egalité, Fraternité, Justice! La Vie et l'oeuvre de Richard Overton, Niveleur*, Berne, 1979.
> M. Heinemann, *Puritanism and Drama*, Cambridge, 1980, Ch. 13.
> N. Smith, 'Richard Overton's Marpriest Tracts' in *The Literature of Controversy*, ed. T.N. Corns, 1986.

PEPYS, Samuel (1633–1703) Born in London, educated at Huntingdon and St Paul's; Magdalen College, Cambridge 1651–54. Entered service of Edward Mountague, later Earl of Sandwich. Married Elizabeth St Michel 1655. Kept diary 1660–68; public offices, mostly in the Navy Office, from 1660–89, apart from brief interlude in the Tower on suspicion of treason 1679. MP for Harwich. President of Royal Society, 1684–86. Suspected of Jacobitism after 1688.

> *The Diary*, ed. R. Latham and W. Matthews, 11 vols, 1970–83 (retranscribed from Pepys's shorthand, unexpurgated; wonderful notes and useful Companion volume).

> See: R. Ollard, *Pepys: A Biography* (1974).
> M.H. Nicolson, *Pepys' Diary and the New Science*, Charlottesville, 1965.

RALEGH, Sir Walter (1552?–1618) Born into Devonshire gentry, became a great favourite at Elizabeth's Court until his secret marriage put him in prison (temporary) and disgrace (permanent). Led expeditions to Virginia and Guiana; his account of the latter published in 1596 and a popular success. Imprisoned in the Tower under James for treason, where he composed his *History of the World* (1614).

> *History of the World*, ed. C.A. Patrides, 1971 (good selections).
> *Selected Writings*, ed. G. Hammond, Manchester, 1984; paper 1986 (contains *The Last Fight of the Revenge* and *The Discovery of Guiana*, and extracts from the *History*, as well as poems and letters).
> *Works*, ed. Oldys and Birch, 8 vols, Oxford, 1829 (the only collected edition; the last reprint of the whole *History of the World*).

> See: P. Edwards, *Sir Walter Ralegh*, 1953.
> S.J. Greenblatt, *Sir Walter Ralegh: the Renaissance Man and his Roles*, New Haven, 1973.
> J. Racin, *Sir Walter Ralegh as Historian*, Salzburg, 1974.
> E. Strathmann, *Sir Walter Ralegh: A Study in Elizabethan Skepticism*, 1951.

SIDNEY, Sir Philip (1562–86) Born at Penshurst, Kent, educated at Shrewsbury School and Christ Church, Oxford, and perhaps most of all on a dazzling Grand Tour of Europe (1572–75). Courtier, much admired, though never powerful, part of a militant Protestant group headed by his uncle, the Earl of Leicester. After various diplomatic jobs, appointed Governor of Flushing in the Netherlands in 1585; died from wounds at the siege of Zutphen 1586. 'Slipped into the title of a poet' (his description), but nothing published in his lifetime; *Arcadia* (1590 and 1593); *Defence of Poetry* (1595); complete edition of poems and prose published 1598.

> *The Countess of Pembroke's Arcadia (The Old Arcadia)*, ed. J. Robertson, Oxford, 1973.
> *The Countess of Pembroke's Arcadia (The New Arcadia)*, ed. V. Skretcowicz, Oxford, 1987.
> *Miscellaneous Prose*, ed. K. Duncan-Jones and J. van Dorsten, Oxford, 1973.

> See: Walter R. Davis and Richard A. Lanham, *Sidney's Arcadia*, New Haven, 1965 (two separate and important studies).
> A.C. Hamilton, *Sir Philip Sidney: A Study of his Life and Work*, Cambridge, 1977.
> A F. Kinney (ed.), *Sidney in Retrospect*, Amherst, 1988 (four articles on *Arcadia* and up-to-date bibliography).
> J.S. Lawry, *Sidney's Two Arcadias: Pattern and Proceeding*, Ithaca, 1972.
> R. McCoy, *Sir Philip Sidney: Rebellion in Arcadia*, New Brunswick, 1979.
> R.W. Zandvoort, *Sidney's Arcadia: A Comparison of the Two Versions*, Amsterdam, 1929.

TEMPLE, Sir William (1628–99) Born into influential Anglo-Irish family, preferred tennis to study at Emmanuel, Cambridge, extended Grand Tour 1648–52. Seven years courtship of Dorothy Osborne (her letters survive) before marriage in 1654. Successful diplomatic career in 1660s and 1670s, pro-Dutch and undermined by Charles's secret pro-French manoeuvres. Enforced retirement from 1681; gardened and wrote. Jonathan Swift his secretary.

> *Miscellanea* in three parts, 1680, 1690, 1701.
> *Early Essays and Romances*, ed. G.C. Moore Smith, Oxford, 1930.
> *Five Miscellaneous Essays*, ed. S.H. Monk, Ann Arbor, 1963.
> *An Essay upon the Original and Nature of Government*, Introduction Robert C. Steensma, Los Angeles 1964.
> *Observations of the United Provinces*, ed. G.N. Clark, rev. edn, Oxford, 1972.

> See: K.H.D. Haley, *An English Diplomat in the Low Countries*, Oxford, 1986 (valuable last chapter on political writings).
> R. Faber, *The Brave Courtier: Sir William Temple*, 1983 (account of Ancients and Moderns controversy as well as public life).
> C. Marburg, *Sir William Temple: A Seventeenth Century 'Libertin'*, New Haven, 1932.

TRAHERNE, Thomas (1637–74) born in Hereford, educated Brasenose College, Oxford. Rector of Credenhill either side of Restoration; later chaplain to Sir Orlando Bridgeman, Lord Keeper of the Privy Seal. Only *Roman Forgeries* (1673) published in his lifetime, then *Christian Ethicks* (1675); some poems published anonymously later. Manuscripts of poems and prose meditations discovered late nineteenth and early twentieth century; some still unpublished.

> *Centuries, Poems, and Thanksgivings*, ed. H.M. Margoliouth, 2 vols, Oxford, 1958 (the standard edition).
> *Christian Ethicks*, ed. C.L. Marks and G.R. Guffey, Ithaca, 1968.
> *Poems, Centuries and Three Thanksgivings*, ed. A. Ridler, Oxford, 1966.
> *Selected Poems and Prose*, ed. A. Bradford, 1991.

See: A.M. Allchin, A. Ridler and J. Smith, *Profitable Wonders: Aspects of Thomas Traherne*, Oxford, 1989 (on the spirituality; a few pages from the unpublished MSS).

M.M. Day, *Thomas Traherne*, Boston, 1982.

A. Leigh Deneef, *Traherne in Dialogue: Heidegger, Lacan and Derrida*, Durham, N.C., 1988.

L.L. Martz, *The Paradise Within: Studies in Vaughan, Traherne and Milton*, New Haven, 1964.

A. Pritchard, 'Traherne's *Commentaries of Heaven*', *University of Toronto Quarterly*, 53 (1983), 1–35.

S. Stewart, *The Expanded Voice: The Art of Thomas Traherne*, San Marino, 1970.

WALTON, Izaak (1593–1683) Born in Stafford; apprenticed to Thomas Grinsell in London, 1618 admitted to Ironmongers Company, though in business as a linen draper. Describes himself as a 'convert' of John Donne, his vicar. Married (1626) Rachel Floud (a descendant of Thomas Cranmer's brother); extensive acquaintance with prominent Anglican clergy, including contact with Great Tew circle. *Life of Donne* (1640) as preface to Donne's sermons. Unswerving Royalist in 1650s, contacts with Great Tew circle. *The Compleat Angler* (1653) a great popular success. Life of Wotton part of *Reliquiae Wottoniae* (1651). *Life of Hooker* (1665) commissioned by Gilbert Sheldon, later Archbishop of Canterbury. *Life of Herbert* (1670), reprinted in *Lives* (1670); *Life of Sanderson* (1678). *Love and Truth* (1680) published anonymously.

> *The Compleat Angler*, ed. J. Bevan, Oxford, 1983.
> *Lives*, ed. G. Saintsbury, Oxford, 1927.

See: J. Bevan, *Izaak Walton's The Compleat Angler: The Art of Recreation*, Brighton, 1988 (despite its title, a good introduction to Walton generally).

J.R. Cooper, *The Art of the Compleat Angler*, Durham, N.C., 1966.

F. Costa, *L'oeuvre d'Izaak Walton*, Paris, 1973.

D. Novarr, *The Making of Walton's Lives*, Ithaca, 1958 (invaluable account of the accumulated revisions).

WALWYN, William (1600–81) Born Worcestershire, younger son of gentry. Apprenticed to London silk merchant 1619. Married Ann Gundell 1627; by 1632 member of Merchant Adventurers. Active and well-read Anglican layman. *New Petition of Papists* (1641) plea for wide toleration. Helped to raise volunteers for war on Parliamentary side. Met Lilburne 1645, began to organise Levellers. Numerous pamphlets. Arrested 1649 as movement collapsed. Wrote *Juries Justified* (1651), and in 1652 published arguments for free trade. By 1654 active as a physician, and wrote some popular medical works.

The Writings of William Walwyn, ed. J.R. McMichael and B. Taft, Athens, Georgia, 1989.

WILKINS, John (1614–72) Born in Northamptonshire, grandson of the great Puritan moralist Thomas Dod. Grammar school at Oxford; BA from Magdalen Hall 1631; MA and tutorship 1634. Early scientific interest: *Discovery of a New World* (1638), a mixture of astronomy and, in the second edition, science fiction, and *Mathematical Magic* (1648), on geometry. Vicar of Fawsley, Northants, 1637 and then Chaplain to Lord Saye; 1641 Chaplain to Lord Berkeley, who became a moderate Royalist; from 1644 associated with the Elector Palatine. Warden of Wadham, 1640, which became a great intellectual centre; contacts with Samuel Hartlib, as well as establishing his own scientific circle. In 1656 married Oliver Cromwell's sister. Instrumental in founding Royal Society. Works on language: *Mercury* (1641) on communication, *Ecclesiastes* (1646) on preaching, *Essay towards a Real Character and a Philosophical Language* (1668) on a universal scientific language. Key member of 'latitude-men' working towards comprehension in Church of England in 1660s. Bishop of Chester, 1668; regular preacher at court. *The Principles and Duties of Natural Religion* published posthumously (1675).

> *Essay towards a Real Character and a Philosophical Language*, facsimile, Menston, 1968.

> See: A.G. Debus, *Science and Education in the Seventeenth Century: the Webster–Ward debate*, 1970 (includes facsimile of *Vindiciae Academiarum* by Wilkins and Seth Ward).
> B.J. Shapiro, *John Wilkins 1614–72, an Intellectual Biography*, Berkeley, 1969.

WINSTANLEY, Gerrard (1609–?) Born in Wigan, son of a mercer with wide Puritan connections; 1630 apprenticed; 1637 member of Merchant Taylors; 1640 married Susan King. Business bad; by 1643 herding cows in Surrey. Early anti-clerical pamphlets (1648). Began in 1649 digging waste ground in Walton-on-Thames with other poor men – the Diggers or True Levellers, following earlier groups in Buckinghamshire. Series of manifestoes. Colony dispersed 1650. Addressed utopian *Law of Freedom in a Platform* (1652) to Cromwell; after 1660 no reliable information.

> *Works*, ed. G.H. Sabine, Ithaca, 1941 (the fullest selection).
> *The Law of Freedom and other Writings*, ed. C. Hill, Harmondsworth, 1968.
> *Selected Writings*, ed. A. Hopton, 1989.

> See: T.W. Hayes, *Winstanley the Digger*, Cambridge, Mass., 1979.
> D.W. Petegorsky, *Left-Wing Democracy in the English Civil War*, 1940.

Index